CONTENTS

Preface

I t was in 1967 during my first term of graduate studies at UCLA that I found myself in Jim Hill's course on 'Archaeological Theory and Method'. Jim was assessing performance on the basis of a single research paper and because I had stumbled across Hugh Hencken's article on 'Indo-European languages and archaeology' (1955) I decided to write my first graduate assignment on the origins of the Irish. This paper has miraculously survived and as I reread it I find myself cringing at countless howlers, albeit at least some generated by the real dearth of archaeological research at the time. As I peruse my list of references, the only one whose author is still among us is the irrepressible George Eogan. Anyway, the search for the origins of the Irish seems to have been an itch that over the years I couldn't help scratching from time to time, although I devoted most of my research activity to other projects. I inflicted a seminar on Irish origins on my fellow members of the Irish Association of Professional Archaeologists in 1984.[1] In 1991 I then took advantage (or abused my position?) as editor of *Emania* to lure six of my colleagues into preparing a diverse assortment of papers on the subject of Irish origins to accompany my own.[2] I returned to the subject briefly in 1999 when Jonathan Bell shanghaied me into editing a volume of *Ulster Folklife* and more recently I touched on the subject for a conference in Monaghan in 2005.[3] Finally, as retirement loomed (and has now indeed become a reality), I determined to complete on my Apple Mac what I started 44 years ago on my 1935 Royal Standard typewriter.

I have seen enough books about Ireland to warn the reader that this one is not filled with personal vignettes of various Irish archaeologists. I hope the reader will not be too disappointed that I have not recounted any nuggets of wisdom imparted to me on a rainy night by Paddy Seandálaí over a pint of Guinness in the back of a pub while he pulls out of his pocket the most beautiful polished stone axe in God's creation with that inevitable Irish twinkle in his eye. I don't do twinkle.

The Origins of the Irish

The Origins of the Irish

J. P. MALLORY

with 122 illustrations

For Molly, Declan and, naturally, their uncle Tom

On the cover: Clouds over Poulnabrone Dolmen; Burren, County Clare, Ireland.
Photo courtesy Design Pics Inc/REX/Shutterstock

Frontispiece: The Rath na Ríogh (Fort of the Kings), Tara.
Photo © Stefano Torrione/Hemis/Corbis

First published in the United Kingdom in 2013 by
Thames & Hudson Ltd, 181A High Holborn, London WC1V 7QX

First published in the United States of America in 2013 by
Thames & Hudson Inc., 500 Fifth Avenue, New York, New York 10110

First paperback edition 2015
This compact paperback edition 2017
Reprinted 2022

The Origins of the Irish © 2013 Thames & Hudson Ltd, London

British Library Cataloguing-in-Publication Data
A catalogue record for this book is available from the British Library

Library of Congress Control Number 2017931376

ISBN 978-0-500-29330-0

Printed and bound in the UK by CPI (UK) Ltd

Be the first to know about our new releases,
exclusive content and author events by visiting
thamesandhudson.com
thamesandhudsonusa.com
thamesandhudson.com.au

On the other hand, I certainly do acknowledgments and would like to thank all my colleagues and students whom I have badgered with a myriad questions and requests for illustrations. I include here over 30 years of students enduring my tutorials on Prehistoric Ireland, who have enlivened my teaching career either with their insightful comments or desperate bullshit, the latter a much undervalued commodity as it too can help fertilize the mind. I especially wish to thank those who read and commented on earlier drafts of the various chapters: Alisdair Ruffel (Queen's University Belfast), Peter Woodman (University College Cork), Rick Schulting (Oxford), Neill Carlin (University College Dublin), Phil McDonald (Queen's University Belfast), Dan Bradley (Trinity College Dublin), Jean Marco, and Peter Schrijver (University of Utrecht). I also would like to offer a very special thanks to Libby Mulqueeny (Queen's University Belfast) for preparing all the line drawings and maps.

Introduction

Open almost any book surveying the span of Irish history and you will see that the issues dealt with here are swiftly dispensed with in the first two or three pages.[1] Most historians believe that they must provide some background information to get the story of the Irish started, but realize that if they actually tackled Irish origins in any depth whatsoever their work would never reach chapter 2. And even if you peruse books on Irish archaeology, from the most academic to the most popular, by and large you will get a trouble-free narrative insofar as the many problems of Irish origins are concerned; most of the issues will either be summarily tabled ('X…remains a matter of debate') or completely ignored.[2] There's good reason that most archaeologists wouldn't touch the subject of Irish origins with a barge pole: the topic involves a very unfashionable cultural historical approach to the archaeological record of a period of Ireland's existence which is clouded in obscurity and entails a morass of issues that most archaeologists spend a lifetime trying to avoid. So an entire book devoted to *The Origins of the Irish* is just asking for trouble.

Let's start with the title itself. Scrape away the definite article and a preposition and we are left with two words whose meaning should not be taken for granted. This book is about *origins* in the plural. The main focus of this book is the various features that might be applied to any human group – physical composition, culture, language, genes – and it should be readily appreciated that these may not all have the same origin. Indeed, the only way the use of *origin* in the singular might be justified is to run an Irish timeline back to the Big Bang. Although I am sadist enough to drag the reader briefly back that far in Chapter 1, I am also aware that such an approach merely results in the Irish sharing the same origin with every star, planet, amoeba, squid, electric toaster, credit card and turkey baster in the universe. That's the problem with seeking a deep origin: go back far enough and all matter and energy in the universe share the same origin. Therefore, we need origins that are not just deep but shallow enough to distinguish the Irish from their neighbours. The origins of the Irish is not a single question and the reader should not expect a single answer.

The second term, *Irish*, is also not particularly transparent once we give its definition some thought. Employing the word as a noun we might follow the standard dictionary definition and presume that Irish simply means 'the inhabitants of Ireland'. This is a broad geographical definition that, if accepted, would certainly exceed the scope of this book. The inhabitants of Ireland today would comprise a substantial number of people whom other inhabitants of Ireland might prefer to call Poles, Lithuanians, Romanians, Chinese, English, American or indeed any other nationality that has settled in Ireland in the recent period. Moreover, the members of all these groups are just as likely not to regard themselves as *Irish*. There are already books about the *peoples* of Ireland[3] that cover this territory admirably and so a simple geographical definition will not serve.

Presumably, the reader will be primarily interested in *Irish* as a member of an ethnic group. The problem here is that ethnic groups are best defined internally, that is, by people who believe themselves to be members of the group. This reduces a lot of the problems raised by our 'peoples of Ireland' definition, but it still leaves some minefields. For example, it withholds the definition from many in Northern Ireland who, from the viewpoint of a hypothetical Irish nationalist, 'just haven't realised that they are Irish, but who sooner or later will come to see the error of their ways.'[4] Add to this the exceptionally thorny problem of identifying *when* the people of Ireland themselves developed a 'national consciousness',[5] a shared Irish identity (and not merely a series of tribal identities), and we can see that a straight ethnic definition will not serve either.

So in the search for a definition that should meet minimal objection and adhere closest to what I imagine the reader has in mind, I have sought my definition of *Irish* in the earlier history of the island and attempted to make my target as concrete as possible. To do so we obviously need to go back beyond the coming of the Anglo-Normans in the 12th century, beyond the Norse raids and settlements that began at the end of the 8th century and, just to be safe, even beyond the 7th century when Northumbrians attacked east-central Ireland and Anglo-Saxon monks came to study in Ireland. For this reason, the target Irishman of this book will be sought in the 5th century AD.

Niall son of Eochaid Mugmedón, nicknamed Noígiallach ('of the nine hostages'), straddles the boundary between Irish mythology and Irish history. While there are a series of tales concerning him that are clearly the stuff of folklore, he is also recognized as an historical person, unlike some of his ancestors who are often dismissed as wholly legendary.[6] While we cannot be absolutely certain how he defined himself, his credentials as an iconic Irishman are fairly solid. He claimed the high kingship of Ireland and established a dynasty that reigned for almost six centuries. He and his sons are credited with carving out power over much, although not all, of Ireland and leading a series of successful raids on Britain. His dates are controversial, although one best guess for his death falls in the years shortly after AD 450. His descendants, the Uí Néill (descendants of Niall), founded many of the commonest surnames in Ireland, e.g. O'Boyle, O'Doherty, O'Donnell, O'Connor, O'Reilly. Obviously, there were many other ancestors of other Irish families in the 5th century as well (e.g. O'Brien, O'Sullivan, Kennedy) who will have slightly different genetic ancestors, but by the 5th century we should feel reasonably comfortable that we are dealing with what the general reader will regard as 'the Irish'. And for the purposes of this book, the origins of Niall of the Nine Hostages and the people who lived in Ireland during his reign will provide us with a recurrent Irish focus for our narrative.

Ireland and its counties.

CHAPTER ONE

The Origins of Ireland

After a night that could not have been entirely pillow talk, Cairenn, the mother of Niall, carried within herself a fertilized egg weighing about 0.000005 grammes. For the sake of illustration we will presume that when the infant grew up to be the famous Niall of the Nine Hostages he weighed about 70 kg (or 155 lbs). In the 4th century young Niall's diet (excepting the odd wine shipment) would have been derived entirely from Ireland and its offshore waters. In short, the future High King of Ireland was in effect a reconstituted mass of Irish geology and hydrology that had been processed into an Irish adult (though recycled back into Irish soil about every two months).

The body of an Irishman contains up to 59 of the 92 naturally occurring elements. One of these, hydrogen, accounts for about one-tenth of the mass of a human being and for a 70-kg Niall, the other very light elements (helium, lithium, beryllium and boron) only provide about 25 mg. Some of the other elements are plentiful, such as the *c.* 43 kg of oxygen (which, like hydrogen, is largely tied up in water molecules) and 16 kg of carbon, while most of the rest are only slightly attested. For example, we could squeeze a lethal dose of arsenic out of about 150 Irishmen but it would take us on the order of 5,000 of them to obtain a gramme of gold. And to turn the Irish into a weapon of mass destruction, it would take about 70 million of them (or of anyone else) to provide enough uranium for a small atomic bomb. As there are an estimated 80 million people who claim Irish descent, this could be managed with people to spare.

It is obvious then that in order to construct Niall we are going to have to combine a great many elements. Some of these, the lighter ones such as hydrogen, may be a residue of the Big Bang. But the rest are heavier elements that make up Niall and the rest of the solar system, and these required a death. Some 4.6 billion years ago the Earth formed out of the dusty residue of previously exploded and obviously nameless stars. We know this because only the hot internal engine of a star can manufacture the range of heavier elements that constitute a planet and the creatures that occupy and sometimes write books about it. Most of our Earth consists of iron (35%), oxygen (30%), silicon (15%) and magnesium (19%), and these elements could only be created in a star much larger than our own sun. To create anything with an atomic weight greater than iron we need the explosion provided by a supernova.[1] Such massive stars as those that made our own existence possible are relatively short-lived and are unlikely to have produced planets on which intelligent life would have had time to evolve, so we do not have to bear the burden of some cosmic guilt that we have prospered on the backs of prematurely dead atomic ancestors. We are now about halfway through the life of our own sun and when it becomes glutted on helium and expands as a red giant to fry our planet in about 5 billion years, the Earth is more likely to go out with a sizzle than a bang. Incidentally, the life expectancy of Ireland is shorter than this, as we will see later, although Guinness's 9,000-year lease on their St James Gate brewery is probably still a safe investment.[2]

It is clear then that at the most basic level any search for the origins of the Irish leads us into the physical composition of Ireland. This is not just a matter of chemistry but also geography. Any search for Irish origins must be rooted in Ireland. Trace if you will the Irish back to a homeland in Britain, France or Spain, and you are led into a logical conundrum that wherever they come from they have no claim to being Irish unless they have lived on the island. Let us imagine, for example, our Proto-Irish sailing out of the Bay of Biscay in two ships. A storm ensues and only one makes it to Cork while the second is forced ashore in Cardiff. Is there anything about the occupants of the second boat that we can now regard as Irish?

The geology of Ireland, then, not only provides a setting in which to tell our story but it also provides one answer to the question of Irish origins. The earliest Irish were direct products of the land they occupied: no Irish geology = no Irish people. And we must be careful here because the physical form of Ireland is deceiving.

Historians have abandoned what they refer to as the essentialist approach to nations, the concept that 'nations are individually prescribed by nature' rather than invented by their populations.[3] But island nations are certainly the most convincing illusions. Bordered by c. 7,500 km of coast,[4] there appears to be a natural border to Ireland that invites us to contemplate a timeless land of lush green fields surrounded by an obviously natural barrier, the sea. A natural scientist would know how illusory this romantic image actually is. Neither the shape, appearance, composition nor location of Ireland has been constant through time, nor will any of these be so in the future. From a geological viewpoint, *Erin go bragh* ('Ireland forever') is wishful thinking. The Ireland that we know today was a geological accident forged between two continents and then frozen, dunked beneath warm seas, lifted in part to the heights of the Himalayas, covered with lush tropical swamps, blistering deserts and vast expanses of molten rock, then again buried under ice and finally thawed out. It took a lot of changes to make the Ireland we have right now, and the processes that forged the present Ireland will ensure that it will keep changing.

From hell to basement Ireland

Out of the remains left after about 10 billion years of the creation and collapse of older stars, both our sun and the planets that circle it were assembled from a spiralling disc of cosmic debris. A superheated Earth passed through the initial period of its history, the Hadean eon (named after Hades), which ended c. 3.8 billion years ago. Throughout this period the Earth's surface was molten, covered by a magma ocean of molten rock, exuding a miasma of noxious gases from erupting volcanoes. It endured a constant onslaught of meteors that pocked its surface to resemble the crater-marked surface of the moon. Although the main period of meteoritic onslaught concluded with the end of the Hadean, the Earth still absorbs 36,000 metric tons of meteorites every year.[5] Incidentally, the last recorded meteor strike of the 2nd millennium was in Ireland.[6]

In the period from 3.8 to 2.5 billion years ago the surface of the Earth had cooled enough to permit the formation of a rocky crust. During this period, known as the Archaean eon, about 80% of the Earth's crustal surface was formed, dotted with small proto-continents. By 3.8 billion years ago it is also believed that the temperature had cooled enough for the water vapour expelled by volcanic activity to fall as rain. The amount of water may have also been supplemented by the giant ice tails left by passing comets and water-rich meteors. The rain first filled the numerous craters and then spilled over to expand eventually into a world ocean. By about 3.5 billion years ago there emerges the earliest evidence of life in the form of bacteria.

As land-dwellers we have a very parochial view of the ocean. Even though we know that the greatest part of the Earth is covered by water we still imagine that it is the water that surrounds the land. In fact, if it were not for the fact that we have a very active planet pushing its crust upwards, there would probably be no land in the first place. The continents that we have are merely floating by virtue of the fact that they consist of lighter material than the basalt bed of the sea. Obviously, the story of Ireland cannot begin before we have some land and, over time, the amount of land has been increasing such that there is now about twice as much as there was 2 billion years ago.[7] Still, the area of the Pacific Ocean alone exceeds that of all the land on the planet.

It is in the next major geologic period, the Protoerozoic eon (2.5 billion to 545 million years ago), that Ireland offers some specific clues to its most distant past. The story does not begin in the north Atlantic, however, but between the equator and the South Pole, around which most of the Earth's landmasses were then clustered. About 1.7 billion years ago the sandy shore of an earlier proto-continent was pushed back deep into the Earth's crust to be heated to about 700° C (1292° F), not hot enough to (re)melt it but hot enough to alter it chemically into a metamorphic rock known as gneiss. Later, when the land buckled to form mountains, the gneiss was pushed upwards to be exposed today on the northernmost part of Ireland, the island of Inishtrahull off the north coast of Donegal (and running under the sea to Colonsay and Islay in Scotland); somewhat later formations of gneiss can be found in the mountainous regions of counties Mayo, Sligo and Tyrone. Such gneisses form the geologic 'basement' of Ireland; while this may seem quite early, northwest Scotland and the Hebrides offer evidence for gneisses formed from still earlier magma (c. 3 billion years old) that were metamorphosed c. 2.75 billion years ago, while the oldest rocks known are gneisses from Canada and Antarctica that date back more than 3.9 billion years.

Partition

By about 1 billion years ago the various landmasses of the world had collided to form a single massive continent comprising portions of the later continents that we know today, hidden within which were some of the fragments that would eventually form Ireland. By about 700 or 600 million years ago the break-up of the earlier supercontinent(s) was under way (1.1). One major section is known as Laurentia which, when it came adrift to be forced northward by the Iapetus Ocean, would comprise portions of northeast Canada, Greenland, northwest Ireland and Scotland. Another section, Avalonia, contained the southern half of Ireland (and Wales and England) and lay on the subcontinent of Gondwana (later India, Antarctica, Australia, South America and Africa). Western Gondwana, the specific area from which we can derive southeast Ireland, lay very roughly seawards of what we would later recognize as the coasts of West Africa and South America.

Geographically, these two portions of the Earth's crust that would eventually form Ireland should not have been expected ever to meet. However, this massive jigsaw

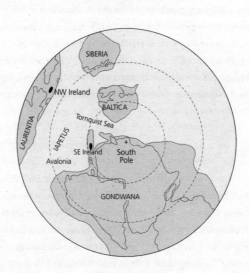

1.1. The break-up of the Vendian supercontinent 600 million years ago set the two components of Ireland in motion.

1.2. The situation 490 million years ago after the break-up of Pannotia had repositioned the two halves of Ireland on opposite sides of a spreading Iapetus Ocean.

puzzle was dismantled when the supercontinent broke apart and then reassembled and then, about 560 million years ago, it began splitting apart again. The good news was that at least the section of Laurentia that held the future northwestern half of Ireland and the part of Avalonia that contained the southeast of Ireland were facing each other. The bad news was that they were drifting further and further apart (1.2).

The driving force for all these movements is the approximately 20 plates (six major and the rest smaller, with Ireland on the major Eurasian plate) that together form the Earth's crust. The plates themselves are generally thought to be about 100–150 km thick (the distance between Dublin and Belfast) which takes them down to a depth where they encounter the asthenosphere, the top section of the Earth's mantle that is so hot (c. 1280° C/2336° F) that it provides a slightly slippery surface over which the various plates can slide at anywhere between 1 cm and 15 cm a year. The surface of the plates is the crust, thicker (c. 40 km) on the lighter continental landmasses and shallower (c. 7 km) on the heavier ocean floors. The continental landmasses may be driven apart by sea floors which expand when molten material wells up to create a succession of mid-oceanic ridges. Currently, the floor of the Atlantic is widening at a rate of about 10 mm per year while the Pacific is shrinking. This rate is quite slow in human terms (it has grown about 16 cm since the birth of Niall of the Nine Hostages and about a metre since Ireland was initially settled by people) but easily fast enough to account for the dispersal of continents that we encounter in geologic time.[8]

The break-up of Pannotia saw the constituent parts of Ireland still divided between Laurentia and now the small continent of Avalonia, the coastal fragment of west Gondwana (southern Ireland, Wales, England, Newfoundland and Nova Scotia). At this time there was a separate continent, Baltica, to account for much of western Europe while Siberia formed yet another continent. The space between Laurentia (northern Ireland) and Avalonia (southern Ireland) as they rifted further apart was filled by the ever-expanding Iapetus Ocean, the precursor to the Atlantic Ocean. Magma poured out through the Earth's crust and a string of volcanoes formed to create an ever-widening ocean floor driving the northern and southern halves of Ireland still further away from each other, although they were now separated by an expanding sea rather than a continental landmass. While the current distance by air between Belfast and Cork is 343 km, about 480 million years ago the distance between the ancestral locations of these two modern towns was 4,000 km! On our present globe, this part of the story of Ireland was taking place roughly where Australia lies today.

The creation of the Iapetus Ocean found northwest Ireland situated on the south coast of Laurentia. Within the shoreline and nearby sea in the period c. 960–450 million years ago there formed a series of sediments, some 25 km thick, built out of marine sands and mud, known as the Dalradian Supergroup; these extend from Shetland south across Donegal and Mayo as far as Connemara. Within these sediments are also the stones and boulders that had been deposited by ice sheets. Today when one refers to the Ice Age we generally have in mind the Pleistocene, the period when the northern parts of North America and northern Eurasia, including Ireland, were covered by ice from 1 million to 12,000 years ago. But these earlier ice ages from *c.* 970 to 570 million years ago were far more extreme and temperatures plummeted to about -50° C (-58° F). Some believe that ice covered all the landmasses of the various supercontinents, forming what is often called 'snowball Earth'. After the gneisses mentioned above, these sediments constitute the second tier of Ireland's basement geology and form about 10% of the surface area of Ireland. Although they should have been buried deep under millions of years of subsequent sediments, we know of them today because about 475–450 million years ago they were greatly uplifted (and deformed) as part of the same process that created the Grampian Mountains of Scotland. We should remember that continental plates do not just move apart from one another – they can also collide. When this happens it forces one plate to slide below the other, resulting in the type of uplift that produces the world's great mountain ranges. In the Himalayas we see the effects of the collision of the northward-moving Indian plate under the southern Asian plate; Mount Everest is estimated to still be rising at a rate of perhaps 4–6 mm per year.

Our knowledge of the earliest geologic history of southeast Ireland is less clear than for the northwest, but we can at least push back its oldest rocks to *c.* 650–600 million years ago when gneisses were also being formed along a portion of the coast of Avalonia (southeast Ireland-Wales) where they are exposed today around Rosslare. After this there is a long period in which the southern portion of Ireland lay either on a geologically quiet coast of Gondwana or under water as sediments accumulated. During the Cambrian period (*c.* 550–500 million years ago) over 5 km of deep marine sediments were laid down in what is now the Leinster coast and they contain the fossilized burrows of sea creatures, the earliest evidence of life within Ireland's geology. In the following Ordovician period (500–450 million years ago) another 5 km of marine sediments and later volcanic rocks formed part of the basis of southeast Ireland.

Throughout the Protoerozoic eon the continual evolution of organisms capable of photosynthesis, converting such noxious gases as carbon dioxide, ammonia and methane into oxygen, set in motion the chemical processes that gradually developed into the Earth's atmosphere. Two billion years ago oxygen made up far less than 1% of the Earth's atmosphere, but by about 500 million years ago this had increased to about 10%; in the next major period it would finally achieve its current proportion of 21%. But whatever goes up is likely to come down, and some earth scientists estimate that within another 500 million to a billion years from now, oxygen will fall again to about 1%.

The unification of Ireland

The creation of the Ireland we know could only happen if the landmasses housing its two halves could be brought together. The process that would make this happen was under way during the Silurian period, some 443–417 million years ago, when warming temperatures melted the earlier Ordovician ice sheets and placed much of the land again below shallow seas.

While ocean floors may expand they also must contract and even disappear through the process of subduction, i.e. after about 10 million years the ocean floors, because they are denser than the part of the crust on which they slide, begin to sink as they slip under the continental crust and settle back into the mantle to be reheated and recycled. This system of subduction means that while we may find traces of continental crust going back billions of years, remains of the ocean floor have not survived for more than about 200 million years. During the Silurian period the Iapetus Ocean closed as its ocean floor was subducted, sliding under both the continental plate of Avalonia and the approaching continental plate of Laurentia, thus drawing the two continents together.

One is tempted to imagine Niall sitting (submerged) in a south-facing pub in the Irish midlands scanning the nearby coast for the southern half of Ireland as it emerged on the horizon and ever so slowly joined with the Laurentian half of Ireland. The two continents did not strike each other head-on but rather slid into position forming an 'Iapetic suture', a 50-km-wide 'scar' that marks the merger and hence formation of the common basement surface of all Ireland (1.3). This scar runs very roughly on a line between Louth (say, Clogher Head) and south Clare (Loop Head). This geological marriage occurred roughly when both landmasses had reached a position still south of the equator in the mid-Pacific between what is now Australia and South America. While a Hiberno-centric view of this process might envisage the two halves of the island of Ireland gradually 'docking' with one another like parts of a space station, what was actually happening was the collision of three separate continents, two of which contained portions of the modern Ireland. Avalonia (southeast Ireland) struck Laurentia (northwest Ireland) and Baltica struck the west of Laurentia and the north of Avalonia. This formed a new continent, Laurussia, that also housed the future North America and Europe.

It is necessary to keep this larger picture in mind in the ensuing account and avoid the temptation of imagining that the geographical entity of Ireland was uniquely experiencing a long series of geological torture. The Iapetus suture, for example, not

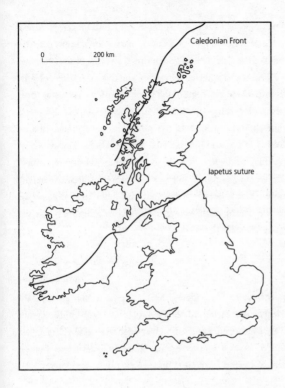

1.3. The unification of Ireland (and Britain) and the Iapetus suture.

only runs across the Irish Sea (which is a continental and not an oceanic part of the crust) to join northern England with Scotland (the suture runs just north of the Isle of Man and the Lake District), but it also extends west into North America. We have the Ireland we have because of the 'accident' of the continental collision that rubbed a specific portion of Avalonia (moving southeast to northwest) against a specific portion of Laurentia. Had Avalonia struck Laurentia a bit further along, we might have had a geological act of union that 18th-century legislators could hardly have imagined, with the future England and Wales appended to Ulster and Connacht. A still greater miss would have found the northern halves of Ireland and Britain appended to western France or Spain. Until the end of this chapter, then, references to Ireland are merely to an abstraction of its present geographical shape superimposed over much larger continents and seas.

The fusion of landmasses joined the basement layers of Ireland together. Along the west of this future Ireland the merger of the landmasses forced upwards the enormous mountain chain of the Caledonides which runs from (the future) Norway southeast to (the future) Nova Scotia and Newfoundland and on to the Appalachians. Magma, molten rock from *c.* 30–40 km deep in the Earth's crust, welled up to leave its mark today as the spectacular granite uplands of Co. Donegal; Leinster also sees a major intrusion of granite about this time, and Ireland is dotted with the remnants of volcanoes such as Lambay Island and Vinegar Hill, the latter better known for its role in the 1798 uprising. It is also during the Silurian that Ireland receives its earliest cover in plant life, a primitive vascular plant called Cooksonia which grew to a height of about 5 cm and whose detritus began creating the soil foundation that would support further forms of life. The Silurian, however, did not just bring life but, as we will later see in Chapter 7, a place for the dead.

Deserts and seas

While Ireland is generally both low and green, this was certainly not an accurate description during the next geological period, the Devonian, *c.* 417–354 million years ago. During this period the Caledonides pushed high enough to rival the Himalayas, preventing rain from falling on the southern plain of the new continent (which included the eastern part of Ireland) so that it became part of a vast desert (1.4).

1.4. Ireland in the Devonian was situated on the coast of Laurentia in the eastern shadow of the massive Caledonides. Its coastal position in the following Carboniferous would expose it to frequent inundation from the sea.

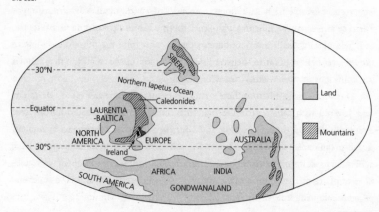

Without dense plant cover, these mountains were also exposed to intense weathering as floods carried earlier sediments down from the mountains towards a distant sea, leaving the layer known today as Old Red Sandstone. In the north the Old Red Sandstone is exposed around Cushendall, Co. Antrim, while in the Munster basin, where it is most marked, the deposits are 6 km thick. As for the once towering Caledonides, all that is left today in Ireland are the eroded stumps that we know, for example, as the Sperrins in Tyrone and highlands of Donegal or the granite uplands of Wicklow. The same processes of erosion account for their North American extension, the Appalachians. It is also at this time that we find slight evidence for Ireland's first four-footed occupant. During the Devonian varieties of lungfish evolved into early amphibians, and the tracks of one such amphibian, estimated at about a metre long, have been discovered in a layer of slate on Valencia Island in Co. Kerry.

By 354 million years ago Ireland entered the Carboniferous, a period lasting some 64 million years during which some of its major rock foundations were established. Sea levels were rising and the sea periodically flooded over the land from southeast to northwest. The parched land of the previous period was now under a warm shallow sea teeming with life, and only some of the higher elevations such as Wicklow and Donegal poked above the water to form small islands covered with vegetation. The coral and shells living on the sea bed gradually formed thick layers of limestone that constitute about two-thirds of Ireland's rock mantle and can be seen at their most spectacular in places such as the Burren, Co. Clare. It was also during the later Carboniferous that massive rivers rapidly dumped sediments in wide deltas. As a geologically mind-blowing exercise, consider that when you stand today on the edge of the Cliffs of Moher or Achill Island (the highest cliffs in Europe) and stare over a sheer drop into the Atlantic, you are perched on the top of sediments dumped there by rivers flowing *downstream from the west* where now you only find the open sea. The missing land that once supported the rivers and provided the sediments would later be forced far to the west with the creation of the Atlantic Ocean. Today we know it as northeast America.

During the Carboniferous there were also periods of lower sea levels when Ireland was covered with freshwater swamps and primitive fernlike trees whose remains eventually formed thick beds of coal. Major geological upheaval was experienced again at the end of the Carboniferous when the main part of Gondwana collided with Laurussia to form the most recent of the supercontinents, Pangaea. The collision of plates fractured the earlier layers of Old Red Sandstone and Carboniferous deposits, allowing hot waters from below to move up channels and deposit various

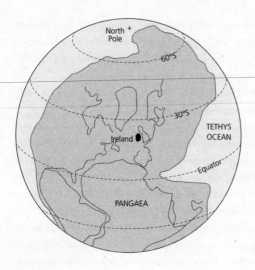

1.5. Pangaea with Ireland
in the centre of a vast
world supercontinent.

metals such as copper, lead and zinc. While the ore fields of central Ireland, consti-
tuting about 0.12 gm lead per person (pp) and zinc (2.3 gm pp), would wait until
the 1960s to be exploited commercially, the pre-Carboniferous deposits of copper
(72 mg pp) in the southwest of Ireland would become critical in establishing a
thriving prehistoric bronze industry (see Chapter 4).

Ireland in a new continent

By the Permian period (*c.* 290–248 million years ago) most of the continents had again
fused together into the supercontinent of Pangaea and the foundations of Ireland
moved with it north of the equator, out of the tropics and into an arid climatic belt
(1.5). As sea levels fell, the coastal seas and swamps evaporated into barren deserts;
Ireland was no longer coastal but occupied the middle of the reassembled continent,
with an extensive mountain chain (the Variscan chain, extending from southern
Ireland across Brittany and on to the Czech Republic) to its south. Ireland felt the
full force of atmospheric erosion, and this would alter not only its geology but also
its later historical trajectory. Before the Permian a science-fiction writer could have
constructed an alternative future history for Ireland in which it emerged as a small
but nevertheless industrialized society – an 18th-century Celtic tiger. For example,

some of the beds of Carboniferous coal (in Antrim, Tyrone, Roscommon, Leitrim, Kerry and Cork) persisted into the modern period and were variously mined from the Middle Ages onward. In the 18th century the Ballycastle works yielded about 10,000–15,000 tonnes a year while a much larger coalfield survived near Castlecomer and the last Irish coalmine, at Arigna, Co. Roscommon, did not close until 1990. But this critical source of energy that would fuel the industrial revolution in England was almost entirely eroded away in Ireland during the Permian (the coal of England and Wales was protected from erosion by further mountain-building activities that largely bypassed Ireland). Although Ireland tried its hand at erecting dark satanic mills as early as Britain, the lack of a widely available and affordable industrial fuel source ensured that Ireland would remain largely pastoral and rural.

Before the late Permian the basin of the east Irish Sea, i.e. the vicinity of the Isle of Man, was filled not with water but with enormous sand dunes. However, by the late Permian the sea had risen again and flooded substantial portions of the northern part of the Irish Sea, but there was no corresponding flooding from the south that would have rendered Ireland into an island (1.6). The new Proto-Atlantic, the Bakevellia Sea, covered extensive parts of northern and eastern Ireland but then

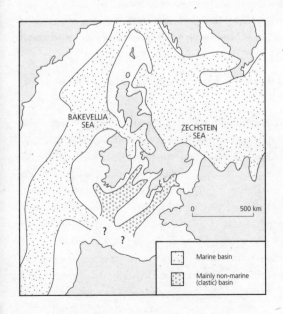

1.6. Almost an island: Ireland in the Late Permian partly surrounded by the Bakevellia Sea.

evaporated, leaving deposits of limestone. The end of the Permian marks the greatest mass extinction of life on Earth; somewhere on the order of 30% to 50% of life in the oceans may have disappeared at this time for reasons that still remain uncertain.

Age of dinosaurs

The Mesozoic, the age of the dinosaurs, had a geologically important impact on Ireland despite the fact that Ireland lags in the dinosaur league.[9] The expanding Atlantic Ocean drove North America away from Ireland and Scotland, leaving Ireland no longer landlocked and situated, by the end of the Triassic era (c. 248–206 million years ago), on the northeast coast of Pangaea. It was well north of the equator, lying roughly at the same latitude as the Azores. The climate was arid, and wind-borne sands laid down deep sediments of sandstone, many hundreds of metres thick. Then, about 230 million years ago, sediments in sea-fed shallow lagoons produced both rock salt and gypsum. The salt deposits of Austria would later become one of the key commodities of the late Bronze Age and Iron Age in western Europe, while clear evidence for salt extraction in Ireland (in the vicinity of Carrickfergus, Co. Antrim) would have to await the historic period. Gypsum was used for medieval tombs and today it is ubiquitous as a major component of plasterboard.

By the Jurassic period (206–142 million years ago), the last supercontinent, Pangaea, was well on its way to breaking up into its constituent modern continents

1.7. Jurassic Ireland with the newly formed Atlantic Ocean separating North America/Greenland from Ireland.

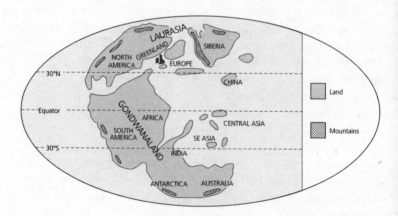

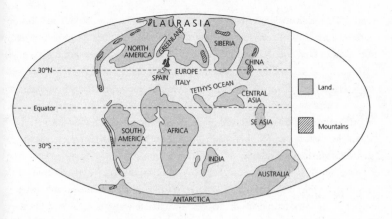

1.8. Rising sea levels in the Cretaceous result in the near complete inundation of Ireland.

while sea levels rose on the order of 100 m, leaving large portions of Ireland's future borders now submerged under a shallow sea (1.7). At this time one could speak of an island of Ireland, although it would have excluded most of the eastern part (then under a shallow sea) and included a large amount of what is now submerged to the west. While remains of marine reptiles have been recovered from the coastal regions, much of the remains of the early Jurassic period in Ireland was eroded away during the later Jurassic and Cretaceous times.

The Cretaceous period (142–65 million years ago) saw a massive rise in greenhouse gases (anywhere between four and ten times the current amount) and this, coupled with the increased ocean floor of the Pacific and Atlantic, drove up the Earth's sea level on a massive scale, some 200–300 m above current levels. The sea was very warm, with estimated maximum temperatures around Britain of c. 28° C (82° F). The result of the sea-level rise was that most of Ireland, along with the rest of Europe as far east as the Aral Sea, was under water (1.8). The only area of Ireland that may still have constituted an island would have been within about a 40-km radius of Carlow, plus some minor archipelagoes.

The geological legacy of the Cretaceous and the preceding period was extremely important to Ireland's future occupants. The organic deposits such as seaweeds that formed at this time ultimately provided deposits of natural gas that are currently exploited off the south coast (and building the pipelines across Ireland has stimulated a wealth of archaeological discoveries). These same seas were also filled with shellfish and other calcareous life that left thick chalk deposits (such as the White Cliffs of Dover or the cliffs of northeast Antrim) in which siliceous material eventually took the form of flint. For 6,000 years flint would serve as the main raw industrial source of tools in Ireland. But like the previous deposits of coal, the thick layers of chalk and flint would also suffer massive erosion over most of Ireland, surviving in abundance only in the northeast for reasons we are about to discover. The Cretaceous, along with the dinosaurs and many other species of life, was brought to an end by the impact of an asteroid in what is now the Yucatan peninsula of Mexico during a period of rising sea levels and climatic change.

The Earth erupts

By about 65 million years ago, at the beginning of the Palaeogene (65–23 million years ago), both sea levels and temperatures had again fallen and Ireland was now roughly parallel with southern France. As a result of collisions in the area of the Alps, Ireland emerged from beneath the sea along with Britain to form a large landmass connected to what is now northwest France. Some 10 million years later a vast hotspot (c. 2,000 km across) emerged, centred on Greenland, that saw the hot interior of the Earth throw up magma over a vast area. The material welled up, expanding the floor of the north Atlantic Ocean as North America continued to be pushed westward (1.9). The magma from fissures and active volcanoes also emerged in the north of Ireland and Scotland. Its effect on the landscape was impressive, producing the Giant's Causeway of north Antrim as well as volcanoes such as Slieve Gullion and Carlingford (and the constituent mass of the Mourne Mountains). Covering the earlier chalk deposits of northeast Ireland, this layer of basalt – estimated to have originally been over 1.5 km thick – provided a protective coating over its flint sources while the unprotected remainder of Ireland experienced the erosion that would remove the chalk and flint. In addition, this period of igneous activity would also provide a series of stone types that were eminently suitable for shaping and polishing as axes: the most widely exploited of these stones was porcellanite, which provided axes in the many thousands. This geological 'accident' helps account for the extremely high density (actually visibility) of early archaeological sites in Co. Antrim compared with the rest of Ireland.

The late Palaeogene saw the formation of the vast basins which would later be filled by Lough Neagh and the Shannon drainage; this was the last geological period in which new rocks were formed in Ireland – or at least that we can find, as the

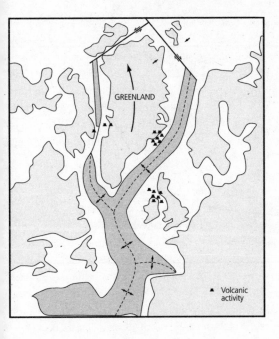

▲ Volcanic
activity

1.9. Ireland enters
the Palaeogene
attached to the rest
of Atlantic Europe.

succeeding Neogene (23–1.6 million years ago) saw a relentless erasing of what had gone before as water continuously attacked the limestone cover and removed many hundreds of metres of sediments, leaving in its wake a deep deposit of clays. It is only during this last of the long geological periods that Ireland finally achieved its current geographical position (1.10) and that its major river valleys appeared, while tectonic uplift began to form many of the hills of Ireland. We must emphasize *current* position, because there is no reason to presume that the geologic processes that have operated over the past 4 billion years have now ceased. In one extrapolation of the present course of continental drift, the world some 250 million years in the future will find the Atlantic vanished and most of the continents again reassembled into a single supercontinent; at its very northernmost tier and abutting Newfoundland will be Ireland, even further north than Scandinavia (1.11).[10] Unless there are suitable advances in technology and changes in environment to prevent this, we have now reduced the life expectancy of Ireland from 5 billion to 250 million years and, as we will soon see, it is about to get a lot shorter yet.

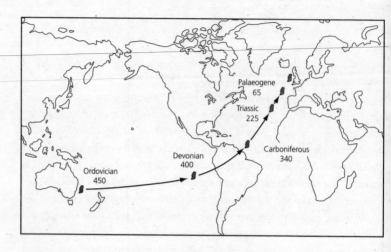

1.10. Ireland's long journey, millions of years ago, to its present position.

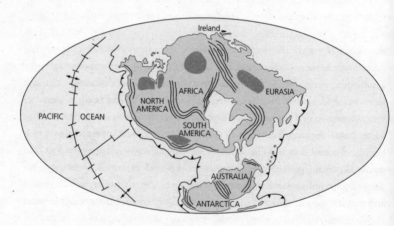

1.11. The future position of Ireland in 250 million years.

Ice

It is at this point, the beginning of the Quaternary (1.6 million years ago to the present), that the main factor in shaping the current surface of Ireland makes its appearance. At 1.6 million years ago a cooling of the Earth's climate resulted in the expansion of ice sheets, especially over the northern half of the globe. The Ice Age saw a series of major cold periods, each lasting on the order of 100,000 years, alternating with warmer periods that might prevail for anywhere from 10,000 to 60,000 years but averaging much closer to the lower end. Ireland's northern position placed it on the front line of these periodic glacial advances, so while we can trace six major glacial periods in Continental Europe, only traces of the final two have survived in Ireland. The earlier of these, the Munsterian (300,000–130,000 years ago), saw large ice sheets (at least up to c. 300–500 m in height) form in the highlands of Ireland and Scotland that gradually expanded to cover the entire island. This was followed by a warmer stage lasting some 50,000 years when forests were once again able to colonize the land, but by 80,000 years ago Ireland had entered the main phase of its last glacial period, the Midlandian.

The Midlandian (c. 80,000–10,000 years ago) is responsible for many of the so-called 'timeless' elements of the Irish landscape (1.12). Ice sheets, armed not only with the sheer weight of the glaciers themselves but also kitted out with the abrasive 'teeth' of the sand and boulders they carried with them, pushed down to form the U-shaped valleys that typify the Wexford Mountains and some of the glens of Antrim. Sand and gravel travelling along rivers at the base of the glaciers would be deposited in long sinuous mounds; the Irish called this formation an *escir* and the word has stuck in the language of the geologist as *esker*. More numerous are the rounded piles of clay and boulders that the ice sheets deposited in their wake. These formed small egg-shaped hills known colloquially as *druimnín* or small ridges, which became distorted into drumlin, another geological legacy provided by the Irish language. The drumlin belt stretches along the southern counties of Ulster and provided the landscape foundation both for Irish towns (e.g. Armagh, Monaghan, Dromore) and some of the earlier sacred sites, both pagan (e.g. Emain Macha) and Christian (e.g. Downpatrick).

Conditions during the Midlandian alternated between intense cold, when glaciers up to 600–700 m thick covered most if not all of Ireland, and somewhat warmer periods, when we find evidence for a variety of mammals. In the period c. 40,000–20,000 years ago there is some evidence for hare, hyena, bear, woolly mammoth, red

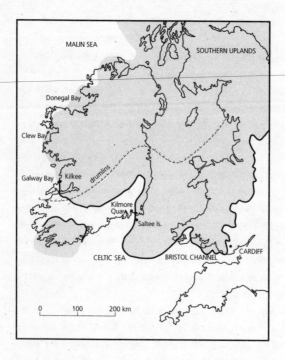

1.12. Ireland under the Midlandian ice sheets.

deer, giant Irish deer, reindeer, horse, wolf, lemming (both Arctic and Norwegian), fox and goose.[11] Then, for a period of about 7,000 years through what was probably the height of glaciation, the solidly dated record of Irish fauna falls silent, and there is certainly a presumption that conditions became so cold and ice cover so extensive that most animal populations were driven out of Ireland.

Making an island

About 16,000 years ago warming conditions had seen off the Midlandian and left Ireland ice free. As the ice disappeared, plants and animals that had occupied refuges further south in Europe during the last Ice Age recolonized Ireland. During the Ice Age the water that would otherwise have been found in the seas was locked up in frozen form as glaciers and ice sheets on land. With the water removed to the land, the result was a massive fall in sea levels that should have made it possible to travel from the Continent across southern Britain and on into Ireland on foot (though the Irish Sea basin may still have been fairly soggy) or directly from northern France to southern Ireland: Then, after the Ice Age, the glaciers melted into rivers that poured water back into the sea and raised the sea level, cutting off the land approaches to Ireland. This event, of course, takes us to the critical point of this chapter – the making of Ireland as a reasonably defined physical entity, no longer simply a component of Laurentia, Laurussia or Europe. Moreover, the dating of this event is central to the entire problem of (re-)establishing the 'native' flora and fauna of Ireland.

To appreciate the problem before us we can compare three different models. In the most optimistic model, land corridors across the Irish Sea remained high and dry long enough to permit a progression of plants and animals to colonize Ireland (1.13). The corridors would have promoted a shift from tundra to open grasslands and the species that fed on grass such as reindeer and giant Irish deer could graze their way across northwest Europe, Britain and on into Ireland. Alternatively, there may have

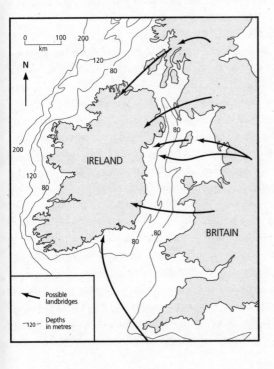

1.13. Potential landbridges into Ireland.

been an extensive enough landmass southeast of Ireland that still connected Ireland directly to the Continent. Along either path moved the various species of trees beginning with willow and juniper, two species that can cope with both the cold and the barren clays and gravels left after the Ice Age. A similar model is employed to explain the migrations of many animals and humans from Asia across the Bering 'landbridge' (an enormous corridor) into Alaska and the rest of the New World. As long as the corridor is left dry, we can populate Ireland with its so-called native flora and fauna, but eventually the Irish Sea must fill up and, so it is argued, nothing else will come into Ireland unless it can swim, fly or be carried by human transport. The critical problem here is the date of this landbridge. Pollen evidence indicates open grasslands by c. 13,800 years ago and then trees – first willow (a very small bush at this time) entering at c. 13,500 years ago and juniper next (13,300 years ago), with a major cold phase (12,700 to 11,900 years ago) succeeded by warmer conditions and the entrance of birch (11,500 years ago) followed by the rest of the native Irish forest.[12] Dated faunal remains record the reappearance of reindeer and giant Irish deer from 13,000 years ago followed by the other species of wild animals (hare, bear, wolf, etc.). In general, we are looking for a landbridge to permit this colonization of plants and animals in the period c. 14,000 to 10,000 years ago.

According to this viewpoint, nothing but a landbridge will do. An impressive series of landsnails dating to c. 10,000 years ago found at Newlands Cross, near Dublin, have been claimed as evidence for the existence of a landbridge (a similar case has been made for moss mites), as they could not have flown nor swum to Ireland.[13] However, the landbridge itself may well have been wet, i.e. bogland, as suggested by the fact that Ireland plays home to the pygmy shrew (which browses on the land's surface) and not the much more abundant common shrew known in Britain (which must burrow for its food). As one can see, the landbridge is primarily supported as the only logical explanation for how the flora and fauna of early postglacial Ireland arrived in Ireland and also why it is less abundant than in neighbouring Britain (because the land connection was severed and thus did not permit the full British suite of plants and animals to arrive in Ireland). Frank Mitchell likened this recolonization to a steeplechase (1.14) in which plants and animals moved northward from southern Europe, the refuge areas they had occupied during the last glaciation, periodically impeded by the creation of new water barriers (as well as more restrictive climatic regimes).[14] France, for example, which included the refuge areas in its south as well as newly colonized territories in its north, possesses c. 3,500 native plants; Britain has only 1,172, while Ireland, cut off earlier than Britain, possesses (according

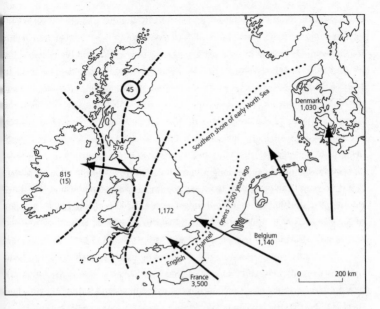

1.14. Frank Mitchell's botanic 'steeplechase' indicating the fall-off in native plants as one approaches Ireland.

to some sources) perhaps only 815 native species. Whereas Britain has 32 species of mammals, Ireland has only 14; British birds number 456 while Ireland has 354; Britain has 6 amphibians while Ireland can only claim 2, and Britain has 4 reptiles to Ireland's one – a lizard (St Patrick can take no credit for ridding Ireland of a reptile it did not possess). It should be emphasized that not all of these disparities are the result of the submergence of landbridges: Ireland is smaller and environmentally much less diverse than Britain, and we should not expect a comparable amount of biodiversity on the smaller island. As for fish, Ireland would have lost all of its fresh-water species during the last glaciation and only received migratory fish (salmon, trout, eels) or once-migratory but then trapped species (pollan, shad and char) after the last glaciation.

The second model is the more pessimistic and asserts that from the time the glaciers began to melt in Ireland, the various basins of the Irish Sea had filled so quickly that there never was a postglacial corridor that permitted flora and fauna to immigrate across land into Ireland, at least not within the time frame demanded by the botanists and zoologists. The entry of plants and animals into Ireland was not so much a steeplechase as a triathlon. This is largely the argument of geomorphologists who study the Irish Sea basin and attempt to model how it may have behaved during the end of the last glaciation. Unfortunately, the issues involved are extremely complicated and cannot be resolved simply by looking at the current sea depths across the Irish Sea and estimating how low the sea was at any given time. During the Ice Age and the subsequent warming period the land levels (and here we are speaking of both the surface of the ground and the height of the Irish Sea bed) were continually fluctuating.

Some geomorphologists have suggested that there is evidence for a series of land-bridges. Robin Wingfield has suggested the existence of landbridges in the period 11,000 to 9,900 years ago (opening progressively northward from southwest Wales) and then again from 9,750 to 9,500 years ago, running to Ireland from just south of the Isle of Man.[15] But in the period before 11,000 years ago he argues for 3–5 km of open water, which makes it awfully difficult to explain the plants and animals that came to Ireland before then. Kurt Lambeck and Anthony Purcell suggest that the only possible land corridor existed c. 16,000 years ago (from southern Britain to southeast Ireland), and even then it would have reached only a few metres above sea level and does nothing to get our most recent fauna to Ireland.[16] And, finally, others such as Robert Devoy have long argued that a case for a postglacial landbridge, at least from the standpoint of the actual physical evidence, still remains unproven.[17] A recent study by Robin Edwards and Anthony Brooks suggests that while a low-lying isthmus joined southeastern Ireland with southwestern Britain about 20,000 years ago, sea-level rise would have broken the landbridge by 16,000 years ago at a time when much of the northern half of Ireland was still under ice sheets.[18]

The third approach falls between the extremes and while it denies any solid evidence of a landbridge, it also recognizes that the sea-level situation during the immediate postglacial period was very different from what it is today (1.15). While there are deep trenches (100–200 m deep) within the Irish Sea, 40% of the sea area is less than 40 m deep. As one can find peat deposits indicating forests up to c. 25 m below current shorelines, we can well expect that the Irish Sea was once not nearly so wide as it is today. Andrew Cooper and others, for example, have suggested that about 11,000 to 10,000 years ago an estimated 30-m drop in sea level would have left a series of shoals and islands across open water between Islay and Malin Head.[19] The conclusion from this approach is that while there may not have been a wide and dry land corridor, the distances between Britain and Ireland in the postglacial period were much less than they are today and this would have greatly facilitated the movement of plants and animals into Ireland. In addition to a British-Irish link, one might also imagine an ever-decreasing archipelago of islands between northwest France and Ireland between *c.* 16,000 and 10,000 years ago that provided a possible route from the Continent to southern Ireland. What makes this attractive are recent studies of the DNA of some of the native Irish fauna (pine marten, house mice, mountain hare, stoats) which reveal that they are genetically much closer to species found in Spain than to those now found in Britain.[20] Also, where we can date the spread of the various tree species, they appear to expand across Ireland from south to north rather than east to west.

Although the jury is still out on the final disappearance of a landbridge and we may have to remain vague about the precise time when Ireland became totally separate from both Britain and the Continent, we can still be fairly certain that Ireland had taken its present form as an island before the time of its first human occupants.

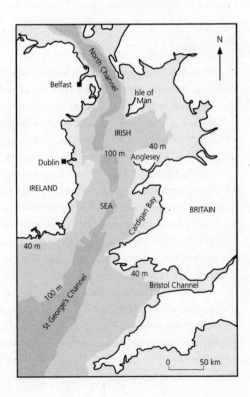

1.15. Sea depths in the Irish Sea.

Finally, we should note that no one has ever declared the Ice Age over, and only an exaggerated sense of our own importance permits us to pretend otherwise. Climatic records over the past 800,000 years suggest that the warm periods in between the advances of ice last on average about 11,000 years, and we have already used up 11,000 years since the last glaciation. There are a variety of explanations for why we are not already under ice – greenhouse gases, the orbital eccentricity of the Earth – that suggest Ireland may be spared for anywhere from a thousand to a few tens of thousands of years (the most optimistic model).[21] But unless human technological ingenuity comes up with a way of staving off what seems to be inevitable, it is entirely possible that Ireland has already enjoyed over half of its existence as part of the inhabited Earth, and it is quite possible that within a time span of the next 20,000 or 30,000 years every trace of its previous people and culture will be scraped clean from its surface by new ice sheets. Guinness might want to think carefully about renewing their 9,000-year lease when it expires.

Conclusions

→ The earliest Irish (like all life on Earth) are composed of elements, most of which were only created after the explosion of one or more supernovas before our own solar system was formed.

→ The early population of Ireland was chemically composed of 59 elements directly derived from the local geology of Ireland.

→ The land that came to comprise the island of Ireland only formed after the collision of two continents c. 430 million years ago.

→ The formation of an island in the approximate shape and size of contemporary Ireland only occurred about 12,000–10,000 years ago, i.e. Ireland has been an island in roughly its present shape for only 1/43,000th of its existence.

→ The relatively rapid separation of Ireland from both Britain and the Continent deprived Ireland of a substantial portion of the native flora and fauna of neighbouring countries.

→ Compared with Britain and the Continent, Ireland would have been regarded as impoverished with respect to potential food supplies.

→ Ireland's future life expectancy is to be measured in thousands rather than millions of years and it may already have entered middle age if not senility.

CHAPTER TWO

First Colonists

Niall could hardly have ignored the relics of the distant past that surrounded him. A claimant to the high kingship would have been aware of the bumps, ridges and mounds that covered the ancient 'royal sites' of Ireland such as Tara, the seat of the High King, or Emain Macha, the Ulster capital that his descendants would reputedly destroy. Niall might have imagined that these earlier monuments belonged to the first settlers of Ireland who had lived on the island since time immemorial. If he had believed this he would have been deceived for two reasons. First, the monuments that filled the landscape over which Niall ruled did not belong to the earliest remains of settlement in Ireland, since the first occupants of the land have not left us anything so obvious. Moreover, in terms of human occupation, Ireland is an extremely young land. While southern Britain has admittedly intermittent evidence for settlement by some form of humans from *c.* 270,000 years ago, there is no positive evidence for the human colonization of Ireland earlier than 10,000 years ago, i.e. *c.* 8000 BC.[1] To put this on a global scale, we have evidence for human populations trekking their way across Asia, crossing the Bering landbridge into North America, and migrating the entire length of the New World as far south as Patagonia, a linear distance of over 15,000 km, earlier than we have for colonists making it over the *c.* 150 km from areas of the earliest human settlement in Wales to Ireland.[2] Can Ireland really have been so neglected?

An Irish Palaeolithic?

During interglacial periods, Ireland enjoyed the same type of warmer temperatures and grazing animals hunted elsewhere in Europe, so there is no obvious reason why Ireland should have been shunned by Palaeolithic (Old Stone Age) hunters. But the closest physical evidence we have for such hunters is a few flakes of flint.[3] One of these was discovered in a quarry near Drogheda, Co. Louth, and has been compared to the type of Palaeolithic tools known from southern Britain *c.* 300,000–200,000 years ago (2.1, 2.2).[4] Found in glacial gravels, the flake would appear to have been dropped by a hunter in what is now the Irish Sea basin at a time when sea levels were so low that this region was dry and could support human occupation. Later glacial activity carried the flint and other gravels to be deposited near Drogheda. But even if more evidence dating to this period could be discovered, it would only indicate the presence of a species of human that long preceded the emergence of our own *Homo sapiens*. In terms of western Europe, we cannot expect to find representatives of people with whom we share a direct genetic line until *c.* 45,000–42,000 BC.[5] And although hunters had made it to Britain by then, and potentially could have reached Ireland, following the herds of mammoth, reindeer, Giant Irish deer, red

2.1. Map of sites mentioned in Chapter 2.

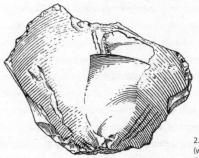

2.2. Lower Palaeolithic flake (width 9.5 cm) from Mell, Co. Louth.

deer and other prey in the period around 35,000 years ago (in this period Ireland shares all the same faunal remains as Britain except for the woolly rhinoceros), we have no archaeological evidence to confirm that this actually happened. Moreover, even if populations did arrive in Ireland at this time, conditions began to deteriorate sharply in what is known as the Late Glacial Maximum, the period in which the glaciers expanded again and intense cold pushed northwest Europe beyond the range of human settlement. Britain appears to have been abandoned by 23,000 years ago. Human populations in Europe retreated to the south, in Atlantic Europe primarily to southern France and northern Spain, and there they remained until warmer temperatures permitted them to expand north again. The attentive reader will immediately realize that this retreat into a southern refuge will provide yet another aspect to Irish 'origins' that we will have to deal with later (Chapter 8).

About 15,000 years ago populations moved north again to northern Germany, Denmark, northern France and southern Britain. Still, there is no evidence that Ireland was part of the itinerary of these hunters, although it is always possible that some did come in pursuit of the Giant Irish deer or reindeer that were present in Ireland at this time. Although archaeologists are always wary of interpreting the absence of evidence as evidence of absence, the fact that Scotland also appears to have lain beyond the reach of these Late Palaeolithic hunters does nothing to strengthen the notion of an Irish Palaeolithic. But we should, of course, make a distinction between 'setting foot' in Ireland – which is possible – and taking up long-term occupation. The resources of Ireland may have attracted occasional hunters to visit but never been enough to encourage them to stay.[6]

If the quantity of the prey was too small to invite sufficient occupation of Ireland to leave any remains, the period around 11,000–10,000 BC should probably have sealed the fate of any potential occupation of Ireland or Scotland. Generally known as the Younger Dryas, or in Ireland as the Nahanagan Interstadial, this marks a major 'cold snap' (immortalized on an exaggerated scale in the 2004 film *The Day after Tomorrow*) that saw temperatures plummet and even glaciers return to high ground in both Ireland and Scotland. This would have discouraged long-term settlement by both animals and humans and, indeed, it is at this time that we see the local extinction of red deer, reindeer and the Giant Irish deer. The latter, whose enormous antlers alone required many times as much calcium and phosphorus as an average human, found the tundra-like conditions incapable of supporting the needs of its own body chemistry.

In the balance of probability against hard archaeological evidence, human occupation of Ireland before *c.* 11,000 BC must be possible, but the evidence remains wholly elusive. Furthermore, it is difficult to see how anyone, once in Ireland, could have survived the Nahanagan Interstadial. The ancestors of the first permanent occupants of Ireland must certainly have belonged to the general range of Upper Palaeolithic hunters who had pushed northward, retreated and then pushed north again in western Europe, but their geographical location lay outside Ireland. It is not they but their descendants who enter the narrative of our own story in the following period, the Mesolithic.

First colonists

The earliest evidence of humans resident in Ireland dates to *c.* 8000 BC, the period known across Europe as the Mesolithic, the 'Middle Stone Age', which encompasses the various regional responses of hunter-gatherers in Europe to new landscapes that were finally free of the ice of the earlier Pleistocene. In Ireland the Mesolithic lasts for 4,000 years and although this comprises about 40% of the period of Ireland's settlement, there are probably fewer archaeologists specializing in this period than any other. The Irish Mesolithic is divided into two periods, the earlier running approximately 8000–6500 BC or perhaps only down to 7000 BC.[7] It is represented by about 20 sites that have produced typical Early Mesolithic tools. Such a small number of sites highlights how little we actually know about Ireland's earliest settlers.

With the exception of a series of huts from Mount Sandel near Coleraine, Co. Londonderry, there is little or no architectural evidence for the actual habitations of Ireland's first colonists; most sites consist only of scatters of tools or chipping waste found in the soil, possibly augmented by occasional traces of fire and animal or fish bone. At Mount Sandel Peter Woodman discovered traces of a series of huts that had been rebuilt from one occupation to the next (2.3). Postholes indicate a slightly oval structure roughly 6 m across consisting of bent rods or poles (hazel or birch?) that were probably covered over by brush.[8] In the centre of the hut was a deep and repeatedly used hearth. On ethnographic analogy such huts probably served a single family and it is possible that several families gathered together at Mount Sandel for several seasons of the year. Most of our evidence suggests that Mesolithic populations were fairly mobile, relocating themselves over the year to take advantage of the seasonally changing resources.

Our main evidence for Ireland's first colonists is stone tools, most of which, because of their small size, are known as microliths. How these small flint blades were used is problematic: while some can be plausibly explained as the geometrically shaped barbs that would be slotted into the wooden shaft of a harpoon or spear, there are also other shapes (rods, needle points) whose purpose remains largely conjectural, and microscopic analysis of damage caused by use suggests a wide range of functions. In addition to the small stone tools there were also larger implements: axes and adzes flaked from flint and polished stone axes fashioned from other types of stone. These tools provide the primary evidence, as we will see below, in tracing the origins of Ireland's first human colonists.

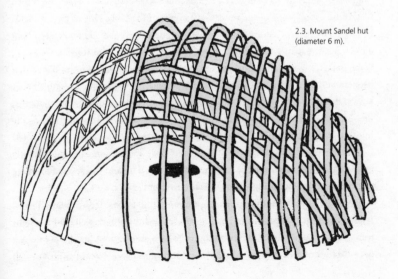

2.3. Mount Sandel hut (diameter 6 m).

As for the 'hard' evidence of Early Mesolithic people themselves, the best that we have are the relatively recently discovered remains of two individuals from Killuragh Cave, Co. Limerick, whose bones have yielded dates of *c.* 7200–6500 BC.[9] There are also at least two cremation burials from Castleconnell, Co. Limerick.[10] One of these comprised a pit with the cremated remains of a complete adult (male?) who was accompanied by a polished stone axe and two microliths and whose grave appeared to have been marked by an upright post; the burial dated to *c.* 7550–7300 BC. Another pit with a cremation dating to *c.* 7000–6600 BC was 100 m away. What should we call these people who lived in Ireland so many thousands of years before Niall? Whoever they are, as we will see, they are hardly going to be able to tick all the boxes of what we might require for the Irish of the 5th century AD, so I am reluctant to call them Irish. With apologies, then, for introducing such a clumsy name, before we can point to the target Irish of Niall's generation, the name for all previous anonymous occupants will be a Germanic-sounding 'Irelander'.[11] Now that we have met our first Irelanders, what type of world did they come to settle?

Bring your own

In the 7th century an Irish monk, Augustinus Hibernicus or the Irish Augustine (to avoid confusion with the famous St Augustine of Hippo), composed a study of the 'Marvels of the Holy Scriptures' (*De Mirabilibus Sacrae Scripturae*) which attempted to 'ground proof' some of the miraculous events of the Bible. One of the problems he tackled was the recolonization of land by animals after Noah's Flood, and he took a brief and apparently first-hand look at this issue in relation to Ireland. He asked: 'Who in fact, for example, conveyed into Ireland wolves, deer, and forest pigs, foxes, badgers, and little hares, and squirrels?'[12] He thought he could come up with a better answer than some of the ancients who had opted for spontaneous generation. Rather, he observed that just as promontories could be observed at present fragmenting into offshore islands (a visit to north Mayo today should convince), so also could Ireland have been joined to land (before the Flood) and the animals that regularly passed back and forth had since become trapped when Ireland was severed from the Continent. So the landbridge theory has been around since *c.* AD 655.

We have already seen that the composition of the earliest Irish is in a very real sense a question of biochemistry, and I have devoted the previous chapter to establishing the geological basis for Irish origins. Yet it is also obvious that people do not draw the bulk of their nutrients directly from stones or the soil but acquire it through the consumption of plants and animals. Thus we are what we eat, and the origins of the plants and animals of Ireland are also very much a part of the origins of the people of Ireland. We have already discussed this in general, but now we must be specific about Mesolithic Ireland. The economy of the earliest inhabitants is problematic and concerns at least two main issues: the composition of the native fauna that had colonized Ireland before humans arrived and the balance among the three main food sources: meat, fish and plants.

As we have seen, unlike the rest of Europe, Ireland was extremely impoverished with respect to wild mammals that might have found their way on to the dinner table. In the case of Ireland, both the timing of the loss of any landbridge and the impact of the Nahanagan deep freeze are critical factors. For example, most Mesolithic societies across Europe engaged in the hunting and consumption of red deer. In Ireland, there is some evidence for red deer before the Nahanagan cold phase, but there is no certain evidence for it on the eve of human colonization or throughout the Mesolithic in Ireland, and it only begins to appear again after 4000 BC when the first farmers arrived in Ireland.[13] So what animals either survived the cold snap or managed somehow to get themselves to Ireland before humans did?

In terms of mammals we can divide them into two groups: prey and their predators.[14] The earliest native prey apparently consisted of the woodmouse and hare. With regard to the earliest human colonists, it is a bit difficult imagining any Mesolithic population sated after tucking into a dinner of woodmice (today they number about 13 million).[15] The Irish hare is another matter, since it is much larger and at least has some potential as an item of diet. Preserves such as the Bialowieza National Park in Poland and Belarus contain the closest approximation to the primeval forest and fauna of Europe and from a few such reserves zoologists have attempted to estimate the potential number of animals in Mesolithic Ireland.[16] The most recent genetic evidence concerning the Irish hare suggests that it may have survived the Late Glacial Maximum (its extreme genetic diversity suggests that it had been separated from its cousins in Britain and on the Continent for a very long time). Population estimates of over 1.5 billion Irish hares have been cited before the forests had colonized Ireland. But it is highly unlikely that the island provided such a vast Watership Down and the recolonization of Ireland by trees made it increasingly uninviting for hares, so that by the time we have human settlement the estimates are on the order of 42,000, i.e. about one hare per 2 sq km. The archaeological evidence does not suggest that the hare was particularly important in terms of satisfying the human diet. Mount Sandel yielded only six certainly identifiable bones (compared with 322 wild pig bones), while none was found at the other major Early Mesolithic site of Lough Boora, Co. Offaly. Hare was also found at a Late Mesolithic shell midden at Sutton and four hare bones were recovered from the very late Mesolithic site of Ferriter's Cove, Co. Kerry. On the other hand, both the hare and woodmouse must have been crucial to the smaller carnivores that required such prey. Among the prey are also the red squirrel (c. 840 for Mesolithic Ireland but of no demonstrably great antiquity, though today they number about a quarter of a million) and the wild pig to which we will return below.

Among the carnivores that appear in Ireland after the Nahanagan Interstadial, we commonly include the stoat, pine marten, otter, wild cat, lynx, badger, fox, wolf and bear. With few exceptions, these are hardly food species on anyone's menu and they do not all have the same credentials as early natives. The stoat (with an estimated Mesolithic population of 3,400; today's stoats number c. 160,000 thanks to the introduction of rabbits) is probably among the most firmly documented natives as it arrived by c. 13,000 years ago if not earlier. It is also genetically as diverse (or old) as the Irish hare and, therefore, seems to have survived the Nahanagan and, presumably, dined on hares and woodmice. Just possibly it had to share its prey with the lynx (estimated numbers of 2,500) and wild cat (remains found at Lough Boora and estimated to number about 2,000 in the Mesolithic), but we cannot be entirely certain. The otter (c. 24,000, roughly the same as today's population) could have swum to Ireland and occurs in archaeological contexts at the very end of the Mesolithic. Most of the other predators are only attested from the Bronze Age, millennia after the colonization of Ireland. Thus it is suspected that the fox (c. 8,400; today numbering c. 90,000) and pine marten were deliberately imported for their fur. Badgers (c. 3,000; today c. 100,000) are edible since we know the medieval Irish dined on them, but they too do not appear any earlier than the Bronze Age. Recent genetic studies indicate that Irish badgers, like the pine marten and the pygmy shrew, are distinguished from their British counterparts and appear to derive from southwest Europe, i.e. southern France or northern Iberia. Ireland did have the bear (c. 840) – remains of an old bear were recovered from the very late Mesolithic site of Moynagh Lough, Co. Meath – that might have been consumed for its fat, but then the bears could say the same thing about humans although they were probably outnumbered. Let's pause for a moment then and consider so far what could have been the earliest Mesolithic meat entrées: woodmouse, hare (though poorly attested on Mesolithic sites) and stoat (no doubt served with an otter and bear roulade).

This leaves then only the wild boar, whose remains predominate on the earliest Mesolithic sites such as Mount Sandel and Lough Boora and without whom many of the larger predators possibly could not have survived. And it is here that we find Ireland in stark contrast to the rest of northwest Europe. The single comparable site in Britain is perhaps the southern English Early Mesolithic site of Faraday Road where the only animal remains in abundance were wild boar, although there were traces of wild cattle, red and roe deer as well as beaver and wild cat.[17] Elsewhere, we generally find hunting economies based on a broad range of ungulates (red deer, roe deer, aurochs (wild cattle), elk and wild pig) rather than the specialized hunting of a single species. Only on the site of Ringkloster in Denmark do we find wild pig the predominant species (at 74%), but of 25 Danish sites, 11 have less than 25% wild pig.[18] At the best-known Mesolithic site in England, Star Carr, pig is in fifth place. Pig was important in Scotland but no more than red deer and roe deer, and there is also some evidence there for the hunting of the aurochs. The evidence of specialist wild pig hunters in Mesolithic Europe is then unique to Ireland. And while the wild pig did provide a sizeable number of calories, the meat weight of a wild boar (c. 124.5 kg) is still less than that of wild cattle (c. 450 kg), elk (300 kg) and red deer (132 kg).

In short, wherever the first colonists came from, they were forced to adopt a far more restricted diet, or worse, bring their own, because we cannot even be certain that wild pig existed in Ireland before human settlement. Wild pig is a creature of the deep forests and these only began to appear about the same time that we have evidence for the earliest human settlement and considerably after any possible case for a landbridge (see below). It seems extremely strange if Ireland could attract natural populations of wild pig to its shores (admittedly they are good swimmers) and yet deny similar entry to red deer (also good swimmers) that would certainly have found its earlier environment more conducive for grazing than would the pigs. It has been estimated that Britain might have had something on the order of a million wild pigs and red deer during the Mesolithic,[19] while the natural wild pig population for Ireland has been estimated at c. 337,000.

There is a good case then for assuming that the wild pig was most likely introduced to Ireland directly by humans.[20] This makes a certain amount of economic sense, for unlike all other potentially hunted large mammals, only pig could provide a substantial increase in meat over a short period of time. Instead of one offspring per year, a wild pig can produce a litter of three to eight piglets, which means that hunters could kill off half the population in a given year and still leave the basic population broadly unchanged. Of course, there are disadvantages as well: the wild pig is capable of fighting back effectively, and the importation of wild pigs into Ireland would probably require multiple crossings. Indeed, if we carry this to its logical conclusion, it suggests that Ireland was first colonized by a human population that deliberately attempted to engineer its native fauna to suit its economic needs.

In addition to red meat, there was also fowl, and while the size of Ireland and the timing and nature of its forests are critical factors, at least we do not have to deal with a landbridge to explain Ireland's birds. The few excavated Early Mesolithic sites suggest that birds were consumed, but not in any great number.[21] The primary species hunted were either waterbirds such as the mallard, or wood pigeons; the finding of a single bone of a capercaillie at Mount Sandel suggests that the early settlers of Ireland could also tuck into more sizeable birds.

In sum then, the meagre evidence that we now have suggests that in terms of prey for hunters, Ireland was one of the poorest places in Europe and one of the least inviting to settlement from any neighbouring region of Atlantic Europe. Unless contradicted by new discoveries (the spectre that hovers over anything an archaeologist chances to write), it seems Ireland's first human colonists also had to introduce a fair amount of their own food.

Balanced diet?

In addition to the meat animals that appear to have been introduced by humans, there were two other potential sources of food. One would have been fish, remains of which are also found on Mesolithic sites. As there was no one to stock the rivers of Ireland after the Ice Age and no way that freshwater fish could have swum to Ireland from Britain or the Continent once there was a saltwater barrier in between, it is unsurprising that the earliest Mesolithic sites have yielded primarily migratory species – eels, salmon and trout – whose main runs are largely during the summer and early autumn. Purely in terms of the number of bones recovered, Mount Sandel yielded 81% fish bones and Lough Boora had 69% fish. Of course, fish bones are naturally far smaller than mammal bones, so we must introduce an element of proportion when we consider that the 2,000 fish bones from Lough Boora derived from a minimum number of 43 eels and 21 salmonids (trout or salmon). While the Irish export rather than consume eels today, we should note that the eel is in a class of its own in terms of nutrition: compared with pork it delivers 1.65 times the amount of calories, over 4 times the amount of fat and, unlike pork or the other migratory fish, it delivers substantial amounts of vitamins A and C.[22] Unfortunately, it would still take about 250 eels to yield the same quantity of food as a wild boar and they have over twice as much cholesterol as pork.

Coastal or estuary fishing was also possible and Mount Sandel yielded the bones of bass, plaice or flounder; at the very late Mesolithic site of Ferriter's Cove, Co. Kerry, there was a wide range of marine species (primarily wrasses, whiting, cod and tope).[23] From this and a series of recently discovered fishing stations it is clear that fish was not simply incidental to the Irish diet.[24]

Finally, we have plant remains, the most ubiquitous of which are hazelnuts, found routinely on both Mesolithic and later sites. Again we are dealing with a seasonal food (gathered during the late autumn), but one that could at least be stored over the harder winter months. Rachel McClean made a study of the full set of Irish plants in terms of their edibility within the ethnographic record and found that there were over 120 species of edible plants native to Ireland.[25] This is a list of the potential rather than that for which we have evidence for exploitation, and other than waterlily seeds, vetch, goosegrass, raspberries, crab apples and wild pears, there is very little else preserved in the archaeological record attesting to the plant diet. Nevertheless, the potential for plants in the diet was quite marked: McClean reminds us that one can collect half a tonne of hazelnuts from one hectare (if squirrels, pigs and birds don't beat you to them) and from a square kilometre one can theoretically collect 20 to 50 tonnes of edible bracken root or 5,000 to 10,000 kg of fungi.

It is apparent that for the first 4,000 years of the human occupation of Ireland, the economy was primarily based on seasonal resources, be they fish or plants, and if meat were wanted in the diet, the early colonists would have had to adapt the necessary skills for importing and hunting wild pig. What is also apparent is that any migration to Ireland involved a people who had to accustom themselves to dealing with an environmentally and gastronomically very different land from the one they had left. In a very real sense, the earliest occupants of Ireland were not merely an extension of their ancestral population but one that was required to adapt to a very different environment and develop uniquely Irish strategies to survive. Ireland really was a place apart.

Rules of the game

From a theoretical perspective, determining the origins of the earliest populations in Ireland should not be too difficult given the fact that Britain was clearly occupied earlier than Ireland and lies closest to the Irish coast; logistically, any other point of origin is going to be increasingly less likely. If we lived in a theoretically perfect world then we should find evidence at a date before 8000 BC for the same type of stone tools in Britain that we find in Ireland, preferably with some abundance along its western shore, from where some brave or foolhardy families would have climbed into their boats (along with some wild pigs?) and crossed over to settle in Ireland. If we could design our evidence at will we might also prefer to find the earliest Mesolithic sites in Ireland concentrated along the northeast coast (if colonization came from Scotland) or along the Leinster coast (from Wales) or, perhaps, even along the south Irish coast (from Cornwall or France?). If we did have this type of evidence, this chapter would have been a lot shorter as we raced to a conclusion that the Irish (here 'Irelanders') are *really* Scots/English/Welsh/Cornish/French! Instead we find a very messy reality, so all we can do is examine a number of hypotheses and attempt to evaluate each one according to the available evidence. But what type of evidence are we looking for? What are the rules of this particular game?

As stone tools are the only item of the Mesolithic that we have in abundance and for which we can suggest cultural affinities, a search for origins is basically an exercise in comparing and dating stone toolkits from Ireland and from any potential foreign source. We should, however, recognize the limitations that this entails, since we are selecting out only about 10% of the potential material culture of the Mesolithic peoples of Britain and Ireland, the rest having almost entirely dissolved in Ireland's unforgiving soils.[26] We are also putting a lot of trust in objects that in themselves are probably not among the most obvious markers of ethnic identity. Stone tools may indeed be imbued with the cultural traditions of their makers, but they are not necessarily the most sensitive expressions of those cultural traditions. Nevertheless this is the hand we are dealt and so these are the cards we must play.

Background to colonization

There is good evidence that after the last Ice Age Britain was reoccupied by Late Palaeolithic hunter-gatherers by *c.* 12,700 BC, thousands of years earlier than Ireland. Hunter-gatherers had entered on foot directly from northwest Atlantic Europe (there was not yet an English Channel) and they kept primarily to the lowlands of south and central Britain, the type of landscape from which they had come. The great cold snap of the Younger Dryas (the Irish Nahanagan) kept them from migrating north into lands that were deteriorating back into glacial conditions and, as Chris Tolan-Smith suggests, they had also run out of familiar lowland territory and were now stalled before the unfamiliar upland landscape of northern and western Britain.[27] Remaining in the south, these early colonists adopted an Early Mesolithic industry.

We can put dates on the various Mesolithic stone toolkits found in Britain. The very earliest Mesolithic assemblages consist of long blades with larger microliths similar to those found in the Netherlands and dating to around 9600 BC. The most famous site of the Early Mesolithic is Star Carr in Yorkshire that dates within the period c. 9000–8500 BC. But the type of stone tools we find in Ireland, i.e. smaller geometric microliths, does not appear until the British Later Mesolithic period that begins c. 8000 BC. This means that there is a serious mismatch of the names for the Mesolithic phases between Britain and Ireland. In Britain the Early Mesolithic has no counterpart in Ireland as Ireland was not yet inhabited. The British Later Mesolithic is the equivalent of the Irish Early Mesolithic. And just to complete the confusion, Ireland has its own Later Mesolithic that dates to the latter half of the British Later Mesolithic but is technologically totally different.

The evidence for the British Mesolithic as a whole suggests that inland hunters depended primarily if not exclusively on mammals; there is no solid evidence of forays to the coast or at least the exploitation of coastal resources over northern England, although there is some evidence for seasonal exploitation of the coast in southern England where we find shell middens, accumulations of discarded shellfish such as oysters and limpets. On the other hand, there is evidence for coastal populations in Wales, both in terms of their settlements and the chemical analysis of human bones which indicates that some at least enjoyed a marine, perhaps sea mammal, diet.

It should be emphasized that we have no reliable point of entry in Ireland for its earliest colonists. While the abundance of sites in the northeast might tempt one to draw an arrow from Scotland to north Antrim, much of this is probably a mirage created by the sheer abundance of flint in Co. Antrim and the stimulus this had on encouraging antiquarians to collect stone tools in the northeast (2.4). The presence of Early Mesolithic sites at Lough Boora in Co. Offaly and also along the Blackwater in Co. Cork indicates that Ireland could have been colonized not just from the northeast but also from the south.

Another problem with both departure and entry points is the nature of sea levels during the Mesolithic. The Irish coast of c. 10,000 years ago – along with any putative evidence of small stone tools, hearths, shelters, etc. – was completely flooded by the rising sea. A later recovery of the land has since lifted these earlier beaches well above the position they occupied during the Early Mesolithic in the northern half of Ireland, but the destructive forces of wave action will have largely destroyed any evidence for the initial coastal sites of the first colonists. In the southern half of Ireland the earlier coast has been sinking, so without underwater exploration almost nothing

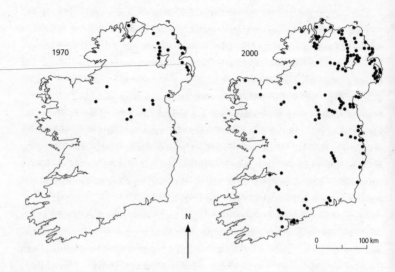

2.4. A map of Mesolithic sites known in 1970 suggested that the Irish Mesolithic was almost entirely confined to the northeast. But finds from ensuing decades indicated that all Ireland was occupied by hunter-gatherers.

of its earliest coastal occupation can be recovered. Any departure points in western Britain have undergone a similar fate through sea-level rise.

Now we can turn to the various models one might propose for the colonization of Ireland that do not require either superhuman logistical effort or extraterrestrials.

Early landbridge crossing

This model proposes that the earliest people in Ireland followed along the same putative landbridge by which the earliest plants, trees and mammals entered Ireland. Logistically the easiest solution, it envisages bands of people unintentionally crossing into Ireland along a land corridor stretching presumably from France, across southern Britain and on into southern Ireland. Once arrived, they found it easier to remain than return as sea levels inundated the land corridor. In a sense this would represent a process similar to the earliest hunters crossing from Asia into Alaska, who would have been equally unaware that they were passing into a new continent. It is also how Britain was colonized from the Continent.

In evaluating this theory we can readily appreciate why the dating or even existence of a landbridge between Ireland and Britain/the Continent is so critical. As we have already seen, many geomorphologists are unhappy with the suggestion of a full landbridge at any time during the last 12,000 years. From their perspective, at some time at least any of the large mammals coming into Ireland had to get their feet wet or be carried by human colonists. A lower sea level would have provided both Britain and Ireland with much wider coastal regions that would have extended far into the present Irish Sea, but this area would never have been entirely dry. Moreover, one might have expected evidence in Ireland of the wild fauna hunted in Britain, such as deer, elk and wild cattle, if such animals could have grazed along this putative dry corridor; and even if there were water obstacles, this would not have prevented deer from swimming across shorter stretches of water. In short, most of the available evidence suggests that hunters did not follow their prey into Ireland because there was no prey to follow (unless you are ravenous for mountain hare and woodmice); there was no landbridge to allow either the prey or human predators into Ireland.

Finally, if we return to the question of toolkits, we see that in this earlier period the type of Mesolithic tools found in Britain tends to be larger and heavier than the microliths we find in Ireland. Had Ireland had tools typical of Britain in the period c. 10,000–8000 BC this model in some form would have been the front runner. But this is not what we find, so the early landbridge model is the least likely explanation of how Ireland was colonized by humans. We are forced to assume that the earliest colonists must have employed boats to reach Ireland, so the question remains: what was their home port?

Scotland

A Scottish source for the first Irelanders is a popular model for two reasons: logistics and resources. Accepting the high probability that the earliest human populations must have come to Ireland by boat, it recognizes that the shortest sea crossing would have been between western Scotland and Co. Antrim. This crossing is not only the shortest in terms of linear distance (the Torr Head-Mull of Kintyre crossing is c. 20 km), which at the time of Ireland's colonization, when sea levels were lower, would have been even shorter (2.5). It is also perceptually inviting in that one can easily see Ireland from Scotland, and it is difficult to imagine any population with an ounce of curiosity not attempting to cross at least to explore the other land. Moreover, as the Scottish islands were also initially colonized during the Mesolithic, the settlement of

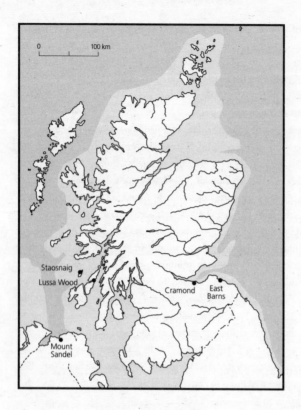

2.5. The Scottish shoreline and Mesolithic sites.

Ireland might be seen as a natural extension of the same process, just one more island in the distance. Further in its favour is what one would encounter on such a crossing. Almost any landfall on the east Antrim coast would reveal a land abundant in flint, the primary raw resource for manufacturing tools during the Mesolithic and a commodity not nearly so available in western Scotland. As to the type of boat, we have only one possible remnant of an Irish Mesolithic boat, what might have been part of an oak dugout from Brookend, Co. Tyrone, although usually it is presumed that sea crossings would have been accomplished in skin boats.[28]

It is little wonder then that a Scottish origin for the colonization of Ireland has been a perennial favourite. In 1921 R. A. S. Macalister could both pose and answer the question of Irish origins:

Whence came these colonists, and how did they make their way to Ireland? The first part of this question admits of but one probable answer. The oldest remains of man in the country have been found in the north-east corner; and it is just at the north-east corner that it approximates most closely to other lands.[29]

The same model is there by implication in Michael Herity and George Eogan's textbook of 1977: 'In the shoreline on the coasts of Antrim and Down opposite Scotland, where the shortest of the sea-crossings to Britain can be made, the implements of a flint industry have been discovered.'[30] But a year later, with Peter Woodman's study of the Irish Mesolithic, doubts were thrown up regarding a Scottish origin.[31] By then there were sufficient discoveries of Mesolithic occupation elsewhere in Ireland to demonstrate that far more of Ireland was occupied during the Early Mesolithic than just the northeast. One response to this was to presume that there were therefore multiple landbridges for a series of colonists all along the west coast of Britain.[32] But as we have already rejected any landbridge for a human crossing, we are going to have to look at the issue a lot more closely. In any event, the Scottish link is still very much on the menu and requires very serious consideration.[33]

The problems with the Scottish model concern both toolkits and dates. Like Ireland, Scotland also lay under massive ice sheets during the Pleistocene (in the western Grampians the ice was up to 1,300 m thick) and had to experience the same processes of recolonization of the land by plants and animals as Ireland.[34] In Scotland it was intensely cold up to c. 13,000 years ago, but within only 500 years the temperature had risen to that of today's climate and it rapidly became ice-free and open for colonization. By 11,000 BC, however, the temperature had plummeted again (like Ireland's), only to rise steadily afterwards to achieve reasonably temperate conditions by 9600 BC. There are somewhat controversial hints that at least hunters had made it into Scotland: there are traces of tanged points that resemble the type employed by Upper Palaeolithic hunters in northwest Europe, including southern and central England, in the period around 9500 BC.[35] These were the first hunters to push both northward (into Norway) and westward (into Britain) after the last Ice Age, where they moved along the coasts in boats and hunted inland reindeer and wild horse.

The next evidence we have for human settlement is associated with a toolkit archaeologists term a 'broad-blade' industry that is best seen in northern English sites such as Star Carr. This reflects the typical Early Mesolithic stone tool technology of Britain and in Scotland it can be found (although undated) from the east coast west to the Irish Sea coast, e.g. Lussa Wood on Jura. Unfortunately, none of these sites has been dated by radiocarbon, so we do not know their absolute date.[36] Moreover, this is not the industry that one finds in the Early Mesolithic of Ireland, i.e. a 'narrow-blade' industry. Nor can we say what these people ate: there are no faunal remains preserved from these sites, although Paul Mellars speculates that inland occupants would have exploited the same species we find at Star Carr (i.e. red deer, aurochs, elk and wild boar).[37] We might also expect that the coastal sites, with their access to abundant marine resources, should have supported sizeable (relatively speaking) populations; at least the quantity of stone tools left at some of the sites suggests this. What we have here then is a potential build-up of population along the west Scottish coast, but there is no evidence that they crossed the sea to settle in Ireland.

Dense coastal settlement in Scotland continues into the next period (Late Mesolithic), when a narrow-blade industry broadly similar to Ireland's does emerge. Kevin Edwards suggests that the most productive areas of Scotland would have been Aberdeenshire and the Tay, Forth and Clyde estuaries.[38] Indeed, the earliest Scottish site according to radiocarbon dates is Cramond on the Firth of Forth (c. 8500–8300 BC), which boasts a narrow-blade industry similar to the type known from Early Mesolithic Ireland.[39] This suggests that narrow-blade industries existed well before 8000 BC, the traditional date for the shift in toolkits, although the dates from this site have always carried something of a health warning.[40] Another point of interest is the discovery at Staosnaig, on Colonsay, of a settlement 'hollow' some 4.5 m across, which has been compared to the hut(s) at Mount Sandel as well as other hut sites in Britain.[41] Also found was a series of deep 'storage' pits, again like Mount Sandel, dating to c. 7000 BC, which contained some 300,000 hazelnut shells. Of the evidence for Scottish 'structures', the largest tend to be about 4.5 m in diameter.[42] Other structural remains are known from East Barns, East Lothian (and from further south in Northumberland), that date a little later than c. 8000 BC and secure a date for scalene triangles, the main type of microlith found in Ireland, about the same time as Mount Sandel.

In general, then, we find some evidence for Mesolithic settlement in Scotland during the Early Mesolithic that should predate the settlement of Ireland, although often we do not have precise dates for the Scottish sites. We also have at least one site, Cramond, with the same type of narrow-blade industry as we find in Ireland and dating before our earliest dates for Ireland (c. 7800 BC). Of course, it would be an extraordinary accident if archaeologists have discovered the earliest Mesolithic site in Ireland at Mount Sandel; there are good reasons to believe that the first settlers arrived at least a few centuries before 7800 BC to account for the peculiarities of the Irish toolkit such as needle points and flake axes.[43]

Although the chronological evidence suggests the possibility of a migration from Scotland to Ireland, this can only be demonstrated by comparing the stone tool-kits found in both regions. While the sites of northeast Ireland were well supplied with flint, as we have seen, Scotland is not and had to make recourse to many other types of stone along with whatever flint they could acquire. In terms of heavy indus-try, Ireland possessed three types of axes: large core axes for chopping, flake axes for planing and polished stone axes (2.6). So far Scotland has only produced about three core axes, two of which are questionable and one of which is probably an Irish import[44] (the site of Mount Sandel yielded 21 of these), and no flake axes (Mount Sandel has 13).[45] Picks and borers are also basically missing from Scotland, although Mount Sandel had 8 of these tools. Finally, Ireland was exploiting polished stone axes since its Early Mesolithic period, while Scotland has so far yielded no more than a few uncertain examples of Mesolithic ground stone axes.[46] In short, in terms of the heavy tools, Scotland does not make a very strong case for foreshadowing the industry we find in Ireland.[47] Moreover, other than the core axe mentioned above, there is really little if any evidence for exchange between Ireland and Scotland during the 1,000 to 1,500 years that comprise the Irish Early Mesolithic.[48] This is potentially criti-cal to assessing Scotland as the source of Irish colonization because one might have imagined fairly persistent coming and going between the two places, especially when northeast Ireland could have provided a good source of raw material. We will see that later in the Neolithic there was nearly constant interaction between Ireland and Scotland, and the absence of such contacts during the Early Irish Mesolithic throws some doubt on a Scottish origin.

When we examine the rest of the toolkit (2.7), we find that both Ireland and Scotland employed large numbers of scalene triangles (the presumed armature of Mesolithic spears), harpoons (2.8) and arrows. On the other hand, in Ireland there are also many narrow microliths termed rods (or backed bladelets) that may be less abundant (though present) in Scotland, while the so-called Irish needle points are very much a minority in the Scottish inventory (Fig. 2.7).[49] A larger tool such as the scraper is common enough in Scotland but, for the Early Mesolithic, it is fairly rare in Ireland (only seven were found in place at Mount Sandel); this might well be explained by the fact that while there was a variety of different animal skins to be scraped in Scotland, Ireland had many fewer mammals with hides that required cleaning. There really is no evidence in Ireland for such common Scottish implements

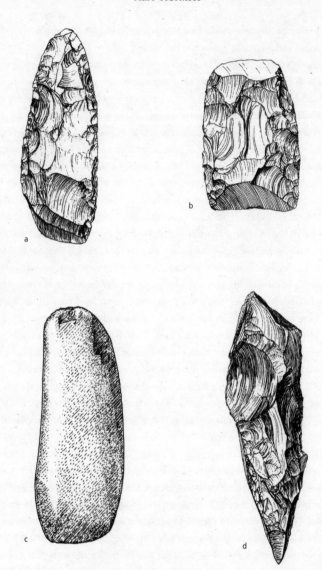

2.6. Irish Mesolithic heavy industry: (a) core axe; (b) flake axe; (c) polished stone axe; (d) pick (length 11.4 cm).

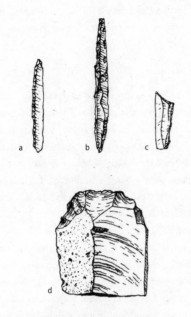

2.8. Reconstruction of a harpoon armed with scalene triangles.

2.7. Irish Mesolithic light industry: (a) rod; (b) needle point; (c) scalene triangle; (d) end scraper (length 2.4 cm).

as bone tools, barbed antler points or antler mattocks. Of course, this may just be due to the absence of red deer as well as the poor preservation of any organic remains in Ireland.

The evidence as a whole, then, acknowledges the possibility of a Scottish origin for the earliest immigrants to Ireland but is seriously lacking in terms of providing a really good ancestral toolkit to those we find in Ireland. One might wish to reformulate the Scottish model to suggest that both Scotland and Ireland were colonized from the same source further south at about the same time, but even then we cannot escape the differences between the two toolkits.

On occasion it has been suggested that we might look to Scandinavia for the origin of the earliest colonists, but a quick glance at a map would suggest that any colonization from Scandinavia, including the broad areas in the North Sea that might still have been above sea level, is most unlikely, since our putative earliest Irish colonists would have had to pass through Scotland first. If we cannot run with the Scottish model, we certainly cannot entertain much hope for a Scandinavian one.

Manx Atlantis

The next model concerns the Isle of Man. After southwest Scotland, the Isle of Man offers the next shortest 'jump' between Ireland and a potential source of colonists. The Isle of Man lies about 60 km from the present coast of Ireland and about the same distance from northwest England; its closest neighbour, southwest Scotland, is only 20 km away (2.9). The superficial case for the Isle of Man is its proximity to Ireland and its medial location (for those who support a landbridge, Ireland and Man should have been connected up to *c*. 7500 BC, while Man was potentially connected to Britain until about 8000–7000 BC). So far we have over 80 sites attributed to the Early Manx Mesolithic (the period in Manx prehistory that accords best with the colonization of Ireland), and the majority of these lie on the north and west of the island, those parts directly opposite Ireland. Sinead McCartan, a specialist in the Manx Mesolithic, suspects that during the Early Mesolithic populations may have occupied fairly stable base camps along the coastal regions with some mobility involved in temporary campsites.[50] Moreover, historically, Ireland and the Isle of Man have frequently been in intense cultural contact: during the Irish Later Mesolithic the Isle of Man is the only region that offers a somewhat comparable stone tool technology and, much later, the Manx language derives from Irish-speaking colonists who were probably arriving on the island during the same century that Niall is reputed to have reigned in Ireland and raided western Britain. Finally, the Isle of Man basin even offers a potential 'push' factor that might explain why a population would wish to expand westward to settle Ireland. The relatively late severance of the Isle of Man from Britain might be seen in the context of its location within one of the shallowest parts of the Irish Sea (less than 30 m deep), and one might speculate that Mesolithic populations once stretched over a broad area between northwest England and the Isle of Man. As the sea level rose, they would have had to relocate and so a movement westward to Ireland (the Mourne Mountains are visible from the Isle of Man) would be an obvious solution.

Our knowledge of the Manx Mesolithic is quite poor in many of the categories of evidence that we need to evaluate if we are to consider it as a potential source of the colonization of Ireland. For example, we have little idea of the range of species hunted on the Isle of Man and to what extent this may have been as restricted as

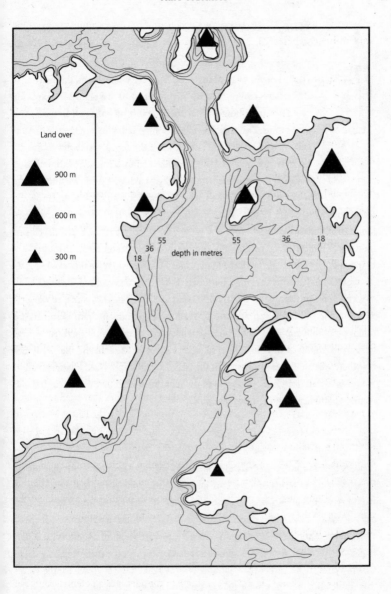

2.9. Sea depths in the Isle of Man basin.

2.10. Manx
hollow-based
point (length
2.16 cm).

Ireland's or as rich as Britain's. The only major source of meat certainly recovered from the Early Mesolithic on the Isle of Man is wild pig; the other species such as aurochs and red deer are simply not (yet?) known from Manx sites. If future research should prove that this reflects reality, then we might at least have a plausible source for our Irish boar-hunters. But the true test of links still lies with the stone tools. The earliest evidence for the settlement of the Isle of Man only dates to *c.* 7000 BC, i.e. nearly a thousand years after our earliest dates for Ireland, but this is likely to be remedied with increased research in Manx prehistory. In the Manx Mesolithic we find a stone tool industry that does bear similarities with that of Ireland (e.g. scalene triangles, needle points), but it is extremely poor in the rods and axes that are found in abundance on Irish sites.[51] Moreover, the Isle of Man has a well-developed industry of hollow-based points, also seen over southern Britain, which are very rare in Ireland (2.10). It is only with the Manx Later Mesolithic that we find closer parallels with Ireland and, by that time, both islands had long been settled.

The main problem with this model is that at present it sinks much of our evidence to the bottom of an admittedly shallow sea, although there is something romantic about peopling Ireland from a Manx Atlantis. A colonization directly from the current shores of the Isle of Man to Ireland is not easy to sell, and the possibility that there was an earlier settlement of the island area that provided a launch pad to the colonization of Ireland, possessed of the requisite toolkit that we find in Ireland, is still hypothetical although also plausible.

Wales

A possible colonization of Ireland from Wales provides another route that makes logistical sense in terms of a sea crossing. It has the same perceptual advantage of the other scenarios in that one can see the Wicklow Mountains from Gwynedd, so any sea crossing was in the direction of known land. We also have some evidence of Wales being occupied by populations using the earliest Mesolithic toolkits known in England, which pre-date those found in Ireland, although the earliest solidly dated sites in Wales are no earlier than about 8500 BC.[52] Finally, the evidence for the Welsh Mesolithic contemporary with that of Ireland suggests a concentration along the Pembroke coast, again inviting the convenient analogy of the modern Fishguard-Rosslare crossing to Ireland (2.11).

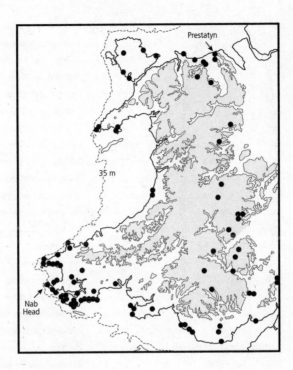

2.11. Mesolithic sites in Wales are especially concentrated along the Pembroke coast.

The problem with Wales is that the earliest dates for the narrow-blade industry known from Ireland are no earlier than the Irish evidence, i.e. *c.* 8200–7550 BC from Prestatyn in the far north of Wales. Here we find a microlith industry dominated by scalene triangles and rods, but it lacks the heavy core axes we find in Ireland (they did appear in the Welsh Early Mesolithic but had disappeared by the Late Mesolithic).[53] The Welsh Mesolithic also possesses other tools – denticulates, basically flint pebbles that have been flaked to give a jagged edge – that are not a customary part of the Irish toolkit, nor does Ireland possess the abundance of perforated stone beads found on some Welsh sites. On the other hand, Welsh sites possess not only a significant series of bevelled tools (beach pebbles) but also three polished stone tools, a phenomenon that one also encounters in Mesolithic Ireland in much larger quantities (2.12). The economic basis of the Welsh Mesolithic is, like that of the rest of Britain and Ireland, poorly known, although sites have yielded remains of wild cattle, red deer, roe deer

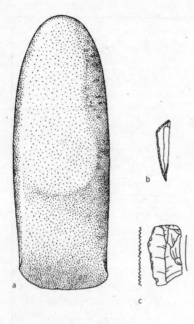

2.12. Welsh tools: (a) bevelled tool; (b) scalene triangle; (c) denticulate (length 3.3 cm).

and wild pig while, like Ireland, there was also a great emphasis on the collection of hazelnuts. Architectural remains are few, but an empty area (i.e. devoid of stone artifacts) about 5 m in diameter from the site of Nab Head II has been compared with the size of the hut structures at Mount Sandel (which seem to have become the 'gold standard' of Mesolithic huts), while there is abundant evidence for burial in caves in Wales, a practice for which Ireland at least can tick the same box.

The evidence thus suggests that the colonization of Ireland from Wales has points to recommend it (some elements of the toolkit, cave burial) but also indicates major differences. Moreover, Wales fails to exhibit a narrow-blade assemblage markedly earlier than the one we find in Ireland.

France

In 1986 Peter Woodman suggested, admittedly as a long shot, a possible origin for the Irish Mesolithic in France. He argued that at least in France we do find a microlithic industry early enough to provide a source for that of Ireland. At Rouffignac, in southwest France, there is evidence for an assemblage of scalene triangles that should pre-date those known in Ireland. Moreover, the *pointe de Sauveterre* (a long narrow-pointed implement) could have served as a possible inspiration for the Irish needle point, which has no obvious British counterpart (2.13).[54] The Sauveterrian expanded over a broad area of southern France and adjacent areas. In order for it to have advanced from France to Ireland it would seem to require a route that travelled up along the Atlantic coast of France to Brittany or Normandy and then crossed, perhaps over a chain of now-submerged islands, to southern Ireland. This is a theory that Woodman has since rejected, and we might have granted it a quiet death except for one rather unscientific reason: there is a sizeable constituency who find it incomparably more attractive to seek the origins of the earliest people in Ireland anywhere on planet Earth other than the somewhat larger island (and certainly not a 'mainland') to the immediate east of Ireland.

2.13. A *pointe de Sauveterre* (length 3.5 cm).

Despite some of the microlithic elements, however, the Sauveterrian and its regional variants do not provide any better fit with the earliest Irish toolkits than do those of Britain. For example, the Sauveterrian lacks the heavy industry that we find in Ireland (axes, adzes, polished stone axes) and possesses a fairly wide range of points, including arrowheads, that are not characteristic of Ireland. It is unfortunate that Brittany, the most likely staging area for a French connection with Ireland, is not particularly well known nor, at least for the period we are interested in, very well dated.[55] Moreover, its ancient shoreline has long been submerged, so that Mesolithic sites once inland are now coastal.[56] While there are some similarities in the toolkits, there are so many differences that one is not encouraged to select this region as the most likely source for the Irish Mesolithic and to trust that more comparable material now lies under the sea between Brittany and Ireland.

From where then?

It is apparent that there is no clear and obvious single source, no Proto-Irish Mesolithic assemblage, from which we can confidently derive the earliest human populations of Ireland. On the other hand, the reader is going to be dissatisfied if I cannot come up with a 'least unlikely candidate', so let us see what we can eke out as a conclusion.

We begin with the observation that so far there is no evidence in Ireland of the type of Early Mesolithic broad-blade industries that we can find in England, Wales and Scotland. This means we are constrained to search for the earliest Irish colonists in the period immediately before 8000 BC, say, c. 8300–8000 BC. It is at this time that we either find or hypothesize the earliest evidence for human occupation in Ireland. This is also the 'eve' or date of the earliest appearance of the narrow-blade industry in Britain. The general focus of the earliest narrow-blade industries tends to be northeast England (Filipoke Beacon in Co. Durham), Ireland[57] and southeast Scotland

(Cramond). As the narrow-bladed sites in southwest Scotland tend to date to *c.* 7500 BC or later, this suggests that perhaps we should concentrate on the spread of the new industry from northeastern Britain southwestward towards the Solway Firth.

We have often employed the specific elements of the toolkits of each region to make our comparisons. We now need to remind ourselves, however, that the various categories are not really fixed and we should not try to make too much out of too little. For example, the difference between a scalene and an isosceles triangle may be more a product of the length of the blade that the flint knapper was working with than any intended cultural statement. Moreover, in some instances the differences between regions may be explained by the function of the tools rather than cultural affinity. For example, any self-respecting Upper Palaeolithic, Mesolithic or Neolithic culture normally has abundant scrapers but, as we have seen, Early Mesolithic Ireland is quite poor in this respect. It does not take a genius to suggest that its inhabitants may not have had that many things worth scraping compared with Britain, where varieties of deer, elk and wild cattle all provided useful skins that Ireland lacked. For this reason the very small number of scrapers from the Isle of Man is suggestive: as an island it too may have lacked a number of the more common mammals whose hides warranted scraping and, like in Ireland, the options may have been largely limited to wild pig.

When we compare the tools from each region we must assess how significant or insignificant the presence or absence of each category of tool is. All of our regions have scalene triangles, so this is merely an indicator that we are looking approximately in the right period, not necessarily the right place, as we could find scalene triangles throughout the west Mediterranean. Rods are common in Ireland and Wales, less so in the Isle of Man and Scotland. Needle points are also common in Ireland but only appear in any number in the Isle of Man, although they are also present in Scotland. In terms of the smaller chipped stone tools, the various regions offer some innovations that are poorly represented in Ireland (or not at all); for example, hollow-based points are very common on the Isle of Man but not in Ireland, while denticulates are very much a Welsh item. It is tempting to see these as local developments in their respective regions over the course of the narrow-blade Mesolithic rather than necessarily a part of the original 'package'.

Where Ireland really differs from its neighbours is in the production of the heavier tools, the flint axes and the polished stone axes. Scotland can only muster three axes, none of which can be entirely trusted. Core axes are also extremely rare in the Isle of Man. On the other hand, both core axes and polished stone axes can be found, although in no great number, in Wales and they are very early (they tend to

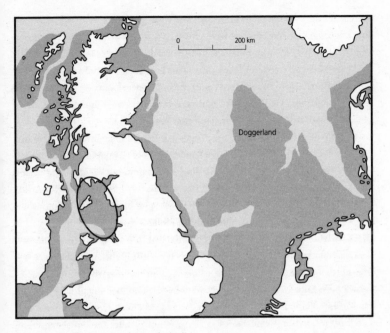

2.14. The source of the earliest settlement of Ireland?

disappear over the course of the Mesolithic). These axes can also be found in British assemblages before the settlement of Ireland but not in the British Later Mesolithic. Axe-rich Ireland, then, contrasts very markedly with contemporary Britain, and it is possible that the entire axe industry in Ireland was a local invention created after the arrival of the first colonists.[58] If this is so, then the Irish heavy industry can itself offer no clue as to where the earliest colonists came from.

If we were to try to select a single source, this would favour some variant of the Manx Atlantis theory that would envisage hunting-gathering bands occupying the territories anywhere between north Wales and the Solway Firth, including the Isle of Man, sometime around 8500 BC (2.14). This is by no means a small area and may have totalled something on the order of 15,000 sq km, about 17% of the area of Ireland. In this region sea travel would have been a necessity and voyages across the sea almost inevitable. The occupants of this drowning landscape would possess a toolkit comprising the residual elements from the British Early Mesolithic such as obliquely retouched blades (found rarely in Ireland) and (just) possibly axes as well as the new suite of geometric microliths that were spreading across Britain.[59] This new industry could be carried by colonists to Ireland before local developments in Scotland, the Isle of Man or Wales diverged from the course taken by colonists in Ireland. This, admittedly, is trusting a lot to a submerged landscape, but archaeologists are now recovering early remains from Doggerland, the enormous expanse of now-submerged land that joined northern Britain to the Continent before sea-level rise.[60]

Setting the original source of the peopling of Ireland in an inundated land may also help explain why the Mesolithic Irelanders did not develop on lines comparable with their nearest neighbours. In dealing with migrations, we often find what is called a 'migration stream' along which populations move back and forth between their homeland and their new colony.[61] The earliest immigrants into Ireland would have left relations behind who would likely have followed over time, settling first near their own kin much as the Irish did who emigrated to America. There would have been a certain amount of coming and going between the homeland and the new settlements that would ensure, over time, a flow of culture between the two regions. Had Ireland been initially settled from, say, western Scotland, one might have expected that kinship relations across the Irish Sea would have seen frequent contacts and, therefore, at least some evidence of exchange if not parallel developments. This is not seen in the course of the Irish Mesolithic, which provides perhaps some weak evidence that the ancestral community that spawned the earliest Irelanders had itself eventually ceased to exist. If their original home had been gradually flooded by the rising Irish Sea, this could well have happened.

Second colonists?

The first major break in the cultural development of Ireland occurs c. 7000–6500 BC, i.e. about 1,000 to 1,500 years after settlement was initiated. It is recognized by a major change in the stone tools. The earlier industry based primarily on microliths disappears and what we now find is a much less sophisticated technology that produced large and heavy flakes. The main cultural marker or type-fossil is the butt-trimmed (or Bann) flake that is found in abundance (2.15). The butts of the flakes were trimmed, presumably, so that they might be inserted into some type of handle and serve as a knife. This shift in technology raises serious questions about function. In the Early Mesolithic we assume the use of spears, harpoons and possibly arrows to hunt or fish, all of which seemingly disappear. The fish and wild pig still

remained on the menu, so the change does not appear
to involve a shift in diet but rather a change in how
the food was procured.[62] It is suspected that the new
procurement method involved manufacturing organic
implements out of bone or wood and the production
of traps and fish-weirs. At Clowanstown, Co. Meath,
archaeologists have excavated a wooden fishing platform complete with large conical baskets, while at a
depth of 6 m at North Wall Quay in Dublin archaeologists have discovered a large Later Mesolithic fish
trap complete with a V-shaped hazel fence leading to a
conical fish-basket/trap that dates to c. 5900–5700 BC.[63]
These provide stationary posts to capture fish and
suggest a different strategy from the more traditional
hunt for wild boar or the spearing of fish along a river
(a fish gorge has also been identified). The location of

2.15. Butt-trimmed or
Bann flake (length 9.5 cm).

the sites sees a great rise in coastal settlement, but this may be more an illusion generated by the relative changes between land and sea levels. Coastal sites occupied in the
Later Mesolithic were often sited along the flint-rich Antrim coast and although they
were disturbed by the same later wave action that should have obliterated any earlier
Mesolithic sites, their sheer size and number preserved them when the land rose to
expose them on top of raised beaches.

A new technology is certain; the question is whether it signifies a new population
or colonization? This was the interpretation accepted in Frank Mitchell's (and later
Mitchell and Ryan's) excellent account of the Irish landscape.[64] To him the cultural
change appeared so marked and unrelated to what had gone before (there are no
transitional sites that reveal both technologies side by side) that some outside source
was suspected. This would involve us in searching for the source of another wave of
colonists and contemplating such possibilities as the collapse of the Early Mesolithic
population of Ireland from disease or some other cause. In fact, such depopulations
were a regular part of the Irish traditional view of its own peopling of Ireland (see
Chapter 7). But unlike the models for the initial colonists, we are not really constrained to accept a new migration.

The reason we may be dismissive of a second colonization is quite compelling:
there is no industrial tradition anywhere that can provide a plausible source for
the Irish Later Mesolithic toolkit. There is no industry in Scotland, England, Wales,

France or Scandinavia that remotely mirrors the developments that took place in Ireland;[65] only the Isle of Man shows any traces of a similar industry and by this time it is generally presumed that Man was being influenced by Ireland rather than the other way round.[66] In such a situation we can invoke the well-worn principle of Sherlock Holmes: when we have excluded the impossible, whatever is left, no matter how improbable, must be true.[67] There should be a local explanation for the change in industry in Ireland and we have no grounds for invoking a second colonization. On the other hand, that explanation still remains a mystery, although there are a number of hypotheses.[68] The most recent attempt to explain this major change in technology is a population collapse at the end of the Early Mesolithic that impelled the survivors to adopt a much simpler technology.[69]

Population

After the question 'from where?' the most obvious problem is 'how many?' Did the colonization of Ireland represent the accidental marooning of six people (the absolute minimum that one might theoretically begin a colonization with) or a larger group, or was it a protracted process rather than a single event, i.e. was Ireland settled by waves (or dribbles) of colonists spilling over from somewhere in Britain to Ireland over the course of centuries? All of these questions can currently only receive the most speculative of answers and we can but offer the musings of the expert in these matters, Peter Woodman.[70]

Woodman rightly recognizes that there is a balance of probabilities: the greater the number of colonists the more difficult it is to explain their presence logistically, as you have more people to transport into Ireland. Reduce the number of initial colonists and the transport problem becomes more manageable, but you then have a problem of viability. Too few people leads to genetic inbreeding. Moreover, reduce the numbers below, say, 100 people, and you could also risk extermination – either by natural disasters, when there is not adequate surplus population to pull through a crisis, or by gender imbalances in which there are insufficient females to supply continual population growth. The general picture then would seem to demand that whether we have a few boatloads of people or more, there must be a viable breeding population within a very few generations to ensure survival. Woodman cites historical examples where the colonization of a new land resulted in a founder's effect, a phenomenon in which we see very rapid population growth, e.g. the Bass Islanders went from an initial 21 adults to a population of 350 in five generations. The upshot of all this is a notional picture of Ireland that, whatever the initial colonization event looked like, speculatively yielded somewhere between 175 and 475 people within the first few generations. Regarding the question of whether we are dealing with a single event or a much longer process, Woodman points to the fact that we find a distinctly Irish toolkit at both Mount Sandel and Lough Boora and this suggests a common background for all the colonists rather than different colonizing events at different periods. If it had been the latter, we might perhaps have expected more exotic finds in the way of tools that would suggest more strongly contacts with Scotland, the Isle of Man or Wales.

The selection of the Isle of Man basin as the most likely homeland of the earliest Irish colonists has an advantage over movements directly from Scotland or Wales in that it postulates a possible motivation – the loss of a large territory. This also helps address the issue of numbers, since we do not have to conjure up a series of adventurous settlers from Scotland or Wales leaving behind the rich hunting of their native lands for the poor pickings of Ireland. Rather, Ireland may have served as a refuge from environmental disaster, playing in a way the same part that America did in the 19th century during the Irish Famine. The initial numbers of colonists may have been sizeable and ensured a viable breeding population.

As for the actual size of the population in Ireland, it is extremely difficult to produce firm figures. Depending on productivity of resources, Woodman calculates population figures ranging from 0.01 to 0.1 person per square kilometre which give a low of c. 800 and a high of 8,000 people in Ireland during the Mesolithic.[71] He compares Ireland with Tasmania, which is slightly smaller but had a native population of c. 4,000 people; attempting to balance out Tasmania's smaller size against Ireland's poorer resource base, he suspects that the Irish Mesolithic population achieved a level of several thousands. If we treat these as ballpark figures, they are not too far off estimates for Mesolithic Scotland, where Clive Gamble suggests a population range of 1,560–7,020.[72] Gamble argued that Britain's Mesolithic population could have ranged anywhere between 4,560 and 20,520. Other guesstimates see figures of 400 to 1,800 for Mesolithic Wales and 6,000 to 27,000 for Britain.[73] If we scaled Ireland accordingly, a probable population might be on the order of c. 3,000 people, somewhat less than 100 people or about 20 nuclear families per modern Irish county.[74] And as for our putative Irish homeland around the Isle of Man, we might estimate anywhere from a low of 150 to as many as 1,500 people looking for a new home.

Conclusions

→ Ireland was not colonized until the late 9th or early 8th millennium BC and is one of the most recently settled lands in Eurasia.

→ Ireland was originally colonized during the Mesolithic, the period when humans adapted to new environments created by the warming conditions following the end of the Ice Age.

→ The earliest colonists in Ireland found a land lacking in many of the resources of neighbouring regions and had to import resources and devise distinctly local strategies in order to survive.

→ The most likely 'homelands' of the earliest human colonists in Ireland are Scotland, the Isle of Man and Wales. All of these share broadly similar toolkits with those found in Ireland, but they also all display some major differences.

→ Although it is impossible to determine for certain the point of departure for the earliest colonists to Ireland, the strongest candidate would be populations that previously inhabited the Isle of Man basin who were forced westward as rising sea levels destroyed their home territory.

→ The population of Ireland over the first 40% of its occupation may have been on the order of 3,000 people.

CHAPTER THREE

First Farmers

A 7th-century account of St Patrick records his visit to Tara where he failed to convert the High King, Loíguire, who explained that his father, Niall of the Nine Hostages, had forbidden him from accepting the new religion but rather had ordered him to be buried as a pagan on the 'ridges' or 'hill' of Tara (3.1).[1] Neither Niall nor indeed anyone else could hardly miss the earthen banks, ditches and mounds that comprise Tara, especially the monument known as the 'Mound of the Hostages' which was, according to a much later medieval legend, raised by Cormac mac Airt, a mythical king who was reputed to have ruled in the 3rd century AD. Actually, this large mound held the remains of people who had died about 3,500 years before the reign of Niall and who had erected the earliest of Ireland's visible monuments. Most spectacular among these are the many hundreds of megalithic tombs that have become focal points not only for tourists but also for promoting an image of Ireland's glorious past, thus providing an iconic expression of Irish identity. But these monuments, generally erected in the 4th and 3rd millennia BC, are merely a partial expression of the changes that swept Ireland during the period known as the Neolithic, the New Stone Age.

Generally, the most obvious and significant event in the prehistory of Ireland (or indeed of almost any country) is the introduction of agriculture. This should be self-evident for Ireland, since over 60% of its landmass is still given over to arable agriculture and pasture. The appearance of farming, however, not only marks a major watershed in terms of economy but also in technology, society, religion and, depending on the nature of its introduction, the linguistic and genetic composition of its population. The prehistorian Graeme Barker has called the transition from hunting and gathering to farming 'the most profound revolution in human history',[2] and it is certainly one of the most significant factors in tracing the origins of the Irish.

While the Neolithic is recognized as a pivotal point in Irish prehistory and it has been described and analysed in great detail, archaeologists tend to get stage fright

3.1. Map of sites mentioned in Chapter 3.

when dealing with its precise origins, about which they often tend to say as little as possible.[3] In a recent opinion poll of 16 Irish archaeologists as to the origins of the Irish Neolithic, the most popular response was 'unsure'.[4] To understand what all the fuss is about, we need to take a closer look at the Neolithic.

Neolithic changes

The Neolithic is the term given to the period when an agricultural economy spread across Europe to replace the hunting-gathering economy of the preceding Mesolithic. It began earliest in southwest Asia, over a broad region stretching from ancient Palestine northward in an arc touching on Syria and eastern Turkey around to the foothills of the Zagros Mountains of Iraqi Kurdistan. It spread beyond this 'Fertile Crescent' by about 8000 BC to arrive in Greece by c. 7000–6500 BC, on the Danube by c. 5500 BC, the French coast by c. 5000–4500 BC and, finally, after a delay, in southern Scandinavia, Britain and Ireland by c. 4000 BC. Precisely how it spread is a matter of controversy, with archaeologists positioning themselves from one extreme

(Europe was essentially recolonized by farmers from southwest Asia, who replaced most of the earlier population) to the other (domestic plants, animals and the new technology spread from one indigenous population to the next without any substantial migration of farmers). Most archaeologists find themselves somewhere between these extreme positions[5] but still argue about the balance between imported or local antecedents. If you don't mind embracing the fallacy of the insidious dichotomy,[6] we could crudely summarize this: were the first farmers in Ireland *really* immigrants from the Near East, or were they native Europeans?

The appearance of the Neolithic in Ireland is marked by major changes in almost every aspect of culture. Later Mesolithic campsites gave way to settlements consisting of from one to perhaps three solidly built timber houses that measured *c.* 6 x 12 m in size (3.2).[7] The settlements, so far as we can determine, would have been occupied throughout the year as the new agricultural economy did not require the whole community to undertake seasonal movements. The settlements are small and accord with the traditional pattern of Irish dispersed settlement rather than the type of nucleated settlement that the earliest farmers engaged in across much of Continental Europe, i.e. most Europeans lived in villages while the Neolithic Irish usually occupied either isolated farmsteads or small clusters of houses.

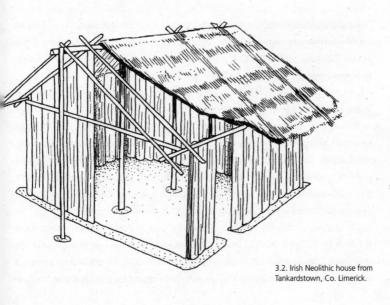

3.2. Irish Neolithic house from Tankardstown, Co. Limerick.

The earlier toolkit was replaced by a new set of stone implements, notably arrow-heads, javelin heads and a variety of new scraping tools, all fashioned according to a different tradition of flint knapping (3.3). A fundamental marker of the Neolithic across most of Europe is the polished stone axe, an implement whose surface was originally flaked into shape and then ground down to a smooth finish by abrasives such as sandstone. We have seen that in Ireland polished stone axes were already in use during the Mesolithic, but the Neolithic marked a virtual explosion in their presence (we have over 20,000 examples). Neolithic craftsmen exploited many new and harder types of stone and exchanged the axes not only across Ireland but also with Britain. Ireland's long apparent isolation from Britain that seems to have typified the Later Mesolithic comes to an end and we find both good circumstantial as well as incontrovertible hard evidence for frequent contacts between the two islands. In addition to new stone tools we also have the introduction of ceramic technology, the fashioning and firing of clay to make pottery (3.4).

The subsistence economy, although not very well represented in the archaeo-logical record, sees the first appearance of domestic cereals and animals. The new cereals consist of wheat, generally the preferred cereal in terms of consumption, and barley, a hardier plant that became increasingly popular in Ireland as wheat all too often proved difficult to grow. At some time during the Neolithic it is likely that a form of wooden plough was introduced. In the Mesolithic the dog was the only domestic animal known, but with the Neolithic we see the introduction of domestic cattle, sheep, goats and pigs.[8] The Neolithic represented a gastronomic revolution as well. This was not just a matter of adding to the meat entrées – now fish, perhaps the main staple of the Irish Mesolithic diet, was apparently off the menu. Chemical analysis of Neolithic skeletons across northwest Europe indicate that there was a major shift from a marine to a terrestrial diet as, at least among many early farmers, fish seems to have become taboo, almost as if the previous staple had been culturally rejected.[9] And both the production of cereals and the need to maintain open pasture for livestock saw the first major human impact on the Irish landscape, as areas of previously virgin forests were cleared for agriculture. A striking indication of how the landscape was brought into use is the Céide field system of Co. Mayo, kilometres of parallel stone field walls that date from *c.* 3500 BC onward (3.5).

The changes in religion are probably the most visible Neolithic innovations: the Irish landscape is marked by over 1,600 megalithic tombs, large stone structures that usually housed human remains and most likely also served as centres for reli-gious ceremony. Although we can say very little if anything solid about the belief

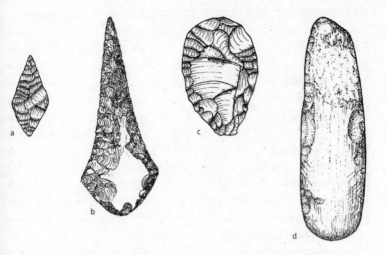

3.3. Neolithic tools: (a) arrowhead; (b) javelin head, (c) scraper, (d) polished stone axe (length 12 cm).

3.4. Neolithic carinated bowl (height 18 cm).

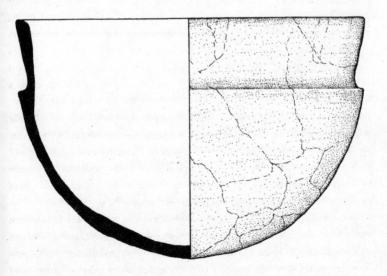

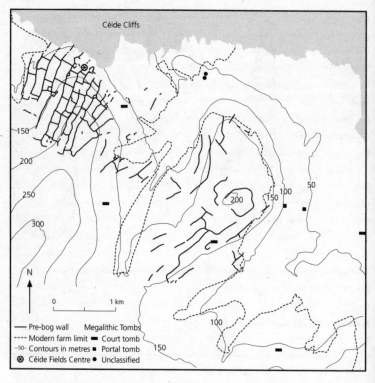

3.5. The Céide fields, Co. Mayo.

systems of Neolithic populations, it seems very likely that they reflected a new religion or religions. These monuments would have met the needs of the world view and social requirements of farmers and, some would argue, may have been one of the mechanisms for enticing local hunter-gatherers into the new cultural system. Many archaeologists emphasize that the shift to the Neolithic was as much a shift in the way people thought as it was a shift in economics.

Society would have changed very much as well. To begin with, farmers must control land on an annual basis and hence concepts of land ownership, largely foreign to mobile hunter-gatherers (unless they found it worth their while to claim particularly advantageous fishing rights), would have accompanied the spread of farming. Stable settlement also impacts on one's ability to accumulate goods (hunter-gatherers

76

regard most material possessions as impediments to mobility) and so the Neolithic generally marks the emergence of a concept of surplus, wealth and social ranking, or, if you prefer, waste, greed and discontent. Stable settlements may also have influenced residence rules, the customs that determine with whom (or with whose relatives) one lives after marriage. The size of the megalithic tombs and the effort required to clear land and erect field walls suggests that labour could be harnessed towards single purposes on a far greater scale than anything imagined in the Mesolithic: while mutual cooperation is always possible, large labour projects have often been seen to indicate the emergence of some form of social elite.

Finally, and for the purposes of our own discussion most importantly, the Neolithic would have brought about a major expansion in population. The size of hunter-gatherer populations must be restricted to ensure adequate resources throughout all seasons. A settled way of life, in which humans can control their own resources, led to major population growth, not only by providing greater food supplies but also, by removing the need for mobility, allowing couples to reduce the spacing between births and permitting larger families. Moreover, because farming involves major cooperative efforts such as field clearances and harvesting, it actually encouraged the growth of family size. It is with the Neolithic that we see the emergence of the 'ethic of fertility', encapsulated in the biblical injunction to 'increase and multiply', which is now being challenged by world overpopulation. An increase in overall population also resulted in an increase in population density and the number of people who would customarily interact with one another.

By the end of the Neolithic the population of Ireland was far greater than in the Mesolithic. Moreover, no other influx of population into Ireland during prehistory would have been anything more than a fraction of the Neolithic population and its indigenous descendants. From a biological point of view, the Neolithic population of Ireland, whatever its origin, provides a base line for defining the genetic origins of the Irish. The big question, then, is to what extent was the Neolithic the product of the local population or the result of new colonists to Ireland?

Origins: the native input

As it is obvious that Ireland lacked the wild ancestors of the domestic plants and animals that appear in the Neolithic, we can exclude the possibility that the Mesolithic people of Ireland, like the people of the Fertile Crescent of southwest Asia, discovered farming on their own. This is not a question of intellect but opportunity: Mesolithic

Ireland simply lacked any wild cereal that could be domesticated, and other than the dog the only potentially domesticable animal was the wild boar. Moreover, as we will see, unless there is some 'push' or 'pull' factor, human societies are unlikely to develop agriculture on their own. This leaves essentially two different models that attempt to explain the origins of the Irish Neolithic: acculturation and colonization.

Acculturation places the primary impetus for the adoption of agriculture on the Mesolithic occupants of Ireland. It still acknowledges that there must have been an outside source that came into contact with Irish hunter-gatherers – an existing Neolithic population from whom the necessary techniques and domestic plants and animals could be acquired. Generally in Continental Europe we see this pheno-menon operating between adjacent communities, e.g. a group of hunter-gatherers in, say, the Lower Rhine basin, living next to existing farmers, begins to acquire from them, perhaps through exchange, certain items of technology (polished stone axes, new chipped stone tools, the idea of manufacturing ceramics) and then, after more intensive interrelationships (perhaps intermarriage or theft) they also begin to adopt domestic livestock and ultimately domestic cereals.[10] We believe we can see such a process, for example, in parts of Atlantic Europe, southern Scandinavia and eastern Europe. But when we attempt to apply this same model to Ireland we have to deal with an added complication – the Irish Sea.

The body of water that separates Ireland from Britain or from direct contact with the Continent complicates the issue considerably by once again introducing the problem of logistics. In order to sustain the acculturation model, one needs to create what Marek Zvelebil and Peter Rowley-Conwy called an 'availability phase', i.e. a halfway house contact area where the processes of transmitting the new economy can take place between existing farmers and their hunting-gathering neighbours.[11] Obviously, this could hardly have taken place in the middle of the Irish Sea. Either Irish Mesolithic populations crossed, for example, to Britain or the Continent where they acquired domestic plants, animals and other elements of the Neolithic tech-nology, or some British/Continental farmers must have established themselves in Ireland where they stimulated local hunter-gatherers to take up the new way of life.

In favour of a local Irish population acquiring the new economy themselves from across the water is their probable skill in seafaring based on their evident exploitation of both coastal and riverine resources. Michael O'Kelly once wrote that he imagined some late Mesolithic Irelanders:

trading animal skins and furs, smoked salmon and other fish and dried venison as well as raw flint out of Ireland and coming back with calves and lambs, kids and young pigs and probably a new wife or two as well as friends *invited* into Ireland. In due time, after other visits abroad, they came back with round-bottomed shouldered bowl pots and sacks full of seed wheat and barley. Thus the Neolithic way of life was introduced by a slow and complicated process resulting from overseas contacts – there was no invasion and no arrival of a great colony of foreigners.[12]

The archaeological support for such a scenario is extremely sparse with by far the best evidence coming from our most recent Mesolithic site, Ferriter's Cove, Co. Kerry. Here there was evidence of a community who seasonally occupied the coast to fish and gather shellfish as well as hunting wild boar inland. The main occupation of Ferriter's Cove falls *c.* 4600–4300 BC, although there is some evidence that it may have trailed on past 4000 BC.[13] However, Ferriter's Cove also yielded several fragments of cattle bones. One has been dated to *c.* 4800–4500 BC and the other to *c.* 4500–4200 BC. As there is no evidence that wild cattle were present in Ireland during the Mesolithic, there is a presumption that the bones derive from domestic cattle and hence indicate contacts between Irish hunter-gatherers and some foreign farming community in Continental Europe. If this is so, it suggests that there may have been a very early horizon of contacts between Mesolithic Ireland and a Neolithic elsewhere, centuries before we have any clear evidence for a local Irish Neolithic, *c.* 3800 BC. Chris Scarre has noted a similar although earlier instance of the introduction of domestic cattle to Mesolithic peoples in Brittany, one of the more plausible sources for the cattle that turned up at Ferriter's Cove.[14] At the site of El Grah in Brittany archaeologists discovered the burial of two whole cattle skeletons that some date to the end of the 6th millennium BC. Similarly, in northern Germany we have the Late Mesolithic (Ertebølle) site of Grube-Rosenhof with domestic cattle remains dating to *c.* 4600 BC, again about 500 years earlier than the appearance of livestock-keeping in the region. This has been dismissed as one of the 'isolated imports of domestic animals, which had no traceable influence on the economic system'.[15]

The emphasis here should be on 'contacts' rather than 'colonization' because there really is no other solid evidence of the Neolithic 'package' in Ireland at such an early date. A minimal interpretation is that the bones were deposited by the local Mesolithic inhabitants and the presence of cattle may have been the result of some form of gift exchange.[16] On the other hand, it is also (remotely?) possible that the bones derive from wild cattle (although they are not particularly large, as one might have expected for wild cattle) and could reflect attempts by Irish hunting communities to import an animal from Britain.

Other than Ferriter's Cove, there seems very little to recommend the long-distance acculturation scenario. Mesolithic Irishmen might have gone abroad to acquire furs, skins and venison but were hardly in a position to export the latter. More importantly, the Irish Later Mesolithic stone tool industry is very different from that of Britain and there is little evidence of contacts between Ireland and Britain, other than the Isle of Man, throughout the entire 2,000 years before the Neolithic appears in Ireland.[17] It is almost as if Ireland had drifted off westward to somewhere beyond Rockall for much of the Later Mesolithic, with the only solid evidence for wider contacts before the formal Neolithic being the cattle bones from Ferriter's Cove and possibly some flint tools in Scotland.[18] Moreover, it is very difficult to imagine why Mesolithic populations should have actively sought to acquire a new technology and economy. A lifestyle that had apparently served for over 2,000 years is not likely to be abandoned easily, and while some popular books might portray the shift from a Mesolithic economy (desperate foragers wandering in search of food) to a Neolithic economy (farmers living off the fat of the land), ethnographic data often reveals the opposite (hunter-gatherers moving contentedly through a cycle of seasonal changes and rejecting the drudge of agricultural labour undertaken by their farming neighbours).[19] What we would look for is some compelling reason such as some form of major stress, for example food shortages, to induce the Mesolithic people of Ireland to purposely acquire new resources and shift to a Neolithic economy.

On the other hand, we can also propose acculturation through an influx of a small number of farmer colonists who might have settled in Ireland and come into contact with the local population. With these farmers already in Ireland, some form of contact, be it friendly or hostile, would be difficult to avoid, so there would at least be a local venue for exposure to the new economy and technology. While this works well enough in theory, there is remarkably little evidence for contacts between native hunter-gatherers and intrusive farmers. What we might hope for would be mixed sites indicating the process of acculturation, where native Mesolithic populations continued to produce their own stone tools while incorporating domestic animals and possibly ceramics and new stone tools into their own society. We can find such evidence elsewhere in Continental Europe,[20] but the evidence for this in Ireland has been really minimal, and even if we accept some of the more questionable sites, these rarely amount to anything more than a few bones of domestic animals found on a Mesolithic shell midden. And we then have another problem: while we do not know how long this process of acculturation lasted, what evidence we do have suggests it was not much more than a few centuries at best and possibly less. The fewer the colonists (and their livestock) one introduces, the harder it is to explain the speed with which the entire island took up the Neolithic way of life. And introducing more colonists to kick-start the process means that at some point one is actually shifting the major impetus for change from the local population to a new people who colonized Ireland with a Neolithic economy.

If it is very difficult to accept the native population as major players in the initial formation of the Irish Neolithic, could they still have had a significant role to play? This indeed was the traditional model advanced over half a century ago in Stuart Piggott's classic account of the Neolithic of Britain and Scotland.[21] Piggott suggested that we should distinguish between 'Primary Neolithic' cultures, those that had been imported from the Continent, and 'Secondary Neolithic' cultures, in which the impact of the Mesolithic natives re-emerges. Piggott wrote:

[with] the first impact of the arrival of agricultural communities over, there is a *modus vivendi* established between newcomers and the old population with hunter-fisher traditions, with a give-and-take of ideas and a consequent series of hybrid cultures growing up in various regions of the British Isles.[22]

This was a persuasive model in the 1950s and 1960s[23] but became far less attractive when radiocarbon dating indicated that the Irish Neolithic was not the brief period of *c.* 300–400 years that Piggott had envisaged but on the order of 1,500 years. This required about 300–500 years before the 'Mesolithic strikes back', and that suggested quite a few generations of hunter-gatherers marking time before they could strut their cultural stuff. That they could have survived has been suggested by Aidan O'Sullivan's excavation at Carrigdirty Rock, Co. Limerick, where the remains of a few stone tools, a woven basket, a fragment of a human skull, wild pig and cattle bones were all recovered.[24] The basket and the human skull date to *c.* 3700–3400 BC, but we lack precise dates for the fauna. The site can be variously interpreted as a very late Mesolithic camp whose hunters had acquired domestic cattle from neighbours or a Neolithic camp for cattle herders. In any event, attempts to discern what have been called 'Mesolithic survivals' in the culture of Neolithic Ireland have invariably come to naught. Peter Woodman, who has been concerned with the transition from the Mesolithic to the Neolithic for over 35 years, has routinely concluded that there is simply no good evidence for 'a positive contribution by the Mesolithic peoples to the range of material found in Neolithic contexts'.[25]

In short, from the perspective of the hard archaeological evidence, there is no solid case for a significant input by the native hunter-gatherers of Ireland with regard to the start or continuation of farming in Ireland. The end of the Mesolithic marked a real watershed with regard to the origins of the Irish.

Neolithic origins: colonists

The model of colonization is not diametrically opposed to the idea of acculturation, but it shifts the explanatory burden more on to a new wave of colonists.[26] It does not deny the possibility that there was some acculturation, some intermarriage and transmission of the new way of life to local populations, but this happens largely against a background of Ireland becoming saturated, within a period of several centuries, by the culture of immigrant farmers and through their descendants.

There is no precise litmus test for determining the size and impact of the putative farmers who may have colonized Ireland, whether it matches a small group who established an availability phase for the local population or a larger group who expanded rapidly across the landscape, quickly absorbing or destroying the earlier Mesolithic communities. Consider the following thought experiment that I have inflicted on my archaeology students and colleagues for 30 years. The question is simple: about how many farmer colonists came to Ireland during the Early Neolithic? If you guess a very small number – say, 20 – then you are up against a serious problem of culture change, i.e. do you really believe 20 people (about four farming families) managed to convince several thousand Mesolithic inhabitants to change almost every aspect of their culture? On the other hand, if you go for a larger number, say, 500, then you are looking for the motivation that encouraged about 100 families to climb into boats with their cattle, sheep, goats, pigs and grain to cross the sea to settle in Ireland. Of course, you may rightly question whether it is necessary to imagine the entire flotilla crossing the sea at once – we will return to the problem of how fast below – but we might expect that this initial colonization lasted no more than a century or so.

The case for a more substantial influx of farmer colonists is supported by the nature of the Early Neolithic in Ireland. While we do not find exact replicas of all Irish material culture outside of Ireland, i.e. clear evidence of its precise origin or source, we nevertheless do find evidence for a fully developed Neolithic culture that fits in every way we can imagine into the general model of other farming cultures of Atlantic Europe. It is not merely the appearance of domestic plants and animals in Ireland. The Early Neolithic houses are substantial timber structures built on the same general architectural principle as Neolithic houses throughout Continental Europe and radically different from anything erected in Mesolithic Ireland. The chipped stone and polished stone technology is nearly identical to that of Britain in the Early Neolithic. The ceramics are well made and in the same general style that one encounters in Neolithic Britain. Some of the Irish megalithic tomb types may also be found in Britain or western France and, as Gabriel Cooney reminds us, 'there is no background in local late Mesolithic funerary practice for the construction of such monuments' in Ireland.[27]

Moreover, the argument for the importance of colonists does not rest entirely on the presence of foreign analogies but on case studies involving acculturated populations elsewhere in Europe. In Belgium, Denmark and the Ukraine, for example, when hunter-gatherers adopted ceramics from neighbouring farming populations, it is the idea of ceramics rather than the precise style that was copied. Generally, hunter-gatherers would manufacture pottery that was bag-shaped and crudely made (3.6).[28]

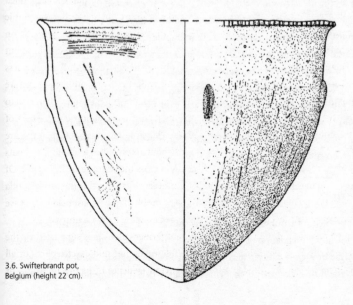

3.6. Swifterbrandt pot, Belgium (height 22 cm).

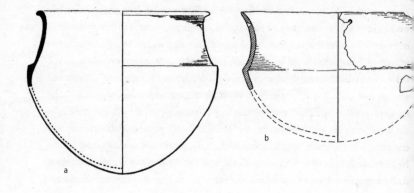

3.7. Carinated bowls from (a) Ireland; (b) Britain (height 15.6 cm).

If the manufacture of ceramics was, as ethnographic evidence generally suggests, a product of female potters who learned their techniques from their mothers, then the replication of the same type of ceramics (carinated bowls, to be technical) in both Britain and Ireland suggests a continuity of tradition (mother to daughter) and not simply the diffusion of an idea (3.7). The only exception to such direct mother-daughter transmission would be when a local woman came to marry a Neolithic colonist where, again on the basis of ethnographic analogy, she would probably make a considerable effort to replicate the local styles so as to fit in.[29] Similar arguments may be expressed for the types of stone tools and their method of manufacture or the architectural traditions we see appearing in Ireland after 3800 BC. The weight of all these arguments suggests that the case for a substantial influx of farmer colonists would seem to fit the evidence much better and, for what it is worth, in that straw poll of Irish archaeologists, colonization was the second most cited preference (after 'unsure').[30]

When?

The problem of chronology or dating is similar to the problem we had in explaining the initial occupation of Ireland in the Early Mesolithic. Ideally, we might like to describe how early Continental farmers crossed the English Channel, for example, and established themselves in Britain about a half a millennium earlier than in

Ireland. We would trace the expansion of agriculture across Britain from the east to west coasts and see an increase of population along Britain's west coast on the eve of our earliest dates for the Neolithic in Ireland. Ireland would be the obvious solution to resolving any problems of population pressure in Britain, and we could then trace the appearance of farming initially along the east coast of Ireland and its expansion westward. Such a persuasive sequence of (hypothetical) events, however, remains a fantasy; we have to deal with a much messier archaeological reality.

As it now stands, there is little evidence that the British Neolithic, with the exception of the extreme southeast, is significantly earlier than the Irish. The earliest Neolithic sites in both Britain and Ireland tend to be somewhat problematic when dated earlier than c. 3800 BC, a period by which time we have substantial evidence for Neolithic houses or enclosures, some tombs, domestic animal remains and evidence for cereal agriculture. But any date before, say, 3800 BC must be fought for almost year by year. One of the problems is that we are dealing with organic remains from archaeological sites (the only things we can really date), and the technique of radio-carbon dating often provides probability ranges of a century or more. So there may be a chance that a radiocarbon date could lie before 3800 BC but, as is often the case, it could also lie after that date. At the moment there are several major research projects trying to tie down the dates of the Mesolithic-Neolithic transition as precisely as possible, employing more advanced statistical techniques, but as yet there is no consensus. The important thing is that for Britain there are really no dates any earlier than, say, 4000 BC that an archaeologist would go to the scaffold for.[31] As for Ireland, there are a series of problematic sites with dates earlier than 4000 BC, but almost all of these have been so seriously challenged that archaeologists are generally unwilling to regard them as part of the evidence to resolve the debate.[32] There are, however, a few sites that are not so much 'toxic' as seriously problematic (other than the cow bones from Ferriter's Cove). For example, one of the major types of monument of the British Neolithic is the interrupted ditched enclosure, formerly known as the 'Causewayed Camp', a large settlement(?) and/or ceremonial(?) site surrounded by anywhere from one to three series of non-continuous ditches, earthen banks and frequently timber palisades. Although primarily a phenomenon of southern Britain, where over 70 are known that date from c. 3800 BC onward,[33] several such sites are also known in Ireland. One at Donegore Hill, Co. Antrim, seems to have been initially built between 3855 and 3665 BC during the main flush of the earliest Neolithic dates, but another at Magheraboy, Co. Sligo, has yielded dates going back to c. 4000–3800 BC and these are difficult to dismiss.[34] Setting aside the Magheraboy dates, the emerging picture suggests that the Neolithic arrived simultaneously in central and western Britain, Scotland and Ireland; if Magheraboy is truly two centuries earlier than the rest of the Irish sites, the Neolithic began simultaneously (and incredibly) in southeast England and northwest Ireland.[35]

Britain and Ireland

Although the dating evidence is problematic, the colonization of Ireland by farmers from Britain is obviously the easiest solution to our problem. We must first confront the lack of evidence that the British Neolithic substantially precedes that of Ireland. In Continental Europe the Neolithic is estimated to have spread at a rate of between one and three kilometres per year.[36] If we imagine that the earliest British Neolithic appeared in, say, Dover and plot the distance to one of the closest points in Ireland such as Wexford, we are dealing with 554 km of which a substantial chunk (over 100 km) is a water crossing. We would still hope for a head start of farming in Britain of 150 to 500 years. On the basis of a recent major evaluation of the beginnings of the British and Irish Neolithic, it seems that it took about 200 years for the Neolithic to spread from southeast England (c. 4000 BC) to south Wales (c. 3800 BC).[37] Also, by c. 3800 BC the Neolithic had spread to both the Isle of Man and Scotland, i.e. at about 3800 BC, over a period of only a few generations, the Neolithic spread from southern England to Wales, Scotland and Ireland (3.8). Chronologically, the spread of the Neolithic through most of Britain and Ireland appears to be almost simultaneous, and when one compares much of the material culture between Britain and Ireland, i.e. the ceramics, stone tools and, to some extent, the timber buildings and tombs, it is difficult to imagine the two islands experiencing different Neolithic origins. While the expected time lag between Britain and Ireland has not been found, a British origin cannot be excluded on chronological grounds, although we may be astounded by the speed at which the Neolithic spread. This takes us to the even more disputed territory of process.

It should be emphasized that archaeologists tracing the origins of the British Neolithic can be divided into the same camps as one finds in Ireland. Some argue that the Neolithic must be explained in terms of local Mesolithic populations adopting or, perhaps better, selecting various features from neighbouring Neolithic communities across the English Channel.[38] Others would argue that there really is a major discontinuity between the Later Mesolithic and the Early Neolithic that can only be explained by some intrusion of farmers who established themselves in Britain.[39]

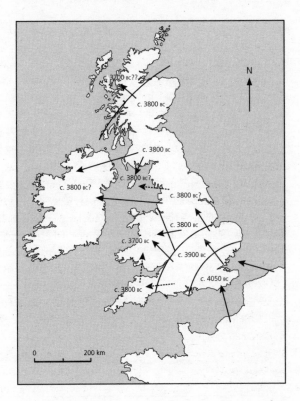

3.8. The spread of agriculture across Britain and Ireland.

What is fascinating is that proponents of both theories emphasize how rapid the shift was and employ this as part of their own argument. Julian Thomas, for example, who supports the local Mesolithic as the agents of change, argues that 'it is hard to see how the arrival of small groups of agricultural colonists on the island coasts could have brought about a sudden and synchronous adoption of Neolithic culture',[40] while Peter Rowley-Conwy, who makes the case for intruding farmers, suggests that the 'whole economic change took at most a century or two, and it was the biggest single upheaval that North-western Europe has ever undergone'.[41] Rowley-Conwy argues that one of the reasons for such a rapid transition is that, according to the ethnographic record, people are primarily hunter-gatherers or primarily agriculturalists; generally, economies that exploit both wild and domestic animals tend to be very few, so we may expect that transition periods will be very short, i.e. about six to eight generations. These are the types of issues that the more recent dating projects have been attempting to deal with.

Both camps do tend to be in agreement about one aspect: Ireland was different from Britain and the rest of Europe in terms of the extreme poverty of its mammalian prey. Britain and the rest of Europe possessed a good range of fauna that were absent in Ireland, so consumer resistance, if you will, in Ireland may not have been as strong as it might have been elsewhere. The shift in Ireland from hunting-fishing to farming may have been a very fast and welcome change.

There is a further factor to be considered. It is abundantly clear that, throughout the course of the Neolithic, Ireland was in regular contact with its neighbour. Polished stone axes, for example, are often made of such specific rock types that their source can be geologically determined. This provides archaeologists with the ability to trace the various exchange routes during the Neolithic. In Ireland, the major material was porcellanite, a stone derived from two sources, both situated in northeast Antrim. These are found in the thousands (there are over 7,000 known so far) in Ireland, but they also occur in Britain from Scotland to southern England and attest the movement of finished goods from Ireland to Britain (3.9).[42] Conversely, the Great

3.9. The Irish axe trade. Left: porcellanite axes from Ireland found in Britain; right: Great Langdale axes from Britain found in Ireland.

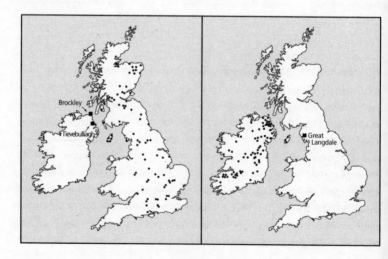

Langdale axe factory not only supplied Britain with axes, but over 100 of these fine axeheads have been recovered from Irish sites.[43] On a lesser scale we have the discovery of pitchstone from western Scotland on Irish sites.[44] In all these cases, we are obviously talking of the circulation of axes across the sea by boat.[45] Cases for contacts can also be made with reference to certain ceramic styles and tomb types which all suggest that, however Ireland received its Neolithic culture, it was in periodic if not constant contact with its Neolithic neighbours across the Irish Sea.[46] The nature of these contacts could have ranged from the obvious, such as trading parties exchanging goods, to the less obvious, the quest for marriage partners, social alliances or esoteric religious knowledge. And once there was a migration path established, i.e. once one had relatives settled across the water, we could expect a migration stream where other family members moved between earlier established points of disembarkation much in the way that modern Irish populations have gravitated to Liverpool or Boston.[47]

How should we explain the initiation of these contacts? There seem to be at least three models that could be suggested. The first would see the contacts as part of the entire process of the spread of the Neolithic from Britain to Ireland that involved a constant stream of coming and going between the two islands. In this way we should not be surprised either by the similarity of culture between them or by the evidence of specific occasions of direct contacts such as the exchange of stone axes. This has been the most popular default position, but it does involve an element of sleight-of-hand: it can describe how the Neolithic progressed but, without earlier dates from Britain, not how it originated in Ireland.

We could also suggest a second model in which both islands received their Neolithic initially under a common Continental influence or influences. A single common source would then explain the similarity and mutual relationships between the Neolithic of the two islands. But this model also has its problems. The best guess Continental source for the earliest Neolithic in Britain is northeast France and adjacent areas of Belgium and perhaps the Netherlands,[48] and one need only glance at a map to see a difficulty. We can imagine a Mesolithic Irishman accosted by a farmer in Calais and asked how to get to Wexford. The Irishman would no doubt answer: 'Well, to begin with, I wouldn't start from here'.

Or we could get a bit more subtle and offer a third model that argues that the contacts between Ireland and Britain were only established *after* both islands had independently adopted the Neolithic from different third sources, Britain from northeast France and Ireland, perhaps, from Brittany or Normandy. This solves one logistical problem by providing two different sources for the very beginning of the

Neolithic, sometime just before or around 4000 BC. Then, once both islands had adopted a Neolithic culture by *c.* 3800 BC, they had begun talking to one another and exchanging material and, possibly, spiritual culture that swamped whatever original differences they might initially have had. Unfortunately, this has the same ring as the legendary student answer claiming that the *Iliad* was not written by Homer but by another poet with the same name. In any event, the latter two models both require a third party, whom we now need to examine.

Ireland and the Continent

As we have seen, the area of northeast France and adjoining regions is the most probable source for many of the Neolithic elements we find adopted in the Neolithic of southern Britain.[49] The closest long-distance source for the Irish Neolithic would seem to be Brittany and Normandy, which do have earlier dates for the Neolithic that fall *c.* 5000–4500 BC (3.10).[50] On current evidence, this is the only region close enough to Ireland and with Neolithic dates early enough to provide the cattle found at Ferriter's Cove. Of course, the more distant the source the greater the logistical problem of explaining the farmer colonists who must not only bring their families but also their livestock. The linear distance between, say, Brest in Brittany and Cork is 483 km or 261 nautical miles. Any would-be colonists would need to row their way to Ireland, presumably in skin boats as plank boats do not appear until the 2nd millennium BC.[51] Humphrey Case suggested that the earliest farmer colonists could have arrived in something like an umiak, a larger version of the Inuit kayak, in which a family with their goods, two dogs and (take your pick) two cows plus two calves or six pigs or ten sheep or goats could be transported.[52] Alternatively, the only actual Neolithic boat remains that we have from Ireland tend to be a series of dugouts, usually oak, one of which was found just offshore of Gormanston, Co. Meath, that measured about 7 m long. Aidan O'Sullivan and Colin Breen have suggested that we should not be too quick to dismiss such boats as being unable to cross the open sea.[53] But assuming that neither the animals nor the crew had been sedated, this was certainly going to feel like a long haul. By the Iron Age, when vessels were no doubt much faster, the voyage from Brittany to the 'Holy Isle' (Ireland) was reckoned to take two days.[54] Nor is it easy to imagine why farmers setting out from Normandy or Brittany would deliberately avoid landfall in southern Britain in order to arrive in Ireland. Nevertheless, a possible French source is regarded as a serious proposition by Alison Sheridan of the National Museums of Scotland.

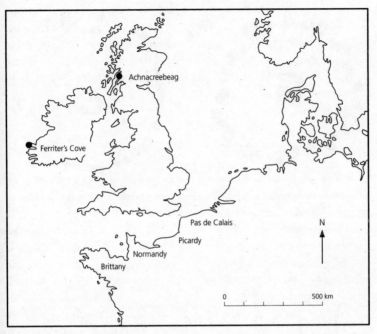

3.10. Ireland and northwestern France.

Setting aside the problem of explaining the cattle bones at Ferriter's Cove (failed colonization? gift-exchange?), Sheridan suggests that before *c.* 4000 BC, farmer colonists from Brittany or Normandy were already settling in Wales, northeast Ireland and southwest Scotland. She provides two lines of evidence. Among the earliest megalithic tombs in Ireland she includes the so-called simple passage tombs (a passage tomb without a passage!). These are small stone chambers covered with a large capstone and surrounded by a ring of stones (3.11). Sheridan argues that they belong to the very beginning of the Neolithic, as four tombs from the Carrowmore cemetery, Co. Sligo, have dates that fall *c.* 4200–3800 BC.[55] Although it is always difficult to compare monuments that are so simple, their closest analogues are to be found in southern Brittany, where there is an older tradition of erecting such stone monuments that goes back to *c.* 4500 BC.[56] It should be emphasized that Sheridan is anxious not to overstate her case, since the number of sites that can be positively linked together is not great and there are differences between the tombs such that

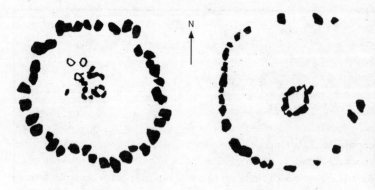

Carrowmore tomb 27, Co. Sligo

Druid Stone, Ballintoy, Co. Antrim

3.11. Simple passage tombs.

NW FRANCE c. 4300–3900 BC

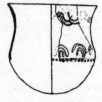

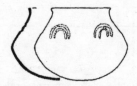

La Castellic, Brittany

Vierville, Normandy

3.12. Comparison of pottery from northwestern France (Brittany and Normandy) with (below) northwestern Scotland and northeastern Ireland.

NW SCOTLAND AND NE ULSTER c. 4000–3750 BC

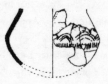

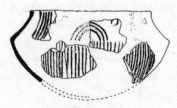

Achnacreebeag, Argyll

Ballymacaldrack, Co. Antrim

there is 'not enough evidence to argue for a widespread, synchronous spread of a specific funerary tradition northward from France'.[57] But she cites a second line of evidence: a pot recovered from a megalithic tomb at Achnacreebeag in Argyllshire, Scotland, which bears a striking resemblance to pre-4000 BC Neolithic pottery from Brittany and Normandy (3.12).[58]

These arguments tend to suggest some movement of people from Brittany northwest up the Irish Sea. Logistically this is difficult, but it does have two points in its favour. First, many archaeologists have commented on the apparent coastal distribution of the earliest (or what they believe to be the earliest) types of megalithic tombs, which are said to exhibit 'a distinct maritime focus' (3.13).[59] Indeed, the coastal location of such tombs has suggested to some possible sea routes between Ireland, Britain and the Continent.[60] It should be noted, however, that in one of the most recent reviews of all the dating evidence for ritual monuments, the authors

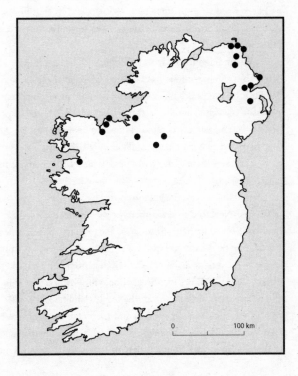

3.13. The coastal focus of simple passage tombs in Ireland.

0   100 km

found 'no grounds to support the existence of very early passage tombs in the west of Ireland'.[61]

Second, how do we explain any potential colonists' need to set off in boats filled with their animals and grain for Ireland? No matter which way we look at it, the sea crossing required to explain the Irish Neolithic has placed the focus on a coastal population as the most likely source of colonists because they would be the only ones with the nautical abilities to build and navigate the mini-arks that could cross the Irish Sea with the types of substantial loads required to recolonize Ireland (it is difficult to imagine inland farmers 'chartering out' boats for the crossing). The spread of the Neolithic across the Mediterranean appears to have consisted largely of a coastal spread, and the appearance of the Neolithic in Atlantic Europe is at least partially the result of similar movements along the coast. Ever since the Mesolithic it is clear that the populations of western Brittany were involved in an economy that took them out to sea, and at least there one might make a case for a build-up of population that led to a need or desire to spread further west.[62] It might also be noted that the Mesolithic had been replaced in Brittany by *c.* 4800 BC, and its transformation from hunting-gathering to agriculture would appear, like Ireland's, to have been very rapid and initiated by an influx of farmer colonists.[63]

Sheridan provides the Irish Neolithic with its best case for a direct Continental origin, but the hypothesis has been sharply challenged in a recent assessment of Neolithic origins in Britain and Ireland by Alasdair Whittle, Frances Healy and Alex Bayliss. They argue that the Breton pottery which Sheridan uses to anchor the date before 4000 BC actually continued down to 3600 BC; that the Achnacreebeag bowl may have just as good comparanda among later Irish wares; and that there is no further trace of these early Neolithic colonists further south on either side of the Irish Sea basin.[64]

Even if one accepts the links proposed by Sheridan, are we discussing the origins of the Irish Neolithic or, again, merely contacts that preceded the 'real' beginnings of the Neolithic? As we have already seen, the primary ceramic type associated with the Neolithic is the carinated bowl, whose links are closest with Britain, and Sheridan speaks of them as 'products of a well-established potting tradition'.[65] As to their more distant Continental origin, Sheridan opts for northeastern France (Calais-Picardy) and not southern Brittany, from where she would trace the initial Neolithic contacts seen in the simple passage tombs and the pot from Achnacreebeag. We have also seen that the Neolithic experienced an explosion in the manufacture and exchange of polished stone axes from a variety of stones, some of which indicate Irish-British contacts. But we also have axes in both Britain and Ireland that appear to derive from the Alpine region and may have travelled up to 1,800 km and over periods of several centuries before reaching their final place of deposition. Sheridan sees these also as potential traces of the Neolithic expansion, because these axes served as 'the treasured ancestral relics of early 4th millennium communities, acquired (and circulated) on the Continent and brought to Britain and Ireland as part of the CB [carinated bowl] Neolithic "package".'[66]

A first contact phase can be interpreted in two very contrasting ways. On the one hand, it might be regarded in the same light as the cattle bones from Ferriter's Cove: initial contacts that did not result in any major influx of population or cultural change. After all, Vikings had settled in North America by the early 11th century, but it was not until the 16th and 17th centuries that substantial European settlement began. However, Sheridan suggests that these initial contacts did bear fruit: although the primary ceramic type of the earliest Neolithic is the carinated bowl found in both Ireland and Britain, there was also a tradition of making decorated bowls that can be found in both Scotland and Ireland which could derive from these early contacts with Brittany.[67] But she believes the 'real' Neolithic, associated with carinated bowls and the new flint assemblage, is more likely to derive from some source in Picardy or the Pas-de-Calais,[68] a good origin for southern Britain but not exactly the easiest place from which to derive the Irish Neolithic. What seems certain is that if we ignore the ceramics for a moment and concentrate on the stone toolkit, one of the most obvious markers of the Early Neolithic in both Britain and Ireland is the leaf-shaped arrowhead, a type of projectile that is totally different from the variety of tranchet arrowheads one finds in Normandy, Brittany and elsewhere along the Atlantic coast of France, among cultures that might have been potential sources of the Irish Neolithic.[69] The type of arrowhead we are looking for is rooted further north in the tradition of the Early Neolithic that spread west across central Europe to northern France and adjacent territories. And the best analogies to those that we find in Ireland are to be found, like the carinated bowls, in Britain.

How?

Whatever the precise geographical origins we give to the Irish Neolithic, we need to consider how it actually happened on the ground in Ireland. All the evidence so far suggests a very rapid transition or, at least, dispersal of farming settlements across Ireland c. 3800 BC. We cannot say what happened to the indigenous Mesolithic population in Ireland: there are too few well-dated Later Mesolithic sites other than Ferriter's Cove, so we simply do not know how long some hunter-gatherers may have hung on. We certainly do not have any meaningful evidence that the Mesolithic communities played a role in the formation of the material culture, economy or ritual practices of the Early Neolithic populations – the story of Ireland's first farmers is almost entirely the story of either new colonists or a local population that quickly emulated the culture of the new colonists. What happened to the people who had occupied Ireland for the previous four millennia? If we exclude acculturation of the native population as the primary cause of change, we must explain how a restricted number of incoming farmer colonists were so successful at obliterating the preceding culture.

First, we might suggest that the Later Mesolithic population is nearly invisible in the Early Neolithic because perhaps there were not many of them to begin with. Prehistoric population estimates are notoriously notional and based on factors such as the carrying capacity of the land that, in the case of Ireland, may have been exaggerated in light of its lack of natural resources. We offered the ballpark figure of c. 3,000 in the last chapter, i.e. about 600 nuclear families, but we also cited ranges that were as low as c. 800 people (160 families). If the Mesolithic population of Ireland had been closer to the lower estimates, then the progressive settlement of Ireland by, say, about 30 to 50 farming families, over several decades, might well have obliterated the local population. This would happen because of the greater growth rate of farmer populations compared with hunter-gatherers, especially in the type of highly mobile economy predicted for the Irish Later Mesolithic. Thus an immigrant farming population of c. 150 (30 families), increasing at an estimated rate of 0.1% per year,[70] would have been more than three times the size of the population of the indigenous hunter-gatherers within 200 years. If the number of immigrants sounds small for such a large impact, one might consider Catherine Perlès's study of the spread of the Neolithic to Greece which, she suggests, may not have involved more than several hundred colonists.[71]

The difference in the potential for population growth is probably the most serious contributor to the rapid shift to the Neolithic, although some have suggested that the Later Mesolithic population may have been reduced by diseases introduced by farmer colonists.[72] The problem here is identifying a truly plausible infectious disease or suite of diseases that might have caused a major drop in population. While it is probable that native Irish Mesolithic populations had been relatively isolated from whatever diseases were passing through the Continent and Britain (and were hence perhaps more susceptible), infectious diseases such as those that plagued

Europe in the Middle Ages or whose introduction to the New World saw major population collapse are generally associated with the type of dense populations that we find in the urban settlements of the later historic period and not among the type of thinly distributed populations we find in western Europe during the Neolithic. The one exception here would be those diseases that are directly associated with domestic animals. Although many of the major communicable diseases may have got their start in animals (e.g. chickenpox, smallpox, influenza), others may be contracted directly from contact with domestic animals or from milk products. Some of these diseases could have a serious impact on human populations. For example, many have argued that human tuberculosis derived from contact with early domesticated cattle that had bovine tuberculosis; today the tuberculosis bacterium is the number one infectious disease and kills over 3 million people a year.[73] Other potential diseases that could be transmitted from domestic livestock include E-coli and swine flu. The spread of new diseases among a society that had had no contact with the wild predecessors of cattle, sheep and goats, much less the domesticated variants, is certainly a possibility. However, at present this remains theoretical speculation: there is no hard evidence for domestic animals producing diseases that seriously reduced the number of Ireland's Mesolithic inhabitants.

How about extermination? It must be admitted that the Neolithic is characterized by an increase in warfare, and there is clearly evidence of warfare in the Early Neolithic of Britain.[74] This involves evidence of attacks on sites, arrows embedded in skeletons, and a recent study of 350 British Neolithic skulls in which about one in 20 gave evidence of trauma.[75] A review by Dermot Moore of the evidence for violence in Early Neolithic Ireland can cite two settlements that had possibly been attacked by both archers and fire, and Moore also notes that many of the Early Neolithic houses show signs of destruction by fire (Ireland also reveals some evidence of death by archery). But he also emphasizes that the evidence for warfare does not appear to involve the local Mesolithic population.[76] The reason is that all the arrowheads are clearly Neolithic (laurel- and lozenge-shaped) and there is no evidence for Mesolithic weapons. Of course, the sites in question cannot really provide evidence one way or the other regarding attacks by farmers on native hunter-gatherers, but if we accept that Ireland's early farmers engaged in fighting among themselves, they could surely have extended such aggression to the native population as well. Moreover, it would have required few acts of overt violence, if the local population were not so accustomed, to instil a sense of fear among the Mesolithic population that might hasten the abandonment of their earlier way of life.

In short, the notion of farmer colonists swamping the earlier inhabitants after several generations is not an impossible scenario, given the advantages of potential immigrants in terms of their ability to increase their population size, engage in aggressive behaviour and, just possibly, resist some of the diseases that might have been introduced with their domestic animals. Moreover, they might also have employed an arsenal of 'pull' factors that could have attracted the indigenous population to abandon their traditional culture and adopt that of the new farmers. One obvious attraction would be the increase of meat in the diet. Also potentially impressive were the erection of stone tombs and the performance of large public ceremonies. A good example has recently been excavated at the Early Neolithic site of Kilshane, Co. Meath, where the remains of no fewer than 58 cattle were recovered from the bottom of a ditch. The bones (over 300 kg) have been examined by Finbar McCormick, who suggests that they would appear to be the result of several, perhaps seasonal, acts of sacrifice and consumption.[77] The potential impact of feasting has long been acknowledged as a serious vehicle for introducing and encouraging social change.

But why should early farmers have come to Ireland in the first place? As we have just seen, when it comes to the origins and dispersal of the Neolithic we tend to look for 'push' or 'pull' factors. The settlement of Ireland is not an isolated question because it receives its agricultural economy at the same time as Britain and southern Scandinavia, i.e. all of northwest Europe seems to be experiencing a similar and contemporaneous expansion of farming. This has encouraged archaeologists to search for a common denominator. One possibility is a shift in climate, because the Neolithic expansion is set to the same period c. 4100–3800 BC when environmental scientists detect a more arid climate with a greater range in annual temperature.[78] This would have resulted in less waterlogged and more easily worked soils as well as a longer growing season, all of which would have made the spread of cereal agriculture more attractive. The Neolithic thus expanded at a time when the climate made it most attractive.

On the other hand, we must also admit that almost from the very beginning Neolithic colonists have a tradition of spreading to islands, and here arguments for population pressure simply ring hollow. For example, about 8000 BC farmers set out, presumably from the Syrian or Palestine coast, to carry themselves and their domestic livestock and cereals to Cyprus,[79] making a sea crossing of comparable length to those who settled Ireland, yet one could hardly argue that the Near East was already 'full up'. Sea-going farmers also carried the Neolithic to Crete, Malta, Sardinia, Corsica and the Balearic Islands, but it is difficult to invoke either population pressure or climate as the primary factor in all these cases, and one might reconsider the arguments of the late Jacques Cauvin, who emphasized the ideological dimensions of the Neolithic revolution for why it spread so fast. He suggested that the earliest farmers dispersed with a 'messianic self-confidence' to carry farming and the mastery of nature into new territories.[80] Or we could reverse the ideological drive, from a desire to spread the new economy to a desire to flee the social consequences of adopting it. Examining the spread of the earliest farming communities in the Near East, Eleni Asouti has speculated that the social cost of abandoning hunting-gathering for life in a farming village was that the new way of life threw up problems that could only be resolved by abandoning a simpler, more egalitarian system of social organization.[81] Extending this to the initial spread of the Neolithic to Ireland (and Britain), we might imagine that the first generations of colonists were putting as much distance as they could between themselves and the more socially complex farming communities from which they came, although, within a period of a century or so, their descendants would be playing their part in the same type of societies as those from which their ancestors had earlier fled.

Making sense of it all?

Are we then really left with a very shaky model involving a so far unidentified coastal population in Britain or the Continent setting out in boats to establish their farms in Ireland at an unverified date and for reasons unknown? Probably yes, but if we have to opt for the least bad hypothesis, then the most immediate source for much of what we describe as Neolithic is still Britain and we live in hope that this will eventually be chronologically easier to swallow. The reason for looking to Britain is that the similarities in almost all areas of material culture, from the Early Neolithic onward, are just too close to ignore. Moreover, as the British Neolithic shed many of the cultural items associated with the carinated bowls found on the European continent, Ireland basically did the same, and this is most easily explained by presuming a British 'filter' rather than the Irish accepting and rejecting the same items independently. Perhaps Charles Thomas, though writing in a different context, put it best: 'Ireland, if far enough from Britain to be a separate country, is nonetheless too close to have experienced a separate history.'[82]

Could there have been still earlier connections with Brittany? This is certainly possible, and if the connections were indeed with both islands that might help to explain Ireland's connections with Britain. It could be argued that Neolithic colonists, having settled on both sides of the Irish Sea, had established the migration stream between the two islands that permitted the rapid flow of ideas, material culture and livestock between Britain and Ireland.

The end of the Neolithic

The types of tombs, both timber and stone-built in Britain and normally stone-built (megalithic) in Ireland, indicate persistent contacts between Britain, Ireland and further afield. The largest of the Irish tombs comprise the passage tombs such as Newgrange in Co. Meath, and this entire class of tomb has many parallels in Atlantic Europe, especially Iberia and Brittany. While some have suggested successions of Neolithic colonists or religious missionaries moving from the Continent to Ireland, archaeologists today generally prefer more muted contacts. One possibility may be indicated by the fact that the largest of the Breton and Irish tombs share great engineering skills, the use of esoteric artistic designs along the passages and interiors of the tombs, and astronomical alignments. These suggest a learned class within society who, irrespective of the various ethnic groups involved, interacted with one another, possibly as pilgrims seeking religious wisdom. Moreover, that astronomical knowledge – most spectacularly evident in the alignment of the entrance of the great passage tomb at Newgrange on the sunrise of the winter solstice – also suggests the type of knowledge that might be required to navigate sailing boats from the Continent to Britain and Ireland.[83]

Without going into painful detail, we can note once again that there is a broad cultural sequence in Britain which is often paralleled by similar developments in Ireland. In both Britain and Ireland, for example, plain undecorated carinated bowls of the Early Neolithic are replaced by various types of vessels carrying a variety of ornaments, while the exchange of polished stone axes between Britain and Ireland reveals the continuous social contacts between the two islands. The interconnections are most marked at the very end of the Neolithic period.

By the Late Neolithic (c. 3000–2500 BC) we find a horizon of a particular type of decorated (though in Ireland frequently undecorated) flat-bottomed vessel ('Grooved Ware'), which, if our radiocarbon dates can be trusted, has its origins in Orkney. This particular type of vessel spread widely over Britain, and in the past few decades it has been uncovered with increasing frequency in Ireland (3.14). The evidence suggests that we are dealing with far more than the spread of a ceramic style, because such pottery is often associated with new ceremonial enclosures built of earth and timber, either located in new areas or in the vicinity of earlier megalithic tombs such as the great passage tomb at Knowth, where one of the few Grooved Ware burials in Ireland is known. These new monuments comprise henges, circular ceremonial structures with a raised bank and a ditch on the inside, precisely the opposite arrangement from that found on later defended sites. Other structures include timber circles and stone circles. The former may include rectangular structures, either roofed 'temples' or excarnation platforms upon which the dead might be placed to decompose (3.15, 3.16).

3.14. Grooved Ware pot (height 31.4 cm).

Some other innovations that appear in Ireland, presumably as part of the Grooved Ware complex, are oblique arrowheads, discoidal knives, clay 'loomweight'-shaped objects, some stone maceheads and, in some areas, the importation of flint from Co. Antrim as far away as Co. Meath. The nature of the ceremonies engaged in is unknown, but feasting appears to be one element, especially the consumption of pork and whatever might have been contained within the Grooved Ware vessels themselves. That the new structures tend to be circular has led to the suggestion that the change in ritual involved an ideology centred on the circle

3.15. Ritual structure at Ballynahatty, Co. Down.

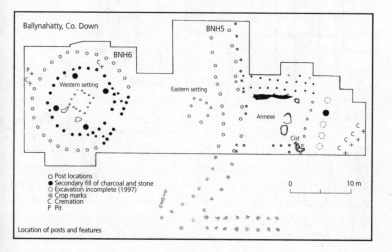

Ballynahatty, Co. Down

BNH5

BNH6

Western setting

Eastern setting

Annexe

Cist

○ Post locations
● Secondary fill of charcoal and stone
◌ Excavation incomplete (1997)
✷ Crop marks
C Cremation
P Pit

0   10 m

Location of posts and features

and that the cosmological system of the Grooved Ware horizon was based on a circle rather than (like the populations of Mesoamerica) a square. This has also been seen as a major shift in religious focus from the cosmology of the earlier periods of the Neolithic, in which ceremonies may have been centred on dealing with the ancestors in megalithic tombs. The spread of the Grooved Ware package has often been interpreted as the very rapid spread of a new belief system that was taken up across both Britain and Ireland.[84] While archaeologists would accept that it may have involved some migration, any full-scale movement of people to introduce and spread the new complex is generally rejected. Alison Sheridan, for example, writes that 'the changes can be seen as an active, deliberate and indeed selective adoption of exotic material culture and practices'.[85]

3.16. Reconstruction of excarnation platform at Ballynahatty.

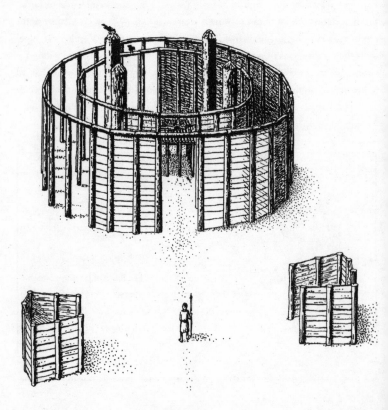

Such contacts suggest that throughout the Neolithic both people and ideas criss-crossed the Irish Sea. This was certainly done at least on an individual or familial basis (the minimum to explain such things as the circulation of polished stone axes) but might have operated at the community level as well. The contacts were likely to have gone both ways. They did not swamp the local cultures on either side of the sea; Ireland was still capable of producing stone tools or tombs that lack any parallels in Britain, and there is no question of the wholesale importation of all the varieties of British Neolithic culture to Ireland, although the Grooved Ware complex does come quite close. But from here on it will be very difficult to discuss cultural change in Ireland purely in terms of a (pre)historic event rather than an ongoing process that also involves its island neighbour.

Conclusions

→ At *c.* 3800 BC Ireland experienced a major revolution in almost every aspect of its culture as it adopted farming as an economic basis.

→ Although there is some very small evidence for contacts between native populations and farming populations, the situation in Ireland does not resemble other areas of Europe where one can track the acculturation of hunting-gathering populations. Thus the cultural contribution of local Irish Mesolithic populations to the Neolithic would appear to be minimal.

→ Despite a few items to the contrary, the spread of farming would appear to have been a rapid affair, possibly taking about two centuries or less to cover most of Ireland, although this does not mean that some Mesolithic populations did not survive longer.

→ There is at present no credible evidence to demonstrate that the Irish Neolithic was appreciably more recent than the Neolithic of central, western or northern Britain.

→ Many items of culture such as architecture, flint tools and especially ceramics and some megalithic tomb types appear to be nearly identical between Ireland and Britain and suggest either a common origin or persistent mutual contacts.

→ The similarities between Ireland and Britain are so strong that, despite some problems of chronology, the source of much of the Irish Neolithic would still appear to be Britain.

→ There is some evidence that the initial impetus for the Irish Neolithic derived from southern Brittany. If so, this may have opened up the seaway connections between Ireland and Britain which promoted the close cultural similarities that developed between the two islands.

→ There were periodic contacts between Ireland and Brittany throughout the Neolithic, but these were never as close as those that obtained between Ireland and Britain.

→ At the end of the Neolithic both Ireland and Britain participated in a similar ceremonial horizon involving the erection of large timber structures and the use of a radically new style of pottery, Grooved Ware.

CHAPTER FOUR

Beakers and Metal

N iall was the youngest of five sons, yet he managed to outstrip his brothers and claim the kingship. In one tale, his primacy was foreshadowed when the five were put to work in a blacksmith's forge. In order to test their worth, a druidical smith set fire to the forge and the five brothers fled the burning building, each attempting to retrieve at least some of the tools. The four older brothers all managed to save some objects (the hammers, a coat of mail, a drinking-vat and the fuel-basket), but it was Niall who carried out the bellows, hammers and even the anvil, and for this he was judged the best of the lot.[1] While the introduction of farming was certainly the main watershed in prehistoric Ireland, the introduction of metallurgy was not merely a technological innovation. It appears to have been associated with a number of other changes that some have seen as evidence for the arrival of a new people from Continental Europe who may also have introduced such iconic Irish emblems as horses, alcohol and even the Irish language.

New pots

Across a broad area of Europe, including Britain, 19th-century antiquarians delving into or outright pillaging ancient burial mounds were routinely discovering a fine form of pottery that was variously termed a *Becker* in German or a *gobelet campaniforme* (bell-shaped goblet) in French; in England the term 'Drinking Cup' (or worse, 'Ancient British fictilia') had been applied to what many would regard as one of the most attractive ceramic styles of prehistoric Europe.[2] In 1912 Lord Abercromby published a catalogue of the vessels from Britain and renamed them 'Bell Beakers' after their distinctive (inverted) bell-like shape.[3] Archaeologists were not only attracted to the pottery but also to the objects that were frequently found with them, such as copper knives and archery kits consisting of barbed and tanged arrowheads of flint, stone plates or 'bracers' believed to protect the archer's wrist from the bowstring, and, in some instances, miniature pendants shaped like bows. To these could also be added occasional ornaments of gold, amber, jet or silver. Generally, the context of their discovery across northwest and central Europe was in single burials under a barrow; the beaker, presumed to have been for consumption of an alcoholic beverage, had been placed in the grave to see the deceased off or quench his thirst across eternity. Beakers were discovered as far north as Norway and as far south as Spain, Sicily and Morocco; they were found as far east as Hungary and Poland and as far westward as Britain (4.1). They were obviously part of a major European cultural phenomenon, but one that had apparently not quite made it as far as Ireland.

4.1. Generalized distribution of Beakers across Europe.

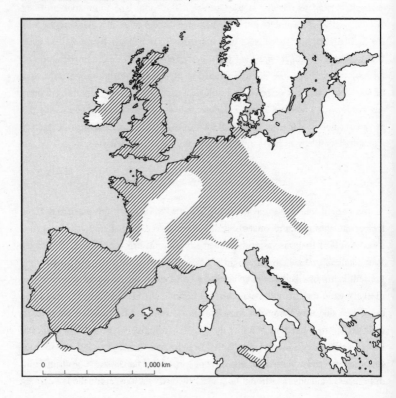

4.2. Map of sites
mentioned in
Chapter 4.

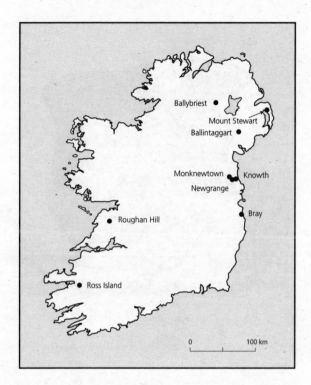

In 1928, in one of his earliest syntheses of Irish prehistory, R. A. S. Macalister lamented that there was record of only a single find of Beaker ware in Ireland (actually a woodcut of an Irish vase, a much later 'offspring' of a Beaker, published in the *Dublin Penny Journal* of 1832), from Mount Stewart, Co. Down (4.2, 4.3),[4] and, following Lord Abercromby's suggestion, he imaginatively explained it away as the product of a captive foreign slave girl producing what she knew best (the small size of fingerprints on Beakers suggested that they had been made by women). To Macalister the absence of Beaker pottery was indicative of a fundamental difference between Beaker-rich Britain and Beaker-poor Ireland: 'for all that the two islands are so near together, *Britain is essentially an island of the North Sea, Ireland of the Atlantic Ocean*; and this difference is fundamental throughout the whole history of their mutual relations'.[5]

4.3. Food Vessels from
Mount Stewart, Co. Down.

Twenty years can be a long time in archaeology and by 1949, when more Beaker remains had been discovered in Ireland, Macalister's attitude had not only changed but turned positively lurid. Gone is our poor Beaker slave girl as we now read how Beaker-using invaders came to Ireland and

> exterminated the men, or at least reduced them to slavery. As for the
> women, they met the usual fate of women in warfare: 'to every man a
> damsel or two,' as the savage old Hebrew paen expresses it…it was the
> only catastrophe of ancient times, subversive enough to have effected
> such a complete change of language.[6]

A quarter of a century later, a cooler assessment of the same problem by Peter Harbison could still conclude that the Beaker-users represented 'the last large-scale "invasion" of Ireland during the prehistoric period'.[7] In subsequent textbooks such as that of Michael Herity and George Eogan, the authors accept that a 'Beaker people' introduced metallurgy to Ireland and arrived in two main groups, one from the Continent who settled in the southwest of Ireland and another group who crossed from Britain to the east of Ireland.[8] And we read that they came 'in strength', sufficient to consolidate their own settlement, expand and 'dominate the existing inhabitants'.[9]

In terms of Irish origins, the Beaker people are obviously relevant players for a variety of reasons. As we have seen, there has been considerable acceptance that the Beaker-users represented one of the more significant waves of invasion in Irish prehistory. They gave to Ireland a new ceramic type (4.4) that some have associated with a new drinking cult. The Beaker people also initiate the appearance of new archery equipment consisting of the barbed and tanged arrowhead and, perhaps, the stone wristguard[10] (4.5). To this we can also probably add the initiation of metallurgy (mining, smelting, casting) of copper axes and other tools along with the production of the earliest gold ornaments. And to the existing range of livestock, some credit the Beaker-users with having introduced the domestic horse to Ireland. Drink, fighting and the Irish Sweepstakes would

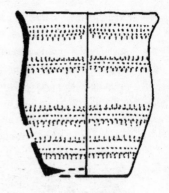

4.4. Beaker (height 11 cm).

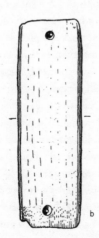

4.5. Beaker (a) barbed and tanged arrowhead; (b) 'wristguard'; (c) gold ornament (diameter 6.3 cm).

certainly tally with Irish stereotypes. Moreover, while we recognize contacts between Ireland and Britain and possibly parts of Atlantic Europe during the Neolithic, it is only with the introduction of the Beakers and copper and bronze metallurgy that Ireland becomes part of a much larger story that generally involves not only Atlantic Europe but also central Europe. This widening picture is critical, because our archaeological canvas must expand beyond simply Ireland and Britain. As we will see later, both islands came eventually to share very similar languages as well as sizeable populations with both Atlantic and central Europe, much of the same territory that comprised the world of the Beaker people.[11]

What are the Beakers?

While we may assert that the archaeological evidence for Beaker-users exists in Ireland, what does that actually mean in terms of their contribution to the origins of the Irish? Are the Irish really the descendants of a randy overlord race of beer-guzzling Beakerfolk? Before we can answer this question we must descend briefly into the morass of Beaker-ology, an interpretive nightmare devised to torment any archaeologist who has the misfortune to work in a land once touched by the Bell Beaker. The problem is that we simply do not have a unified coherent vision of what finding a Beaker actually means – anywhere. And to compound the mystery, Beaker-users tend to behave very differently in different regions of Europe. Generally, archaeologists refer to the larger assemblages of material they find as a 'culture' or 'horizon', but when it comes to the Beakers we often encounter the word 'phenom-enon'. When an archaeologist uses the word phenomenon to describe something, you know we are in trouble. So we will oversimplify and pretend that we can reduce the Beaker problem to two major opposing models that archaeologists, depending on the region they are studying, either embrace or reject, and which model we opt for will have serious repercussions regarding Irish origins.

The traditional model sees the Beaker-users as the expansion of a single ethnic group, involved in the manufacture and circulation of copper and gold artifacts, who settled among local populations across much of Europe at the end of the Neolithic. The broad expansion of a single ceramic type (the Beaker) coupled with the very poor evidence for substantial dwellings suggested the existence of a conservative yet highly mobile population. The fact that cemeteries were generally quite small argued that the social groups who buried their dead in the cemeteries were also likely to have been small. That Beaker burials are accompanied by exotic ornaments such as amber, jet, copper or gold and in some regions were also associated with the earliest evidence for metallurgy further rounded out the image of the Beaker people as either traders of exotic material or a wealthy elite. Some have further argued that the people buried in Beaker graves, at least those in central Europe, Britain and Ireland, reflect a different physical type than their Neolithic predecessors.[12] One is left with a conservative, physically distinctive mobile group of families possessing fine metalwork who lived among various native populations of Europe (in many areas local ceramics continued alongside Beakers). At this point the ethnic model divides into several different variants. We have already seen one of them in Macalister's interpretation: the Beaker people were an elite ruling over local populations or, in the words of the great prehistorian V. Gordon Childe, the Beaker-users formed 'a relatively thin governing class, dominating and organizing older alien societies'.[13] In all these models, the Beaker people either come en masse or form an elite who superimpose themselves on a local population.

Others have stripped this model of some of its broader ethnic connotations to portray the Beaker-users, at least in some regions, as migrant craftsmen who not only helped establish metallurgy in different regions but also are precursors of a much wider phenomenon of mobile elite craftsmen who would become increasingly important over the course of the Bronze Age. The fact that the Beaker-users seemed to maintain a conservative material culture (in terms of ceramics), travelled much and in small groups, and were involved with metallurgy invited them to be compared with the later gypsies or tinkers.[14] This model keeps the ethnic elements of the previous model but does not make them out as elites.

But while this 'ethnic' model of Beaker expansions was popular before the 1960s, later there was a backlash in archaeology against attributing culture change to new populations. John Waddell's excellent *The Prehistoric Archaeology of Ireland* captures this mood when he tackles the question of the Beaker phenomenon:

> The hypothesis of a distinct population group, 'the Beaker Folk' of
> older archaeological literature, has therefore been replaced by a func-
> tional model in which various artifacts including Beakers are
> considered as expressions of individual status. While this model does
> not preclude the possibility that some users of Beaker pottery travelled
> from place to place, it does obviate the need to presuppose complex
> population movements to account for the European spread of 'the
> Beaker assemblage'.[15]

The replacement of a Beaker-using ethnic group and its immigration into Ireland by some form of social diffusion can be found widely in the syntheses of Irish prehistory, and migration has been placed on the back burner.[16] Nevertheless, recent studies of human remains associated with Beaker burials in Continental Europe have revealed evidence that a considerable number of people buried in Beaker graves were not likely to be local and that migration is still on the cards. One study of Beaker cemeteries in central Europe suggested that somewhere between 17.5% and 62% of its occupants were not local.[17] The most celebrated instance of migration is the remains of a man associated with a Beaker from near Stonehenge, the 'Amesbury archer', which suggested that he had originated from as far away as central Europe.[18] Similar studies have not yet been carried out in Ireland but might be employed to determine whether there was some population movement into Ireland (if we could find well-preserved inhumations instead of cremations). We will return to the physical evidence for this in a later chapter, but the possibility of a migration to Ireland is certainly no less plausible than the one that required a 325-km journey from Sardinia to bring the Beaker phenomenon to Sicily.[19]

The second model of Beaker expansions minimizes or denies population movements and explains the spread of Beakers in terms of either exchange systems or social ideology. Are we dealing with the movement of prestige pottery rather than a people? Such an argument has been used to explain the density of Beakers along the Atlantic coasts or major rivers, as water transport would have been the most efficient way of carrying Beakers over long distances.[20] The idea that Beakers were merely an exchange item has been tested on a number of occasions by examining the inclusions inside Beakers compared with the local geology of where they have been recovered. Most of the evidence for Continental Europe suggests at best very limited exchange and generally local manufacture.[21] Crucially, in Ireland the local manufacture of Beakers has been consistently supported by the few petrological examinations that have been made.[22] In short, there is so far no case for Irish Beakers attesting to long-range ceramic exchange networks, and the same probably goes for any idea of an extensive Bell Beaker ceramic exchange system.[23] Irish Beakers tend to look like they were homemade.[24] Their context supports this, as Beakers are not found solely confined to elite burials where we might suspect a long-distance exchange item. In France, for example, both well-made and substandard Beakers may be found in the same grave, and they are rarely found with other prestigious Beaker weapons or ornaments.[25] But they are also found as kitchen rubbish. In these cases archaeologists have suggested that we may be dealing with emulation, i.e. while elites may have originally marked themselves off by possessing imported wares or fine-quality specialist products (Beakers), lower social orders attempted to enhance their own prestige by producing inferior 'knock-offs' and swamping the market (like imitation Rolexes). One could then argue that the fine Beakers of the Continent have been debased to serve as standard domestic ware in Ireland.

An obvious issue here is what were the practical and social functions of Beaker pottery? Some have argued that the expansion of the Beakers reflects the spread of a cultural package[26] employing alcoholic drinking kits and archery. We cannot be certain what the beverage served in the Beakers was, but in at least one case the residue of a Beaker from Scotland may indicate that people were drinking mead or perhaps simply gobbling honey;[27] recent analysis of a Spanish Beaker suggests that it served beer laced with some hallucinogen,[28] while residue from a French Beaker was analysed as '*caramel alimentaire*'.[29] Whether or not they held an alcoholic beverage, they were not ideally shaped for drinking in that the imbibers would probably have dribbled some of the liquid because of the wide flaring necks and expanded bodies.[30] But if they were for consuming alcohol, Irish national pride is certainly upheld, as Ireland has yielded what is just about the largest Beaker in Europe: a Beaker from Ballybriest, Co. Londonderry, would have held about 9.5 litres.[31] A parallel for the importance of drinking kits occurs later in Europe when Iron Age elites routinely went to their graves accompanied by imported wine-serving sets from the Mediterranean. Again the emphasis here is on the spread of a cultural phenomenon and not primarily the movement of a people. In this case the elites would be local and they would be buying into a new ideology to mark themselves off from the rest of their communities. How this new ideology worked remains highly speculative. Humphrey Case suggested that the Beaker kit reflected a sequence of ritual symbols involving the hunting of animals (with bow and arrow), the dispatch of the wounded animal by slitting its throat with a copper dagger (found more routinely outside Ireland), and the collection and drinking of its blood in the Beaker.[32] But this model is also challenged by those who find no real evidence for the type of elite society suggested as the driving force behind the adoption of Beakers.[33]

Finally, one might think that if archaeologists can't explain in any detail what Beakers actually mean, we could at least say from where they originated. Wrong again, although here the two camps are at least fairly discrete: Iberia or the Rhine (Dutch model). Iberia has the advantage of earlier radiocarbon dates while the Netherlands has the edge on demonstrating archaeological antecedents, i.e. pots and some other Beaker-associated artifacts that appear immediately ancestral to the earliest Bell Beakers.[34] The Iberian camp attempts to deal with the local evolution of Beaker ceramics in the Rhineland by suggesting that Iberian potters obtained, saw–and/or were influenced by ceramics from northwest Europe in their exchange contacts with the north, and that the reason the Dutch Beakers look so much like their earlier pottery is that they are hybrids.[35] This requires one to interpret Dutch Beakers as copies of an Iberian copy of an original Dutch pot.

In Continental Europe the Beakers first appear *c*. 2900 BC and tend to have died out by *c*. 2100 BC.[36] They appear in central Europe by *c*. 2600–2500 BC and in Britain also by *c*. 2500 BC. And about this time they also begin to appear in Ireland.

Beaker settlement in Ireland

The discovery of Beaker sites in Ireland is now very much a growth industry, and in the most recent assessment of the nature of Irish Beaker sites, Neill Carlin has identified 213 sites with Beakers.[37] Once believed to have been largely confined to the northern half of the island, they are now found in marked concentrations along most of the east coast and at least to some extent in both the south and west of Ireland.[38] Despite the number of sites, it is still very difficult to generate a coherent description of the Beaker presence in Ireland. While the number of sites with Beakers or objects that we would normally associate with Beakers is very much on the increase, actual Beaker structures are few and far between and are generally reduced to pits, some postholes or hearths. In Carlin's study, the primary context for Beakers in Ireland are pits (91 sites) which, at least in some cases, may have been part of more extensive settlements. Carlin treats these pits as largely the product of the deliberate deposition of Beaker sherds, i.e. a form of offering. The second largest context (30 sites) comprised spreads of Beaker material in the soil that were not associated with any architectural features. Carlin has suggested that these may have represented ploughed-out heaps of accumulated Beaker material, possibly collected during communal feasts. One might imagine here the 'altars' of beer tins and empty wine bottles that decorate university students' rooms, commemorating more secular social occasions. Although Beaker sites seldom reveal any clear floor plan or indicate what the superstructure may have looked like, what little evidence does exist suggests just possibly round or oval huts, measuring on average somewhere between 5 and 6 m in diameter.[39] This paucity of Beaker settlement is also typical of Britain[40] and, as we have seen, has led to a tendency to view Beaker sites as merely temporary camps of a mobile population who may have engaged in stock-raising or occasional settings of communal feasts. But the quantity of material on a number of sites is suggestive of something more than seasonal stopovers by temporary squatters. Around the great passage tomb of Knowth, for example, were five concentrations of Beaker material associated with several hearths, pits and postholes.[41] While little if anything could be made of the architectural features, the fact that there were the sherds of well over 200 individual Beaker vessels,[42] both fine pottery and substantial quantities of Beaker domestic wares that may have served for storage or cooking and not just the quaffing of fermented beverages, might lead one to presume that the site saw more substantial activity. We might compare the quantity of pottery found here with a recently exca-vated Early Neolithic settlement at Ballintaggart, Co. Down, where three rectangular Neolithic houses and the adjacent area yielded sherds from about 140 different pots.[43] In short, the quantity of waste at the Beaker site is comparable to that from a presumably permanent Neolithic settlement. Moreover, Beakers also occur on earlier ritual sites. At Knowth the cremated remains of an adult and child, associated with an undecorated Beaker, were recovered from one of the smaller megalithic tombs.[44] Extensive Beaker remains are also found nearby at Newgrange and at another ritual site at Monknewtown.

The tendency for Beaker remains to appear on earlier ritual sites, especially those previously erected by those employing Grooved Ware, raises serious problems of interpreting precisely what Beaker-users were doing in Ireland. As Carlin warns us, it is extremely difficult to determine whether a site is essentially a long-term settlement site or perhaps a seasonally occupied ritual site where people have come together for feasting and celebrations.

At Newgrange we find evidence for cattle and pig-raising. The Beaker settlement there also yielded what was claimed as the earliest evidence for the horse in post-glacial Ireland.[45] However, the ascription of the horse remains to the Beaker period is now being seriously challenged by new radiocarbon dates, and it is hard to find any really solid evidence for the domestic horse in Ireland before the Later Bronze Age, c. 1000 BC.[46] On the other hand, it is equally hard to come up with substantial collections of Irish faunal remains before c. 1000 BC, so the domestic horse could have arrived at an earlier date.

Beaker burials

The concept of a Beaker-using elite is primarily prompted by the fact that much of the evidence for Beakers in northwest and central Europe, including Britain, is found

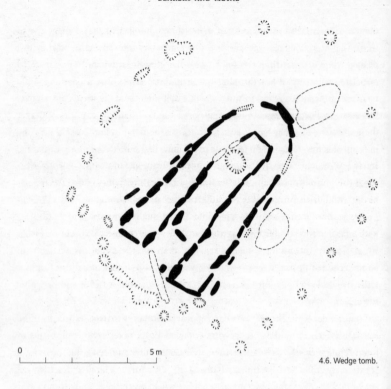

0   5 m

4.6. Wedge tomb.

in 'classic' Beaker burials. These comprise a single individual buried in a pit with an assortment of items from the Beaker 'kit' and the entire affair covered by a mound of earth.[47] In Ireland, where Beaker burials now number about 40 individuals,[48] there is not a single 'classic' Beaker burial.[49] Instead, we find Beaker burials primarily in wedge tombs, the most numerous and most recent class of megalithic tomb in Ireland (4.6). Here the burials are not single but collective, with up to eight burials found together at Ballybriest. In its use of collective burial in a megalithic tomb, we find Ireland behaving more like some regions of north and south Atlantic Europe.[50] But there is a subtle distinction to be made between the Irish evidence and that of any of its potential Atlantic homelands. Throughout Atlantic Europe the Beaker burials are found as secondary burials in earlier Neolithic tombs, i.e. burial monuments already ancient were re-employed by Beaker-users to bury their own dead. In Ireland, there is indeed evidence of Beaker remains inserted into earlier Neolithic tombs, especially the court tombs where Beaker sherds have been found in 14 tombs.[51] But here we are only talking (with certainty) of Beaker sherds and not necessarily of whole pots accompanying the Beaker dead. Here we may well be dealing with votive offerings (to the ancestors?) rather than actual burials. Neill Carlin has discovered that only in wedge tombs do we recover the remains of whole Beakers along with burials, and these tombs generally appear to date no earlier than the Beakers.[52] So after their Continental Beaker-using kin had abandoned erecting new megalithic tombs (but were content to employ earlier tombs), the Irelanders created a new megalithic monument, the wedge tomb.[53] Also, while most of the Atlantic burials are inhumations, the majority of the Irish burials continue the Neolithic practice of cremation.

As we have seen, a set of associated items that might be found with a Beaker burial in the rest of Europe includes an archery kit.[54] The other weapon found is the copper dagger (4.7). To these might be added an innovation in dressing: the button, conical in shape and fastened with a cord through a V-shaped perforation. Gold ornament also begins to appear. All of these are known from Ireland, although generally as stray finds or dissociated from a distinctive burial complex. It looks as though the Irelanders ordered various items from the Beaker catalogue but did not buy the whole package.

Metallurgy

The earliest metallurgy in Ireland involves the exploitation of copper that, as we have seen in Chapter 1, was locally available. In the period *c.* 2500–1800 BC we find evidence of the extraction of copper ores, their smelting to produce metallic copper, and their working into shape to produce, in particular, simple copper and later bronze flat axes. The production of such axes in Ireland was a major social phenomenon; sources credit Austria with 243 such axes, Denmark with 600, Iberia with 893, but Ireland with over 2,000.[55]

In some countries this earliest horizon of metallurgy is associated with the Beakers, and evidence from Ross Island, Co. Kerry, strongly suggests that Ireland should be included.[56] Here were found copper mines, thousands of stone hammers and a campsite for miners along with smelting furnaces and sherds from over 20

4.7. Copper dagger (length 22 cm) and V-perforated button.

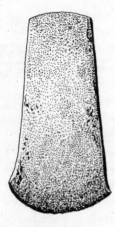

4.8. Copper flat axe
(length 17 cm).

beakers. The beakers were for domestic use, serving as cups or other water containers. The composition of the copper from the mines makes an excellent match against the type found in the hundreds of earliest copper objects known from Ireland, generally fairly heavy, thick-butted axes (4.8), and Ross Island could well have served as the main source for Irish copper objects in the Early Bronze Age. Indeed, there is some reason for suggesting that Ireland also produced some of the earliest copper objects found in western Britain. In addition to copper metallurgy we may also include Ireland's earliest gold objects. By far the most spectacular of these are the gold crescent-shaped collars known as lunulae (4.9). Recent chemical analysis suggests the possibility that the gold was locally derived from rivers in the Mourne region of Co. Down.[57]

4.9. Gold lunula
(width 18 cm).

A Beaker invasion?

It takes little imagination to see that explaining the Beaker presence in Ireland is an exceedingly complex problem. Invasion scenarios are seldom easy. Sometimes there are cases, such as the Anglo-Saxon settlement of England, where the evidence for migration is well accepted although the scale of it can be debated.[58] One specialist suggests that Anglo-Saxon immigrants constituted somewhere between 20% and 33% of the total population in England.[59] This level of population movement is very high and, generally, archaeological evidence for invasions rarely constitutes a 'smoking gun'. The agenda of this book forces two questions upon us. To what extent can we regard the Irish Beakers as the result of a substantial influx of new people? And whether by invasion or some other mechanism, from where does Ireland derive its Beakers?

The 'package'

In the traditional approaches employed a century ago, the main key to tracing the movement of a people was often their burial rite, which was regarded as one of the most ethnically sensitive elements of a people's culture. For example, the discovery at Bray, Co. Wicklow, of burials in the extended position with Roman coins placed in their mouths provides strong support for the idea that at least some people from Roman Britain had managed to make it to the Leinster coast during the Iron Age and were buried according to proper Roman custom.[60] We have already seen that if we were to employ burial practice as a criterion for evaluating a Beaker-using migration, the Irish evidence falls at the first hurdle, as we simply do not find the classic individual Beaker burials of Britain and northwest Europe in Ireland. The full Beaker kit seen in central and northwest Europe and often in Britain, where we find clear marking of gender with emphasis on male warriors (or drunken male warriors), cosmological settings, etc.,[61] is simply absent from Ireland, where the evidence more closely resembles that of the Beakers of south Atlantic Europe. Not all Beaker burials in Britain were of the classic type,[62] but any argument that the Beaker populations crossed from northwest Europe into Britain and then travelled on to carry the same ideology to Ireland finds little or no support in the burial evidence.[63] In Ireland we lack such evidence for intruders, but this does not mean we can exclude the possibility of intrusion. In Ireland Beakers are found in contemporary wedge tombs or, presumably as votive deposits, in earlier (court) tombs. Our attention may focus on France and Iberia, where megaliths were routinely employed for Beaker burials. Coastal Brittany offers abundant evidence for Beakers in megalithic tombs that would make a potential embarkation point for the Beakers of Ireland, and here we find at least some of the elements of the Beaker kit assembled together in the tombs.[64]

It is useful to dwell on Brittany a moment longer, as it is frequently suggested as the departure point for immigrants to Ireland. We should note that while the Beakers are attested in Ireland primarily from settlement sites (or ritual sites that might pass for settlements), over 80% of the Beaker sites in Brittany are from burials.[65] Moreover, while Brittany has yielded only six wristguards, Ireland has over 100 and the great majority that have a known provenance come from Co. Antrim which, we may suspect, was hardly the immediate holiday destination of French tourists; only a very small handful are known in the southern half of the island, and none of these are among the earliest types.[66]

Portugal, another of our potential source areas for Beaker-using immigrants to Ireland, also has burial in megalithic tombs like Ireland; however, here again it is only able to muster some 20 wristguards.[67] These and other Beaker-associated objects that are not found together in Ireland all suggest that the original Beaker package was disassembled before it ever arrived in Ireland, Portugal or Brittany or, alternatively, it was only put together in central and northwest Europe from where it was then imported to Britain but not to Ireland. Indeed, there is some radiocarbon support for this theory, as the well-dated 'classic' Beaker burials in Britain occur only from 2200 BC onward, i.e. after the main floruit of Beakers in Ireland. A review of Irish Beakers suggests that if we try to follow them according to the details of shape and ornament, they will lead us both to northern Britain and to southern Atlantic Europe (France, Iberia).[68]

Irish metalwork, at least in terms of its chemical composition, does not reveal an outside source. Chemical analysis of early Irish copper suggests that 95% of it is similar to the type of copper that one could have mined at Ross Island and, indeed, some of it may have been exported to Britain.[69] In this sense, we cannot follow a series of imports back to their source to determine whence metallurgy came to Ireland. On the other hand, the Early Bronze Age mines of both Ireland and Britain tend to be very localized. In Ireland they are found exclusively in the southwest while in Britain they are largely confined to the west, between mid-Wales and the Isle of Man.[70] It is obvious that the most efficient way these regions could be accessed by potential early metallurgists would have been by sea, presumably (?) from Atlantic Europe.

Contexts

Across many regions of Europe, Beaker-users are seen as elites living among native residential populations whose own existence is indicated either by different material culture or behaviour or by the confinement of the Beakers to restricted areas.[71] So what can we say about Irish Beakers? In Ireland, although Beaker finds tend to be most prolific all along its eastern shore, we would be hard pressed to see Beakers as anything other than an all-Ireland phenomenon.[72] Moreover, for the period of the Beakers it seems that if the archaeological sites yield evidence of ceramics, they are exclusively populated with Beaker ceramics, i.e. there does not seem to be any trace of Late Neolithic native wares.[73] The main overlap is with Grooved Ware pottery, which appears to have been the exclusive ceramic type that preceded the Beakers.[74] This is, frankly, rather difficult territory for archaeologists. Recall in the last chapter how the evidence for the rapid dispersal of the Neolithic all over Britain was simultaneously interpreted by some as a clear sign of the rapid spread of immigrant farmers while others took it as proof that the transition must have been based on the local population.

Perhaps we can still wrestle some conclusions from this. We find no evidence for Early Beaker-using elites in confrontation with locals, mixed sites where locals were enticed to join the Beaker way of life,[75] nor regionally restricted regions of Beakers, so Macalister's Beaker-using overlords are not supported by the archaeological evidence. All that we can say for certain is that, whatever the Beaker people were selling, the people of Ireland bought it in spades. But why? How can anyone argue that the Beaker was a major status item when everyone in Ireland appeared to use Beaker pottery? Also, the range of ceramics (cups, bowls, storage jars) fills the general run of all vessel functions and is not solely confined to luxury drinking goblets.[76] Nor should the manufacture of Beakers have been regarded as a specialist craft.[77] We are left with what appears to have been the very rapid dispersal of a primarily domestic craft, presumably the product of women potters, across all Ireland. How is this likely to have happened? A study of how women potters behave who have moved into a foreign community suggests that they would have adopted the styles of their new social network (Grooved Ware) and tried to pass themselves off as well-integrated locals to ensure their social acceptance.[78] Indeed, any archaeologist can cite examples of imported wares in foreign contexts that remain just that – foreign imports. This makes it more probable that we are dealing with some immigration on the community level, where women felt no pressure to conform to local styles but continued their own tradition of Beaker pottery. So also certain changes in the stone tools that we associate with Beakers, such as barbed and tanged arrowheads, might be understood as male-produced items that were replicated in Ireland. There is a case here then for some immigration of Beaker-using families or larger communities from both Britain and Atlantic Europe.

What was the social mechanism by which Beakers would rapidly replace earlier wares? Beakers must have had inherent advantages and a social context that people found attractive. They did not obviously extend the range of functions of a set of Grooved Ware vessels: it has been suggested (though not conclusively demonstrated) that Grooved Ware vessels could also have been employed in the brewing and consumption of alcoholic or hallucinogenic beverages (milk and barley are the only substances identified so far),[79] so the Beakers may not have had an advantage there either. Beakers do, however, have a greater variety of shapes (especially those with a curved profile) and often far more decoration than many Irish Grooved Ware vessels. There is also a class of Beaker ceramics known as polypod bowls, vessels with feet that were made out of clay or wood and may have had some ritual function, which have no parallels in Grooved Ware. How about the social context?

It is certainly no accident that we find both Grooved Ware and Beakers associated with ceremonial sites at which we might imagine seasonal gatherings involving both religious ceremonies and a good deal of social interaction (gossip, boy meets girl, verbal and physical contests, exchange) that small dispersed families would be eager to experience. The Beaker-users do not seem to have been major innovators in Ireland with respect to ceremonial centres such as timber circles or henges. Rather, the Grooved Ware culture did all the hard work earlier and it would appear that the Beaker 'phenomenon' mapped itself on to the earlier Grooved Ware social-ceremonial circuit.[80] This included meetings or settlements around still earlier major ceremonial monuments such as the Boyne passage tombs. In this way, Grooved Ware may have 'softened up' Britain and Ireland to accept further pan-island cultural packages.

So why did Beakers replace Grooved Ware? Here speculation replaces any hard evidence. We can see that the Beaker network did have some things that the Grooved Ware-users in Ireland did not. First of all, it had a pan-European network of interrelations. Archaeologists have recently emphasized the prestige that might have been associated with distant travels and ideas imported from foreign lands. The Beaker and its associated objects could be understood, at least initially, as exotic items connected with powerful people from abroad who possessed 'wonderful things'.[81] One of those wonderful things was metal.

Under the presumption that the techniques involved in prospection, mining, smelting and casting are unlikely to have been passed on by simple word of mouth, we may expect that there were immigrant metallurgists belonging to the Beaker-using social network who settled in Ireland and created objects that would have been highly regarded by the local population. Other than the copper axes – not really demonstrably superior to their polished stone counterparts – most copper items were not utilitarian, so the movement of prospectors into Britain and Ireland was hardly driven by the need to discover new metallic resources for an expanding market. It probably had far more to do with foreign miners, skilled in the techniques of metallurgy but not in a position to turn their skills into social rewards in their home territory, setting off to find new fields in which they could become mine operators and traders and not simply mine workers. With shining copper axes and other metal objects, early Beaker-using metallurgists could convince the local population of Ireland to desire what it didn't need and thereby integrate themselves within the Beaker network. The copper sources that we know so far in Ireland are peripheral to most of our evidence for settlements, so it was this Beaker network that managed the circulation of metal goods all across Ireland.

Some have associated the Beaker people with a new solar cult that spread across the Continent.[82] The evidence for such a cult in Ireland is not abundant, but one could at least construct an argument for it. Neil Brodie suggests, for example, that 'copper contained the fire of the sun and the significance of this was that both the sun and the "Beaker Folk" came from the east, a significance not likely to be overlooked.'[83] Better yet perhaps are the occasional finds of small circular discs of gold that appear to date to the Beaker period and which might have been sun symbols (4.10). Finally, in terms of celestial imagery we also have the large assemblage of gold lunulae (little moons).[84] These latter objects (there are 85 from Ireland and adjacent regions), assigned to the Beaker period because they appear to have their terminals decorated in the Beaker style, are believed to have originated in Ireland, perhaps as gold copies of necklaces that are found in Britain made of amber or jet. If we can assume that they are the product of Ireland it is useful to note that they have also been found in both Scotland and southwest Britain, with 18 recovered from the Continent, particularly northern France.[85] This again emphasizes the extent of the Beaker network that may also have served as a conduit for population movements (4.11).

As we have seen before, one of the characteristics of a migration is that it often involves a migration stream, a path between the 'auld country' and the new that facilitates migrating individuals and families who can count on kinsmen at the other

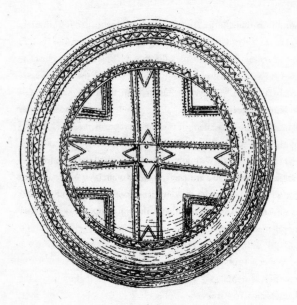

4.10. Gold sun disc (diameter 11 cm).

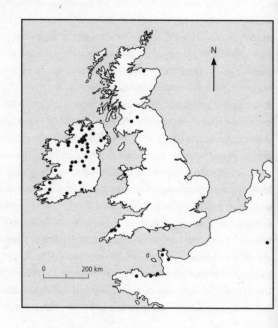

4.11. Distribution of gold lunulae.

end of their journey.[86] Moreover, once this has been established, we also frequently encounter return migration, as some people eventually return to their place of origin (think of wealthy Irish returned from America). One of the clues we might expect as a sign of migration is evidence for ongoing contact between Ireland and some potential source of Beaker-using migrants such as northern France. The movement of these objects of evident prestige (personal, religious, community?) between Ireland, Britain and the Continent is hardly unexpected if Beaker-carrying colonists came from these latter regions.

In short, intuition screams that there must have been an ideological component in the conversion to Beakerism even if we are very unsure of what it was. Like a future Martian archaeologist on Earth pondering the significance of crosses, crescents and stars (of David), we know they must have signified something important even if we have no idea what they actually meant.

New ceramics: new people?

By the late Beaker horizon we find a new series of ceramics associated with burials, e.g. Irish bowls, Irish vases, and various types of urns. A recent study has placed them within fairly tight chronological parameters. Irish bowls, found primarily in the north and east of Ireland, date to c. 2200–1800 BC (4.12). Their appearance coincides with what some archaeologists have seen as the Irish version of the classic Beaker package, since we now find burials that more closely resemble the individual Beaker burials of northwest Europe, including Britain (4.13). These are followed by vases that occupy roughly the same regions and date c. 2150–1700 BC. During this period there was a shift from primarily inhumation to cremation burials and out of the preceding ceramic types evolved the Food Vessel or Encrusted Urn, a highly decorated urn that dates c. 2000–1700 BC. The distribution of these includes the north, east and south of Ireland but largely avoids the west. All of these vessel forms can be derived locally or with occasional influence from corresponding types in Britain. The only widely regarded intrusive form was the Collared Urn (1900–1650 BC), which has no precedent in Ireland and whose finds are concentrated in eastern Ulster and eastern Leinster (4.14). This type of mortuary vessel appears to have evolved in Britain and spread to Ireland along with several other items (ribbed daggers, Bann type stone battleaxes) 'for reasons which are not clear'.[87] The final ceramic series, the Cordoned Urn (1880–1500 BC), is located in mid-Ulster and east Leinster and derived from the intrusive Collared Urn tradition and local wares. This unremitting series of Early

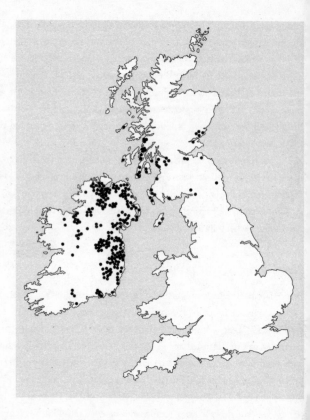

4.12. Distribution
of Irish bowls.

Bronze Age vessels and burial traditions emphasizes the continual links between Ireland and Britain before *c.* 1500 BC. All these pottery types are directly associated with the disposal of the dead, and the circulation of the furniture of burials may also be indicating the movement of ideas associated with religion and death. Yet ever since the Neolithic it has also been obvious that there were periods of intense contact between regions of Ireland and Britain that suggest streams of migration, perhaps both ways. By about 1500 BC ceramics are no longer the best marker of outside contacts, as Ireland begins employing fairly coarse domestic ceramics and abandons fine wares associated with burials; by the end of the Bronze Age, the people of Ireland will abandon the making of pottery altogether.

4.13. (a) Irish bowl; (b) vase (height 17 cm); (c) Food Vessel urn; (d) Collared Urn (height 23 cm).

4.14. Distribution of Collared Urns.

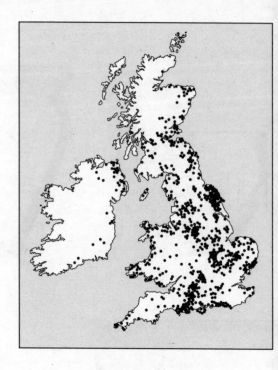

Conclusions

→ The Late Neolithic Grooved Ware horizon was completely replaced *c.* 2500 BC by the Bell Beaker culture.

→ The Beaker-users introduced a new ceramic type that fulfilled both ritual and domestic functions. It is most likely that this entailed a certain amount of immigration.

→ The Beaker-users introduced metallurgy and established a network of exchange both throughout Ireland and between Ireland and its neighbours, both in Britain and on the Continent.

→ The Bell Beakers integrated Ireland into a network of communication that covered most of western and central Europe.

→ The mechanism for the spread of the Beaker culture to Ireland initially involved some immigration from both northern Britain and Atlantic Europe.

CHAPTER FIVE

The Rise of the Warriors

Niall was noted for his periodic and allegedly successful raids on Britain. His society valued both the prowess of a warrior and the material rewards available to a warrior elite. There is little if any trace of such a society in Ireland before *c.* 1500 BC, but after that, during the course of the full Bronze Age, we can discern the emergence of a wealthy class in Ireland marked by weaponry and ostentatious ornament. Combativeness is embedded in the English language as an inherent component of the Irish stereotype: 'Irish' can be defined as 'fieriness of temper or passion'.[1] From an archaeological perspective, one can at least symbolically anchor in the Bronze Age the common expression 'to get one's Irish up'. But do we really need to discuss the Bronze Age in our quest for Irish origins? The ability to alloy tin with copper is hardly the primary defining element of either origins or identity and, excepting the Beaker-users of the previous chapter, archaeologists have regarded the Irish Bronze Age as relatively free of foreign invasions. It was the one period in which the local population could take the credit for filling Irish museums with many of their most spectacular objects. Nearly 80 years ago R. A. S. Macalister posed the question of cultural change in early Ireland, wondering whether it was:

the result of successive migrations, each tribe as it arrived bringing into the country its own contribution to civilisation; or was Ireland continuously peopled by one stock, who adopted from their over-sea neighbours, the various discoveries and inventions whereby civilisation was from time to time advanced?

With regards to the Bronze Age Macalister concluded (on rather spurious racial grounds) that 'the Bronze Age culture was introduced into Ireland by trade rather than by conquest or invasion'.[2] In short, accounts of Bronze Age Ireland generally focus on the many changes in tools, weapons and ornaments or on the emergence of greater social differences in society, but they devote little or no time to the concept of immigration, as there seems to be no strong case to make for intruders aside from a handful who may have slipped through the tradesman's entrance.[3] So why not omit the Bronze Age from the overall discussion of Irish origins and leave the natives in peace for at least one of their prehistoric periods? In fact, there are several reasons for not ignoring the Bronze Age.

First, the introduction of bronze metallurgy saw Ireland enter a more intense Continental European orbit than we have seen up to now. Clearly, in the preceding periods the population(s) of Ireland were ultimately derived from or heavily influenced by other peoples of Continental Europe and Britain. The Beaker horizon is a clear example of Ireland as part of a greater European 'story'. But with the cultural developments of the late 2nd and early 1st millennium BC we find Ireland not simply 'kick started' from a Continental base but in near constant contact with Britain and, more distantly, the Continent. Only in this way can we understand the parallels in architecture, burial, material culture and religious practice that we find between Ireland and Britain. These are not simply the logical consequences of the earlier Beaker phenomenon but the result of such persistent interactions between the two islands that we must envisage some movement of populations, presumably in both directions.

Compared to both earlier and later periods in prehistory, Bronze Age Europe developed an unparalleled level of interdependency. Ireland was at the end of a long chain of contacts that extended back to the industrial centres of the Bronze Age, the metal-rich regions of what is now southern Germany, Austria, the Czech Republic, Slovakia and Hungary, where the technological breakthroughs were initially made and then spread along established trade routes to the peripheries of Europe. Having reached the Atlantic, these trade routes naturally developed sea crossings and it is in the Late Bronze Age that we can imagine routine long-distance sea travel, presumably in sewn plank boats or leather-covered boats akin to the Irish currach.[4] So unlike the earlier Neolithic and the later Iron Age, the Bronze Age, with its circulation of relatively rare metals and finished goods over large territories, resulted in an extraordinary level of mutual dependency. It should also be emphasized that Ireland was not simply on the periphery of such an exchange system. Bronze Age societies required three main minerals (copper, gold and tin) and Ireland possessed at least the first two of these resources, so it was not only a recipient of foreign influences[5] but also an exporter of finished products as well as, probably, raw metal. Ireland was thus a real player. And while these kinds of contacts may be hidden under the umbrella term 'trade connections', they are critical to the social organization and identity of any society.[6] We need to understand the nature of these foreign contacts if we are to deal with the very real linguistic relationships between the Irish and other west Europeans. Some, for example, have suggested that the extensive Bronze Age trading systems should have promoted the spread of a trade language as a *lingua franca* between the diverse communities of Atlantic Europe. Eventually (in Chapter 9) we will assess whether the Irish language entered Ireland as a Bronze Age trade language or was carried into Ireland by Bronze Age immigrants.

A second major feature associated with the Bronze Age is the suspected rise of ethnic or at least tribal identities. The hard evidence for domestic settlements (houses) during the Early Bronze Age is extremely sparse, but by the Middle and Late Bronze ages we have abundant evidence for stable settlements. By about the 12th century BC, hillforts and other enclosures begin to appear that have been interpreted as the chief places of social elites and/or the ritual centres of self-defining political or tribal groups. This is the first time we have some evidence for the type of tribal society that we associate with the earliest Irish of the historical period. Moreover, the appearance of regional centres or even super-regional territories may hint at the possibility of ethnic divisions within prehistoric Ireland, also alluded to in our earliest Irish literary sources.

Finally, there are early historical and literary descriptions of the Irish that play an important part in fashioning a real or imagined image of a prehistoric Irish identity. A society characterized by a warrior elite (Ireland has the greatest number of Bronze Age swords per area in Europe[7]), practising a religion that emphasized making offerings to the gods in watery places and devoted to feasting (read 'drinking'), finds its origins and some of its most dramatic expression during the Bronze Age. When it came to locating Ireland's 'Heroic Age', for example, Michael O'Kelly found it in the Bronze Age.[8]

The Bronze Age sequence

After the introduction and spread of copper metallurgy during the Beaker period and subsequent Early Bronze Age, archaeologists divide the cultural development of Ireland into two further major periods (a Middle and Late Bronze Age), the last of which is further subdivided into two phases, based essentially on changes in the types of metal objects.

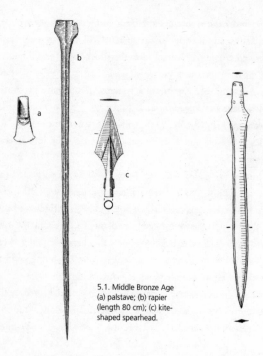

5.1. Middle Bronze Age (a) palstave; (b) rapier (length 80 cm); (c) kite-shaped spearhead.

5.2. Roscommon period sword (length 51 cm) from Ballintober, Co. Mayo.

The Middle Bronze Age dates to *c.* 1600–1200 BC[9] and is a period in which there is abundant evidence for extensive land clearance for agriculture;[10] the erection of circular dwellings and enclosures; improvements in transport (at least across bogs, over which wooden trackways were laid); the rise of what is known as hot-stone technology; and changes in bronze technology, e.g. the evolution of the palstave (an axe-shaped tool/weapon that was held in its haft by very high flanges and a stop ridge), the rapier (a long, very narrow-bladed piercing sword), and the kite-shaped spearhead (5.1). The burial rite initially showed continuity with the previous Early Bronze Age burials, beginning with cremation in cordoned urns, but gradually saw a reduction in the care given to the deposition of the cremated remains (the bones were increasingly pulverized, or only token portions were deposited) and in the quality of the pottery (a shift to increasingly undecorated coarse wares). Prominent among the burial goods were beads and what are termed razors or razor knives.[11]

The earliest part of the Late Bronze Age (*c.* 1200–1000 BC),[12] the Roscommon phase, sees substantial reforestation of the land – although perhaps not around a new

5.3. Map of sites mentioned in Chapter 5.

monument on the Irish landscape, the hillfort, where we do find evidence of land clearances. It is also the period of the introduction of the true sword, whose blade can be used to both cut and thrust (5.2). It has been argued that around 1200 BC the entire nature of connections between the Continent, Britain and Ireland began to change, with far greater evidence for overseas contacts seen in the abundant exchange of bronze artifacts. These are initially expressed in styles of swords and spears that tie together northwest France, southern Britain and Ireland.

This is followed by the Dowris phase (1000–600 BC), the period in which Ireland truly flourished in its production of both bronze and gold objects. The name is derived from the great Dowris hoard that was discovered in the 1920s (5.3). It may have included more than 200 objects, primarily ornaments such as pendants (48 examples) followed by weapons (36 spears), tools(?) (35 axes) and a large collection of musical instruments (26 horns). Although there are occasional implements such as an anvil, tongs and a saw from an earlier hoard discovered at Bishopsland, Co. Kildare, actual tools (other than axes) constitute a very small proportion of the metal objects.[13] We seem to be dealing with warrior elites who ritually disposed of their wealth (bronze and gold) in hoards that may be uncovered either on dry land or in water (lakes, rivers, bogs).[14] The metal surplus is often presumed to have been a product of an agricultural surplus because this is also a period when we again see extensive land clearance, although the economy is suspected of being largely pastoral rather than arable – not the economic basis on which one normally postulates complex social elites.[15]

Dowris objects range from a series of sword types to gold ornaments such as necklaces and clothes fasteners (which were also exported to Britain); the hoard also includes an impressive supply of bronze horns and cauldrons (5.4, 5.5). The manufacture of the latter was centred in Ireland whence they were exported all across Atlantic Europe from Denmark south to Iberia. What is of interest is that some of the artifact types are very widely distributed over Atlantic Europe while others are more restricted. For example, Ireland was militarily, at least in terms of its sword styles, part of the Atlantic arms race until about 950 BC, when a new sword type, the so-called carp's tongue sword (from the shape of its blade; 5.6), was made in

5.4. Bronze cauldron (width 49 cm).

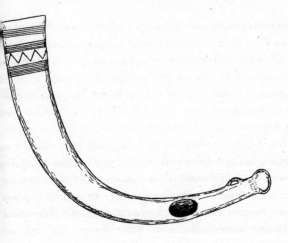

5.5. Bronze horn (50 cm from mouthpiece to end).

5.6. Carp's tongue sword (length 72 cm).

its thousands across Atlantic Europe yet is barely represented in Ireland, despite the fact that other objects often associated with the carp's tongue swords are found in Ireland.[16] It is also during this phase that we suspect hillforts ceased to be built or occupied. Dowris C, the final phase of the Bronze Age dated *c.* 750–600 BC, falls within a climatic downturn when we also witness a decrease in agricultural activity. Ireland then descends, at least insofar as the archaeological record is concerned, into a limbo between the end of the Bronze Age and the beginning of the Iron Age.

Settlement and centres

As was the case with Neolithic houses, the discovery of Bronze Age houses has also been a growth industry insofar as Irish archaeology is concerned. In a recent survey John Ó Néill indicates that we now know of 583 structures dating to the Bronze Age.[17] Of these, over 200 occur as single houses each known from a different site,[18] while about 50 sites have produced two houses and 18 sites have yielded three houses. Few sites offer more than this, so with a few important exceptions the traditional pattern of dispersed settlement of from one to three houses obtained for most people in Bronze Age Ireland, although there seem to have been a few who lived in larger communities.

These houses generally measure about 8–10 m across and, like most houses in Atlantic Europe at this time, were circular (5.7).[19] It should be emphasized that aside from hillforts (see below) the structures are rarely more than 10 m across. Houses would remain circular in Ireland into the early medieval period. One generally presumes that these reflect single farmsteads or, at most, several contemporary families living together near to their fields for both arable agriculture and pasture. Also, like those of similar houses in Britain, the entrance to the majority of Irish houses is located at some point between east and south. The constancy of such an orientation, irrespective of prevailing wind conditions, has been interpreted by some as evidence for a shared ideological vision of how a house should be oriented, a sort of British and Irish Bronze Age feng shui. It should be emphasized that in the Early Bronze Age the orientation of houses tended to be to the north, and it was only after c. 1750 BC that houses were routinely built with their entrances to the southeast.[20]

The major exception to this pattern of dispersed settlement is the recently excavated site of Corrstown, Co. Londonderry,[21] where in the course of expanding a modern housing estate, builders encountered an adjacent prehistoric estate of about 70 round houses, the majority of which can be dated to the Bronze Age (5.8). This site might not be entirely unique: two other large sites of round-house foundations (now destroyed) were reported by early antiquarians, also along the north coast, at Whitepark Bay, Co. Antrim (c. 20–30 huts), and Dunfanaghy, Co. Donegal (c. 50 huts).[22]

The 'meaning' of the round house has been queried by archaeologists who have contrasted the Atlantic European tradition of round-house building with the rectangular-house tradition of central Europe. Some have seen the roots of the Atlantic round house in the circular tentlike structures that prevailed millennia earlier in the Mesolithic. Challenged by the introduction of rectangular houses in the Early Neolithic, the reappearance of the round house has been interpreted as 'the survival of long-held ideological conceptions and expressions of structure'.[23] From an Irish perspective, round houses or, at least, sub-rectangular houses had already appeared by the Middle Neolithic (c. 3500 BC) and it is difficult to imagine that Bronze Age houses reflect some form of suppressed architectural urge among the native population. Rather, we seem to be dealing with a phenomenon that involved the spread of a common house form over both Britain and Ireland at least from the Middle

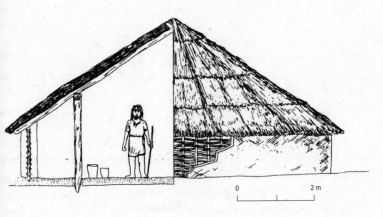

5.7. Bronze Age house.

5.8. Corrstown settlement, Co. Londonderry.

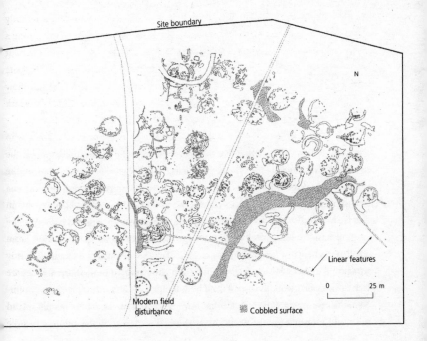

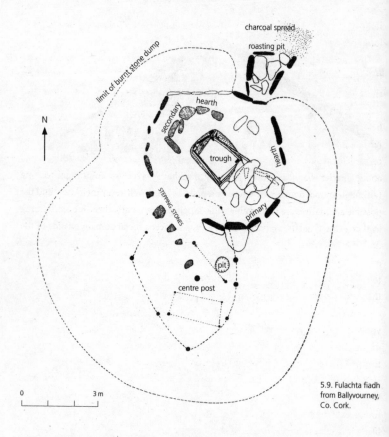

5.9. Fulachta fiadh from Ballyvourney, Co. Cork.

Bronze Age, along with a belief that the proper place for the doorway was toward the southeast. This suggests the type of persistent contacts between the two islands that permeates the entire Bronze Age and may reflect the movement not only of ideas but also of people, possibly in both directions. We should add that a sizeable minority of Bronze Age houses tend to be rectilinear, although often with rounded corners.

The basic building block of Irish Bronze Age society would appear to have been small settlements of single families or, less likely, small clusters of families.[24] But something is obviously missing, as a dispersed population of yeoman farmers would lack the social network to sustain itself both biologically and culturally. Just as in the Neolithic, we might expect that some form of central places, where people might meet and exchange goods, would be established to deal with the growing bronze industry. We will deal with these central places in order, starting with the smallest or least spectacular.

Outside the actual household, there is one common site type that could potentially have provided a venue for meetings – the fulachta fiadh (5.9). These enigmatic sites, which number nearly 5,000 for all of Ireland, generally consist of a trough constructed out of timber and built to hold water that was then boiled by dropping in heated stones. The purpose of this hot-stone technology is unclear, although the preferred option is generally the cooking of food. Since this function was also carried out on settlement sites in more traditional ways, there may have been something special about fulachta fiadh. For example, they may have served for communal feasting (although animal remains are a rare find on such sites). Whatever their use – and the possible alternatives are remarkably wide-ranging (steam baths, brewing ale, tanning leather, extracting fats, preparing dyes) – they suggest a social domain outside of the domestic household. These sites span the Bronze Age but are not found uniformly over all Ireland. Fulachta fiadh are primarily concentrated in the southern third of the island, with nearly 60% from Co. Cork alone. How such sites are associated with the actual evidence for Bronze Age houses is far from clear.[25]

Another type of Bronze Age site that suggests public gatherings is the hoard or votive deposit, comprising collections of bronze objects that were deposited either on dry land or, very frequently, in wetlands, either bogs or rivers. Their numbers increase through time: some 40 hoards are known from the earliest part of the Bronze Age, rising to 130 from the Dowris phase of the Late Bronze Age.[26] Interpretations of hoards vary and there is no single reason that explains all deposits, although those found in wetlands and rivers are particularly likely to represent religious offerings that were deposited in conjunction with public ceremonies.

In an important study of the Bronze Age of north Munster, Eoin Grogan has proposed a model for the social organization of the region that envisages several tiers of society.[27] According to him, the individual farmsteads were organized into communities of 5 to 15 or more families with their surrounding field systems (5.10). These were then grouped into territories of about three or more communities

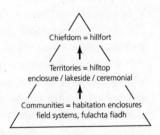

5.10. A model of Late Bronze Age social and spatial organization according to Eoin Grogan.

Chiefdom = hillfort

Territories = hilltop enclosure / lakeside / ceremonial

Communities = habitation enclosures field systems, fulachta fiadh whose central place was a hilltop enclosure, a structure too large to have been built by a single family but probably the product of those who owed labour obligations to an elite.

At the top of Grogan's model is the largest of our central places, the hillfort. In the case of north Munster one of the most striking is Mooghaun, Co. Clare, which theoretically 'ruled' an area of about 450 sq km that was occupied by an estimated 1,500 households, or 9,000 people. I would be cautious extrapolating such a figure to the entire island, as it would suggest a population on the order of 1.6 million! North Munster may be extremely rich with respect to settlement evidence compared with many other regions, and the actual population of Ireland is likely to have been a fraction of our extrapolation.[28] If one assumes that tribal chiefs governed territories on the order of 500 sq km, then Ireland would have yielded something like 168 chiefdoms, a figure not far off the (possibly groundless) estimates for the number of early medieval tribes in Ireland.[29] We could instead dispense with an assumption of a uniform area and estimate the number of tribes on the basis of the number of known hillforts, currently reckoned at about 74 although more are likely to be discovered.

Hillforts

Whether or not one accepts Grogan's model or believes it can be extrapolated over the rest of Ireland, the hillforts are nevertheless very likely to be important in our quest for the origins of the Irish. This is because they are the largest architectural structures of the Bronze Age and are, therefore, the product of the cooperative labour of surrounding communities, either under a single authority or at least as an expression of communal cooperation.[30] Setting aside for a moment their precise function(s), they appear to provide a central focus for communities during the later part of the Bronze Age and hence offer a political or religious means of parcelling Ireland into different social groups that at least approximate the size of a tribe.

The hillforts are usually defined as bank-and-ditch enclosures occupying the more defensible contours of hilltops and enclosing an internal area of generally more than one hectare (roughly one-and-a-half football pitches) (5.11). The majority of hillforts range between 1 and 3 hectares (ha), although 30% are larger than 5 ha. They may be surrounded by anywhere from one to three ramparts, constructed largely of earth, but there are also many stone-walled ramparts such as Mooghaun. Excavation suggests sizeable ditches such as those at Haughey's Fort, Co. Armagh, that descend into V-shaped profiles (ankle-breakers that are difficult to exit once you have gone

5.11. Distribution
of Irish hillforts.

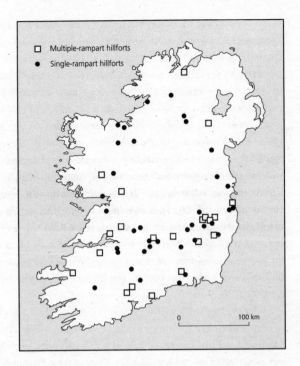

□ Multiple-rampart hillforts

● Single-rampart hillforts

0   100 km

into them) several metres deep. There are at least three aspects of Irish hillforts that
demand special attention: their function, date and origin.

Function

The purpose of hillforts is less transparent than their name might suggest. A compendium of possible functions for Continental and British hillforts would at least
include defended settlements of elites; defended settlements of the general population; refugia – temporary shelters in times of war; defended centres for exchange;
strategic defended sites to protect specific natural resources or trade routes; and
ceremonial centres.[31] To discern the purpose of hillforts in Ireland we need to investigate all the possible activities and hence functions that seem to have occurred on these
sites. It must also be emphasized that not all sites may have had the same functions.[32]

The Irish hillforts vary considerably with respect to location, although a substantial majority occupy prominent places in the environment with excellent views of the surrounding landscape. Moreover, a considerable number appear to be set along natural routeways or overlook fords in rivers.[33] The hilltop location and the surrounding earthen banks or stone walls and ditches all suggest defence, although archaeologists are certainly aware that there are problems with such a simple answer. In some cases, the enclosing banks are so long that it is difficult to conceive of there ever being enough defenders to cover the walls. About 20 hillforts occupy areas of over 5 hectares that would require fairly sizeable numbers of defenders,[34] while the 130-ha fort of Spinnan's Hill, Co. Wicklow, is on a scale of its own. Enclosures with multiple banks and ditches may have them spaced so far apart that it would seem to defeat the supposed intended purpose of confining an attacking force within a narrow area. Alternatively, some defences are such that they offer the defender no hope of escape. Still, the notion that many of these sites were built to offer protection is still the most attractive hypothesis. Deep ditches cut to a V-shape as we find at Haughey's Fort would constitute a formidable barrier to an attacker, as would the stone walls that surround other sites. And it is difficult to see other purposes for the banks and ditches that cut off promontories such as that recently excavated at Knockdhu, Co. Antrim.

Who were the defences for? There have long been three schools of thought: livestock, permanent settlement or temporary boltholes. Obviously, many sites are of a sufficient size that one can well imagine livestock being herded within the enclosure in times of threat and, indeed, this is one of the most popular explanations for the defences found around Irish ringforts of the early medieval period, when cattle raiding was endemic. In some cases where we find evidence for houses within the hillfort, they may have served to defend its permanent occupants, but in other cases, where we find large forts at high altitudes that would militate against year-round settlement, the sites may have served as refuges to which people fled during times of conflict.

Did the hillforts serve as the residence of substantial communities? In his review of domestic structures within the excavated hillforts, Eoin Grogan suggests that the evidence as it stands indicates no more than the residences of 'a few families at most'.[35] On the other hand, he also acknowledges that the amount of labour required to build such forts would certainly have exceeded the numbers living within them, and this suggests an organized workforce under the direction of a chief. In short, most hillforts appear to be a central component of a larger system of settlement.

Other than cower or fight, what else did people do inside the hillforts? There is some evidence for metalworking (at Rathgall, Dún Aonghusa and Haughey's Fort

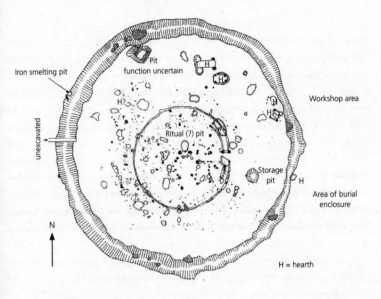

5.12. Late Bronze Age house at Rathgall.

(King's Stables)), the preparation and consumption of food (grinding stones, animal bones, cereals), and shelter (houses). On rare occasions finished metal objects have been recovered, suggesting that at least some of the population dwelling within the hillfort belonged to the elite who wore bronze and gold ornaments.

Finally, it is likely that some of the evidence that might be interpreted as reflecting domestic settlement was actually associated with rituals.[36] Large circular post-built structures at Haughey's Fort may have been ritual enclosures rather than domestic houses, and Rathgall similarly has a structure larger than the usual round house (5.12). The fact that a significant proportion of hillforts enclose earlier barrows also suggests at least a concern with the earlier ritual landscape. How this should be interpreted is crucial. Some have argued that the positioning of hillforts on earlier ritual sites reflects a continuity with the ancestors, i.e. it highlights the local evolution of the site among *native populations*. On the other hand, one could just as easily argue that any *intrusive population* might also select earlier ritual sites in order to legitimize their own authority and replace that of the indigenous tradition, as we find later when missionaries 'Christianized' earlier pagan sites.

Date

Although only about 9% of the Irish hillforts have been excavated so far (i.e. 7 out of 74), the dates for the excavated hillforts tend to lie within the period *c.* 1200–800 BC. This is extraordinary because the far better known hillforts of Britain usually begin to appear *c.* 800–700 BC,[37] and the Irish hillforts have such significant differences in both morphology (shape) and date from these later British hillforts that it is very difficult to see them as similar phenomena. When the hillfort in Britain is at its height, we find little or no evidence for its existence in Ireland.[38]

Origin

So, are Irish hillforts wholly independent of what was going on in Britain? This has certainly been a common view, and among its adherents was the late Barry Raftery, Ireland's foremost authority on Irish hillforts. He suggested that the evidence we have

> implies that the forts were constructed by indigenous Late Bronze Age
> peoples, perhaps during a period of internecine tension. There is
> nothing in the available evidence to indicate the presence of intruders
> among the occupants of Irish hillforts.[39]

But was the development of hillforts in Ireland purely a local phenomenon? Obviously, the ability to surround the top of a hill with a ditch and a bank made from the upcast earth would not require a great leap in imagination for the native population of Ireland. On the other hand, Irish populations had every opportunity to build hillforts centuries before we actually have evidence for them. So why do they begin to appear when they do, about 1200–1000 BC?

If we look at the emergence of hillforts in Britain, their appearance coincides with the disappearance of any really visible burial rite and a rise in making offerings of metal objects in rivers.[40] Very similar changes occur in Ireland at the same time. Although British terminology sets the earliest phase of hillfort building to *c.* 800–600 BC,[41] in fact, there is also a shadowy horizon of Late Bronze Age hillforts in Britain (or, at least, hilltop enclosures) that appear roughly contemporary with those of Ireland. Ram's Hill, Berkshire, shows evidence of a timber rampart being constructed to face an earthen bank sometime *c.* 1400–1100 BC, and there are several comparable sites, although perhaps not so well dated, that suggest the erection of fortified sites in the Late Bronze Age in southeastern Britain. Richard Bradley reminds us specifically that eastern England does offer some evidence of defended hilltop enclosures as early as those of Ireland.[42] The British Bronze Age 'ringworks' date to *c.* 1100–700 BC, and an obvious question arises: were the British ringworks and Irish hillforts part of the same phenomenon?

Comparing the few excavated Irish hillforts with British ringworks suggests common features but also some that would tend to differentiate them. British ringworks are generally just that – rings, i.e. circular enclosures. In fact, they tend to be so circular that they were originally confused with Late Neolithic hengiform ceremonial sites, especially as they might show two opposed entrances as on henges. Irish hillforts are hardly so geometrical and tend to be oval in shape, although Rathgall, Co. Wicklow, might come close in form to a British site. But Rathgall also indicates a difference in scale, as it is substantially larger than a British ringwork; indeed, Irish hillforts are generally much larger than the British ringworks. We can deal with this in one of two ways: look for something smaller in Ireland, or ignore the shape and scale and examine the associated features. As for something smaller, Ireland offers what are known as hilltop enclosures that range from *c.* 0.2 to 0.8 ha in area and are generally surrounded by an earthen or an earthen-and-stone bank, sometimes with a ditch. Only two have been excavated and they are poorly dated but presumed to lie within the Late Bronze Age.[43]

On the other hand, if we focus on contexts, there are some interesting similarities between British ringworks and Irish hillforts. One such feature is a series of one or more concentric enclosures surrounding a single very large round house. At Mucking, Essex, and Thwing, Yorkshire, we find circular enclosures made up of concentric rings with an unusually large circular building in the centre (5.13).[44] This is precisely the pattern that Barry Raftery uncovered in his excavations of the hillfort at Rathgall, whose inner enclosure (45 m in diameter) surrounded a large timber-post structure about 15 m in diameter.[45] Sometimes British ringworks have several large timber structures; for instance, at Springfield Lyons, Essex, there were three large circular structures within the enclosure. This can be matched by Haughey's Fort, Co. Armagh, where aerial photographs suggest two circular buildings, each on the order of 15 m or more in diameter (5.14).[46] Recalling that the average Bronze Age house in Ireland measures 8 to 10 m across, these hillfort structures are on the extremes of Irish house sizes, and there is considerable doubt that the Haughey's Fort structures were ever roofed.

Richard Bradley has also noted that some of the British sites are associated with places of offering,[47] and this is certainly true of some of the Irish hillforts. Near the hillfort at Mooghaun, Co. Clare, was located the 'great Clare find' of 1854 (most of

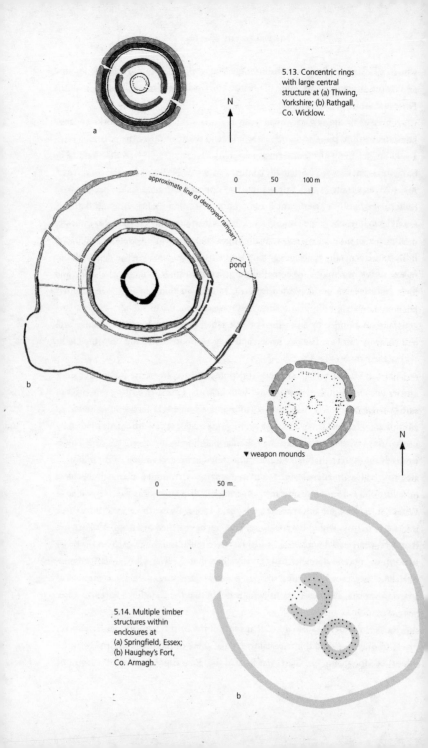

5.13. Concentric rings with large central structure at (a) Thwing, Yorkshire; (b) Rathgall, Co. Wicklow.

N

0   50   100 m

approximate line of destroyed rampart

pond

a

▼ weapon mounds

0   50 m

N

5.14. Multiple timber structures within enclosures at (a) Springfield, Essex; (b) Haughey's Fort, Co. Armagh.

b

which was subsequently lost or melted down) that comprised at least 146 gold objects and constituted the largest find of gold objects in Ireland.[48] Adjacent to Haughey's Fort, Co. Armagh, lies a contemporary artificial pond known as the King's Stables wherein were deposited remains of animals (cattle, pig, dog, red deer antler, sheep, horse, badger) and part of the skull of a young man.[49] To the west of the hillfort was a small deposit of Late Bronze Age objects which comprised a ring, a native Irish bronze sword and two bronze vessels that had been imported from central Europe.[50] Another possible comparison is the deposition of fragments of sword moulds that have been found on British ringworks, which is paralleled by Chris Lynn's discovery of 18 fragments of clay moulds for casting swords at the King's Stables,[51] while moulds for sword manufacture were also recovered from Dún Aonghusa.[52] Hillforts in southeast England have also been found to associate with earlier ritual monuments, which has been interpreted as an attempt by their builders to claim some form of descent from the earlier occupants of the area.[53] As we have seen, a similar phenomenon can be found among a number of Irish hillforts, and John Waddell lists at least 12 Irish hillforts where there is evidence of a presumably earlier burial mound or a cairn.[54]

But not all British features can be matched in Ireland. One conspicuous characteristic of southeast English hillforts is the tendency for double entrances on the east and west.[55] This feature, which helps explain why many of the sites were identified as earlier henge monuments, is not apparent at Irish hillforts nor the hilltop enclosures, although determining the location of an entrance on the Irish sites is admittedly not always easy. Another problem is location, since most of the verifiably early ringworks are situated between Yorkshire and Kent, i.e. the east of Britain. Any staging area for their spread to Ireland might presuppose sites in either the west of Wales or Scotland. Unfortunately, the earliest fortified hilltop enclosures in neighbouring Wales date no earlier (so far) than the end of the 9th century BC[56] and are characterized by timber palisades rather than the bank-and-ditch or stone-built enclosures that we find in Ireland. At Mam Tor in the Peak District there is clear evidence for Late Bronze Age settlement (c. 1600–1100 BC), but the precise date of the surrounding ditch and rampart may fall later.[57] In one way they do resemble the Irish sites in that a number of them also seem to have been abandoned after a century or two, which has prompted the suggestion that whatever stimulated the need for such defensive sites had disappeared.

Hovering over all this discussion is a further question. Even if one can support a connection between the earliest British sites and Irish hillforts, how do they fit into a larger picture? As both islands will broadly come to share a group of closely related languages, attested on the Continent since the Iron Age, where do we find our Continental connection? How do the hillforts of Ireland, for example, relate to those of Continental Europe?

Hillforts in Continental Europe have an older pedigree than those of Britain and Ireland with some examples stretching back to the Early Bronze Age, although these are largely confined to east-central Europe and the Alpine region.[58] By the Later Bronze Age there was an explosion of hillfort building, primarily in central Europe, that provides an initial horizon a few centuries earlier than the Irish examples. These hillfort defences were constructed either out of stone or from clay and stones deposited into a set of timber frames. They also varied considerably in size, shape and location. Margarita Primas has suggested that these Late Bronze Age hillforts in central Europe were associated with some form of control over local territories that lasted down to c. 800 BC, when the nature of settlement shifted again.[59] In Richard Osgood's discussion of hillforts, he suggests that 'new ideas of defence and warfare thus spread from central Europe to north Europe and then to the peripheral areas such as the British Isles'.[60]

What are we to make of all this? We have compared Irish and British hillforts and some of the specific parallels such as large circular internal structures, weapons manufacture and ritual depositions in the vicinity. These are similarities, but they could simply be attributed to generic patterns of behaviour. On the other hand, it is difficult to see the horizon of Irish hillforts as wholly independent of the contemporary spread of hillforts across Continental Europe and their earliest appearance in eastern Britain. Nor is it likely that the adoption of circular houses with entrances between south and east was merely coincidental in Ireland and Britain. This is about as far as the architectural evidence alone will take us, so we need to turn briefly to the evidence of material culture.

People or products?

Recalling R. A. S. Macalister's assessment of the Bronze Age as having been introduced by trade rather than invasion, it is worth considering the material culture of the Bronze Age. For the Neolithic and Beaker periods we have often employed ceramics as one of the most sensitive indicators of population movement. This is much more difficult in the Bronze Age. From c. 1500 to 800 BC the characteristic ceramic type on settlements is a coarsely made, seldom decorated (with at best minimal

5.15. Late Bronze Age
pot (height 24 cm).

ornament) bucket-shaped pot. On the one hand, it appears to have a local origin in
the earlier decorated urns (specifically the Cordoned Urns) found not only accompanying burials but also at settlements.[61] On the other hand, a very similar ceramic was
being produced in western Britain, so it might be difficult to distinguish whether the
grotty pot (5.15) recovered from Late Bronze Age sites was manufactured by a local
potter following generations of tradition or by an equally inept but intrusive potter
from western Britain.[62] Besides their unimpressive pottery, Ireland and western
Britain shared another ceramic characteristic: they both gave up making ceramics at
the end of the Bronze Age.[63] As the use of clay moulds for casting continued, we are
not dealing with a sudden onset of technological amnesia but a deliberate cultural
choice that appears roughly simultaneously in Ireland and along the coastal region of
western Britain (but not the Hebrides). Again, it seems easiest to explain this in terms
of closely interacting populations.

Generally, it is not the ceramics but the metal objects that attract most of our
attention during the Bronze Age. Metal objects play by different rules than ceramics.
Poorly fired ceramics are easily broken and do not travel well, while a bronze sword
or golden pendant could be exchanged over vast distances without being the worse
for wear. This makes it far more expedient to interpret similar items of metal as either

the products of trade or local copies of foreign objects rather than presume that they provide evidence for the actual movement of peoples. So what do the metal objects – the tools, weapons, ornaments and other items – indicate about Ireland's relationships with the outside world?

One way of approaching the material culture of the Bronze Age is to examine distribution maps of the various objects. On a number of occasions, John Waddell has attempted to read from the maps the close contacts between Ireland, Britain and the Continent in terms of extensive exchange systems.[64] Irish gold bar torcs (neck rings), for example – which would certainly be regarded today as high-status items that one might expect to be worn only by an elite – are found primarily across central and northeast Ireland, southern Britain and northwest France (5.16). These have been interpreted as evidence of a possible network of alliances that spanned the Irish Sea and continued on to Brittany.[65] Similarly, Irish razors in northern France have been

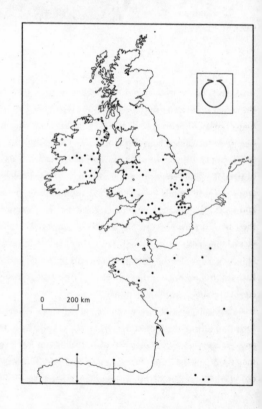

5.16. Distribution of Irish bar torcs.

0   200 km

5.17. Circular enclosures in Ireland and the Thames Valley; shaded areas reflect 'weapon zones'.

seen as possible evidence of high-status males relocating to the Continent to find a mate.[66] Maps showing slightly different patterns can be found for other objects, such as swords: for example, Ireland and Britain share similar types of Late Bronze Age swords over a long period.[67] There has even been an attempt to link the distribution of weapons with that of the earliest hillforts. The distribution of weapons in Britain and Ireland has been divided into two zones of concentration: the Thames Valley and central Ireland (5.17).[68] Not only are weapon finds specifically concentrated in these two areas, but the specific types of weapons, such as rapiers or later swords, are virtually indistinguishable. One interpretation of this pattern is that we are dealing with two zones of an elite warrior class who were in contact with one another, and Richard Bradley suggests that we seem to have a pattern that embraces both circular enclosures and weapons.[69] When one actually considers the specific distribution of Irish hillforts and their weapon region, the pattern is more problematic: Irish hill-forts are largely concentrated along the outer periphery of the putative 'warrior zone' and hardly appear within the core of this zone where we do find lakeside sites or material recovered from rivers. As the River Shannon has produced more Bronze Age objects than any other Irish river and the types of objects recovered from rivers tend to be heavily biased towards weapons, there seem to be other factors at work here.[70] It must be noted that weapons are rarely found on hillforts, either in Ireland or on the Continent.[71]

John Koch has termed the period of the Later Bronze Age the 'Age of Depositions' and contrasted it with the earlier Neolithic and Early Bronze 'Age of Megaliths'.[72] The earlier period, he argues, is marked by priest-leaders who jointly held religious and political authority, which was reflected in the archaeological record in the form of megalithic tombs, stone circles and other types of ceremonial enclosures. His 'Age of Depositions' is characterized by the large-scale manufacture and conspicuous consumption of metal artifacts, with the appearance of an elite warrior class kitted out with weapons (and sometimes in armour) similar to neighbouring elites in Britain and western Europe. He and others have seen Ireland as a network of intermarrying (and perhaps inter-raiding) elites, held together by close systems of gift-giving and exchange, and participating in the same value-laden practices. While not excluding the possibility of intrusive warrior bands, the emphasis here is clearly on the spread of values through exchange rather than population movements.

More recently, however, Kristian Kristiansen and Thomas Larsson have attempted to put some human legs on the movement of objects across Europe.[73] Obviously, trading systems, some of them quite extensive, would seem to be the most economical explanation for the movement of some ornaments or weapon styles across the Continent. In addition to this, they believe there was also a very active system of gift-exchange among elites, especially involving the giving of weapons and metal vessels. Both weapons and metal vessels are known from Ireland, although they are generally regarded as of local manufacture. Just occasionally do we find evidence of something more exotic. One of the major items of the great Dowris hoard was a bucket that is generally presumed to have been manufactured in central Europe, although some have suggested that it might be an Irish copy.[74] Recently, the remains of two unquestionably imported bronze vessels were uncovered at Tamlaght near Haughey's Fort, one of the Late Bronze Age hillforts, situated in the Navan complex in Co. Armagh.

The Tamlaght hoard consisted of what is technically known as a Fuchstadt bowl within which were fragments from at least one so-called Jenišovice cup. In addition there was a bronze ring and an Irish bronze sword, the latter possibly encased in a leather scabbard. They had been deposited in a small bog and constitute what is generally recognized as a votive deposit, i.e. a hoard of objects placed in the ground ostensibly for some ritual purpose. The remarkable aspect of this deposit is that the two types of metal vessel, as their names might suggest, are essentially a central and north European phenomenon and, with the exception of Co. Armagh, completely unknown in Atlantic Europe (5.18). Both types of vessel are found primarily in one of two contexts in Continental Europe – as grave gifts or in hoards – and their occurrence on actual settlements is extremely rare.[75] For this reason they are presumed to be objects of high status, political or religious, although we are uncertain as to what might have been consumed in them (a Fuchstadt bowl averages about 0.47 litres, a Jenišovice cup 0.39 litres – about the size of a soup bowl).[76] While in Austria and southern Germany they are more prone to turn up in burials,[77] they usually occur in hoards in Bohemia, Poland and northern Germany. Although the two types of vessel are rarely found together, there are several such instances from eastern Germany.[78] Where bronze vessels (especially those that precede the Fuchstadt bowl) are recovered from graves, they are sometimes found to accompany males and may even be found along with swords or other weapons. This is suggestive that they may have played some part in a male warrior cult. The fact that the objects have been ritually buried in a fashion similar to that of their homeland may indicate that they are not simply items passed between peoples across a long distance but may attest the presence of foreigners in Ireland. On the Continent, Kristian Kristiansen envisaged such hoards as part of a network of exchange systems, transported by traders and perhaps warrior escorts from one fort to the next.[79] In Continental Europe the further such goods strayed from their source and main network of exchange, the greater the

5.18. Map of Tamlaght-type finds.

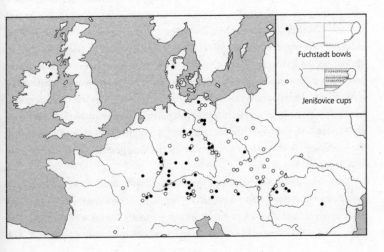

chance they would become associated with local objects such as at Tamlaght, where an Irish sword has been found as well. Kristiansen and Larsson emphasize that the Bronze Age probably marked the emergence of the professional warrior, at least one who could serve as a mercenary, and that long-distance travel would have been encouraged. They go so far as to suggest that 'Bronze Age society was obsessed with travel and esoteric knowledge brought home from the outside'.[80] The travellers would include warriors, smiths and bards/priests, all seeking out valuable foreign skills and knowledge that they might bring back home (should they make it), which would enhance their own prestige.

Death

In one area Ireland refuses to behave like much of the rest of Europe and, consequently, deprives us of absolutely critical information. At the height of the Bronze Age in Continental Europe, when we can best identify the warrior elites and their households, we often find our most spectacular evidence in tumulus burials. In Ireland, the evidence for burial during the Late Bronze Age is so sparse that it is difficult to attribute our ignorance entirely to bad luck: other than a handful of cremation burials surrounded by a ring ditch, the possessors of the enormous wealth of the Irish Bronze Age elude us so effectively that we can only suspect they were disposed of in some manner (exposed on scaffolding, placed in rivers, cremated without any accompanying grave goods or buried with no recognizable monumental association) that is largely outside the traditional grasp of the archaeologist. The fact that hoards increase as burials decrease has long been regarded as a sign of related phenomena, and some have suggested that hoards are effectively the deposit of grave gifts without a burial. To the hoards should be added the material retrieved from rivers, which is heavily biased towards weapons and suggests that if burials were not actually made in rivers (and there is some evidence to support such a possibility), the commemoration of a warrior's death may have involved depositing weapons in rivers.[81] But again, while Ireland does not look like the Continent, it does share this lack of Late Bronze Age burial with Britain, where similarly we see the disappearance of an earlier series of well-attested burial rites.

Some may object to employing a shared absence between Britain and Ireland as an indicator of cultural influences, but the comparisons between the two islands do not simply rest with the lack of Late Bronze Age burials. Remains of the dead were still around in Late Bronze Age Britain, largely confined to the south, but they do not appear in traditional funerary contexts. For example, Joanna Brück lists some 135 human skulls, many of which were fragmentary, found on British settlement sites.[82] Human remains are also recovered in some frequency from watery locations such as bogs. All these practices find parallels in Ireland. To the example of the frontal part of a skull from the King's Stables, adjacent to Haughey's Fort, one could add the finds of human skulls at Moynagh Lough and Lagore crannog, Co. Meath, plus a series of other sites.[83] Explanations for this practice in Britain have focused on a changing relationship between those wishing to express their power and the ancestral dead, and that somehow the ritual use of parts of the human anatomy served to express one's 'control over land and agricultural production'.[84]

Population movements?

In the Early Bronze Age, similar funerary wares – such as the Cordoned Urns that were concentrated in northeast Ireland and southern Scotland, or the pan-British (except northern Scotland) Collared Urns that are also found along the east coast of Ireland[85] – make a fairly convincing case for contacts that would appear to have been so intimate they suggest migration streams. In general, archaeologists have not found similarly convincing evidence during the Middle and Late Bronze Age that suggests much more than occasional craftsmen or, possibly, brides exchanged between elite populations in Britain and Ireland. To suggest anything more than this involves swimming upstream against current archaeological opinion, as many archaeologists today find it difficult to accept the concept of migration in general, much less migration where the evidence is hardly inescapable. Kristiansen and Larsson's model of Continental Europe integrated by chains of local elites who exchange gifts, goods and genes and regularly engaged in long-distance travel cannot simply be extended to the situation in Ireland, although the Tamlaght hoard certainly suggests the possibility of foreign visitors.

The course of the Irish Middle and Late Bronze Age suggests that Ireland was in intimate contact with Britain over the course of at least a thousand years. Some of the contacts would appear to be persistent and deep, going back to the Middle Bronze Age. The basic settlement form of the circular dwelling with southeastern orientation and surrounded by a ditched enclosure provides a clear example of a parallel shared between both islands. From the Late Bronze Age the contemporaneous rise of the hillfort c. 1200 BC, the erection of unusually large circular structures within the hillforts, their association with ritual depositions and, possibly, sword manufacture, are again parallels. While the practice of depositing votive offerings in watery places goes well beyond Ireland and Britain, the composition and behaviour associated with that of Britain and Ireland are strikingly similar. Both islands see a parallel collapse of a formal burial rite, but also the employment of human remains on settlement or ritual sites. In terms of material culture we find what appear to be clear examples of the export of Irish ornaments, e.g. gold bar torcs, or the import of objects manufactured elsewhere (the Tamlaght hoard). On a more general level we see the sharing of identical weapons and ornaments between Britain and Ireland. And at the end of the Late Bronze Age both western Britain and Ireland make a conscious decision to reject the manufacture of ceramic containers. Many of these similarities have nothing ostensibly to do with the manufacture of metal artifacts, and to attribute all these parallels – ranging across domestic architecture, defensive centres of the elite, burial, religious ceremonies and material culture – to the activities of a few blacksmiths or traders requires no less faith than it does to accept some movements of communities across the Irish Sea. In short, throughout the Middle and Late Bronze Age the cultural behaviour of the people of Ireland was very often shared with their neighbours from Britain.

Conclusions

→ The Middle and Late Bronze Age in Ireland was both initiated and maintained through intimate contacts with Britain and the Continent.

→ Many features of Middle Bronze Age settlement in Britain were adopted in Ireland.

→ The erection of hillforts in Ireland may have been related to their earliest appearance in Britain and suggests at least the possibility of some population movement from Britain into Ireland.

→ Ireland shared with Britain many elements of ritual behaviour, especially associated with the treatment of the dead and the deposit of metal artifacts as offerings to the gods.

→ Ireland adopted from western Britain (or the reverse) the abandonment of ceramics.

→ Deposits such as the Tamlaght hoard suggest the presence of Continental foreigners in Ireland.

The Iron Age

I f we assign the Irish Iron Age to the period roughly between 700/600 BC and AD 400, then our target Irishman, Niall of the Nine Hostages, should have been born in the last decades of Irish prehistory and died during its earliest historical period. And if we follow our rather personal definition of the Irish as anyone related to Niall and the people of Ireland at the time of his rule, then it is clear that the centuries immediately before his birth are of critical importance. There are in fact several very specific reasons why the Iron Age looms so large in any discussion of Irish origins.

Most of the material culture of the Irish Iron Age, at least that which now graces Irish museums, belongs to the La Tène – a major cultural period and stylistic horizon across much of central and western Europe (6.1). In terms of the formation of the Irish ethnic identity, the spread of the La Tène 'culture' to Ireland has often been presented as the single most important event in Irish prehistory, despite the fact that most general accounts have not portrayed it as the result of a major colonization.[1] On the other hand, revisionists have used it as a paper tiger to dismiss its importance.[2] The interpretation of the Irish La Tène thus runs the gamut: from a full migration of Iron Age communities, through restricted raids by Iron Age warrior bands (with their attendant smiths), to some form of artistic osmosis in which local Irish bronze-smiths absorbed the aroma of a new style that enjoyed a certain west European vogue and then produced their own versions. In short, as for the Beakers, we must deal with a La Tène 'phenomenon' in Ireland as a key problem in the study of Irish origins.

In almost any account of Irish prehistory, it is with the Iron Age that one generally finds discussion of the arrival of the Irish language.[3] The other populations of Europe who spoke languages closely related to Irish are often associated with the La Tène culture. We will deal separately with the issues of language in Chapter 9, but first we need to establish the archaeological background.

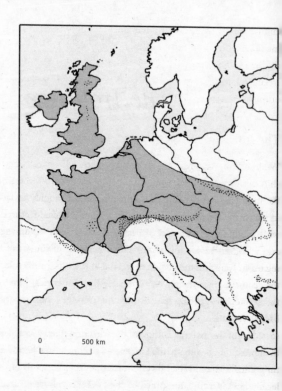

6.1. Generalized map showing distribution of the La Tène art style in Europe.

0 ___ 500 km

The earliest Irish literature and (pseudo)historical works purport to describe, whether in great narrative detail or more sober though spurious chronological precision, the heroic deeds of Ireland's Iron Age warriors. Kenneth Jackson once described these tales as offering a 'window on the Iron Age',[4] and although we will find good reason to be sceptical of such claims in a later chapter, it must be admitted that the landscape of the heroic tales of early Ireland is anchored in monuments that archaeologists date to the Iron Age.

Finally, it is during the Iron Age that Ireland comes into contact with the Roman world, either directly via Roman traders or Irelanders travelling to Britain or by proxy, through Romanized populations of Britain. Niall sits on the edge of this final transformation; indeed, he is sometimes credited as the raider who carried off the son of Calpurnius, the future St Patrick, into slavery.[5] The attendant changes that came with the expansion of Romano-British religion (Christianity) and material culture to Ireland were so profound that they provide us with our iconic image of the medieval Irish occupying an island of saints and scholars. There is a certain irony in this image of the early Irish who would soon follow Niall, as it was largely built on Ireland's acceptance of the dress, customs, technology, behaviour and religion of the outpost of a dying civilization that lay immediately across the Irish Sea.

The Iron Age

While an Iron Age involves a shift from bronze to iron technology, the nature of this shift can vary considerably. In Continental Europe we witness the abandonment of the industrial use of bronze (i.e. for tools and weapons) in favour of an industry in which the corresponding items were primarily manufactured in the much more widely found iron. In Ireland we cannot recover such a dramatic technological shift and, while some evidence for iron metallurgy does appear in Ireland, the overwhelming bulk of metal artifacts from the Irish Iron Age are in fact still bronze, and this is the general pattern for the Atlantic Iron Age as a whole.[6] Some have suggested that the iron technology may have been purposely rejected or resisted in Atlantic Europe because its population had seen how the new technology had destabilized earlier societies further east.[7] Recall that communal interdependence was required during the Bronze Age if one wished to obtain via extensive trade networks the copper and tin needed to manufacture bronze ornaments, weapons and tools, but iron was often locally available and would not have required such close contact; the shift to iron could thus have led to a breakdown in trading and social networks, which may also have stimulated greater regional identities. As for the exceptional dearth of early Irish iron, it is very likely that the new metal was recycled, and this plus the tendency for iron to corrode to the same colour as Irish peat might help explain why so little is found in the earliest period.[8] Moreover, some argue that there was not so much a rise in the use of iron as a collapse in the creation of bronze, with Late Bronze Age hoards appearing as the profligate dumping of a commodity whose social value – the bronze standard – was decreasing.[9] Another resource that is distinctly lacking compared with the previous Bronze Age is gold.

Hallstatt raiders?

The beginning of the Iron Age in western Europe dates to about the 8th century BC and is assigned to the so-called Hallstatt period, which is divided into an earlier

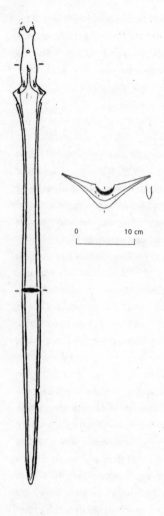

0   10 cm

6.2. Gündlingen
sword (length 79 cm)
and chape.

Hallstatt C (*c.* 800–625 BC) and a later
Hallstatt D (625–450 BC). In Continental
Europe, the Hallstatt period sees the introduction of iron metallurgy, including the use
of a long iron sword that has generally been
interpreted as the weapon of mounted warriors. This period has also been associated, at
least in western Europe, with a greater emphasis on a more mobile pastoral economy and
(another) rise of warrior elites, who engaged
in long-distance raids and spread an Iron Age
'elite warrior ideology'.[10] Superior weapons
and itchy feet are just the combination that
might promote the incursion of warrior
bands into Ireland. While Macalister was
content to explain away any of the Hallstatt
artifacts known from Ireland as the product
of 'traders or of travellers',[11] there have been
some who have argued otherwise.

Nearly 40 years ago Colin Burgess briefly
presented the case for some form of Hallstatt
military incursion, which was supported
by a number of arguments. First of all, the
Hallstatt C presence is primarily indicated
by a specific weapon type, the Gündlingen
sword, and its presence in Britain and Ireland
is hardly trivial.[12] Gündlingen swords from
Britain and Ireland constitute more than
a third of this class of sword, and as many
come from Ireland (*c.* 50) as are known from
Britain (6.2). In addition to Hallstatt-derived
swords are chapes of bronze that secured the
base of presumably leather or wooden scabbards. Second, the distribution of Hallstatt
swords is primarily riverine with some finds
from the coasts, which according to Burgess

suggested a 'classic raiding pattern', very different from the familiar 'trade-based dis-tributions'[13] that Macalister seemed to envisage. Third, Hallstatt material is only very rarely found in contexts alongside locally made material, which suggests that it was culturally apart, i.e. intrusive and not the material culture of the native population. In fact, Burgess argued that it was unlikely that the swords were made by local smiths, as not only are they not found with local material but they appear to have influ-enced the local production of native Irish swords. Burgess qualified his description of a Hallstatt intrusion by emphasizing that the limited material evidence points to raiders, traders and smiths rather than the wholesale settlement of foreign families; in short, the women and children stayed at home.

Burgess's initial model (apparently abandoned by Burgess himself by 1980)[14] generally received a rough ride among Irish archaeologists, who have not interpreted the evidence as being indicative of intrusive warriors.[15] First, the Gündlingen swords in Ireland, like their British counterparts,[16] were made in bronze and not iron[17] as they were on the Continent, so it is questionable whether they constituted an advantage for putative invaders, although it must be admitted that they were longer than the earlier Bronze Age swords. It might be added that the source of these swords seems to embrace both southern Britain and the adjacent area of Continental Europe, so the earliest swords were actually in bronze to begin with and need not have originated exclusively on the Continent (6.3).[18] While such swords are found with horse gear on the Continent and in Britain, this is not the case in Ireland, so it is difficult to put our sword wielders on horseback.[19] The swords themselves would also appear to be copies of British swords rather than direct copies of Continental imports.[20] The distribution of these Gündlingen swords is just about the same as the earlier Bronze Age weapon horizons that we saw before, i.e. the Thames and the inland waterways of Ireland, so they do not differ markedly from other patterns for which raiding parties are not the preferred explanation. While 8 Gündlingen swords are known, for example, from the River Bann, the same river also yielded 24 swords of other types, including 14 from the previous 'native' Late Bronze Age period.[21] The swords can easily be explained in the same terms as the other types, i.e. a continuation of making votive offerings in rivers. This is an important distinction, because on the Continent these same swords are generally found accompanying burials.[22] That such swords do not occur in hoards with local material is neither entirely accurate now nor particularly remarkable, considering that there are not many Irish Late Bronze Age hoards that include both swords and other accompanying items, although there are hoards of Late Bronze Age swords on their own.[23] Moreover, Gündlingen swords

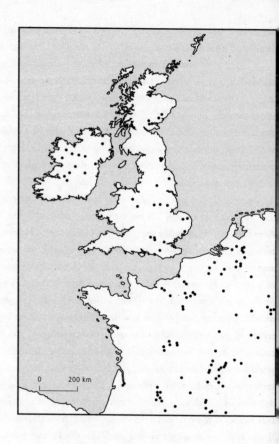

6.3: Distribution of
Gündlingen swords.

in Britain are also characteristically absent from hoards.[24] As for the segregation of
Hallstatt material from native Late Bronze Age items, this is still largely true with only
a few exceptions.[25] Among the few other Hallstatt-associated objects are ornaments
such as dress fasteners.[26] In short, it is very difficult to make a convincing case for a
Hallstatt C intrusion into Ireland. In addition, when it comes to the following period,
Hallstatt D, during which long swords were abandoned for short swords and daggers,
these new forms do not find their way to Ireland at all, suggesting that if there had
been Hallstatt intruders, they had by then lost contact with wherever they had come
from. As this dearth of Hallstatt D material is similar across Britain, it suggests that

the major exchange routes between the Continent and its western periphery had largely collapsed by *c.* 600 BC.[27]

In short, the evidence of Hallstatt C swords does not make a convincing case that Ireland was on the receiving end of an influx of warriors from the Continent in the period *c.* 800–600 BC. In other respects, Ireland behaves very much like Britain in terms of the reception of Hallstatt material (river deposition, similarity of sword types, lack of cemeteries), and we can presume that Ireland remained in close contact with Britain, borrowing some of the weapons technology and ornaments spreading from the east as it had done in earlier periods.

Ireland's earliest iron

After 600 BC and before the start of the La Tène in Ireland about 300 BC there seemed to be a profoundly obscure Dark Age, at least in terms of settlements and artifacts, and when the curtain rose again during the La Tène, the overwhelming majority of metallic remains were confined to the northern two-thirds of the island, with Munster traditionally appearing as either poorly settled or a backwater of the rest of Ireland.[28] This image of a final Bronze Age collapse, whose potential causes I rehearsed over 20 years ago[29] and have inflicted on a generation of students as a tutorial topic, needs some correction now. In 2008 the Irish Heritage Council funded a project to examine the new evidence thrown up by developer-funded excavations in Ireland that pertained to the Iron Age.[30] The project leaders divided the Irish Iron Age into three main periods – Early (700–400 BC), Developed (400–1 BC) and Late (AD 1–400) – and found that the number of sites assigned to the first period (our 'Dark Age') was not materially different from those of the most recent period (the centuries just before the coming of Christianity to Ireland). In the Early Iron Age there was some, admittedly questionable, evidence for ironworking at Rossan 6, Co. Meath, Kinnegad 2, Co. Westmeath, and Reask, Co. Kerry,[31] and the distribution of sites clearly covered all of Ireland, including Munster. It now seems probable that a new technology of ironworking spread across Ireland at about the same time that it penetrated Britain, so contacts between the two islands were clearly still taking place. The authors of the report to the Heritage Council indicated that they believed that the period around 700 BC (the beginning of their Early Iron Age) marked one of the two significant transitions witnessed during the Iron Age.[32] There is also some evidence of continuity between the earlier Hallstatt period and the following La Tène that can be seen in the largest of the Iron Age sites, the ancient royal sites of Ireland.

6.4. Map of native
Iron Age sites
mentioned in
Chapter 6.

Ceremonial centres

The early medieval Irish believed they could access their pagan past through a series
of tales centred largely on the exploits of the prehistoric Ulstermen and their less
than friendly relationships with their neighbours in the other provinces, especially
Connacht. The major set piece of tales, known as the Ulster Cycle, was the *Táin*, the
great cattle raid that included a series of duels between Ulster's champion CúChulainn
and the warriors of Queen Medb. The stories are set in a series of ancient provincial capitals such as Emain Macha in Ulster and Cruachain in Connacht, which are
archaeologically identified respectively with Navan Fort (6.4), outside Armagh,
and Rathcroghan, near Tulsk, Co. Roscommon. Other 'royal' sites are Dún Ailinne
(Knockaulin, Co. Kildare), the ancient seat of the kings of Leinster; Cashel, the royal site
of Munster in Co. Tipperary; and Tara, the legendary capital of the (equally legendary)
High King of Ireland.[33] To these one might add the more overtly ceremonial
site of Uisneach, Co. Westmeath, the ritual 'centre' of Ireland. Most of these sites have

seen either excavation or surveys, and they all exhibit features that indicate they were important Iron Age centres. From the perspective of the Irish of the early Middle Ages who, as we will see in the next chapter, imagined themselves as the last of a very long series of invaders, these Iron Age sites were very much part of their own ancestry and not the ruins of remote and ancient peoples. While earlier races of heroes or gods might be confined to much earlier megalithic tombs, the Iron Age centres are the earliest monuments that the Irish attributed to themselves and, indeed, they may have deliberately associated themselves with these sites in later historic times in order to emphasize claims of legitimacy.[34] For this reason it is important that we understand these sites.

Although the centres are far from identical, some share a number of important common features. Navan, Knockaulin and Tara, for example, all present their ceremonial centre in a henge-like enclosure. Unlike the Late Bronze Age hillforts that, as one would expect of a defensive structure, had their ditches outside their earthen, timber or stone ramparts, these Iron Age enclosures reverse the relationship. The henge was a relic of the distant past, the type of ceremonial enclosure that was widespread in both Britain and Ireland c. 3000 BC. Where dating evidence is available, it suggests that these Iron Age enclosures, measuring anywhere from c. 285 to 500 m across, were built c. 100 BC. The main ritual site at Rathcroghan was also surrounded by a ditch, although there is no trace of what side its bank lay on.

The interior of the enclosures was not, so far as we can tell, densely filled with houses. Rather, at least in two of them, we find an early phase of figure-of-eight structures. These consist of a smaller round structure attached to a larger enclosed 'courtyard' that was approached by a funnel-shaped walkway (6.5).[35]

Both Knockaulin and Navan replaced the earlier figure-of-eight structures with very large circular structures, built of concentric rings of upright timber posts, measuring 40 m or more in diameter (6.6). At their centre was a post (Navan) or tower (Knockaulin). At the Rath of the Synods at Tara there are two adjacent enclosures that were perhaps comparable to the figure-of-eight structures and, as at the other sites, these were subsequently replaced by a larger multi-ringed structure.[36] A recent survey of Rathcroghan mound has revealed the presence of a 32-m circular structure.

Finally, three of the sites also possess sizeable mounds. The enclosure at Tara, the Ráith na Ríg, surrounds an earlier Neolithic passage tomb (the Mound of the Hostages)[37] that later featured as a cemetery for Early Bronze Age burials. At Navan the mound covers both an earlier figure-of-eight and the 40-m structure, while the circular structure at Rathcroghan is also encased within its mound. To these we might

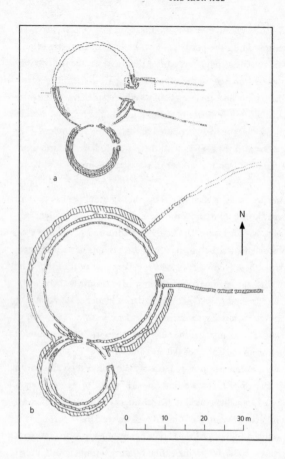

6.5. Figure-of-eight
structures at
(a) Navan;
(b) Knockaulin.

N

0   10   20   30 m

add a very low (0.8-m) mound at Knockaulin.[38] At Navan there appears to have been a well-ordered sequence of events in which the earlier 40-m ceremonial structure was first filled with limestone cobbles, then its timber outer structure was set on fire, and finally sods were placed on it to form a mound. Such behaviour has sparked no end of archaeological speculation, but one potential explanation is that the occupants of Navan were copying those at Tara and felt the need to erect their own mound that might have provided a ritual access to the Otherworld.

Henge-like enclosures, figure-of-eight structures, large circular ceremonial buildings or precincts consisting of concentric timber circles and mounds appear to

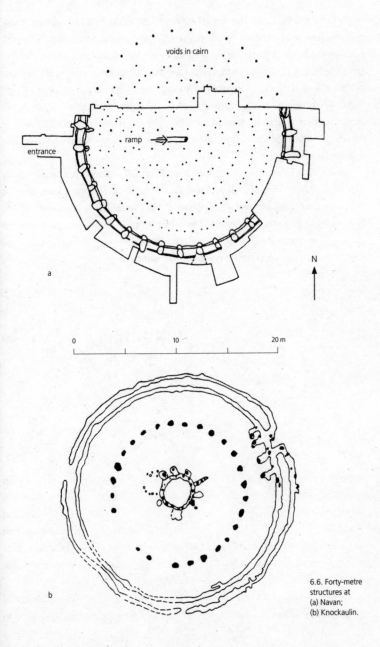

6.6. Forty-metre structures at (a) Navan; (b) Knockaulin.

be part of a ritual package that spread across Ireland in the first centuries BC. There may well have been some other elements as well. For example, next to Navan Fort lies Loughnashade, a lake from which four spectacularly large Iron Age horns were recovered, suggesting an adjacent ritual lake. Here we find nature imitating art, because not too distant is the earlier Haughey's Fort with its adjacent artificial pool, the King's Stables. Although undated, a similar pond lies near Tara.[39] Moreover, some of the features appear to continue beyond the time of the major royal sites; Raffin Fort, Co. Meath, also possessed a hengiform enclosure that is dated some time between the 4th and 6th centuries AD (6.7).[40]

As to what ceremonies might have been practised at these sites, we have very little idea. The one element that archaeologists do agree on is that the sites offered a venue for feasts, perhaps on a seasonal basis.[41] The primary meat consumed at both Navan and Knockaulin was cattle, followed by pig (at Navan pig was the numerical majority but in total provided less meat than cattle). At Navan the animal remains are confined to the period of the figure-of-eight structures.

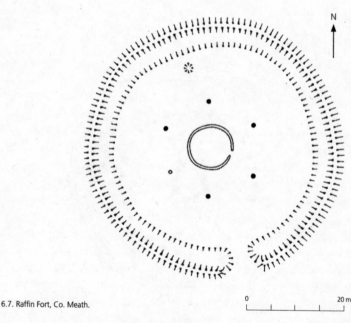

6.7. Raffin Fort, Co. Meath.

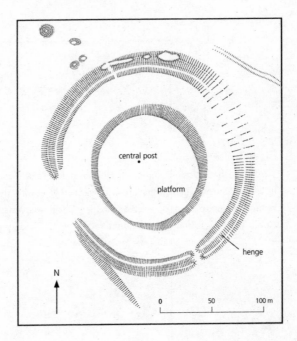

6.8. The Goloring.

We have then an extremely interesting phenomenon. A series of elements, some apparently incorporating ancient ceremonial features (henges, barrows), spread across Ireland to form what were later imagined to be royal provincial capitals of the earliest Irish. When one compares Navan and Knockaulin, there is a real sense that we are witnessing variations on the same theme. This roughly simultaneous dispersal of what would appear to have been a new ceremonial architecture (new religion?) is the type of archaeological evidence that clearly indicates something important is going on (even if we don't know precisely what it is). Of critical importance is whether these 'royal' sites were home grown or the ritual centres of a new population.

There is some evidence that figure-of-eight structures might already have appeared in the Late Bronze Age part of Raffin Fort, but this is only a possibility.[42] As for the large circular 'temples', the best parallel so far cited is the Goloring near Koblenz in Germany (6.8).[43] It too was a henge-like enclosure, though at 175 m it was somewhat smaller than those at Navan and Knockaulin. Inside was an earthen platform some 100 m across and towards its centre was a single posthole that suggests

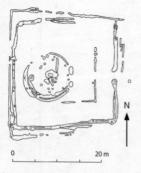

6.9. Hayling Island.

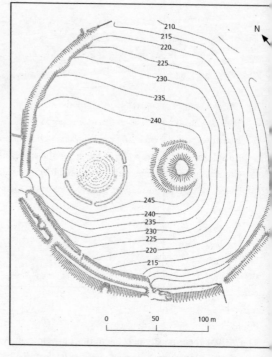

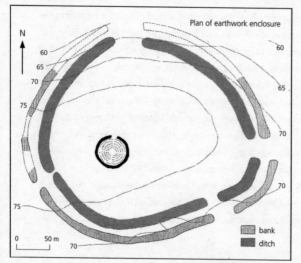

Plan of earthwork enclosure

bank

ditch

6.10 Navan Fort (above) and Mount Pleasant, Dorset.

a post about the same size as the central post at Navan. But this is about as far as the comparison goes (no figure-of-eight structures, no circular post-built structure); the Goloring is over 1,000 km from its closest Irish parallel and may date anywhere from about 300 to 800 years earlier. In fact, this new Irish ceremonial horizon centred on figure-of-eight structures and large circular 'buildings' so far lacks any really close foreign analogues. Let's be explicit here and quote Barry Cunliffe:

> The monumentality of the Irish religious sites sets them apart from
> their British and continental European counterparts. The huge timber
> structures, and the enclosing earthworks which invariably have banks
> outside the ditches, are features which hark back to Neolithic and Early
> Bronze Age times and provide a firm reminder of the strength of
> indigenous traditions in more remote areas of the Atlantic fringes.[44]

We simply do not find similar sites or even some of the major elements anywhere else, including Britain.[45] There, the ritual sites so far known tend to comprise rectangular structures set within rectangular enclosures or circular structures whose dimensions do not differ from what might be regarded as domestic houses.[46] On occasion there are round structures such as at Hayling Island, but here it was little more than 10 m across and set within a rectangular enclosure (6.9). Moreover, it produced an impressive assemblage of votive offerings that we do not find on the Irish sites.[47] Only a few very general comparisons can be made. For example, at Tara there were fragments of human skull found within the surrounding ditch of the Ráith na Ríg, which finds parallels on British sites. Some human remains were also found within the composition of the mound at Navan. But human remains are encountered on sites of both islands throughout the previous Bronze Age as well. Also, at Tara, we find evidence for the consumption of horses and dogs, another pattern matched within ritual contexts on British sites.[48] Probably the best comparisons are natural sanctuaries involving water such as Llyn Cerrig Bach in Britain and, we suspect, Lisnacrogher in Co. Antrim. But these comparisons are too general. Disturbingly, if we were forced to look to Britain for a 'source' for the 40-m Irish structures, the best parallels would have been Late Neolithic sites such as Mount Pleasant in Dorset or Durrington Walls, where we find large circular enclosures, also about 40 m across, built from five or more concentric rings of posts (6.10).[49] But these buildings are separated by nearly 3,000 years from the Iron Age Irish sites, so we can hardly talk of a connection between the two unless we invoke time-travel. In short, it is very difficult to derive either the figure-of-eight structures or the large ceremonial 'temples' from outside of Ireland.

The 'invisible people'

Once outside the major ritual centres of Iron Age Ireland we enter the world of what Barry Raftery once termed 'the invisible people'.[50] Writing back in 1994, he found little evidence for the habitations of the ordinary Iron Age family in Ireland. In some ways this dovetailed very well with the evidence of environmental scientists. From about 4000 BC onward, when farming began in Ireland, the landscape had become progressively less forested and more open, with continual evidence for the growing of cereals. But in the centuries around the BC/AD divide there was a major closing of the Irish landscape, when the forests reasserted themselves and the evidence for arable agriculture diminished or disappeared altogether. It looked like the worst collapse in agriculture in the past 6,000 years, which might be also read as a dramatic fall in population or at least a shift to a more mobile economy based on pasturing livestock.[51]

As we have seen, the Irish Heritage Council project assembled evidence from at least 250 Iron Age dated sites.[52] The majority of these sites are not, unfortunately, primarily settlements of the Iron Age but rather features of sites of other periods for which the archaeologist has often received a little 'surprise' when the results from the radiocarbon lab were returned. The Late Bronze Age site of Haughey's Fort, for example, also produced a pit whose contents were deposited during the Iron Age, and this pattern can be found across Ireland from sites of just about every period. Often the date comes from a hearth, pit or some postholes in a site of a different period. House structures are still fairly rare. We have an Iron Age house among the many Bronze Age dwellings from Corrstown, Co. Antrim; an oval hut from Muckridge 1 in Co. Cork dates to the first centuries AD, while a round hut from Scrabo, Co. Down, can also be broadly set to the Iron Age. The closest to a real settlement is perhaps Cloongownagh, Co. Roscommon, with traces of eight houses (circular to sub-rectangular) that date from c. 200 BC to AD 200. The general impression is that the people who built such magnificent ceremonial structures lived in extremely modest dwellings or, as some suspect, employed an architectural form designed to thwart archaeological recovery, i.e. flimsy shelters or tents or even substantial structures built on now disintegrated timber sleepers.

But alongside the dearth of substantial domestic sites, we do have considerable evidence that associates the Iron Age occupants of Ireland with transport, industrial sites and the relics of earlier ritual sites. The evidence for transport is clearly seen in the presence of wooden trackways that have been known in Ireland since the Neolithic and are especially frequent during the Bronze Age.[53] They also continued in use through the Iron Age, when some of the most spectacular are found attempting to provide a dry pathway across the bogs of Co. Longford.[54] With such a long history, duplicated elsewhere in Europe including Britain, one might regard the Iron Age roads in Longford as entirely native – except for the fact that here it is something rather special (6.11). The trackway, Corlea I, consisting of two sections totalling about 2 km in length, was built of large oak timbers set horizontally on wooden runners or brushwood, and formed a truly massive road on the order of 3–4 m wide. It dates to the 2nd century BC and while there were many earlier trackways, there is very little evidence for trackways in the centuries immediately before the building of the Iron Age trackways. What is particularly striking is that the best parallel for the Corlea trackway is nearly identically constructed trackways in northern Germany that date to the same period.[55] As Barry Raftery notes, the German examples are part of a clearly seen evolution in construction techniques while the Corlea trackway seems to appear out of nowhere and within a generation of the German ones. This raises the question of whether there is a connection between the two regions, reprising perhaps the connections we have already seen with the Tamlaght hoard of the later Bronze Age and the far less secure parallels with the Goloring. Raftery notes that, according to our earliest map of Europe by Ptolemy, both the area of Co. Longford (roughly) and the area of northern Germany where the trackways are found were occupied by a tribe known as the Cauci. The German Cauci have generally been presumed

6.11. Corlea trackway.

to have been Germanic in language, and this has set off speculation that an Iron Age Germanic tribe may have settled in Ireland.[56] But before we imagine Irish trackways littered with billboards proclaiming 'Vorsprung durch Technik', it should also be noted that the tribal names may not be related and that there are other examples of the name Cauci in western Europe.[57]

As well as for traversing bogs, we naturally have some evidence for navigating the waterways of Ireland and possibly crossing the sea. Among the gold objects recovered from Broighter, Co. Londonderry, was the model of a boat, complete with oars, a steering oar, nine thwarts and the mast for a sail. The best guess as to its composition tends to favour a wicker frame over which were stretched skins; this accords well with a series of contemporary classical descriptions of the boats employed in British and Irish waters.[58]

A second area of Iron Age transport comprises Ireland's linear earthworks which were commonly thought to have been erected to prohibit rather than promote movement, although there is a recent theory that they may have actually been erected for portage, i.e. the conveying of boats across boggy land between waterways.[59] Generally, however, these quite imposing monuments consisting of earthen banks, timber palisades and parallel ditches are believed to have served as barriers to discourage cattle raiding in areas not otherwise defended by natural impediments such as rivers. Traces of these earthworks may run for kilometres across the landscape, and both their size and the extent of the area that they appear to 'defend' suggests that like the trackways they were major labour projects involving a large number of people. The best-dated linear earthworks such as the Black Pig's Dyke and the Dorsey are located in southern Ulster and have been treated as indications of the marking out of political territories in Iron Age Ireland. But there are also Iron Age earthworks of a similar nature 'protecting' a ford on the Shannon and also further south in Munster. While they are traditionally assumed to have served as defences against such practices as cattle raiding, their effective purpose may rather have been to provide vast labour projects that would bring families together and help provide a common social identity.[60] Whatever their proclaimed function, large earthmoving projects would certainly have provided opportunities for elites to reinforce their status and bring what may well have been a very dispersed population together, welding them into more coherent social units and providing them with distinct identities.

There are linear earthworks in Britain, especially south-central England, that date somewhere between c. 1000 and 600 BC, which Barry Cunliffe sees as part of the evidence indicative of a marked break from earlier settlement patterns with an increased focus on 'land and territory'.[61] While there is no technique involved in the building of the Irish linear earthworks that was not already present in Late Bronze Age hillforts or promontory forts, there again seems to be a hiatus between the erection of these structures and the linear earthworks, unlike in England where they are roughly contemporary. Moreover, if the purpose of the linear earthworks in Ireland was to define and defend the territories of early tribal groupings, this operates at a scale far greater than those commonly found in Britain, where archaeologists generally ascribe a more economic function, e.g. land divisions or droveways for livestock.[62]

Another frequently encountered type of Iron Age site is associated with iron metallurgy. As we will see below, the overwhelming majority of metallic remains of the Iron Age in Ireland are actually bronze, and iron objects are exceedingly rare. But the evidence for ironworking is, thanks to the Heritage Council project, not so rare. There are at least 30 sites indicating metalworking scattered across Ireland, e.g. Derrinsallagh 5, Co. Laois, with 44 bowl furnaces and iron slag. We will need to keep this in mind when we review the evidence for Iron Age metalwork below.

Finally, while we have evidence for an interest in earlier ritual monuments seen at the large ceremonial sites, there is also plenty of evidence that Iron Age peoples could not resist leaving traces of their activities in earlier megalithic tombs. The tomb type was not important, as we recover evidence for Iron Age activity at Annaghmare court tomb, Altar wedge tomb and a series of passage tombs from Carrowmore; only the portal tombs seem (so far) to have been untouched by Iron Age people.[63]

The La Tène

Maps of Europe depicting the Iron Age generally portray a vast area comprising modern France (or ancient Gaul), southern Germany, Austria, Switzerland and the Czech Republic under the umbrella of the La Tène culture (6.12). Out of this blob extrude a series of arrows, some pointing east into Hungary and the north Balkans (justified by archaeological evidence) and then pushing further east into Greece and central Turkey (ancient Anatolia), the latter justified almost exclusively on historical and, occasionally, linguistic evidence. Arrows also push southward into Italy, often reminding us that the Gauls under Brennus sacked Rome c. 390 BC. And, of course, appearing as the most natural thing in the world, arrows also point across the English Channel and around Britain (or through it) into Ireland. In the Heritage Council project, the 3rd century BC, the period in which we find our earliest La Tène objects

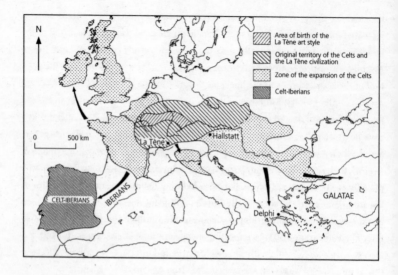

N

	Area of birth of the La Tène art style
	Original territory of the Celts and the La Tène civilization
	Zone of the expansion of the Celts
	Celt-Iberians

0   500 km

La Tène   •Hallstatt

CELT-IBERIANS

IBERIANS

GALATAE

Delphi •

in Ireland, is regarded as the second major transition period. And, as we have seen above, the spread of the La Tène to Ireland has often been portrayed as the single most important factor in the creation of an Irish identity. We will need to examine in some detail what all this means in terms of the origins of the Irish.

If we are forced to place dots on a map to indicate all of the evidence we have for Irish La Tène items (6.13), the distribution of such objects is largely confined to the northern two-thirds of the island; Munster has remained largely terra incognita with respect to La Tène objects, although we now know that there is good evidence for settlement there throughout the Iron Age.[64] The overriding problem here is that La Tène metalwork is not the Irish Iron Age but merely a component of it, assigned to the elite and hence, in Barry Raftery's words, 'culturally confined and numerically small'.[65] For some reason, it did not appear to 'take' in Munster.[66]

As we will soon see, the La Tène period yields a series of objects and styles that do represent a radical break from the Later Bronze Age. But in attempting to make links between Ireland and specific regions of either Britain or the Continent, archaeologists often find themselves dissecting artistic motifs and techniques and searching for parallels among an enormous variety of objects recovered across western Europe. An object found in Ireland might be on the stylistic receiving end of a host of influences emanating from various parts of Britain and the Continent with no consistent narrative. An object may well have been made by a craftsman along the Danube and later influenced bronzesmiths in France who, in turn, stimulated some stylistic change in Britain that was then further altered by smiths in Ireland. Or, quite possibly, Irish smiths may have received their influences directly from the Continent, either travelling there themselves or coming into contact with Continental craftsmen in Ireland. Alternatively, some archaeologists find little difficulty in declaring an object of clearly local manufacture. But even if we are secure in our ability to identify direct imports, there is really no consistent and substantial horizon of securely imported La Tène artifacts in Ireland that can be regarded as the stimulus for the emergence of the Irish Iron Age. Barry Raftery's catalogue of La Tène objects numbered 774 and, although the number has increased somewhat since he compiled the catalogue, the additions are not numerous.[67] Of these objects some 539 could be located to their find spot and of these, more than one-third were recovered from bodies of water such as rivers, bogs or lakes, sustaining the argument that votive offerings were still in vogue.[68]

6.12. (opposite) Map of La Tène art style with arrows suggesting expansions.

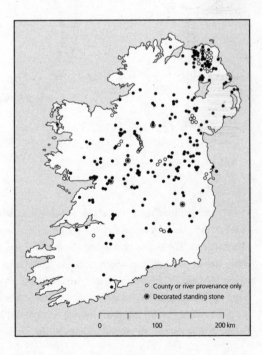

County or river provenance only
Decorated standing stone

0   100   200 km

6.13. Distribution map of Irish La Tène objects (excluding beehive querns).

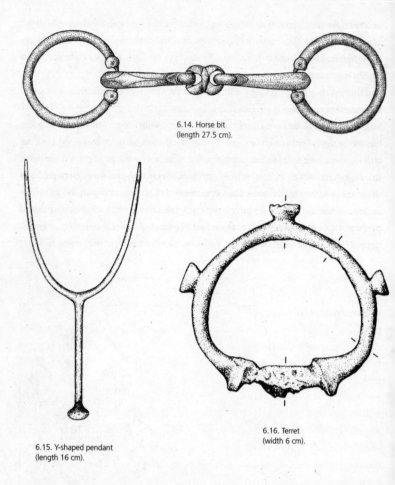

6.14. Horse bit
(length 27.5 cm).

6.15. Y-shaped pendant
(length 16 cm).

6.16. Terret
(width 6 cm).

We can divide all the Irish La Tène metalwork into broad classes of objects, in order of their abundance: transportation, ornament, weapons, tools and miscellaneous objects. The largest class (over 230 items) is associated with the driving or riding (we are not really sure which) of horses. There are at least 135 horse bits (6.14), nearly 100 large (Y-shaped) pendants that have been presumed to be part of horse trappings (martingales?; 6.15) and a few cart fittings. When decoration occurs it is in the general style (tendril-like floral motifs) encountered across central and western Europe during the La Tène period, although there are decided differences in British and Irish La Tène art. Unfortunately, any attempt to pin these specific items to the arrows pointing at Ireland on the maps must deal with the fact that the overwhelming majority are presumed to have been of local manufacture rather than imported. The horse bits, for example, are made in a distinctly local fashion with three links, and finding an appropriate precursor, be it in Britain or France, is more than problematic. There are a few two-piece bits that do have British or Continental parallels, but these do nothing to explain the appearance of the majority of La Tène horse bits in Ireland. Even worse are the Y-pendants that are entirely confined to Ireland, although there are some vague and distant Continental parallels. In Britain the horse drawing a chariot would be controlled by reins that would pass through metal hubs or terrets mounted on the pole. These terrets are well represented with 585 examples in Britain, but in Ireland we only have a single example from Co. Antrim that is presumed to be an import from southwest Scotland (6.16). Incidentally, all of the items of Irish horse gear are bronze, with the exception of four iron horse bits and one iron Y-pendant.

So what conclusions can we draw from this class of material? The evidence for either horse riding (most horse bits are single finds) or chariot driving (some horse bits are found in pairs, with asymmetrical wear patterns suggesting draft teams) supports the notion that transport in Iron Age Ireland involved objects manufactured in the La Tène style. We can also say that, in focusing so strongly on horse gear, Ireland behaved precisely like Britain, where horse harnesses and chariot fittings also constitute the most numerous type of La Tène artifact. And we can emphasize the obvious: we now have substantial evidence to indicate the presence of the domestic horse in Ireland. In other words, both Ireland and Britain undergo the same revolution in transport with a cultural emphasis on horse gear, and this should indicate an intimate cultural connection between the two islands. However, it is also clear that they did not employ vehicles or horse gear of the same status. The Irish have a distinctive horse bit, and if they were driving carts or chariots, they did not use the same steering system that was employed on British models (the terret). Nor do we find evidence for the wheels, although these are abundantly represented in Britain, e.g. 132 linchpins[69] and 38 nave bands.[70] And while Britain offers a series of vehicle-associated objects known as 'cheek-pieces' (30), these are not found in Ireland, whereas Ireland possesses nearly 100 Y-shaped pendants, a type not found on British sites, although the same function may have been fulfilled by strap unions.[71]

The next most numerous class of objects comprises ornaments employed in fastening clothes as well as items worn directly on the person such as neck rings,

and a series of decorated 'mounts' that were probably detached from larger ornaments, in some cases quite possibly headgear. The clothes fasteners may have been
straight pins (ring-headed pins) or fibulae, the technical name applied to prehistoric safety-pins. Some are imported objects: the 'Clonmacnoise'[72] gold torc from Co.
Offaly (6.17) was manufactured on the Continent (presumably the Middle Rhine,
c. 300 BC), and gold torcs and wire necklaces from Broighter are derived from the
Mediterranean.[73] But the overwhelming majority of ornaments are again regarded
as locally manufactured, either because the maker has taken a foreign prototype (the
ring-headed pin; 6.18) and created new styles, or because the type (e.g. the Navan-
type brooches; 6.19) simply has no parallels anywhere else. However, we do at least
have some likely foreign stimuli for some of the Irish fibulae. There is reasonably
widespread agreement, for example, that some of the Irish fibulae were developed
through some form of contact with southwest England, possibly as early as the 3rd
century BC, while other fibulae may have better Continental parallels. There are also
instances of more obvious imports, e.g. a fibula from near Galway, its origin attributed to the north Alpine area with no intermediaries, and an iron fibula and axe from
Feerwore, Co. Galway. It is clear that comparisons between ornaments in Ireland and
abroad do not lead to any consistent pattern of origin, i.e. parallels in ornaments
may be found localized in Britain from Scotland south to Wiltshire or Dorset or generalized over Britain as a whole. The parallels may also derive from the Continent,
but even there the proposed areas of manufacture range widely, from the Middle
Rhine (Clonmacnoise torc) to Gaul or the Mediterranean (gold-wire necklaces of the
Broighter hoard). In short, if we attempt to follow the track of elite ornament, it leads
everywhere and, consequently for our purposes, nowhere.

When we turn to weapons, the story appears to be the same. Of the 30 swords
dated to the Iron Age, only two are imports. The more interesting of these was discovered in a fishing net in Ballyshannon harbour, Co. Donegal, and survives only as a
bronze hilt (to an iron sword) shaped like a man (6.20); it was most likely imported
from southern Gaul and, possibly, deposited as a votive offering in Ireland.[74] The
bronze scabbards in which iron swords were carried have all been identified as of
local manufacture; indeed, the very short blade of the swords also emphasizes their
local rather than foreign origin. Ultimate stylistic sources are variously set directly
from the Continent (middle Danube region through eastern France) or via Britain.
An intriguing aspect is that the site of Lisnacrogher, Co. Antrim, has yielded three
hollow bronze rings that would appear to be direct imports from eastern France, and
it is reasonably possible that the rings were used to suspend the scabbards from a belt.

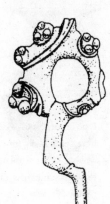

6.18. Ring-headed pin (length 12.9 cm).

6.17. The 'Clonmacnoise' gold torc (diameter 12.9 cm).

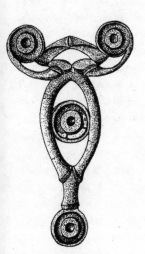

6.19. Navan-type brooch (length 9.2 cm).

6.20. Ballyshannon sword hilt (length 13.6 cm).

6.21. Irish 'spear butt' (length 8.6 cm).

While there are only a small number of spearheads (5) that we can confidently assign to the Iron Age, Britain does not fare much better, with only about 13. But here again Ireland and Britain appear to part company, as Ireland also yields over 70 bronze objects of various shapes (doorknob, cone) that have tentatively been identified as spear butts (6.21). These are probably later than most of the other La Tène items and are far better represented in Ireland than in Britain.

Miscellaneous metal objects include a series of large bronze horns (some now lost) that were apparently part of votive offerings, placed in watery homes. Parallels outside Ireland are few; the best are an undated object recovered from Nice in southern France and a fragment found in Llyn Cerrig Bach in Britain. A series of bronze bowls have been dated to the first centuries (BC or AD) and are related to (some would claim exported from) the territory of Belgic tribes settled in southeast Britain, as also is a bronze tazza (shallow bowl). To all of these may be added a very non-La Tène import of a bronze figure that was apparently introduced from the Mediterranean around the 3rd century BC. A single wooden tankard found at Carrickfergus and dated to the first centuries AD is suspected of being an import from Wales.

Finally, there are objects of stone. The most numerous (over 220) are the beehive querns (6.22), two large stones used for grinding grain. That these objects were both heavy and primarily domestic (unlike elite metalwork) has suggested to some that they may reflect more obviously the intrusion of a new people into Ireland in the first centuries AD. Beehive querns are also known from northern Britain and Scotland and it is presumed that they spread from there to Ireland. The beehive querns, which employed a rotating millstone, were more efficient than the

6.22. Beehive quern (diameter 27.2 cm).

primitive saddle querns, and one would presume that they should be associated with an intensification in agricultural activity. Might this be evidence for a major Iron Age population movement? Quite some time ago Seamus Caulfield suggested as much when he noted that the distribution of the beehive querns was largely restricted to the northern two-thirds of Ireland, precisely the same area where we find La Tène metalwork.[75] As an argument for population movement, this had far more bite than those based purely on metalwork, which could easily be explained away as either exchange items for the elite or local copies of high-status imports. Grinding stones take us down to the foundation level of society and might be far more suggestive of population movement. But Richard Warner has since complicated matters – disturbingly or intriguingly, depending on your point of view.[76] Warner demonstrated that while the querns were indeed confined to the northern two-thirds of the island, on the local level their distribution and that of the La Tène metalwork were

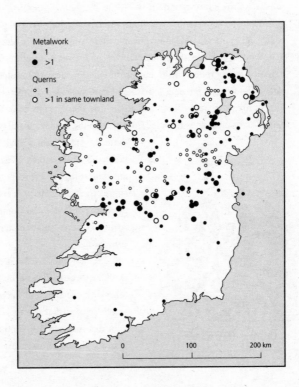

6.23. Distribution of beehive querns and La Tène metalwork.

mutually exclusive (6.23). This summons up the incongruous image of two discrete populations – the metal people (who did not eat) and the quern people (who lacked metal), both living in a forested landscape where there is little evidence for agriculture. When Warner plotted the soil types against the metal and querns, the results were counter-intuitive: the metal objects were found on the best soils and many of the beehive querns were restricted to the poorer soils.[77] One explanation for these differences might be economic, in the sense that the elite metal users may perhaps have enjoyed a largely livestock economy, supplemented with the agricultural products of the surrounding(?) quern population, who may have belonged to the same culture but were not of the same status.

Also in stone are a number of pillars clearly of local origin (the Turoe stone is more obviously phallic) that are finely decorated with La Tène ornament (6.24). The idea of erecting stone pillars (and presumably also wooden pillars that have not survived) does have parallels in Brittany, but the artwork itself is regarded as local or of southern British inspiration.

When we look at the potential source of the imported objects there are only some slight patterns indicating possible trade routes. Initially, almost all the La Tène material was regarded as probably being of British inspiration, largely because so much of it was found in the northeast. Subsequently, archaeologists have tried to isolate the various possible sources and have provided conflicting models. Etienne Rynne, for example, believed that there were two streams of La Tène imports: the earliest coming directly from the Continent to the west of Ireland while a later stream derived from Britain with its finds largely concentrated in the north.[78] He even saw in this an archaeological expression of the tensions suggested in early Irish literature between the provinces of Ulster and Connacht. Since Rynne wrote, however, matters have become more complicated.

6.24. The Turoe stone (height 1.68 m).

The amount of La Tène material that would appear to have been imported is very limited (Table 6.1), and the pattern of imports would suggest that the earliest material seems to be derived from the Continent (the Rhine or France), while the material from Britain tends to date from after the 1st century BC (Table 6.2). From the perspective of material culture, the Continental material is certainly limited, and Barry Raftery concluded that 'there is no evidence to support the notion of a substantial folk movement from the Continent to Ireland.'[79]

Table 6.1 Early Continental La Tène imports in Ireland

La Tène period	Site	Object	Source
B2	Clonmacnoise	Buffer torc	Middle Rhine
B2	Clonmacnoise	Ribbon torc	?Middle Rhine
B2/C1	Lisnacrogher	Chapes	?E France
B2/C1	Lisnacrogher	Rings	?E France
C1	Lisnacrogher	Scabbards	?E France
	Bann	Two-link bit	?E France
	Ballyshannon	Sword hilt	?W France
	Broighter	Collar	?N France
	Feerwore	Fibula, axehead	?W France

Table 6.2 Some later British La Tène imports in Ireland (AD 1–100+)

La Tène period	Site	Object	Source
	Newry	Armlet	Scotland
	Antrim	Terret	NE England
	Lambay	Torc	NE England
	Loughey	Fibula	S England
	Derrybeg	Fibula	S England
		Earliest horse bits	Yorkshire
		Beehive querns (type B1)	E England
	Ballymoney	Mirror handle	E England
	Carrickfergus	Tankard	Wales
	Lambay	Bronze plaque	Wales
	Dunmore	Linchpin	SE England
		Ring-headed pins	SW England
	Edenderry	Tazza	S England
		Nauheim fibulae	S England

Britain offers considerably more instances of La Tène imports into Ireland, as one might expect from an adjacent island.[80] There are several aspects of Ireland's connection with Britain that need to be emphasized here. First, although the evidence for contacts appears to begin perhaps a little later than the Continental evidence, it increases markedly through time, especially in the early centuries AD. We have already seen that the sources of the British parallels are not localized within Britain, and there is no suggestion that there was a specific region from which La Tène connections with Ireland were initiated or sustained. There are very strong ties in material culture with western Scotland (e.g. there too we find the manufacture of bronze spear butts), but the dating evidence is insufficient to indicate whether the Irish material is older or younger than that found in Scotland. In addition to Scotland, there were also close contacts with northern England, including some evidence that people migrated from northern England to Lambay Island, off the coast of Dublin, where they left their cemetery and an assortment of British and Roman goods dating from the 1st century AD.[81] It is also from this area that we can most easily derive the beehive quern. Conversely, there is also evidence of Irish cultural influences on Scotland in the first centuries BC and AD.[82] Similarly, one can make a case for contacts with northwest Wales, the Isle of Man and southern England. Moreover, the evidence also suggests that Irish material was exported to all of these regions of Britain.

Finally, among the purported foreign objects there is one that everyone agrees must have come from abroad: in the Iron Age levels of Navan Fort were found the remains of the head and jaw of a Barbary ape, an animal that is hardly native to Co. Armagh. Barbary apes were regularly kept as house pets across the Mediterranean and presented as royal gifts, and one of the more likelier contexts for its presence in Ireland is as a gift carried along the coasts of Atlantic Europe, presumably by a Carthaginian ship that exported apes from North Africa or southern Spain.[83]

Burial

Irish Iron Age burials continue the Late Bronze Age tradition, employing cremation in a ring barrow (a mound circled by a shallow ditch and an external bank) or in the ditch surrounding the barrow. A good example is Carrowjames, Co. Mayo, where at least 25 cremations were recovered from under the mound. The Carrowjames burials occur within a cemetery of Middle Bronze Age burials, and this association with earlier monuments occurs sufficiently often to be a striking feature. For example, the passage tomb cemetery at Carrowmore, Co. Sligo, also yields the later insertion of

Iron Age remains, while a passage tomb at Kiltierney, Co. Fermanagh (6.25), became the centre of a series of Iron Age satellite tombs involving cremations accompanied by fibulae and glass beads. Again, the great passage tomb at Knowth later became the centre of Iron Age burial activity where some 30 inhumation burials, two of which were decapitations, date from about the 2nd century AD and later. In the ditch surrounding Carrowbeg North, Co. Galway, a Middle Bronze Age mound, four Iron Age inhumations were inserted, while Iron Age cremations were found in two Bronze Age mounds of Pollacorragune, Co. Galway.

6.25. Iron Age burials around Neolithic passage tomb at Kiltierney, Co. Fermanagh.

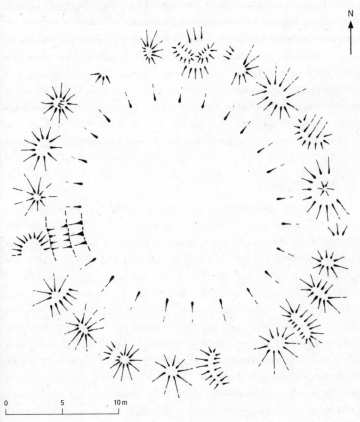

0   5   10 m

This reuse or attempt to associate with earlier monuments might be explained in a practical way: an existing barrow and ditch provides an already 'sacred' area for the disposal of the dead, and later burials can be inserted with much less labour than preparing a ring barrow from scratch. The reuse of such mounds has been cited as evidence of continuity between the Bronze Age and the Iron Age.[84] But in the Ukraine and southern Russia, earthen barrows erected in the period *c.* 3000 BC were reused repeatedly for burial until at least the Middle Ages among a wide variety of presumably unrelated ethnic groups, so continuity cannot be guaranteed as an explanation. All we can say is that after a dearth of mortuary evidence in the Late Bronze Age we may be dealing with a cultural shift and that in the first centuries BC and AD there was a deliberate attempt by people in Ireland to associate themselves with the physical monuments of a distant past. However, it is exceedingly difficult to attribute these Iron Age burials to a foreign population, including those from immediately across the Irish Sea. While Iron Age burials in Britain also occur only sporadically (on a regional basis the British dead are also archaeologically invisible), what little we do know suggests that they come in a variety of categories (e.g. inhumations with carts, inhumations in long stone cist graves) that are conspicuous by their absence in Ireland.[85] Generally, British burials remain inhumation except for those in southeast Britain, where cremation emerges in the first centuries BC but the remains are then placed in an urn. None of this is really comparable with what we find in Ireland.

La Tène colonists?

Did foreigners settle in Ireland and introduce the La Tène horizon or 'Developed Iron Age'? The evidence, as we have seen, is far from clear. In favour of at least intimate contacts is the adoption of a totally new artistic style of Continental origin. It might be argued that this provided an emblematic shift in identity among the elite in Ireland, one that was not shared across the entire island as it is so sparsely known from Munster. Furthermore, in terms of its heavy focus on horse gear, the Irish La Tène parallels the La Tène adoption in Britain as well. That La Tène objects in Ireland are overwhelmingly regarded as being of local manufacture does not militate against some migrant smiths who, once removed from their original clientele, were free to develop local styles and extend La Tène decoration to objects not found in Britain or to abandon certain types of artifacts. That we are dealing with some movement of population hardly strains credibility, but that it betokens a substantial influx of colonists is also hardly in evidence. We would need evidence from the domestic sector to support anything more than some smiths, traders and warriors. There we have two lines of evidence. The spread of beehive querns to Ireland does relate to the economic foundation of society and might be regarded as evidence for some population movement. Another possible strong cultural link with Britain may be the abandonment of ceramics. It might seem odd to regard the absence of ceramics in western Britain and in Ireland as points of comparison, but the apparently simultaneous rejection of a domestic craft that had existed in both regions for nearly 4,000 years (and which would resume again after the Iron Age) appears to be a conscious cultural rejection that links the two regions where it occurred.

Yet after such comparisons we must deal with some rather profound differences. The ceremonial architecture of the Irish 'royal sites' finds no parallels in Britain, and the Irish linear earthworks also seem to be on a scale not seen in Britain. Both the ceremonial sites and the earthworks (if not themselves also ceremonial) involved the largest-scale workforces that we can see in the Irish Iron Age: that they are unique to Ireland seems to speak for the emergence of local elites rather than foreigners. It is not just the fact that Irish ritual sites lack British predecessors, but that British sites are so different from what we find in Ireland. That the sites may at times appear to anchor themselves deliberately in earlier local sites or traditions is, unfortunately, a double-edged argument which could equally signal locals emphasizing tradition and foreigners attempting to foster the illusion of continuity.

The Roman problem

In popular accounts of Irish history, the Romans play little or no part in discussions of the origins of the Irish, although the course of Irish history is often seen to have been 'irradiated' by its proximity to Roman culture in Britain. In short, Romans have traditionally been explained in terms of 'influence' but not 'presence' when dealing with the development of Ireland, and much of that influence was seen to have ridden on the back of the Christian missions to Ireland. Returning to our occasional guide, R. A. S. Macalister, this is what he wrote in 1928:

> The Romans made no direct impression on the country.
> A provincial king invited Agricola to invade the country, in order to
> further some interests of his own; and it is possible that Agricola so far
> accepted as to send a legion on what proved to be a tentative and
> abortive expedition. Something of the kind seems to be required to

explain a reference in Juvenal. But this expedition, if it ever took place, passed away, leaving no sign except, perhaps, a lost coin or two; and Ireland remained outside the empire.[86]

As we will see in Chapter 9, already by the 2nd century AD we will have conclusive evidence that the predecessor to the Irish language was in place, so one might imagine that we have a straight run between the Iron Age (c. 700–600 BC to AD 400) and our target Irishman of the 5th century. By AD 500–600 the impact of Christianity from Roman Britain could be reduced to a paraphrase from the well-known joke: aside from major improvements to agriculture and stock-raising, and changes in settlement type, dress, ornament, tools, weapons, literacy, vocabulary, art and religion, what did the Romans ever do for Ireland?[87] Or, less flippantly, we can quote Harold Mytum, who attributes the changes to:

the new religion and with it the institution of the church. Even though many were not initially converted, the whole nature of society was transformed; the change was far more than just one of religion. Indeed, archaeologically most of the change appears to be related to settlement, subsistence agriculture and technology. The old order was completely revolutionised in all aspects of life.[88]

The traditional view would thus hold that the major changes in Irish society were the product of contacts between Ireland and Britain around and after the time of the first missions in Ireland of Palladius and Patrick (c. AD 430–60). We would conclude our chronological survey of Irish origins by imagining a pagan La Tène Ireland (c. AD 100–400) passing directly into an early Christian Ireland (c. AD 400–1200), largely through the spread of Christianity as well as the closer association between Ireland and Britain brought about by the brief period of early Irish colonialism when the Irish settled in both Scotland and Wales.[89]

Yet there is some evidence that contradicts Macalister's rejection of the Romans making a 'direct impression' on Ireland. He might reduce their presence to a 'lost coin or two', but in fact, it has been claimed that Ireland boasts something on the order of 2,500 Roman coins, though even this number is trivial when compared with Britain.[90] The real irony is that in some ways it seems easier to demonstrate a Roman presence in Ireland than it is to prove an Iron Age intrusion. Clearly, we need to have a better grasp of what happened in Ireland in the centuries before the advent of Christianity. This is the period termed the Late Iron Age (*c.* AD 1–400) according to the systematizing of all Irish Iron Age radiocarbon dates.[91] It is roughly contemporary with the period from the Roman colonization of Britain under Claudius (AD 43) until the end of the Roman period (*c.* 410–30) or beginning of the Sub-Roman period. In Ireland this is naturally still known as the Late Iron Age and not the Roman period because we seem to have a continuity of the local population across the island. The survey of radiocarbon dates recovers most of the types of sites we saw earlier during the first centuries BC. So for the 'native Irish' we still have dates from hearths, pits, postholes and ditches; trackways continue, as do furnaces for producing iron and the occasional fulachta fiadh. And there is Iron Age activity at earlier ceremonial sites such as a wedge tomb at Altar, Co. Cork, and the ditch surrounding a stone circle from Reenascreena South, Co. Cork. But we should also note that the number of Late Iron Age dates is less than for the preceding period and, as suggested above, there may have been a reduction in population.[92]

The material culture dated to the four centuries before *c.* 400 is difficult to interpret. Some of the material fits well within the La Tène, but its parallels in Britain would generally seem to be confined to the 1st century AD as the spread of Roman culture there brought the British La Tène to an end. Ireland probably continued to make objects in the La Tène style *c.* 100–400, but these cannot be confidently dated.[93] Some material has been dated using radiocarbon; however, it is rather meagre and often dates to the 1st century AD at best. So we seem to have an Ireland characterized by its La Tène component, now on its last legs and disappearing at an unknown date, and radiocarbon-dated pits, postholes, furnaces and the like. The rest of the material culture, on the other hand, may be associated with Roman Britain. Of this material, no one disputes that by the 5th century it is connected with the impact of Christian missions from Sub-Roman Britain and the mutual connections between Ireland and Irish colonists in southwest Britain. The problem is the evidence for the impact of Romano-British culture on Ireland before the 5th century.

Romans and the Holy Island

Ireland was known to the ancient world by a variety of names. Most of these are Romanized variations on one of the Irish self-designations: **Iweru* as 'Hibernia',[94] *Iérnē* or *Iwernia*,[95] or, via Greek, the 'holy island'.[96] Other names that obviously did not stick were 'little Britain'[97] and, on one occasion, *Scotia*.[98] Why the Romans or indeed anyone else should have wanted to come to Ireland is a mystery if the early classical descriptions of the island had provided copy for Roman travel brochures.

Ireland was at the western edge of the world in Ptolemy's atlas and – like Timbuktu, paired with Sri Lanka in later times – was representative of the far ends of the known world.[99] As its geographical location was at the northern margins of human knowledge it was generally presumed to be so cold that human existence was barely possible.[100] So far from 'civilization', the Irish were naturally wild and crude, even 'more savage than the Britons' and 'unfriendly and warlike'. Strabo depicted the occupants of Ireland as cannibals and gluttons who copulated with their mothers and sisters.[101] When St Jerome wanted to ridicule his theological opponent Pelagius, he accused him of Irish (Scotti) ancestry, glutted on Scotti porridge.[102] Was there anything at all positive that one could say about the place? Well, it did have such abundant plains of grass (according to Pomponius Mela) that the livestock could eat their fill in a very short time and, unless checked in their gluttony, would burst.[103] And Solinus observed that the island lacked snakes.[104] Although the historical evidence is quite meagre, the Romans did take some interest in Ireland that went beyond the niche tourist market for those who longed to see cows explode in a serpent-free environment.

One of the most oft-cited sources is Tacitus's biography of his father-in-law, Agricola, the general who pushed the Roman conquest of Britain past its southern enclave to include northern England and Scotland. Agricola is credited with claiming that he could take and hold Ireland with a force of a legion (c. 5,000–6,000 men) and auxiliaries (100–1,000 men), about a quarter of the force that had been employed in seizing southern Britain – perhaps not quite an insult to Irish manly pride when one considers that Ireland is about one-fourth the size of Britain. About AD 82 he built forts along the western coast, facing Ireland, not 'out of fear but hope', presumably intending that these would serve as staging ports for an invasion. He even held a political card, an Irish king who had been driven out, so Agricola could have played Strongbow to this anonymous Dermot MacMurrough.[105] So far we have intent but hardly enough evidence to convict. This comes (if at all) from the Roman writer Juvenal, who wrote that the Romans:

> have advanced arms beyond the shores of Iuverna [Ireland] and the
> recently captured Orkneys and the mighty Britons with their short
> nights…[106]

Interpretations of these lines run the gamut from poetic exaggeration to concrete evidence for a Roman invasion of Ireland.[107]

Perhaps the clearest thing we can take from these accounts is Tacitus's observation that 'the approaches and harbours [of Ireland] are [better] known due to trade and merchants'.[108] This is best borne out by over 50 names of tribes, rivers, islands and other places recorded in Ptolemy's gazetteer of the known world that begins with Ireland. Such geographical detail has generally been attributed to British merchants in Irish waters and attests to at least a fair knowledge of the ports and major inland waterways of Ireland.

The concrete evidence for a Roman presence in Ireland, and here we mean anyone in the Roman empire who had embraced Roman culture, is fairly far-ranging but always open to various interpretations.[109] Obviously, portable objects such as coins – as many as 1,506 in a hoard from Ballinrees, Co. Londonderry (6.26), which also included 5.7 kg of silver ingots and plate,[110] sourced to southern England – have

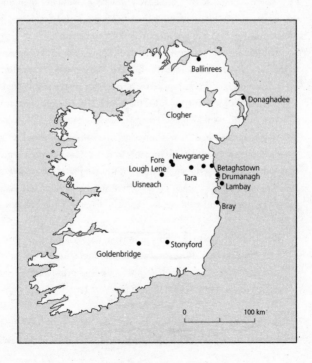

6.26. Map of Roman period sites mentioned in Chapter 6.

been treated as anything from ritual deposits to merchants' hoards, booty taken back to Ireland by Irish raiders in the early 5th century (the most recent coin dates to c. AD 420), payments made to Irish soldiers serving as auxiliaries in the Roman army or an official bribe to keep the Irish from raiding Britain. The first of these interpretations is the most likely explanation for the 25 Roman coins found around the entrance of the famous Neolithic passage tomb at Newgrange that date from the 1st to the beginning of the 5th century, though mainly from the 4th century. Also found in addition to the coins were gold ornaments, including the terminal of an Irish Bronze Age torc that had been cut up and inscribed in Roman letters. All of this points to Newgrange as a place of pilgrimage and while we cannot be certain of the identity of the pilgrims, one at least appears to have been literate.[111] Charles Thomas has suggested that the offerings might have been made by Roman merchants who employed such ceremonies to impress the local population and secure rights to the Irish market.[112] Similar finds have been recovered at other ritual sites such as the Rath of the Synods at Tara and at Uisneach, Co. Westmeath. While some of this could be explained as the activity of native populations who, like their ancestors, utilized exotic materials as offerings, other evidence is more easily explained by accepting the presence of visitors or immigrants from Roman Britain.

The literary sources speak of merchants plying the Irish coast and their presence in Ireland is archaeologically supported. The discovery of a Roman storage jar 240 km off the west coast of Ireland suggests the presence (and possible fate) of one of these merchant ships. More enigmatic are the remains of a wooden boat from Lough Lene, Co. Westmeath, fashioned according to Mediterranean techniques as if a Roman boatwright himself had been involved.[113] In all there are about 85 Roman ceramic vessels known in Ireland,[114] presumably trade objects, although it must be admitted that some (much?) of the single sherds of Roman pottery may have been brought to Ireland long after the Roman period.[115] We also have about 25 Roman fibulae.[116] By the 4th century we might therefore expect, as Charles Thomas has written:

> Roman Britons actually living in Ireland; engaged in trade, perhaps
> managing boats, staffing small mercantile concerns, buying the
> necessary protection from Irish potentates and priests, and in one
> degree or another involved in Irish life.[117]

By the 5th century (if not before) the Roman Britons had also brought Christianity to Ireland, either as settlers or, like St Patrick, as slaves. By 431 their number was sufficient to induce the pope to send Palladius as the first bishop to the Christians of Ireland,[118] and St Patrick arrived in the following year. But again, is there still earlier evidence for the Roman impact that would indicate a prehistoric Romano-British presence in Ireland?

Two sites provide serious evidence for the earlier settlement of foreigners in Ireland. At Clogher, Co. Tyrone, Richard Warner excavated a hillfort that has an un-Irish sub-rectangular shape and appears to date within the Iron Age, although strict dating evidence from the site is admittedly quite poor. So too is the context of the finds from within the fort, but here at least some objects can be cross-dated. A Roman-type brooch, for example, is set to the 1st century AD as well as some imported ceramics. Warner observes that the fort failed to produce any native Iron Age objects but it 'did produce a not-insignificant number of imported Romano-British objects'.[119] A survey of finds from the surrounding region suggests both native Irish and Romano-British material from the first centuries BC and AD. But as for the occupants of Clogher, Warner argues that they were 'settlers from Britain'.[120]

The other case for substantial foreign settlement is Drumanagh, Co. Dublin, a coastal promontory fort defended by three closely spaced ditches. The site yielded Roman pottery (1st century AD), coins (2nd century AD) and ornaments, in quantities unspecified as it has been the subject of litigation for many years.[121] The site has been interpreted as anything from a Roman military camp (and the clearest evidence for invasion) to a trading emporium (implying peaceful exchange, especially as the site produced native Irish material as well) and is reputed, within certain archaeological circles, to offer the most spectacular Roman material ever recovered from an Irish archaeological site.

Finally, we have the evidence of imported Roman material in burials. In almost all cases, the presumption is that the individual interred was a Roman or Romano-Briton who was buried by fellow Romans or Romano-Britons. One of the earliest of these, dating to the 1st century BC, comprised cremated remains deposited in a bronze bowl found in a pit at Fore, Co. Westmeath. The bowl (and presumably the individual buried within it) came from southern Britain. Another presumably cremation burial from near Donaghadee, Co. Down, was accompanied by a set of foreign grave goods (beads, fibula, tweezers, two rings) that came either from southern Britain or possibly the Continent. Most other intrusive burials bear witness to contacts with the Roman (British) world. At Lambay Island, off the coast of Dublin, we have a series of inhumation burials accompanied by Roman fibulae and other goods (including a long iron sword) that appear to derive from northern England in the late 1st century AD, the territory of the Brigantes. At Stonyford, Co. Kilkenny, we have a classic Roman burial, possibly of a woman, whose ashes were placed in a glass urn and accompanied by typical Roman goods (a mirror and bottle; 6.27). At Bray, Co. Wicklow, there are inhumations accompanied by Roman coins of the 2nd century AD, and a series of inhumations from Betaghstown, Co. Meath, also derived from the Roman world. Indeed, it is argued that a shift from native cremation burial to inhumation was prompted by contacts with the Roman world after the 1st century AD.[122] A series of other such burials have been discovered, including an intriguing one from Goldenbridge, Co. Tipperary, which included a stone stamp that was used to identify an eye-salve that had been prepared for the son of one Marcus Tutianus.

What does all this add up to? Obviously, one explanation for the portable goods such as coins, toilette kits, pottery, etc. could be that they were the possessions of people from Ireland who had visited, served in the army and/or raided Britain and brought Roman material home with them. Nevertheless, there is also some fairly convincing evidence for foreign populations in Ireland in the first centuries AD. This is particularly seen in the burial evidence, especially the Stonyford burial, where we find thoroughly Roman(ized) material culture and behaviour. The dead do not bury themselves, and such an exotic burial, complete with the appropriate kit of Roman objects, is hardly the work of a distraught husband burying his foreign wife in a strange land. It is more likely, especially when taken with the other evidence for Roman burial, to reflect small communities of Romans and/or Roman Britons that were of sufficient size to sustain their own cultural practices.

Archaeologists do not treat objects, especially exotic imports, as merely items of trade but recognize that they probably had a meaning to the people who acquired them. Changes in ornament, dress and the importation of new toilette kits, for example, may have been ways of adopting and signalling new identities.[123] If one, for example, follows Warner's discussion of the 1st-century AD material from around Clogher, Co. Tyrone, some of the population may have worn traditional Irish La Tène material and others adopted Romano-British kit. Did these objects mark a symbolic battlefield between those who regarded themselves as La Tène and those who now wished to identify with the new Roman way? To some extent this depends on how the owners came by these goods. If the foreign objects were plunder, retrieved during Irish raids on Britain, it is doubtful that they would have provided a new identity to their owners (one could have worn both La Tène and Romano-British bling). Indeed, Harold Mytum has dismissed raiding as a likely source of social change in Ireland, as it was probably already endemic in Irish society and resulted in the taking

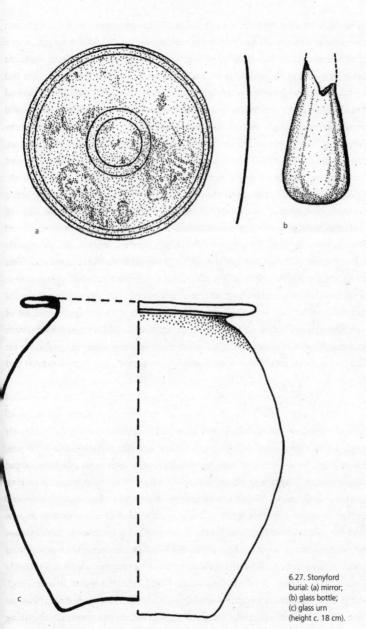

6.27. Stonyford
burial: (a) mirror;
(b) glass bottle;
(c) glass urn
(height c. 18 cm).

of slaves, who were hardly role models that one might want to emulate.[124] He also raises the possibility of Irish mercenary veterans as the vehicles for Romanization. That some of the Roman material belonged to returning soldiers has been advanced as an attractive explanation for the Ballinrees hoard of silver coins and plate, but Mytum also questions the returning veteran as a vehicle for altering identity in Ireland. He reasons that soldiers abroad would probably stick to their own kind and hardly integrate deeply enough into Romano-British society to return to Ireland spreading Roman culture. The most likely vehicle for Romanization would have been kinship ties among people whose families were spread between Ireland and Britain. This became a serious factor with Irish settlement in Britain, especially southwest Wales, where Irish colonists from Munster settled in the 4th and 5th centuries, retaining their identity or at least their Irish names (as indicated by inscriptions). But all these mechanisms – raiding, veterans, colonists – are probably features of the 4th and 5th centuries. The major Irish (Scotti) raids into northern Britain, for example, are dated historically to AD 360, and the shift to Scotland of the royal house of the Dál Riata, the dynasty that came to rule both northeast Ireland and southwest Scotland, is set to c. 500, while the Irish settlement of southwest Wales is similarly dated to the 4th century[125] or later.[126] The evidence of the first two centuries AD speaks perhaps for something different and, while the evidence for traders and Romano-British settlers in Ireland may not be abundant, it does come from a significant percentage of the sites uncovered from this extremely poorly known period.

Summary

As generations of Irish archaeologists have indicated, there is really no convincing evidence for a substantial migration into Ireland by either Hallstatt or La Tène communities. If we were to compare, for example, the evidence for the Anglo-Saxon migrations to Britain with all the evidence adduced for Iron Age Continental or British migrations to Ireland, the difference in terms of plausibility is at several orders of magnitude. This is not to say that there were no population exchanges over the course of the Iron Age. But the most convincing evidence for any intrusive populations comes not with the onset of the Iron Age but during the first four centuries AD and is associated with the Romano-British populations who had settled in Ireland. This accounts for the foreign burials found in Ireland that suggest the establishment of some small foreign communities. Whether they occupied elite positions that went beyond the realm of traders and craftsmen depends to some extent on how one interprets the foreign finds from Clogher, Co. Tyrone. But at least we can imagine trading outposts with ethnically Romano-British populations, especially where we find imported material on coasts or along rivers. That there may have been some British settlement of a more substantial nature is supported to a certain extent by the linguistic evidence that we will review in Chapter 9.

As for earlier periods, we find ourselves acknowledging that contacts between Ireland and Britain can be clearly discerned and may well have involved the movement of restricted numbers of craftsmen and possibly families throughout the entire Iron Age. This would help explain the introduction of iron metallurgy and the spread of material either originating in Britain or at least passing through, e.g. Gündlingen swords and La Tène metalwork, especially horse gear. The presence of such material in proportions comparable to those found in Britain also suggests that Irish elites, at least in the northern two-thirds of the island, were adopting the same symbols of prestige as their British counterparts. On the other hand, Ireland was far from just being the end recipient of a series of innovations, but clearly also had its own regional identity in the manufacture of La Tène decorated items that were not common or were completely unknown in Britain or on the Continent. In addition, there are probably as many Irish objects known from Britain as British objects recovered from Ireland.

Conclusions

→ There is no convincing evidence that the Irish Iron Age was introduced by a military incursion from abroad.

→ There is some evidence that the comparability of material culture and the earliest iron metallurgy in Britain and Ireland during the Early Iron Age does allow for some movement of populations between the two islands.

→ The Irish La Tène is primarily an elite art style that appears to derive from no specific part of the La Tène world, although it does reveal imports from both Britain and the Continent.

→ The Irish La Tène was restricted to the northern two-thirds of the island while Munster was engaged in an Iron Age that did not privilege the La Tène art style.

→ The Irish La Tène in general includes the same categories of artifacts as in Britain but shows a number of distinct regional developments.

→ The major ritual sites of the Irish Iron Age lack any convincing foreign antecedents and should be regarded as the creation of native elites.

→ There is some possible evidence for population movements into Ireland during the so-called Developed Iron Age, seen in the spread of beehive querns and the abandonment of ceramics.

→ The best evidence for foreign populations in Ireland appears during the Later Iron Age, when material and behaviour of a clearly Romano-British origin are found in Ireland.

CHAPTER SEVEN

The Native Version

T he career of Niall predates almost but not quite all our evidence for what the Irish tell us of their own origins. Several centuries after his death, from about the 7th or 8th century, we get the first hints of what would become the native version of Irish origins.[1] Earlier pagan traditions were absorbed into an entirely new Christian model, allowing Irish ancestral figures to claim genealogies that could be traced back to Adam. The pagan past was effectively incorporated into a new narrative that constituted, as Kim McCone has described it, 'a kind of "Old Testament" of the Irish race'.[2] The various legends, myths and, as we will see, learned borrowings (in some cases outright plagiarism) were formally put together in the 11th century in what is known as the *Lebor Gabála Érenn* (LG) – literally, the 'book of the invasions of Ireland' – which relates a series of failed colonizations before the final settlement of Ireland by what an 8th-century Irishman would regard as his own people.[3] Much of the information was incorporated into the Annals of the Four Masters,[4] admittedly a very late source, which at least provides us with spurious but convenient absolute dates reckoned according to a chronology that set the creation of the world (*Anno Mundi 1*) to 5200 BC.

Earliest settlers

The first settlement of Ireland is attributed to Cessair, the granddaughter of Noah, who came to Ireland (in AM 2242 according to the Annals of the Four Masters, i.e. 2958 BC). Finding that there was no room for her on the Ark, Cessair was advised by her grandfather to take a ship and flee to the western edge of the world: Ireland, a land with no people and hence no sin. She led a demographically intriguing group of 50 women and three men, who came ashore in Co. Kerry. One of the males, Ladhra, died and was buried in Wexford. The second, Bith, then died (according to one account he overdosed on women, as he found himself servicing not only his own 17 women

Tory Island

Lough Derg

Emain Macha

Teltown   Slieve Beagh
Uisneach   Tara

Slieve Mish

Kenmare

Bull Rock

0   100 km

7.1. Map of places
mentioned in Chapter 7.

but also those of Ladhra) and was buried on Slieve Beagh (7.1). Some versions also kill off the third male, Fintan, the husband of Cessair, who is buried at Lough Derg, Co. Donegal, but a far more entertaining version has the entire troop of grieving widows charging after Fintan. In order to escape what could have been an endless series of extremely exhausting nights he either hid in a cave (in Co. Tipperary) or dived into Lough Derg, turned himself into a salmon to survive for thousands of years and was later reconstituted as a man to relate (in verse) the history of Ireland's colonizations. Excepting Ireland's first archaeologist, Fintan, no human survived the Flood that washed over Ireland 40 days after Cessair's arrival. Although one version of the *Lebor Gábala* also credits Cessair with introducing sheep to Ireland,[5] they were presumably drowned as well.

Although the Flood ends the first attempted colonization of Ireland (in what we would recognize as the late Neolithic), it sets in motion the eventual emergence of the Irish. After the Flood, Noah's three sons – Shem, Ham and Japheth – and their descendants populated the world. From Shem derive the Semites, Ham is the ancestor of the Hamitic peoples and Japheth colonized Europe. This is the basic medieval paradigm that was widely accepted across Europe, so much so that scholars interested in the linguistic relationships between European languages in the 17th and 18th centuries would use the word Japhetic (or Scythian, as Scythia was regarded as a major part of Japheth's territory) to describe the languages of Europe. While Shem fathered 27 nations and Ham was the ancestor of 30, Japheth only founded 15 peoples. After the biblical sources dried up, Irish monks had a field day creating the names of the descendants of Japheth who might serve as the founding fathers of the various peoples of Europe, e.g. Grecus, Espanus, Romanus, Francus, Britus, Gotus, Saxus and Vandalus. The Gaels (Irish) descended (their name derived) from Gáedel Glas, whose mother (incidentally, the daughter of an Egyptian pharaoh) Scotta gave her name to the Scotti (Irish). From a linguistic point of view we should probably assume that Cessair and her people spoke Gorthigern (Hebrew), but all other settlers were *rifath Scot* 'the progeny of Scotta' and hence spoke the same language as the Irish. The Irish language was synthesized after the Tower of Babel, when the world fragmented into 72 languages and peoples. Gáedel Glas is credited with having distilled the Gaelic language out of the best elements of these 72 languages, although students of Old Irish might have cause to be sceptical of this claim. Anyway, the presumption that all other colonizers spoke Irish suggests that language alone was an insufficient guide to whether one was *really* Irish.

The second colonization occurred in AM 2520 (2680 BC) under Partholón, identified as the great-great-great-great-great-grandson of Japheth, who came to Ireland from Sicily (by way of Spain) to arrive on 17 May (a Tuesday, according to the LG). This was a serious colonizing force that introduced into Ireland cattle-raising (four oxen), the plough, land clearance, house building, querns, gold and brewing (fern ale, no doubt an acquired taste as it had to be drunk through a tube of red gold). Partholón also fought a major battle against the (one-armed and one-legged) Fomorians in Ireland. But in AM 2820 (2380 BC) the entire population of Ireland was wiped out by a plague.

Thirty years later (AM 2850 or 2350 BC) Nemed led the third group of colonists. We are told that he had 44 ships sailing about the Caspian Sea for a year and a half, but only his ship reached Ireland (a remarkable achievement nevertheless, considering that the Caspian Sea is landlocked). Nemed himself died of plague, but his followers occupied Ireland for 216 years and under their supervision the plains were cleared and the Fomorians were forced to build the first forts (though the workers were slain before they could finish the job). The Fomorians eventually managed to turn the tables on the followers of Nemed, whom they reduced to servitude. Harried by the Fomorians, Nemed's followers finally attacked the Fomorian capital at the Tower of Conand (Tory Island, Co. Donegal), where the mutual slaughter reduced Nemed's men to a handful who were then scattered across the world. Among them was Semeon, who settled in Greece, where his descendants swelled in number but were placed in servitude. From these people emerged the Fir Bolg, the next colonizers of Ireland and the first whose descendants survived into the historic period.

Fir Bolg and Tuatha Dé Danann

While still in servitude in Greece, the Fir Bolg were forced to work on a major landscape project by dragging soil in bags (the popular etymology of their name is 'Bag men') to convert barren mountains into tillable fields. Five thousand of them managed to escape (along with their bags) and set off under five kings to arrive in Ireland in AM 3266 (1934 BC). The *Lebor Gabála* emphasizes that this represented a 'return' to Ireland, as they were the descendants of the earlier Nemed. This theme of return migrations is deeply embedded in Irish tradition. The Fir Bolg occupied Ireland for 37 years through a succession of quarrelling kings. It was during their reign that spears were introduced into Ireland – not too bad a guess, as bronze-tipped spears appear about this time during the Early Bronze Age. On the other hand, associating the first knots in trees with the Fir Bolg is simply weird.

Meanwhile, other distant descendants of Nemed were off in the north learning magic and sorcery. These emerge as the Tuatha Dé Danann, 'people of the goddess Danu', who arrived under cover of dark clouds in the year AM 3303 (1897 BC). Challenging the Fir Bolg for the kingship of Ireland, they defeated the Fir Bolg in the first Battle of Mag Tuired. After severe hardships under King Bres, the Tuatha Dé Danann fought a rematch at Mag Tuired (AM 3330 or 1870 BC) which involved a host of characters familiar to anyone who has studied the mythology of the ancient Irish. The Irish account of this battle has been widely compared with the major eschatological, i.e. end-of-the-world, battles of other peoples of Europe and Asia.[6]

Cultural contributions of the Tuatha Dé Danann are not numerous other than the specific four gifts (talismans) that they brought to Ireland: the Lia Fail (stone of destiny), the spear of Lug, the sword of Nuadu and the cauldron of the Dagda. They also introduced board games, ball games and horse racing.

Sons of Míl

The final conquerors of Ireland arrived in AM 3500 (1700 BC) from Spain. These were the followers of Míl Espáine, the 'soldier of Spain'; however, they had an impeccable pedigree as descendants of Gáedel Glas who had come across the Mediterranean and conquered Spain. From there, atop the Tower of Bregon, Íth son of Bregon caught sight of Ireland and sailed there with 150 warriors. In contrast to the negative descriptions of Ireland that permeate most Roman accounts, Íth described it as rich in acorns, honey, wheat and fish, with a balanced climate.[7] Jealous of Íth's ability to make wise judgments, the three resident kings of Ireland murdered him, after which the Sons of Míl set off to take Ireland in revenge. Where they first landed is uncertain because there are conflicting accounts. One would have them land in Munster while the other indicates Ulster.[8] They were victorious in a series of battles at Sliab Mis (Slieve Mish, Co. Kerry) and Tailtin (Teltown, Co. Meath), thus destroying the power (kings and queens) of the Tuatha Dé Danann and establishing Irish rule over the island in the following year. It might be emphasized that among the Sons of Míl were Éber(us), i.e. 'Irishman' (from *Hībernus* 'Ireland' in Latin) and Éremón 'Irishman' (from *Ériu* 'Ireland' in Irish) and that each arrived with his followers in different halves of Ireland.[9]

The ensuing history is a story of further battles, usually internal but also periodically against the Fir Bolg or Fomorians, and cultural innovations: e.g. the establishment of many forts (1671 BC), the introduction of gold smelting and the covering of brooches and vessels with gold and silver (1544 BC), the colour coding of clothes to indicate status (1536 BC), the presentation of silver shields to the men of Ireland (1383 BC), the wearing of gold chains by kings (1328 BC) and then gold rings ten years later, the establishment of the feast of Tara (1278 BC), the digging of the first wells for water (1209 BC), the introduction of the four-horse chariot (1024 BC), and the establishment of Emain Macha as the Ulster capital (668 BC). It should be noted that while some have suggested there is a level of historicity to some of these dates, by and large they are obviously wrong (for example, the presence of silver in Ireland is generally 1,500–2,000 years later than the dates given; gold was worked in Ireland many centuries before the Annals suggest; no four-horse chariots are known, etc.).[10]

Interpretations

The traditional account of Irish origins may seem pure fable, but it has had a lasting impact on how the Irish imagined their prehistory up into the 20th century.[11] More relevant, perhaps, is whether traditional lore has any bearing on our pursuit of Irish origins, other than providing us with an indication of how the medieval Irish explained their own origins. While parts of the story can be fairly easily dismissed, there will always be some who object to dismissing all the Irish internal evidence as fantasy. For example, Seamus Caulfield's study of Irish origins suggests that his contention that the southern half of Ireland possessed a non-La Tène Iberian orientation during the Iron Age receives some support from the Milesian legend of Ireland being divided between two brothers, one ruling the southern half of Ireland and the other the north.[12] Employing the linguistic evidence that we will review in Chapter 9, Miles Dillon suggests that one way of resolving the question of the linguistic origin of the Irish is to assume 'that the Milesian Goidels did come from Spain as the Book of the Invasions says'.[13] Indeed, the geneticist Stephen Oppenheimer notes that a series of genetic expansions from Iberia is still consistent with the narrative in the *Lebor Gabála Érenn*.[14] Probably the greatest exponent of employing the literary evidence to resolve the problem of Irish origins was Thomas O'Rahilly in his 1946 study *Early Irish History and Mythology*.

While acknowledging that the *Lebor Gabála* might generally be 'described as a deliberate work of fiction', O'Rahilly argued that the modern scholar can still derive value from both the agenda of its compiler and the content of the work itself.[15] The agenda, according to O'Rahilly, was to deal with the fact that the early medieval Irish knew that the island had seen a series of invasions of different peoples from whom various dynasties or families might trace their origin. The LG acknowledges the multiple origins of the people of Ireland but then unites them all by providing a common descent from Míl Espáine and his offspring. In fact, as Kim McCone has observed, the *Lebor Gabála* was continually expanded to incorporate more dynasties and afford them all with a legitimate Irish origin.[16] Only the Fir Bolg were set aside as a resident lower class. A key element of O'Rahilly's argument was the suggestion that some of the earlier invaders, such as the Fir Bolg, were also linguistically related to Irish but belonged to the Brittonic rather than Goidelic (Irish) branch. This suggested that the Goidels were the last group of invaders, who superimposed themselves on still earlier linguistically related peoples. To make sense of this, O'Rahilly rejected the deep chronology provided in the *Lebor Gabála*, where the Sons of Míl arrived *c.* 1700 BC, and argued that the Goidels came to Ireland around the 1st century BC. He also rejected an invasion from Spain but, accepting the LG's notion of a Continental origin for the Goidels, he opted for a departure point in southern France.

Native and foreign elements

Whether or not native Irish tradition has a serious role to play in the search for Irish origins depends on our ability to discern how much of the tradition is native and how much has been pillaged from classical or Christian sources. Many of the 'nations' of early medieval Europe were very much preoccupied with providing themselves with an origin rooted in either classical or biblical antiquity. The Romans had already established a blueprint for such origin myths by tracing their ancestry back to Aeneas after he had managed to escape from Troy. The Britons derived themselves from Aeneas's son Brutus, from whom, they mistakenly argued, one can derive the name of Britain. The Germans sought their origins among the offspring of Japhet, the son of Noah, in particular Ashkenaz. As we have seen above, the Irish did one better and selected ancestors (or failed ancestors) from the classical, biblical and presumably their own native worlds. Their mythical sojourn in the Near East, for example, provided them with enough biblical credentials that they came close to passing themselves off as a lost tribe of Israel.[17] In other cases they lifted nearly directly from the origin myths of other European peoples such as the Franks.

John Carey has probably done more than anyone else in trying to ferret out the native from the purely imported elements of the Irish origin story.[18] Cessair, for example, in her role as Noah's granddaughter, derives from a biblical background but may be associated with native stories in which a woman, brought across the sea, induces a flood. Needless to say, these elements of inherited belief have little specific bearing on the question of Irish origins, and indeed many of the 'native' elements that have been drawn into the story may originally have served a different purpose. Partholón, whose name has been presumed to be derived from 'Bartholomew', i.e. 'the son of the one who holds up the waters', as the first post-flood occupant of Ireland, initiates the clearing of plains. This introduces a human agent into the formation of the Irish landscape, which was further augmented during the course of subsequent 'invasions'. The third invasion under Nemed was at least led by a king with an Irish name that designated 'privilege' or, perhaps, 'sanctuary', but this does not really get us any closer to their 'true' origins.

Into the list of early peoples the medieval Irish monks inserted their ancient deities as well, the Tuatha Dé Danann. This is also found elsewhere in early Christian accounts of the peoples of Europe, most notably in Snorri Sturlusson's account of the origins of the Norse in which the Norse god Othinn is presented as a human leader. In the *Lebor Gabála* there is still some ambiguity as to whether the Tuatha Dé Danann are demons or humans. Carey emphasizes that the Gaels, the earliest Irish, must take Ireland from a semi-divine race that ruled Ireland as part of the Otherworld. The Tuatha Dé Danann also present us with the deeply embedded notion that Irish kingship involves the mating of a male with a goddess of sovereignty or of the land. When Íth, the first Milesian leader to come from Spain, arrives in Ireland he encounters three Tuatha Dé Danann kings whose wives (Ériu, Fótla and Banba) all bear names that can be translated as 'Ireland'.

The Spanish connection

But what about the crucial geographical element of the *Lebor Gabála*, the tradition that the Irish derive themselves from Spain? Why Spain and not, say, France or Britain? Those who find the Spanish connection unconvincing argue that almost all the elements involved in constructing such an origin can be explained as essentially non-native. The name Míl Espáine is easily enough dispensed with, since it is merely an Irish translation of the Latin *miles Hispaniae* 'soldier of Spain', which can be found in the earliest account of the Milesian story recorded in the 9th-century *Historia Brittonum*, which contains in summary many of the elements of the later *Lebor Gabála*. In short, the Spanish origin myth involves the Irish being descended from someone whose name is merely Irish translation of a Latin description.

The geographical association between Iberia and Ireland can also be explained (away) by our knowledge of the geographical sources employed by the medieval Irish to embellish their origin myth.[19] Over the classical period Ireland underwent its own version of continental drift. Our earliest sources have Ireland safely tucked up to the northwest of Britain, but by the time of Julius Caesar it had drifted south. In the account of his invasion of Britain in 55–54 BC, Caesar described the location and dimensions of Britain. He wrote:

> The second side of the island [Britain] faces westward, towards Spain.
> In this direction lies Ireland, which is thought to be half the size of
> Britain and is the same distance from Britain as Gaul is.[20]

So Caesar has Ireland lying to the Spanish side of Britain and suggests that Ireland is as close to Britain as Britain is to France. The geographical relationship was repeated by the Roman writer Tacitus in AD 98:

For the possession of Ireland, situated between Britain and Spain, and
lying commodiously to the Gallic sea, would have formed a very
beneficial connection between the most powerful parts of the empire.[21]

The Spanish cleric Paulus Orosius compiled his *History against the Pagans* in AD 417,
and his description of the geographical relationship between Spain and Ireland
continues the earlier refrain. He writes that 'the island of Ireland is located between
Britain and Spain' and that the nearer portion of Ireland is situated at a good distance
opposite the Galician city of Brigantia. Moreover, in Galicia, he reports, there was a
very high tower, built to 'keep watch on Britain'.[22] This provides a fairly clear basis for
the story of Íth, who spies Ireland from the tower of Bregon.

Each of these we may merely treat as ancient accounts of the geographical relationship between Ireland and its neighbours. But the description in the *Etymologies*
of Isidore of Seville is much more than historical background. By the 7th century the
intellectual powerhouse of Latin learning in the West had moved from North Africa
or Italy to Spain, and the encyclopedic nature of Isidore's writings ensured the widest
possible audience, especially in Ireland. J. N. Hillgarth, for example, mentions that
there were at least 10 different Irish scholars who were familiar with the *Etymologies*
in the 7th century.[23] In a world where contact between scholars was distant and difficult, Isidore's encyclopedic *Etymologies* was plundered by Irish monks in the same
way that university students now pillage Wikipedia for their essays. Isidore provides
a brief description of Ireland, incorporating many of the usual classical conceptions
of the island. We read that it lacks snakes, has few birds and that the land was so
hostile to bees that Irish soil or pebbles sprinkled on a beehive would drive out the
swarm. He also, of course, tells us a little about the location of Ireland and how it got
its name:

> Ireland (*Scotia*), also known as *Hibernia*, is an island next to Britannia,
> narrower in its expanse of land but more fertile in its site. It extends
> from southwest to north. Its near parts stretch towards Iberia (*Hiberia*)
> and the Cantabrian Ocean [i.e. the Bay of Biscay], whence it is called
> *Hibernia*; but it is called *Scotia*, because it has been colonised by the
> Scoti.[24]

Isidore provides the Irish *literati* with two reasons to look to Spain for their
origins. Obviously, he again takes up the theme that Ireland and Spain are in a close

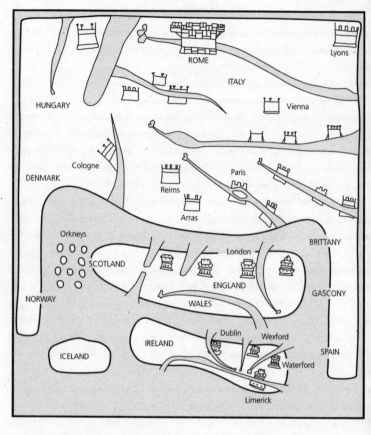

7.2. A 13th-century map of Ireland suggested that Ireland was situated opposite Iberia.

geographical relationship, the island lying distant but still off the coast of the Bay of Biscay (7.2). But here he also introduces another argument: it is because its closer parts stretch (*intendunt*) towards *Hiberiam* that it is called *Hibernia* (*unde et Hibernia dicta*). The geographical link is reinforced by the fact that the name of Ireland derives from that of Spain. Does it in fact?

Few works can beat Isidore's for justifying Voltaire's famous dismissal of etymology as an exercise in which vowels count for nothing and consonants for very little. In reality, there is absolutely no relationship whatsoever between the two words under discussion. As we have already seen, *(H)ibernia* is not an Irish name but a Latin rendering of a native Irish word that is generally reconstructed as **(h)iwerno* or *(h)iwernā* (it occurs in Ptolemy's gazetteer of Irish place and tribal names as, for example, *Iérnē*, and because it would have been written in classical Greek sources as *HIBERN- it was adopted into Latin (for example, by Julius Caesar) as *Hibernia* (there is another theory that it was helped along by the more familiar Latin word for 'wintry', *hibernus*, to give *Hibernia*). In any event, the word has nothing to do with *Hiberia* which is from *Iberia*, the ancient name of the river Ebro. The writings of Isidore, who had labelled Spain as the 'mother of races' in his *History of the Goths*, still provides no evidence for deriving the Irish from Iberia.

And while our main narrative of the Spanish origin myth is elucidated in the *Lebor Gabála*, it was actually known in outline earlier: it first appears in the *Historia Brittonum*, which dates to *c.* 830 and clearly relies on access to Irish scholarship, possibly dating to the 7th century.[25] According to the 'History':

> *Novissime autem Scotti venerunt a partibus Hispaniae ad Hiberniam*
> 'The Scotti [i.e. the Irish] came very recently from parts of Spain to
> Ireland'. The first to come was Partholomus [Partholón] who died in a
> plague with his followers. Then came Nemeth [Nemed] whose ships
> were wrecked on arrival in Ireland and he and his people stayed for
> many years before they returned (*reversus*) to Spain. Then came *tres*
> *filii militis Hispanie* 'three sons of a soldier of Spain'. They settled in
> Ireland for a year but, on seeing a glass tower in the sea, they attacked it
> in their boats except for a single damaged boat consisting of thirty men
> and thirty women. After the attackers landed at the tower, the sea
> drowned them all and only the sixty survivors in a single ship survived
> and it is from them that *tota Hibernia impleta est usque in hodienum*
> *diem* 'all Ireland was populated to this day'.[26]

So how useful is the literary evidence that associates the earliest Irish with Iberia? On balance, I think, it should not be regarded as having any bearing whatsoever – we simply cannot apply the traditional story of Irish origins to our problem. Distant folk memories, possible inklings of past historical relationships and so on are attempts to assign significance to the results of a concatenation of geographical and linguistic errors enlivened with folk motifs from other nations as well as a generous dash of imagination. There are good reasons for discussing the traditional account of Irish origins, but in terms of providing an historical solution to the problem, it offers absolutely nothing to any argument. However, we should also recall the old cliché that just because someone is paranoid, it does not mean that people aren't out to get them. The Irish could still have come from Iberia, but it will take evidence other than Irish mythology to prove it.

The House of Donn

Although our medieval learned sources do not appear to provide us with any real insight into Irish origins, within the attempt to manufacture Irish tradition as historical narrative there does seem to lie a kernel of earlier pagan beliefs. These yield some clues as to how the question 'where did the Irish come from?' might have been answered by Niall of the Nine Hostages in the 5th century. [27]

Leading the invasion of Ireland were Míl Espáine's two sons, Donn and Amairgen, and their stories seem to reach back into the kind of genuine pagan Irish tradition that should have been familiar to the man who claimed the high kingship of Ireland. When Donn and Amairgen arrive in Ireland they encounter at different locations the three queens, each of whom bears one of the ancient names for Ireland (Banba, Fótla and Ériu). At the first two meetings Amairgen, the sweet-talking brother, repeats his agreement that he will name Ireland after the woman in question. Ériu is met at Uisneach (in Co. Westmeath), seen as the centre of Ireland, and there she prophesies that the Sons of Míl will possess Ireland forever. Amairgen thanks her and promises that hers will be the main name for Ireland (a promise that has obviously been kept). Donn, however, withholds thanks, indicating that it is to his own gods that he should be giving thanks. Recalling the ancient Irish concept that kingship comprises selection by a female goddess of sovereignty, Amairgen has taken the appropriate course. Niall, if he believed the later tales of his own rise to power, would have appreciated this, as he reputedly rose above his four brothers because he had the wit to kiss an old hag who promptly turned into a beautiful woman, the figure of sovereignty.[28] Donn, on the other hand, is arrogant and aggressive and asks, as John Carey puts it: 'Is Ireland a territory to be conquered, or a woman to be wooed?'[29] The brothers continue to Tara where they encounter the three kings of the Tuatha Dé Danann and where Amairgen takes the first judgment made in Ireland that the Milesian forces should retreat back to the sea for a distance of nine waves and then approach again. The Tuatha Dé Danann take advantage of this to summon up a storm to drive the fleet away, but Amairgen, whose name seems to mean 'born of song', settles the wind and sea by chanting, while the ever aggressive Donn boasts that he will put Ireland to the sword. The wind rises again and drives Donn's ship aground, and he drowns off Kenmare, Co. Kerry. A cairn was erected in his memory and there, on an island known today as Bull Rock, was located the Teach Duinn, the 'house of Donn', at which it was imagined the dead gathered (there is now a helpful lighthouse on top that flashes every 15 seconds). Amairgen would go on to further the Milesian conquest until it broke down into a civil war and he was slain by Eremon, the legendary ancestor of all the major dynasties.

Here we find ourselves poised on the cusp of identifying both the ancestor of the Irish and, to some extent, his mythical identity. The choice lies between the wise and articulate Amairgen and the aggressive, warlike Donn, which neatly polarizes Irish identity between two stereotypes: one possessed of the gift of the gab and the other epitomized as the 'fighting Irish'. Today the academic smart money would seek the ancestor of Ireland in Donn, the lord of the dead.

One very good reason for accepting the Donn story as an ancient belief among the Irish is that there are comparable stories in earlier attested mythologies. For the ancient Gauls, who we will soon see spoke a language closely related to Irish, Julius Caesar relates that they believed themselves to be descended (according to the druids) from Dis Pater. Caesar applied the name of a Roman god to whatever the Gaulish god was actually called, probably because he had the same function as the Roman god, i.e. lord of the underworld and the dead. So both the Irish and the Gauls believed that their ancestor was the god of the dead and, in the case of the Irish, the afterlife was off the west coast of Ireland. This belief probably goes back to much earlier times; we also find the idea of the ancestor of mankind serving as the lord of the dead to whom the dead are called in the religion of the early Indians and Iranians. While geographically distant, both the Indians and Iranians belong to the same language family as the Irish (as we will see in Chapter 9), and many members of this language family, Indo-European, either share the same names for some of the deities or describe them in such a way that we expect they were all derived from the same ancestral form.

As to the 'real' identity of this god among the Irish and Gauls, Kim McCone has provided an intriguing solution. The Irish name 'Donn' is unlikely to have been the real name of Míl's aggressive son, any more than the Latin Dis Pater was the name for the Gaulish god. Donn simply means 'the dark brown one', which sounds much more like a nickname than his 'official' name, although it does conjure up images of someone who is obscure (like the application of 'prince of darkness' to Dracula).

McCone finds our equivalent of Irish Donn in the underlying meaning of the name of one of the ancient peoples of Europe, known in Greek as *Keltoi* and Latin as *Celtae*. The root meaning is 'hidden' (giving us the English word *hell*) and the underlying linguistic form **kḷtos* would mean 'offspring of the hidden one', suggesting that the Irish saw themselves as the offspring of a god who served as both ancestor and lord of their underworld. Niall would have known from whom he was descended and where he would be heading after death. But while we might be able to locate the entrance to the world of the dead in Ireland, native tradition does not really provide any solid basis for determining where Niall's ancestors dwelt before they came to Ireland.

Conclusions

→ The official account of the peopling of Ireland was constructed by Christian monks between the 7th and 11th centuries.

→ The Irish origin legends were modelled on biblical accounts depicting the wandering of the Jews.

→ There is no convincing native Irish testimony that might associate Irish origins with Iberia.

→ The earliest native traditions derived the ancestor of the Irish from a figure who also served as the lord of the dead.

CHAPTER EIGHT

Skulls, Blood and Genes

The Uí Néill, the descendants of Niall, claimed the high kingship of Ireland until they lost it in 1002 to the leader of the Dál Cais, Brian Boru. It was in the waning century of Uí Néill dominance that surnames began to emerge in Ireland, making it one of the earliest countries in Europe to employ surnames. Out of the descendants of Niall arose such common Irish surnames as O'Boyle, O'Connor and O'Donnell, while the new dynasty of the Dál Cais engendered the family names of O'Brien and Kennedy. Today we consult surname records in tracing our ancestry, but when we go beyond the historical record we no longer have access to surnames. And we are not just seeking the ancestry of a family but that of an entire people, so other techniques must be employed. Establishing the physical ancestry of the Irish was first approached through the most durable remains of any prehistoric population, the human skeleton. But other evidence has also been used, including blood types and an entire series of characteristics that can help track genetic inheritance. Foremost among these techniques is the analysis of DNA in population genetics to trace the composition and origins of a people.

Skulls

Throughout the 19th and early 20th centuries one of the major tools of any prehistorian attempting to trace either the origins or movements of a people involved analysis of the human skull. In the mid-19th century the purpose of studying skulls was to link current populations with their appropriate prehistoric ancestors and ensure that one would be in a position to 'assign to each race its true influence, or to award to it its proper share in the general scheme of social progress'.[1] Cranial analysis varied from the purely impressionistic to increasingly systematic measurements of the skull. The ratio between length and breadth of skull assumed critical importance, with human skulls being classified as brachycephalic, mesocephalic and dolichocephalic, i.e. wide-, middle- and long-headed. Entire populations could then be grouped according to their average cephalic index[2] and their movement in time and space could (supposedly) be tracked. The cultural loading on the crania became incredible depending on national prejudices. Georges de Lapouge, for example, argued that the high civilizations of Europe and southern Asia were dolichocephalic while 'the brachycephalics were probably still living like monkeys'.[3] In contrast, the geographer Griffith Taylor believed the most highly developed languages and civilizations belonged to the brachycephalics and that it was the dolichocephalics who were most primitive. In Taylor's table of languages and cephalic indices, Gaelic, the language of Ireland, was ranked the most primitive (though in good company with Latin and Greek).[4]

John Beddoe in his *The Races of Britain* (1885) believed that the Irish (and their immediate neighbours in Britain) were a 'cross of the Iberian with a long-faced, harsh-featured, red-haired race, who contributed the language and much of the character'.[5] Acknowledging the Iberian connection, Beddoe even describes one Irish racial type (whatever that means) as 'the ideal portrait of Sancho Panza'.[6] As at this time skull, hair colour, eye colour and a people's personality were believed to go hand in hand,[7] we learn that when Beddoe attempted to examine such 'Atlanteans' in western Ireland, this type would not allow themselves to be measured. Beddoe dismissed these specimens, who did not seem to enjoy having their heads squeezed between an Englishman's callipers, by observing that 'though the head is large, the intelligence is low, and there is a great deal of cunning and suspicion'.[8] The different ethnic and regional groups of Britain and Ireland were also classified in terms of moral categories, where we find that both the Welsh and Irish lacked 'any love of order and regularity' (possessed, of course, by the English) while the Welsh and Irish parted company because the former were characterized by 'prudence, frugality, caution, and secretiveness'.[9]

Such studies were accelerated in Ireland when in 1891 the Anthropometric Laboratory of Ireland was established at Trinity College Dublin (where it was hoped that Trinity students would come to be measured at six-month intervals).[10] But the major metric survey of the Irish population was undertaken in the 1930s as part of the Harvard University Mission. A thousand Irish males queued 'for the glory of Ireland to submit to being measured by the good doctor from America'.[11] The purpose of the mission was to provide a good picture of the physical variation of the Irish according to religion and region. Males averaged 171.9 cm in height and 157.3 (±22.5) pounds in weight; the Irish cephalic index was 78.84, rendering the Irish mesocephalic, so hardly a valid target for those obsessed with the length or breadth of the head. A more bizarre product of the study was the discovery that Presbyterians outweighed members of the Church of Ireland by 2.7 pounds and Catholics by 3 pounds; they were also the tallest. Applying a morphological typing index originally designed to classify American criminals by sub-race, the largest single physical type in Ireland was those with dark hair,[12] blue eyes and long heads, but there were also other types such as Nordic Mediterraneans and Dinarics (southeast Europeans). Incidentally, Irish tradition describes our target Irishman, Niall of the Nine Hostages, as having long light-coloured hair (*find*) and eyes the colour of woad.[13]

As for the prehistory of these different types, Cecil Martin attempted to assemble what information he could find about the physical anthropology of the prehistoric and early historic populations of Ireland. He believed he could discern at least four physical types. The first for which he had any adequate data was what he termed Early Neolithic – medium stature with long and narrow high skulls (also represented in Britain at this time). He saw those buried in the megaliths as a later race with lower and slightly broader heads and described them as Iberians, rejecting the fanciful but widespread notion that dark-haired Irishmen were the offspring of randy Spanish sailors who had survived the destruction of the Armada. This type was followed by a radical change in the Bronze Age (the evidence was to be found with Food Vessels) when skulls became very short and round. The final prehistoric invaders were attributed to the Iron Age, but its population appeared to be similar to the earlier burials in the megalithic tombs.[14]

We could pass over much of this as comic relief, except that the few attempts to examine the physical anthropology of Ireland from an historical perspective have employed statistical means that are not so easy to dismiss and these have also indicated some changes in physical type. In a brief survey of the evidence, the physical anthropologist Don Brothwell distinguished Irish Neolithic skulls (which did resemble those from long barrows in Britain) from Bronze Age skulls.[15] These differences have also been recorded between Beaker-using populations in Britain and earlier Neolithic skulls.[16] Finally, Brothwell notes that Iron Age skulls differ from those of both the Neolithic and Bronze Age, although they suggest an admixture with earlier populations. This would suggest that there is at least a case for suggesting some influx of foreign population during the Early Bronze Age and the possibility of some outsiders entering Ireland during the Iron Age. But the samples for all periods so far examined are extremely small and the source of some of those measured is not always clear.

In addition to skulls, teeth have also recently been examined, where it is argued that a close analysis of dentition (both the size and the characteristics of the teeth) can provide useful evidence for establishing genetic ties. In a study presented in 2004 of 681 individuals from the Neolithic up to the early medieval period, Jaimin Wheets was able to establish that there was a reduction in tooth size over time but that changes in the characteristics of the teeth, while they helped distinguish those of the Irish from other populations, did not suggest any major influx of population, although one could not rule out small-scale migration.[17] Attempts to compare the Irish data with a world dental base threw up a variety of potential links that found Ireland most similar to populations in North Africa, western Europe, India and even east Africa. Making any historical sense out of patterns like these is no easy task.

Blood

In his novel *Dracula* Bram Stoker has Dr Van Helsing administering blood transfusions to the doomed Lucy from her various male suitors. This could have finished her off even faster, but if Stoker had shifted the scene from England to his native Ireland and had the count sink his fangs into an Irish lass with suitors from her own country, Van Helsing would at least have escaped a malpractice suit. Ireland is a good place for a transfusion as it has one of the highest proportions of universal donors (Type O) in the world. This was not known when *Dracula* was written back in 1897, but by the first decade of the 20th century scientists had discerned four main blood groups: A, B, AB and O. Which type of blood you possess is determined genetically according to basic rules of inheritance. Everyone inherits a gene for blood type from both their father and mother. They develop the blood type from whichever of each parent's two genes is passed to them according to the rule that A and B are dominant and O is recessive. If one parent donates an O, then the child will be whatever the other parent has contributed (an A or B). To be Type O both your parents must have contributed an O. If, on the other hand, one parent was Type A and the other Type B, the offspring will be the much rarer Type AB.

The plotting of the frequency of blood types by country, region or ethnic group tends to throw up patterns that suggest possible migrations. This was already indicated in the 1940s by J. B. S. Haldane, who observed that Type B was more common in eastern than western Europe and particularly high among some Asiatic populations.[18] Today we would find that Type B is about 10% of the population in Ireland, 11% in Germany, 13% in Austria, 16% in Hungary and 18% in the Ukraine, and by the time we get to China it is at least 25%. Haldane suggested that Europe was originally (at least in the Neolithic) mainly Type O with very little Type B and that the gradient across Europe reflected successive migrations from the east of Type B populations.

Reading historical origins from blood groups has been employed outside of Ireland but hardly with clear results. For example, although Iceland historically traces its settlement from Norway, in terms of the ABO blood groups the modern Icelandic population is more like the Irish than it is like the Norwegians. This has been interpreted as evidence that much of the settlement of Iceland was done via the Norse in Ireland, where wives and slaves were obtained from Irish populations. Alternatively, it has also been suggested that medieval Norwegians may have resembled modern Irishmen more than they do contemporary Norwegians. Or perhaps the current composition of the Icelandic blood types is a product of genetic drift.[19]

One complicating factor is that blood type may provide greater susceptibility to or protection against particular diseases, and hence the proportions may have as much to do with natural selection and past plagues as the geographical origins of a population. This is true, but the types of diseases against which Type O is generally regarded as providing some extra resilience are probably not ones that plagued prehistoric Ireland, e.g. malaria and syphilis.[20] What has generally emerged from the blood type surveys is that Type O, which was not only highest in Ireland but also higher in the west than the east of the island, reflected more closely the 'aboriginal' population while Type A (about 35% in modern Irish populations) was more likely to be associated with later migrations from across the water, especially as Type A is much higher in north European populations (Norway 50%, Sweden 47%, Denmark 44%, Germany 43% and England 42%).[21] In short, Type O became shorthand for 'native Irish' and Type A might be interpreted as 'Norse' or 'English'. Of course, there is no direct relationship between these blood types and these ethnic designations, as all the blood types in Ireland can be found all over the Old World. Ireland and Iceland have high proportions of Type O blood, but in Saudi Arabia it is even higher. So blood types provide only the crudest of arguments for population movements.

Beyond the ABO system there are many other more sophisticated indices of genetic affiliation, and these have also been brought to bear on the problem of origins. While blood type is determined on the 9th chromosome, a far more sensitive potential marker is found on the 6th, where six genes make up the HLA (human leukocyte antigen) system. The white blood cells contain proteins that form antibodies, and their practical importance in medicine is that they help determine whether a skin graft or organ transplant is likely to be accepted or rejected. It has been observed that populations in Wales, Scotland and Ireland share a particular combination (HLA-A1 B8) in greater amounts than their English neighbours, and Walter Bodmer has suggested that this coincides with the observation that the native languages of these three nations were closely related.[22]

The ABO and HLA systems are just part of a much larger battery of genetic markers that can be employed to help determine the similarities or differences between populations. In a famous exercise undertaken by L. L. Cavalli-Sforza and his colleagues, the distribution of 88 different genes was analysed across 26 European populations and the peoples of Europe were divided genetically according to these 'classical' markers into a series of subgroups. Here the Irish and the Scots are found to occupy a single peripheral branch of the genetic tree (8.1). That this was not purely the result of geography is suggested by the fact that the English were subgrouped with the Dutch and Danes and somewhat more distantly with the Swiss, Germans, Belgians and Austrians, i.e. broadly the same general geographical and linguistic group (ignoring Romance languages in Belgium and Switzerland).[23] The same data can be displayed differently in terms of principal component analysis, where

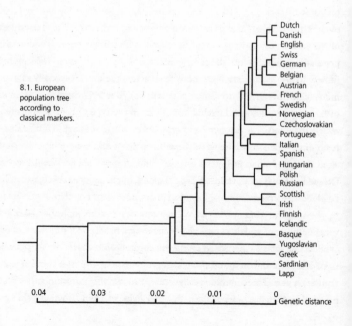

8.1. European population tree according to classical markers.

220

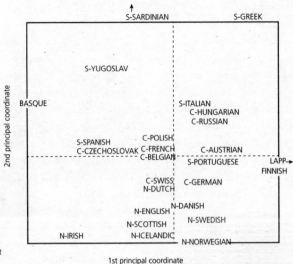

8.2. Peoples of Europe according to principal component analysis.

we find the Irish situated at the periphery (8.2). The geographical representation of the genetic data has been mapped on to the continent of Europe where the first principal component has indicated a gradient running from the Near East across Europe to the Atlantic periphery (8.3). The interpretation of this map has long been the subject of debate: the original authors regarded it as indicating the expansion of farming from the Near East across Europe.[24] Essentially, it was seen to map the migration of farming communities from the Near East, and the fall-off as one moved from southwest Asia to Ireland could be considered the diminution of the southwest Asian contribution to the European gene pool. In short, while we might expect that Greece and the Balkans were heavily populated by peoples stemming from the Near East, the further west that one went the local (pre-Neolithic) contribution was likely to increase. Others suggested different causes such as the original peopling of Europe, which also came via southwest Asia, by *Homo sapiens*.

The impact of these studies on tracing Irish genetic origins was problematic. Generally, Ireland was found to be closely linked with Scotland (and Wales when the data was included) but not to possess markedly clear connections with other Europeans other than Iberia (Type O blood). Genetically, Ireland occupied the same

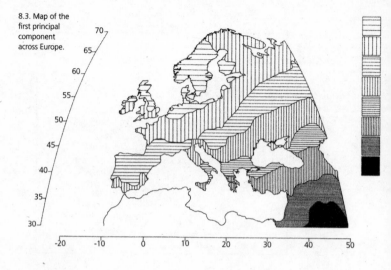

8.3. Map of the first principal component across Europe.

position as it did geographically – on the western periphery of Europe – and appeared to be further removed from Near Eastern immigrants than were other populations.

Disease

Other evidence of genetic past rests with genes specifically associated with diseases. Ireland has an unenviably high rate of cystic fibrosis, hemochromatosis and phenylketonuria.[25] In Ireland, phenylketonuria (PKU) has been examined from the perspective of what it can tell us about the genetic history of the Irish.[26] PKU is a genetic disorder that, if left untreated, can lead to retardation and brain damage. Fortunately, in many countries including Ireland all newborn infants are monitored for it. There are a variety of PKU mutations that can theoretically be organized into chronological layers and thus provide an indication of past relationships. For example, the mutation known as I65T is common in Ireland, Britain and Spain but uncommon elsewhere in Europe.[27] Confined to the periphery of Europe, one might then suggest that I65T spread with the repopulating of northwest Europe after the last Ice Age (8.4). Recall that during the Ice Age humans were confined to refuge areas far to the south but when the ice sheets retreated, populations moved from Iberia and southern France northward through Atlantic Europe. Another mutation, R408W, is the most frequent in Ireland and Scotland but is far less common in southwest

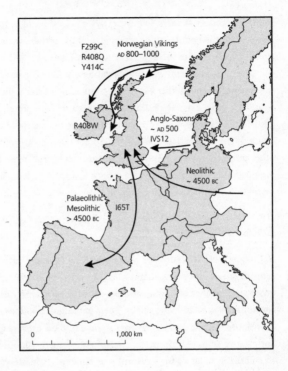

8.4. Patterns of PKU mutations and their possible spread to Ireland and Britain.

England and is not found in Spain at all. This suggested a second mutation, possibly local to Ireland, that spread after the first settlement of Ireland.

Classical genetics: interim view

By and large, the evidence of classical genetic markers and genes associated with specific diseases could be summarized as follows. The Irish gene pool shares markers with other populations of Atlantic Europe, particularly Iberia, that might be accounted for as derived from the spread of human settlement after the Ice Age into the north of Atlantic Europe. There is also evidence for genetic influences from southwest Asia that may have been associated with either the earliest humans in Europe (*c.* 40,000 years ago) or the spread of farming (*c.* 7000 BC). The second hypothesis seems to be more popular, so the Irish might be regarded as substantially 'native' Atlantic Europeans since the Mesolithic but with a substantial minority of genes derived from Near Eastern farmers. In most analyses Ireland could be found associated most closely with the population of Scotland, and often there were some genetic differences that marked out these two regions from England.

One of the problems with interpretation invariably involved the lack of clarity as to how specific any marker was to any population. In short, there was no such thing as an 'Irish gene', a characteristic that was unique to Irish populations and that distinguished the Irish from other populations or provided a specific origin for the Irish. Much of the genetic data could be found not only throughout Europe but also on other continents; it was only the percentages that varied. All of these techniques thus provided only a rough view of the genetic history of Ireland, but other approaches began to emerge from the 1990s onward.

DNA

In Chapter 1 we deconstructed Niall of the Nine Hostages into a variety of elements, some of which had been around since just after the Big Bang (e.g. hydrogen) and others that had formed only in the explosion of stars (oxygen, carbon). These elements constitute 98% of all living things. Their physical origin does not get us very close to Irish origins, but the arrangement of some of these elements just might. In Niall's body the elements of hydrogen, nitrogen, oxygen and the all-important carbon joined chemically in different ways to form four different molecules: adenine (A), guanine (G), thymine (T) and cytosine (C). These four molecules or bases along with a sugar molecule and phosphate are the building stuff of DNA, the genetic code that has been replicating itself since life first appeared on Earth about 3.5 billion years ago. The specific arrangement of these molecules provides us with an evolutionary trail that springs from Luca, which stands for the 'last universal common ancestor' of all life, and passes through every subsequent life form to Niall and on to all of his modern descendants. Obviously Niall's relationship to lichen, sea slugs, dinosaurs or the ancestors of chimpanzees do not really narrow things down, but once we enter the realm of anatomically modern human beings, *Homo sapiens*, the arrangement of these molecules within the peoples of Europe, both in space and time, can provide clues to the relationships between these peoples and the paths of their earlier migrations.

The critical evidence for all this, the DNA, is predominantly concentrated in the nuclei of cells, where it is organized into chains of various sizes known as chromosomes. A chromosome averages something on the order of 100 million bases which are arranged in enormously long strings, e.g. ...CCATGGTACTGAATCCTT....

These strings provide a code that is 'read' in units of three letters. About 3% of the code actually leads to a chemical product and is recognized as a gene, which codes for the production of an amino acid or enzyme. In short, genes 'do something' such as determine eye colour, susceptibility to disease, blood type, etc. Although some of the rest of the code serves as 'punctuation' for chemical instructions, most of it appears to be wholly superfluous.

With such an enormous set of copies to be made in the reproduction of every generation, it is natural to suspect that there will be some miscopies of the chemical sequences. These are the mutations that involve such changes as the substitution of one base for another (e.g. CCAT > CCAC), the deletion of a base (e.g. CTG > CG), or the insertion of one or more bases (e.g. CC > CTGTC). It is these mutations that provide a trail for the geneticist as they are passed on, so we can follow the different paths of mutational baggage that various individuals have picked up through their ancestors. Imagine that air passengers could never remove the destination tags from their baggage and so one would always be able to determine when and where various passengers made their journeys. Those more closely related, such as members of the same family, would be more likely to share the same destination tags than any randomly selected travellers.

The DNA sequence, as we have seen, is largely confined to the chromosomes, of which humans possess 23 pairs, half of each pair inherited from each parent. Of these, 22 are known as autosomes, i.e. the first 22 chromosomes, numbered from largest (1) to smallest (22). These autosomes are not involved in determining what sex an individual is and they are the product of the combining of the DNA from both parents. Since the mixture of the mother's and father's contributions to their offspring's DNA is so thorough, autosomal DNA cannot provide a clear trail differentiating between the mother's and father's line.

The 23rd chromosome is the sex chromosome and it comes in two very different types: a larger X (female) and smaller Y (male). A female possesses two X chromosomes while a male possesses an X and a Y. During mating each partner has an equal chance of contributing either one of their two sex chromosomes. Niall was produced because one lucky sperm from his father managed to deliver a Y chromosome that penetrated his mother's egg. Had his father donated an X chromosome there would have been a daughter, and we would have lost our archetypal Irishman.

Most research on the origins and dispersals of human populations rests on the analysis of the DNA that can only be inherited from a single parent so that there is at least a fighting chance of following a single genetic trail. The Y chromosome serves this purpose very well as it is passed exclusively between father and son. The genes associated with it are primarily concerned with producing males, i.e. the presence of a Y chromosome ensures that a foetus will develop into a male, but not much else.[28] Tracking the Y chromosome is essentially tracking the male bloodline that in most western societies is the genetic equivalent of the surname. In contrast, the female chromosome is not specific to women, as an individual may obtain an X chromosome from either their mother or father. This means that analysis of mutations on the X chromosome cannot give a clear indication of one's maternal ancestry. Fortunately, there is another way – mitochondrial DNA.

Mitochondrial DNA (mtDNA) draws its name from the fact that it is not found on a chromosome but rather in the mitochondria, small areas of a cell outside the nucleus that provide energy for the functioning of the cell. In the female egg cell there are about 100,000 mitochondria while the male sperm only hosts about 50 to 75, which are not passed to the fertilized egg. So the DNA that lurks in the new cell's mitochondria only comes from the mother. It is thus passed to both daughters and sons but cannot be passed further on by the sons. In short, analysis of mtDNA tracks the genetic history solely through the female line.

Before we attempt to survey the evidence for the genetic origins of the Irish, a word of caution. We are dispensing with the 22 autosomal chromosomes because they tend to leave a very confusing genetic trail. But although the sex-specific DNA provides an easier genetic trail, it is only a tiny fraction of who we actually are. While mtDNA is heavy in 'information' compared with the Y chromosome, it still only carries about 37 genes and 16,569 base pairs. The rest of the DNA found on the other chromosomes contains about 6.2 billion base pairs and governs an estimated 20,000 genes from each parent. And this inheritance has been passed down and remixed every generation in a geometric progression, i.e. we each share the genes of two parents, earlier mixed across four grandparents, still earlier mixed across eight great-grandparents and so on. A good example of an autosomal gene is that which governs lactase persistence, i.e. the ability to consume milk past infancy without very unpleasant side effects. It is governed by a gene on the 2nd chromosome and in Europe it is found in greatest concentrations in the northwest and in the lowest amounts in the southeast. It is generally assumed to have emerged with the development of dairying during the Neolithic,[29] and Ireland shows one of the highest concentrations of this gene. A human being is a composite of all his or her genetic inheritance across all the chromosomes and not only the product of a Y chromosome or mtDNA.

Mother Ireland

The evidence of mtDNA provides us with the trail of the female line of the Irish population. Most of the 16,569 bases of mtDNA are devoted to producing energy and if a mutation occurs among them, the host is unlikely to live long enough to pass the mutation on. There are, however, about 1,000 bases that serve another purpose: they control the way mtDNA replicates itself during cell division and this sequence is known as the 'control region'. Within this region there are 400 bases in which mutations may occur without causing any serious damage to the system, and this is where geneticists look for the evidence for past history. A mutation that occurs in this region will be passed on to the next generation but will have no effect on the individual, at least that we can discern.

Mutations have been discovered among these 400 bases and their recurrent patterns of similar mutations permit them to be divided into seven major groups, popularized by Bryan Sykes as the 'seven daughters of Eve',[30] the seven mothers whose mutations have continued into today's European populations. The mutations that define the groups are found at certain positions along this 400-base sequence, e.g. at position 126 or 294. Some individuals might have one mutation, others more, and the pattern that emerges permits geneticists to fit each individual into the branch of a genetic family tree. When individuals show common mutations on a chromosome, they form a haplotype, and when a series of haplotypes all seem to be closely related variants in the same general area, they are known as a haplogroup. The haplogroups are the largest entities that geneticists work with in tracing population histories.

The seven haplogroups that comprise about 95% of the population of Europe all have alphabetical designations: H, T, J, X, V, K and U. Each of these mutations occurred within a single woman at some time in the past and so they also designate a distant female ancestor for a section of the modern population of Europe. Assuming that these mutations occur at a constant rate, there are estimated ages for each group.[31] It has also been possible to propose the areas where each group is most prevalent, and these have been identified as the home territories. This information is summarized in the first three columns of Table 8.1.

Table 8.1 mtDNA of modern Irish population

Haplogroup	Age (years ago)	Proposed home territory	% Irish
U	43,100–65,200	Greece	13
X	19,700–44,600	Caucasus	2
H	14,700–22,600	S France	39
V	9,100–18,200	N Iberia	4
T	18,100–35,800	N Italy	2
K	22,700–40,400	N Italy	11
J	22,400–43,200	Near East	10

The dates in column 2 indicate the beginning of the ancestral female line and one could draw a series of arrows from each home region to Ireland if you wanted to trace the 'ancestral mothers' of the Irish back to the Palaeolithic. This would not be a very rewarding exercise, of course, since Ireland was not settled during the Palaeolithic (at least as far as we can tell). Moreover, there would be nothing specifically about Irish origins, as modern Hungarians would show almost the same constellation of haplogroups.[32] In fact, tracing such paths back to these seven 'daughters' (whose starting points are still regarded as debatable) is almost the genetic equivalent of the Big Bang, an origin anchored in the too distant past. Also, we should emphasize that in any of these tables, space is factored by time: the distinction between J, which derives from the Near East, and the various European haplogroups is purely temporal, as all the European haplogroups must ultimately lead back to the Near East as well and then down into Africa, the home of the first modern woman, mitochondrial Eve.

In order to move forward we need to work with a higher degree of resolution and go beyond the main mtDNA branches to the smaller sub-branches. For example, the most frequent mtDNA haplogroup is H, which accounts for something like 40–50% of the European gene pool and is the highest group in Ireland (39%).[33] It is argued that this haplogroup emerged in the Near East and came into Europe about 25,000–20,000 years ago. There it remained until about 15,000 years ago, when distinct variations of H began to evolve and spread across Europe. Table 8.2 indicates some of the main varieties of H that occur in Ireland.

Table 8.2 Subgroups of mtDNA haplogroup H

Haplogroup	Age estimate (years ago)
H1	9,100–15,400
H3	8,400–15,400
H4	7,300–17,900
H5a	6,400–16,800
H6	10,500–20,300
H7	10,300–21,000
H13	13,300–21,700

This is only a minor improvement on the haplogroup analysis seen in Table 8.1, but it at least brings some of the potential ancestors into existence about the time Ireland was first settled (if we opt for the shallowest date in some of the enormous ranges). On the other hand, we are not much closer to finding anything specifically Irish, as we could also find all of these same subgroups in Bulgaria. In order to push on, one needs to keep refining the groups much further into yet smaller and more recent subgroups. First, you need to observe the mutations within each of the groups in Ireland and determine whether these match populations from outside Ireland (to scrape away the ancestral mothers of Hungarians, Bulgarians, etc.). Second, you need to determine if any of the Irish samples lack any outside parallel, as this would indicate that the mutations only occurred within Ireland, i.e. the trail goes cold in Ireland itself. Bryan Sykes conducted such an exercise and his dates for the emergence of the locally found subtypes of the main groups within Ireland are provided in Table 8.3.[34]

Table 8.3 mtDNA haplogroups in Ireland

Haplogroup	Proposed home territory	In Ireland (years ago)
U	Greece	7,300
X	Caucasus	c. 5,500
H	S France	c. 5,500
V	N Iberia	c. 5,500
T	N Italy	c. 5,500
K	N Italy	c. 5,500
J	Near East	4,500

These dates are exceedingly rough – far more so than anything that an archaeologist would dare serve up. If we were naive enough to take the dates literally, they suggest that 10% of today's Irish population have a maternal Irish female ancestor who was probably in Ireland during the Mesolithic. Almost all the other groups exhibit dates that would place them in Ireland either at the end of the Mesolithic or within the Neolithic. The most recent mutation (J) shows the most recent date, about the beginning of the Beaker period, and this is the one that has an ultimate geographical origin in the Near East. Before we get carried away, we should emphasize that these are not radiocarbon dates, and even if these are ballpark dates supplied by geneticists we have no idea how big the ballpark actually is. We will revisit these dates below.

What ultimately tends to emerge from most such studies is a separation of Irish mtDNA into two broad temporal and cultural groups (Table 8.4).

Table 8.4 **Genetic composition of modern Irish according to mtDNA haplogroups**

Pre-farming	**Farming**
D, H, HV, I, K, T, T2, T4, U, U2, U4, U5, U5a, U5a1, U5a1a, U5b, V, W, X	J, J1a, J1b1, J2, T1, U3

As one can see, most of the different haplogroup types are regarded as having emerged in Europe after the last Ice Age. When precisely they entered Ireland it is difficult to say, although the popular press has often portrayed this as evidence that the modern Irish were genetically anchored in Ireland since the Mesolithic before the spread of farming. The smaller second group of J, T1 and U3 are designated Near Eastern in origin and are usually interpreted as the genetic descendants of the earliest farmers who came from the Near East. While this Near Eastern cluster of genes averages about 20% across Europe, it falls to c. 13% of the Irish population.[35] It should be emphasized that we are still working at very crude levels of genetic subgrouping and that those with Near Eastern ancestral mothers need not have arrived as early as the Neolithic but could have entered Ireland at a later date. But the bottom line of this interpretation is that coursing through the blood of most Irish women is 'native European' blood associated with the recolonization of the north Atlantic from southern France, Iberia and Italy after the last Ice Age. On the other hand, a little more than 10% of Irish women might have an innate craving for pitta bread and kebabs that could be explained by their more recent arrival in Ireland.

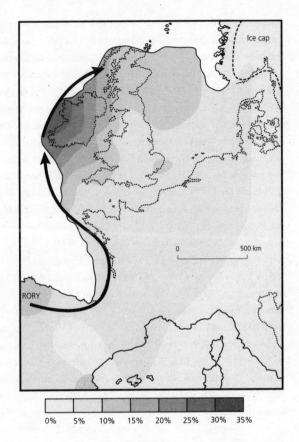

8.5. The proposed migration of R1b-14 ('Rory') from Iberia to Ireland.

Father Ireland

The haplogroups of the Y chromosome, summarized in Table 8.5, can be arranged to tell a story comparable to that of the mtDNA. Again we see that the majority of haplogroups are traditionally associated with the pre-farming populations of Europe and that only a few are regarded of more recent Near Eastern origin, usually associated with the spread of the Neolithic, although we must emphasize here again that the ultimate origin of a haplogroup may not reflect the staging area of its introduction into Ireland. Although some haplogroups have been interpreted as having an Iberian origin, they may not have arrived in Ireland until the Neolithic or later, i.e. they may have been 'local' residents in Atlantic Europe who adopted agriculture and helped bring it to Ireland.[36] Stephen Oppenheimer has controversially suggested a series of very early migrations from Iberia around the Atlantic coast of Europe and Ireland such as R1b-14 (which he nicknamed 'Rory') that he assigns to a period at least 3,000 years before any evidence for the settlement of Ireland (8.5).[37] From an archaeological perspective this is a hard sell, as there is not the slightest evidence for either a human presence in Ireland at this time or for any plausible cultural connections suggested by this hypothesis that would link Ireland to the material culture of any putative homeland. Part of the problem lies with the types of dates suggested for genetic 'events'. Oppenheimer cites the date of R1b-14 in the British Isles as 15,760 years ago with a standard deviation of 8,440.[38] This means that it should fall somewhere between 24,200 years ago (c. 22,200 BC) and 7,320 years ago (c. 5300 BC). The dates of the different haplogroups and their offspring range from the critical to the diabolical. For example, in 2010 three different studies dated the same haplotype from a low of 4,577–9,063 years ago to a high of 25,000–80,700 years ago![39] The second problem concerns how meaningful the dates are in human terms. The date of a mutation will certainly be earlier than whatever one can track back to the 'Most Recent Common Ancestor' (MRCA) on the basis of whatever haplotypes one's survey is able to sample. The haplogroups may well have histories that extend much deeper in time than their appearance in Ireland, so it is exceedingly difficult to anchor genetic evidence with human migrations unless there are exceptionally clear correlations between the two types of evidence. In the case of Ireland, nothing is ever that clear.

Table 8.5 **Major Y chromosome haplogroups in Ireland**

Pre-farming	Farming
R1a, R1a1, R1b3, IJK, PN3, N3	E3b, G, J
I1a, I1b2, I1c	

Surnames

The male sex chromosome offers much more to those interested in origins than simply the haplotype. As we have seen, Irish surnames began as early as the 10th century, so one can attempt to trace the original founders of these surnames by examining the genetic record of the members of each family. For example, we could take what we would regard as the classically Irish surnames (excluding therefore any Norse, Norman, English, Scots or Welsh) and work our way back to the founding father of each surname.[40] This has been attempted at several levels of resolution.

Table 8.6 Distribution of Y chromosome haplogroup R1b among populations in Ireland

Sample source	Percentage with R1b
Connacht	98
Munster	95
Ulster	81
Leinster	73
English	63
Scottish	53
Norman/Norse	83

The most basic attempt to relate surnames to the Y chromosome was undertaken in 2000, when DNA samples were drawn from males with Irish surnames and then arranged according to province and compared with those of men living in Ireland whose surnames were not Irish (Table 8.6).[41] This emphasized the importance of R1b (then known as haplogroup 1) and the fact that it was concentrated highest in the west of Ireland, traditionally regarded as the repository of the earliest or most authentic Irish (one popular account of this research employed the subheading: 'Connaught men are the most Irish of the Irish').[42] But before the citizens of Galway begin boasting about their racial purity, we should recall that the association between the surnames and the haplogroup actually has little to do with anything specifically 'Irish'; it is rather a result of the marginal position of Ireland in Europe, genetically speaking, where a haplogroup (R1b) has had less chance of being swamped by more recent migrations. That it is not specifically 'Irish' can even be seen by the percentage figures, which would seem to suggest that someone with an Anglo-Norman surname (for example, me) was actually *more* Irish than someone with a Gaelic surname from Ulster or Leinster. And who would have imagined that the English are 'more Irish' than the Scots? Nor, obviously, could we suggest that 1.8% of Turks have an uncontrollable urge to break into 'Danny Boy' because that is the percentage of Turkish men who carry R1b. In short, at this degree of resolution we can only say that an Irish identity has been mapped on to the distribution of an earlier genetic type, not that the genetic type is in any way specifically associated with being Irish.

A more detailed study has been attempted involving the examination of 43 Irish surnames.[43] This revealed that there was certainly some correlation between genetic makeup and surname which suggested that many sharing a common surname did indeed share a common ancestor. But this varied, with the highest correlation (about 50%) occurring among those named O'Sullivan and Ryan. For others, most notably the two surnames with the greatest number of members (Kelly and Murphy), the results suggested that their ancestors fortuitously acquired the same surname. Alternatively, people with different genetic signatures and Irish surnames may have found themselves lumped into a single surname after the adoption of Anglicized names.

The children of Niall

Throughout this book I have held up Niall of the Nine Hostages as our archetypal Irishman, and we might wonder whether we could reconstruct Niall's DNA as at least one clear case of a genetic Irishman. In fact, this has already been attempted by geneticists at Trinity College Dublin.[44] As we have seen, Niall was the founder of the Uí Néill (descendants of Niall) who, according to Irish genealogies, survive today in common surnames such as O'Donnell, Molloy and Quinn. Analysis of men bearing these and other surnames indicated a statistical association between these surnames and an ancestral mutation (M222) of haplogroup R1b. This haplotype, labelled the Irish modal haplotype, is concentrated in the home territory of the Uí Néill in north-west Ireland and Scotland as well as the US, where we might expect large numbers of Irish immigrants. It is presumed that Niall and his male progeny (he reputedly had 14 sons) were highly prolific, putting about a genetic signature that can be found among just under 5% of modern Irish males. On the one hand, this speaks for a potentially strong correlation between political rulership and the ability to mate and disperse one's offspring. On the other hand, it must be admitted that our archetypal Irishman can only explain about 5% of the Irish male population. Moreover, attempts to extend this kind of analysis to other major medieval Irish dynasties such as the Dál Cais and Eóganacht of Munster do not reveal similar evidence for a single major founder, although the surnames through which the dynasties have been analysed do show some coherent patterns of lineage, e.g. the O'Briens and Kennedys do go back to a single ancestor, as also do O'Sullivan and McGillycuddy.[45]

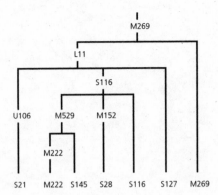

8.6. The Irish modal haplotype (M222) and its ancestors.

The ancestors of Niall

If we start from the premise that we have identified Niall's Y chromosome, we can hardly resist trying to follow the trail back further and recover a still earlier 'Irish gene', something that might account for both Niall and the rest of the lads. Only in this way can we avoid the problem that the Irish modal haplotype[46] originated in Ireland and is, therefore, a genetic dead end insofar as retrieving the genetic signature of most Irish males.[47] For our purposes, the family tree begins very distantly with haplogroup R (which includes about 50% of European males) through R1 and then down to R1b. Haplogroup R is believed to have emerged in Asia *c.* 34,000–20,000 years ago, while R1 has been dated to *c.* 18,500 years ago. Its offspring, R1b, has traditionally been treated as a product of the Iberian refuge during the last period of glaciation from whence it spread into Atlantic Europe, i.e. it was one of the classic 'native European' genes that anchor the genetic composition of the Irish to the spread of human populations northward after the last Ice Age. To go any further we need to move down the genetic tree of R1b (8.6). Our target is the Niall gene (R1b1a2a1a1b4c),[48] whose mutation is designated M222. To simplify matters we will dispense with the long and frequently changing haplogroup names and simply trace the descent of Niall's group according to the sequence of mutations: M269 > L11 > S116 > M529 > M222 (Niall). The first of these (M269) is found among about 70%

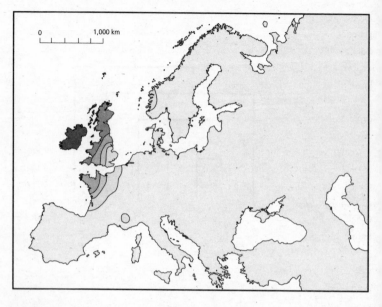

8.7. Distribution of M529.

of the males of western Europe (i.e. more than 100 million men) and decreases as one moves east (e.g. Ireland 85%, Germany 32%, Turkey 19%, Iraq 11%, Iran 6%).[49] This only tells us that Niall's ancestors probably came from western Europe, so no surprise there. Further down the line (more recent) comes L11, which is similarly dispersed over western and central Europe. Moving still closer to Niall (M222) we have S116, which covers essentially the same territory as L11, although with a slightly higher density in western Europe, especially Iberia, France, Britain and Ireland. Finally, we move immediately upstream of Niall to M529 (8.7), which is mainly concentrated in Britain and Ireland but can also be found elsewhere in western Europe, although much more likely in France and further north (Norway) than Iberia. We have already seen that M222 is primarily concentrated in Ireland and Britain, so the ancestors of Niall look like they came from somewhere between France and Norway.

We see that searching for Niall's ancestors according to his Y haplogroup only tells us that they came from somewhere in western Europe – hardly a result that would get a geneticist on the front page of a newspaper. But what was it that we hoped to find in the first place? Obviously, if there was a large cluster in Ireland and another one concentrated in northern Iberia, we could be tempted to conclude that genetics had supported the legend of the Sons of Míl invading Ireland from Iberia. But even if we found such evidence, we would still have to ask when the linkage was established. And here is where the rough time depth estimates in genetics cause real havoc. Throughout this study I have repeated the popular paradigm: Irish genes are essentially derived from the postglacial recolonization of northwest Europe which explains their west European, often specifically Iberian, connections. But as geneticists themselves acknowledge, the difference between human expansions dated at c. 10,000 years ago compared with the spread of farming about 7,500 years ago are 'exceedingly difficult to discern with genetic tools'.[50] In a number of recent papers there has been a move away from the assumption that the descendants of R1b were all rooted in Late Glacial refuges. We began our climb of the genetic tree at M269, which some geneticists now associate with the spread of agriculture.[51] If this were to be accepted, it would render all the mutations that occurred 'downstream' of this as Neolithic or later, challenging the entire notion that the population of Ireland was essentially rooted in its initial colonization and instead bringing the main male genetic foundation of Ireland forward to the Neolithic or later.[52] In so doing, Ireland would move from being essentially 'European' (which we can now see as essentially a temporal rather than spatial definition) to 'Near Eastern'. But no sooner did this new model appear and take hold than a still more recent (2011) and more extensive re-analysis of M269 concluded that the distribution of this sub-haplogroup does not look like a phenomenon of Neolithic expansions after all (it is far more prevalent in the northwest than in the southeast, from whence farmers should have dispersed), and the later 'downstream' branches seem to have very localized concentrations, although M529 is still very much localized to Ireland, Britain and western France. Recognizing that 'dating of Y chromosome lineages is notoriously controversial', the authors of the article would not hazard a date for M269 other than suspecting that the more recent (Neolithic) dates cited in some recent papers are likely to be too recent.[53]

What about the local women who were great-granddaughters of Eve? The dates for them are also problematic, but the evidence of ancient DNA suggests that we can find some of the variants of mtDNA haplogroup U that occur in Ireland among Mesolithic populations elsewhere in Europe.[54] For example, mtDNA U5 is found in about 6% of Irish women and appears to be well grounded in pre-Neolithic Europe. On the other hand, many of the other mtDNA haplogroups found in Ireland are neither certainly pre- nor post-Neolithic.[55]

Ireland and the Magyars

If one still believes that the genetic composition of Ireland was largely fixed in the Mesolithic or Neolithic, then Ireland would seem to have been largely static from the Neolithic onward. Perhaps one exception is haplogroup I2a2a1 (M284), which tends to be rare in Ireland but is found among males with the surnames McGuinness and McCartan and is also found in Britain and the Continent. McEvoy and Bradley have dated the foundation of this haplogroup in Ireland to about 2,300 years ago, i.e. to roughly the beginning of the La Tène, and speculate about it providing possible support for the idea that there may have been some gene flow from Britain into the north of Ireland during the Iron Age.[56] But other than this exception, most of the archaeological or anthropological models for Bronze or Iron Age population movements appear unsupported (contradicted?) by the evidence of genetics. Does this, for example, mean that the Irish language must have been introduced either during the first colonization of Ireland (whence most of the Irish trace their genetic origins) or during the Neolithic? The problem here, admitted by geneticists themselves, is that relatively small population incursions that might have produced thorough cultural or linguistic changes may not be amenable to recovery by looking at the genetic composition of modern populations. Often one imagines that a small foreign population may have assumed leadership and brought about language change. When this happens, there is no expectation that this process of language shift 'be accompanied by a high degree of genetic admixture, and, if this is so, populations such as the Hungarians and Turks are unlikely to be separated from surrounding populations by genetic barriers'.[57] And this is precisely what we do find. This example concentrates on the Turks and Hungarians (Magyars) because both are traditionally represented as people who undertook distant migrations before they found their historical seats among populations very different from themselves. And a millennium after they settled, they tended to look like everyone else around them.

According to the classical markers the Magyars are closest to their neighbours, the Poles (Fig. 8.1). The land they occupy has been a thoroughfare for a variety of different language groups throughout its history. In the first centuries BC it was probably occupied by people whose language was related to Irish; by the 1st century AD it was occupied by Sarmatians, presumably Iranian-speaking people, who were then absorbed into the Roman Empire where the language was Latin. In the 4th to the 6th centuries early Germanic tribes (Gepids, Langobards) settled Hungary under the leadership of the Huns, who spoke an Altaic language (Turkish and Mongolian are good examples). From the 7th to 9th centuries the land was occupied by the Avars, another Turkic-speaking group, but it was also settled by Slavs at this time. Finally, about AD 900 the Magyars, the ethnic group that defines Hungary today, arrived on their long trek from the Ural Mountains that had begun around AD 500. The Magyars, incidentally, belong to a third language family that also includes the Finns and Estonians. The mtDNA of modern Hungarians simply reveals to us the same basic outline of development that we find in Ireland or anywhere else in Europe: early Palaeolithic lineages followed by Near Eastern lineages associated with the spread of agriculture. In short, the genetic evidence leaves out all the different peoples and languages that have been attested in the historical record. As a cautionary tale, this is about as scary as it gets for anyone relying on the genetics of modern populations to elucidate their origins. Fortunately, genetics has one more trick.

Although far more difficult than obtaining a swab from someone's mouth to gain a sample of modern DNA, there are ways of extracting the DNA from the bones of long-dead people. Hungarian researchers along with colleagues from the University of Ulster have made a comparison between the genetic composition of modern Hungarians and ancient DNA retrieved from the remains of burials of what are presumed to be the Magyar elite as well as the local population of the 10th and 11th centuries AD.[58] The results indicated 'that significant genetic differences exist between the ancient and recent Hungarian-speaking populations, and no genetic continuity is seen'.[59] Of 27 ancient DNA samples, two possessed haplogroups that were classically Asiatic, and the general composition suggested that the ancient Hungarians were genetically a different population from the modern Hungarians.[60] In short, at the time of the Magyar settlement the basic population were Slavs, and this may account for why the classical markers indicate a close connection between the Hungarians and the Poles. But in the modern Hungarian population there seems to be little or no evidence of the previous movements out of Asia or indeed of the arrival of the Magyars themselves. A smaller study of the Y chromosome evidence revealed a somewhat similar story.[61]

The lesson from these studies is that analysis of modern DNA may be an exceedingly crude and, in some cases, totally ineffective method for recovering the past genetic history of a population. On the other hand, it also offers some encouragement that with the recovery of ancient DNA, something that is still in its infancy in Ireland, there might be eventual hope of resolving much of the existing speculation regarding the time and place of the different haplotypes that currently makes it so difficult to write a genetic history of the population of Ireland.

Pure Irish?

Finally, a word of warning for those who seek some form of Irish genetic purity: it doesn't exist.[62] Throughout this book I have employed Niall as my target Irishman and we have even seen that geneticists have made a good attempt to recover his Y chromosome. What I have not revealed so far is that Niall's mother, Cairenn, had been carried off from Britain by Niall's father, Eochaid Mugmedón. My archetypal Irishman was in fact half British! In targeting Niall, I have simply drawn an imaginary line across the 5th century and declared anyone who had managed to get into Ireland by that time as 'Irish'. What happened before is genetically irrelevant insofar as the definition of an Irish identity is concerned, because anyone, any gene, that had found its way into Ireland by my census date has an equal claim to be called Irish. To appreciate how arbitrary my definition is, imagine for a moment that you are a Martian scientist attempting to reconstruct Irish genetic history in the distant future. A digital virus has wiped out all the historical records for many intervening centuries, but that doesn't matter: you are going to analyse the DNA of all the population of Ireland who have surnames recorded in the only surviving census, that of the year 2525, which is sufficiently ancient for your purposes. So you assemble the DNA from the current Irish sample population, which includes Brendan O'Hare, Seamus Naujokaitis, Ciaran Kostrzewski and Sean Wang. From the perspective of the Martian scientist, every one of these people has an equal claim to being 'native Irish'. This is not a matter of political correctness but rather the whole nature of the question. Distinguishing a Lithuanian, Pole or Chinese from a 'real' Irishman would be as idle and meaningless as distinguishing someone whose genes had come from an early Mesolithic colonist from northern Britain, a Neolithic farmer from Scotland, a pilgrim from the Church of the Holy Megalith from Brittany, a mead-drinking Beaker-using metallurgist from the Rhineland, or anyone else who had sunk their roots into Ireland by the time Eochaid had dragged poor Cairenn from Britain.[63]

The genetic overview

Although genetics holds much promise for elucidating the past, it is currently moving so rapidly that it is difficult if not impossible to determine a consensus of opinion on even the most fundamental issues concerning the genetic history of Ireland. Paradigms seem to rise and fall within a matter of months and it is difficult to determine what might still be standing when this book sees print. At present, there would appear to be two very different models.

The first model asserts that the modern population of Ireland, identified as Irish through surnames, are primarily derived from the expansion of human populations from southern France and Iberia after the last Ice Age. It also recognizes an influx of people whose genetic signature would appear to derive more immediately from the Near East and whom geneticists believe to have been descended from the initial expansion of farmers from southwest Asia into Europe. After the Neolithic, there is little evidence for any further human immigration until the historical period.[64]

This model is structured as a series of extreme positions that might well be tempered. For example, if the earliest farmers in Ireland were the result of a colonization from anywhere in Atlantic Europe, it is highly probable that they would retain much the same genetic signature as Ireland's earliest inhabitants, i.e. they would once have been local hunter-gatherers who adopted farming from more easterly neighbours. The difference between someone who entered Ireland in 8000 BC (Mesolithic colonization) and 4000 BC (Neolithic colonization) is only 4,000 years, and there is nothing in the previous discussion of founder dates for the various subgroups that instils much confidence that genetic dates operate at this level of precision. Moreover, the same goes for migrations that have been pegged to the beginning of the Irish Neolithic: here again, these may reflect the movement of genes into Ireland during the Bronze Age or later. One gene that may well have entered Ireland during the Neolithic is that associated with lactase persistence, as we now have evidence for milk in Early Neolithic Ireland.[65]

The second model, reflected in the writings of those who have argued that the Y chromosome R1b, for example, is better seen as associated with the Neolithic or later, suggests a very different composition of the modern Irish. Rather than being essentially 'good Europeans', the majority of the population are reinterpreted as descending from Near Eastern farmers with very little echo of the Mesolithic occupants of Ireland. The cautions suggested for Model 1 also apply here, especially as this theory has very recently taken some very hard knocks. Movements of populations may not have been restricted to the Neolithic but may also include later influxes of people during the Bronze and Iron Age. The geographical message of R1b suggests that the later variants are more likely to have derived from north of Iberia in Atlantic Europe rather than Iberia itself.[66]

The fortunate thing about these two models is that we may ultimately be able to test them with the hard evidence of ancient DNA. In the near future it is entirely possible that we will be able at least to ascertain whether, for example, R1b was found in Ireland before the introduction of agriculture, with the first farmers, or still later.

More Mesolithic human remains will need to be found, but at least we can hope that the many uncertainties of this chapter may ultimately find some resolution.

There are two sets of contradictory conclusions for this chapter.

Conclusion 1

→ The principal genetic basis of the Irish population derives from male and female lineages who entered Europe during and after the last Ice Age. These populations branched into different subgroups while isolated in southern refuges and then moved northward when the ice sheets melted.

→ Geographically, most Irish genes would appear to link with a refuge area in southern France or northern Iberia.

→ A minority of Irish genes carry a legacy derived from the spread of the first farmers from the Near East. It is probable that at this time the gene for lactase persistence was also introduced.

→ Most surveys of Ireland's genetic profile fail to find any significant evidence of migrations after the Neolithic.

→ The denial of any further population incursions on the basis of modern genetics is unsafe if we follow the results of studies of Hungarian DNA that reveal that the genetics of the modern population may fail to reflect the actual history of the region.

Conclusion 2

→ The principal genetic basis of the Irish population derives from male and female lineages who entered Europe after the last Ice Age, possibly with the advance of farming from the Near East.

→ There are some traces of population continuity from earlier populations who had been resident in Europe before the end of the last Ice Age, e.g. mtDNA U5.

→ The major male genetic line associated with Ireland (Y R1b) may have entered from the Neolithic period onward.

→ The evidence of current Irish population genetics can neither confirm nor deny the possibility of later gene flow into Ireland during the Bronze and Iron ages.

The extension of ancient DNA testing to the prehistoric population of Ireland should help decide which (if any) of the above models is valid.

CHAPTER NINE

The Evidence of Language

A bout the 5th century AD we find evidence for inscriptions in the earliest form of the Irish language, so we can be reasonably certain that when Niall shouted at his sons or sweet-talked the sovereignty goddess, he did so in an early form of Irish. This is one of the critical reasons why Niall has been selected as our target Irishman, because when one asks people today about the origins of the Irish, they often have in mind the origins of the Irish language and the date and circumstances under which it initially appeared in Ireland. In this way the Irish language has become intimately associated with the entire definition of being Irish, or as it might be expressed in the Irish saying: *ní tir gan teanga* '[there is] no country without a language'.[1] On the other hand, few today would regard competence in the Irish language as the essential characteristic of anyone who claimed to be Irish, and even its earlier role in identifying people as Irish is somewhat ambiguous. We have seen in Chapter 7 that the tradition that derived the Irish from the Milesian invasion from Iberia (1700 BC) overlooks the earlier 'invention' of the Irish language by Gáedel Glas[2] and the presumption that everyone who set foot in Ireland from Nemed (2350 BC) onward should have spoken Irish.

To investigate the origins of the Irish language we will need to begin with the earliest evidence for Irish and then progressively examine the linguistic evidence in increasingly wider contexts in the hope that this may provide some hint as to where Irish originated, when it arrived and how it spread. After we have taken the linguistic evidence as far as we can, we will see whether any of the other disciplines, especially archaeology, can help us resolve the problem.

Of course, we have to deal with more than the question of language, because the Irish language is closely tied up with the whole concept of the Celts. Any popular introduction to Irish history will usually include some reference to the Celts or Gaels entering Ireland sometime around 500–300 BC where they introduced the Irish language. A survey of some of the more recent work suggests that relentless hammering by archaeologists has had some impact, as we no longer find reference to mass invasions of Celts but generally the immigration of small groups.[3] Nevertheless, there is still a serious problem with the word 'Celt'; it is so loaded in meaning and import that I have done everything I could to avoid using the 'C' word in earlier chapters. But now I must acknowledge the elephant in the room and, before we take up more strictly linguistic matters, we need to get past the troublesome concept of 'the Celts'.

Celts

The Celts as the name of an ethnic group derives from the testimony of both Greek and Roman geographers and historians, who referred to one of the major peoples of ancient Europe as *Keltoi* in Greek sources or *Celtae* in Latin. By the 4th century BC the Greeks divided the barbarians (non-Greeks) of the world into four major peoples: Ethiopians in Africa, Indians in south Asia, Scythians to the north and east of the Greeks (on the steppelands of the Ukraine and Russia) and the Celts who dwelt near the source of the Danube (which the Greek historian Herodotus had relocated to Iberia). Later classical writers subdivided the western part of Europe among the Iberians in the south, the Celts in the middle, and the Germans in the north. References to the Celts in classical literature begin about 700 BC and, in terms of contemporary accounts of what was recognized as a distinct ethnic group, ceased about AD 500.[4] They describe, usually in unflattering terms, the behaviour of the Celts (prone to drunkenness, incest, cannibalism) and they also record the expansion of Celtic peoples both southward (where they attacked Rome around 390 BC) and eastward (where they sacked Delphi in Greece in 279 BC, invaded and settled in central Turkey, and served as mercenaries across the Near East and Egypt). The Celts are most closely identified with the Gauls whom Julius Caesar described and conquered, although the relationship between the two terms (Gauls and Celts) is complicated and can be ambiguous, depending on the author concerned.[5]

That the ancient authors never referred to the ancient British or Irish as 'Celts'[6] has attracted an enormous amount of publicity and debate over whether we can legitimately apply the term 'Celtic' to the Irish (and ancient British) or whether the 'Celtic' name represents a recent myth constructed by modern nationalists in Ireland, Scotland and Wales to put distance between them and the dominant English.[7] Celto-sceptics argue that the concept of the Irish or ancient British (and modern Welsh) being Celtic only arose in the 16th century when the Scottish poet and scholar George Buchanan (1506–82), examining the evidence of the language of the Gauls, concluded that 'the ancient Gaels and the Britons were branches of the ancient Celtic people of the Continent'. This idea gained in popularity when the writings of the Breton monk Paul-Yves Pezron were published in 1703 and was provided with abundant linguistic cover in 1707 by Edward Llwyd (1660–1709) in his *Archaeologia Britannica*. A Celtic bandwagon had begun to roll that brought the Celts well within the Romantic movement in Matthew Arnold's (1822–88) *On the Study of Celtic Literature*. The Celts seemed to be the ancestral population of both Britain and Ireland, but there was still a major problem that the Irish historian Eoin MacNeill had to confront in 1919:

> From the earliest traceable traditions of the Gaelic people down to the
> time of George Buchanan, there is not the slightest glimmer of
> recognition that the Celts of Ireland were Celts, or that they were more
> nearly akin to the Celts of Britain than to any other population of
> white men.[8]

In a nutshell, not only was there no evidence that anyone on the Continent ever extended the name Celts to the people of Ireland but also, until the time of George Buchanan, no one in Ireland ever imagined that they shared any particular kinship with their British neighbours, irrespective of what cover name might be applied. While a clever medieval Icelander had worked out that his language (Old Norse) and Old English were two branches of the same family tree, his contemporaries in Ireland failed to recognize their own cross-water kinship. Time and again, medieval Irish scholars seem to have turned a blind eye to their Celtic relations. Golden opportunities such as the preparation of Cormac's glossary around the 9th century,[9] for example, found no privileged position for Welsh. More importantly, as Eoin MacNeill recognized nearly a century ago, when the Irish came to deriving themselves from the various peoples of Europe, ironically the one they avoided was the only one to whom they were clearly related. We may recall from Chapter 7 that the earliest classical geographies of Europe divided the Continent into thee main groups: the Scythians of the east (from whom the Irish traced some of their deepest origins), the Celts of the west and the Iberians in the western Mediterranean. The Irish accounts looked to both Scythians and Iberians but totally ignored the one ancient people, the Celts, whose language, customs and religion were most akin to their own.[10] Perhaps we should not be too surprised, because by the Middle Ages the Irish and Welsh languages were significantly different. Patrick Sims-Williams provides a good example when he cites the opening lines of the Lord's Prayer in their medieval Irish and Welsh versions:[11]

Middle Irish: *A athair fil hi nimib, noemthar th'ainm.*
Middle Welsh: *Yn tat ni yr hwnn ysyd yn y nefoed…kadarnhaer dy enw ti.*

On the other hand, as we will soon see, there is absolutely no question whatsoever that the languages of the Irish, Welsh, Cornish and the immigrants who left Britain to form the Bretons are closely related to one another and also to ancient languages attested widely over Atlantic Europe and beyond.

The main critics of the use of the term 'Celtic' are archaeologists who reject or at least want to mitigate how much baggage the term 'Celtic' has accrued. Celto-sceptics would argue that there is no evidence that there was once a uniform Celtic culture that covered western Europe, Britain and Ireland, nor can one utilize the archaeological or ethnographic evidence concerning the Celts of the Continent to explain the behaviour of the 'Celtic' peoples of Britain or Ireland nor, conversely, can the literary evidence of the medieval Irish or Welsh be used to explain the behaviour of the ancient Gauls or indeed of their own prehistoric ancestors. Nor do we have any reason to suppose that populations in Britain or Ireland ever imagined themselves to be 'Celts' or, indeed, a single people (rather than members of whatever tribal grouping they belonged to).[12] We are into sensitive political territory here, with 'Celticity' regarded by some as an inherent element in the national self-identification of the Irish. When a recent popular introduction to Irish history boasts that 'Ireland is now the only remaining Celtic nation in the world'[13] you can understand why, in the eyes of some, dismissal of the Irish as a Celtic 'people' may be regarded as a form of intellectual genocide perpetrated largely by insensitive or even malicious English academics. On the other hand, one can also marvel that people really want to embrace a Celtic identity that the 19th-century American anthropologist Daniel Garrison Brinton dismissed as follows:

> Their mental traits are quite conspicuous: turbulent, boastful, alert, courageous, but deficient in caution, persistence and self-control, they never have succeeded in forming an independent state, and are a dangerous element in the body politic of a free country. In religion they are fanatic and bigoted, ready to swear in the words of their master, rather than to exercise independent judgment. France is three-fifths of Celtic descent, and this explains much in its history and character of its inhabitants.[14]

Nevertheless, the Celtic brand name sells very well indeed and is applied to art, language, literature, women, warfare, music, new-age healing traditions and a host of other subjects marketed as 'authentic' Irish culture. There seems to be so much ambiguity about the meaning of the term that Raimund Karl toyed with a highly flexible definition:

> A Celt is someone who *either* speaks a Celtic language *or* produces or
> uses Celtic art *or* material culture *or* has been referred to as one in
> historical records *or* has identified himself *or* been identified by others
> as such &c.[15]

That the languages of Ireland, Britain and Gaul were closely related had been suggested by the 16th century, and shortly after 1700 this closely related group of languages was sometimes referred to as Celtic. By the early 19th century suggestions and speculations were grounded in sound linguistic analysis when Celtic was recognized as a constituent branch of the Indo-European family of languages.[16] Linguists today have absolutely no problem referring to Irish as a Celtic language, and indeed it is the only term employed; there is no alternative. In some ways it is safer than some of the other names for branches of the Indo-European family. It is used in the same way that English is termed a Germanic language (although I wouldn't recommend calling anyone from England, or for that matter anyone from the Netherlands or Scandinavia, a German). Moreover, we cannot by any means be certain that the ancient tribe of Germani actually spoke a Germanic language (their leaders bore Celtic names). In short, the designation of the Germanic language family may be far more flawed than the Celtic, but this does not seem to inspire the emotional hysteria that 'Celtic' does.

Anyway, to get around the problem, this chapter is about the Celtic languages and does not presume any other form of 'Celticity'. On the other hand, I would also emphasize that a language is not some trivial veneer, superimposed over one's 'real' culture.

Irish through time and space

In *Gulliver's Travels*, we meet a race of immortals, the Struldbrugs, who could not understand members of later generations and after about two centuries were incapable of communicating with the local mortals. Gulliver (or Jonathan Swift if you insist) blamed this on the fact that 'the language of this country [was always in a state of] flux'. In this, he was very much on the mark: all languages are in a continual process of change.

An English speaker will find the language of Shakespeare 400 years ago difficult enough at times. For example, while the abusive intent is fairly obvious, the modern reader may find the following verbal assault less than clear:

'You scullion! You rampallian! You fustilarian! I'll tickle your catastrophe!' (*Henry IV, Part 2*)

You low-order kitchen help! You rascal! You fustilarian [a made-up term of abuse]! I'll beat your arse!

A glance at a proverb from Chaucer, whose language is a mere 600 years away from us, can also throw up some rather opaque lines:

'Alwey the nye slye maketh the ferre leeve to be looth' (*Canterbury Tales*, The Miller's Tale, 3392–93)

Always the near sly one makes the distant dear one to be unwanted [out of sight, out of mind].

And the text of Beowulf, even comparatively 'easy' passages where the vocabulary has been retained in Modern English, is usually incomprehensible after 1,200 years:

'Léoht éastan cóm beorht béacen godes' (*Beowulf*, 569–70)

Light from the east came, bright beacon of god.

These examples are taken from the three different stages of English: Old English (700–1100), Middle English (1100–1450) and Modern English (1450–). The Irish language trumps English in that it enjoys a longer textual tradition that can be divided into four periods: Ogam Irish (400–700), Old Irish (700–900), Middle Irish (900–1200) and Modern Irish (1200–).

As we can see (Table 9.1), the most abrupt change across the four periods is that between Ogam Irish, the language of the earliest Irish inscriptions, and Old Irish. Although we have some Irish names from classical sources that go back earlier, the

Table 9.1 **Irish through time**

Ogam Irish	Old Irish	Modern Irish	English
alattos	*allaid*	*allaidh*	wild
battigni	*baíth*		
cattu-	*cath*	*cath*	battle
cuna-	*cú*	*cú*	hound
druta	*drúth*		
eqo-	*ech*	*each*	horse
-gusso(s)	*gus*		
inigena	*ingen*	*iníon*	daughter
maqi	*maic*	*maic*	(of the) son
ol-	*oll*	*oll*	
qeno	*cenn*	*ceann*	head
qritti	*creth*		
tigern	*tigern*	*tiarna*	lord

earliest native writing employed ogam, a script comprising incised notches along the edges of an upright stone, almost exclusively utilized to produce dedications (9.1). Ogam is dated to about the 5th through 8th centuries and the inscriptions are primarily known from Munster, although some are found across the rest of Ireland (9.2). For anyone who has studied a classical language such as Latin, Ogam Irish is in some ways less strange than Old Irish. For example, it still retains many of the case endings of its nouns (*-os*, *-a*; cf. Latin *-us*, *-a*). But the same words when they emerged in the earliest Irish books in Old Irish had often been radically shortened and mangled.[17] They lost their original case endings (although the 'ghosts' of the original case endings would haunt the word that followed) and every other syllable was also dropped. Hence all that survived into Old Irish of the names of men inscribed in ogam as Cattubuttas, Cunagussos and Cunavali was Cathbad, Congus and Conall. Possible reasons for this radical shift will be explored later in this chapter.

9.1. The ogam alphabet.

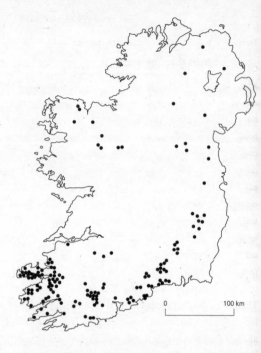

9.2. Distribution of ogam inscriptions in Ireland.

0   100 km

Not only did the Irish language pass through different stages but, as we know from the distribution of ogam stones, it also spread from Ireland to Scotland and the Isle of Man (and, abortively, to southwest Britain). These expansions are set to the 1st millennium AD (the Ogam and Old Irish periods) and account for why Irish, Scots Gaelic[18] and Manx form a single group of closely related languages with a common ancestor in the earliest form of Irish. This group is known to linguists as Goidelic because the Irish, amazingly enough, came to refer to themselves as Goidels, the unflattering name given to them by the Welsh (*gwyddel*) which meant 'wild men' or 'raiders'.[19] The search for the origins of the Irish language is, in effect, a search for the origins of Goidelic.

Insular Celtic

The nearest geographical relations to Goidelic are the various Brittonic languages, first encountered by the Romans in their conquest of Britain. These comprise Ancient British (AD 1–600), Welsh (600–), Cornish (800–1800) and, after migration from southern Britain to the Continent, Breton (800–). To illustrate their neighbourliness, let's briefly examine a list of some animal names from early Irish and the various Brittonic languages (Table 9.2).

Table 9.2 **Insular Celtic animal names**

Old Irish	Modern Welsh	Middle Cornish	Modern Breton	English
abac	afanc	-	avank	±beaver
art	arth	ors	arzh	bear
bó	buwch	bugh	buoc'h	cow
brocc	broch	broch	broc'h	badger
cú	ci	ci	ki	dog
cuilén	colwyn	coloin	kolen	puppy
elit	elein	elen	-	deer, hind
gabor	gafr	gaver	gavr	goat
loarn	llewyrn	lowarn	louarn	fox
loíg	llo	leugh	leue	calf
oss	ychen	oghen	oc'hen	ox, deer
tarb	tarw	tarow	tarv	bull

This table as well as a much more thorough comparison of Irish with the pre-Roman languages of Britain makes it absolutely clear that they are all closely related to one another and thus Goidelic and Brittonic are grouped together as the Insular Celtic languages. The table of animal names suggests systematic similarities, but we need to be aware of systematic differences as well. In Table 9.3 we list a series of other words, specifically chosen to illustrate one major difference between Goidelic and Brittonic.

Table 9.3 **Irish and British words**

Old Irish	Modern Welsh	Middle Cornish	Modern Breton	English
cethir	petguar	peswar	petguar	four
cóic	pump	pymp	pemp	five
coire	peir	per	per	cauldron
cré	pridd	pri	pri	clay
cruth	pryd	pryd	pred	form, time
ech	ebol	ebel	ebeul	horse
macc	mab	mab	mab	son

A quick glance indicates that wherever we find a 'c' in Irish we find a 'p' (or 'b') in the Brittonic languages. Indeed, the name Brittonic is another example, since the early British name for the island was *Prettanía*, which we also find in Middle Welsh

Prydein, but in Irish the same word is expressed as *Cruithne* with a 'c'. The reason for the difference is that the original sound was what linguists term a labio-velar, involving a back of the throat sound ('k') modified by pushing it through one's rounded lips ('w'), which may be written as 'kʷ' or 'q'.[20] There are other systematic differences between Goidelic and Brittonic, but the shorthand way of describing these is to refer to Goidelic as 'Q-Celtic' (because it retained the 'q' sound in the oldest Irish inscriptions, e.g. *maqqa* which later became *macc* 'son') and to Brittonic as 'P-Celtic', because it only retained the labial (lip-sounded) part of the original sound (e.g. Old Welsh *map*). We will soon meet this distinction again.

Continental Celtic

Although the Insular Celtic languages are the best known as they survived the expansion of the Roman Empire, the largest area of Celtic speech, mostly attested in the first centuries BC before and during the expansion of the Roman Empire, is western and central Europe. The Celtic languages of Continental Europe are generally divided into three groups with some smaller (attested) outliers such as Galatian in Turkey.[21] Gaulish was the language of southern and western Gaul, the territory conquered by Julius Caesar, which is attested in inscriptions (and later in loanwords in French) from about the 3rd century BC into the first centuries AD. There was also a small enclave in northern Italy in the region of Milan where we have inscriptions in the Lepontic language, another Celtic language. Lepontic dates from about the 6th century BC into the first centuries BC. Like British, both of these branches of Celtic had made the shift from 'q' to 'p'. To these we may add a large area of Iberia where we have inscriptions in the Ibero-Celtic or, perhaps better, Hispano-Celtic languages, an undoubted separate branch of the Celtic languages. Hispano-Celtic inscriptions generally date from the first centuries BC, but John Koch has recently argued that we should now include the language of southwest Iberia, Tartessian, in the Hispano-Celtic group, which would push the dates for this branch back to the 8th century BC.[22] Hispano-Celtic, like Irish, retained the 'q' sound. Finally, we have a handful of words that survived the eastern expansion of the Celts into Anatolia (Turkey) where they settled in Galatia.[23] Irish is clearly related to these Continental Celtic languages, e.g. Hispano-Celtic *ebur* 'yew' = Gaulish *eburos* 'yew' = Old Irish *ibar* 'yew'; Hispano-Celtic *briga*, Gaulish *briga*, Old Irish *brí* 'hill'; Hispano-Celtic *uiros*, Gaulish *uiros* and Old Irish *fer* 'man'.

The earliest testimony

Although Ogam Irish provides the earliest *native* testimony of the Irish language in Ireland, we also have somewhat earlier evidence that people speaking a Celtic language had been settled in Ireland by at least the 2nd century AD. The great geographer Ptolemy (AD 100–180), writing in the library of Alexandria in Egypt, compiled an atlas of the known world, beginning in the west with Ireland and proceeding eastward to the frontiers of China. From this atlas we retain a gazetteer with the names of peoples and places and their coordinates within the Greek cartographical system. Ptolemy lists 53 names for Ireland (9.3).[24] These come to us through a truly baroque game of Chinese whispers. The ultimate source was probably British merchants who coursed the Irish Sea and obtained the names of Irish peoples and places. They would have passed the information to the Romans where it was gathered by Philemon in the 1st century AD and then recorded in Latin by Marinus of Tyre, but Ptolemy then transposed the text into the more academic language of Greek. His work was preserved through being written down by generation after generation of scribes, for whom much of the text would have been unremitting gibberish. Although there is

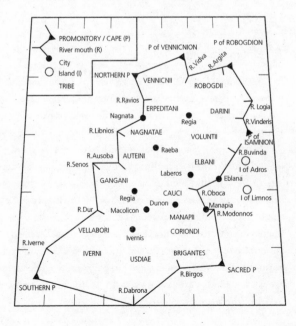

9.3. Ptolemy's Ireland.

an earlier 12th-century Arabic translation, the earliest preserved Greek text dates to the 14th century, so the scribes had over a thousand years to get the names distorted beyond all recognition. Remarkably, that is not always the case and there are some names for Ireland that are relatively transparent. For example, Ptolemy provides the coordinates for *Bououinda potamou ekbolai*, 'mouth (*ekbolai*) of the river (*potamou*) *Bououinda*' (which is not only in the right position but makes the right sound to be the Old Irish river name *Bóand*, the modern Boyne, which would have meant 'the cow-white' river). Ptolemy's *Sēnou potamou ekbolai* designated the mouth of the *Senos*, now known as the Shannon, 'the old (river)', a name matched also in Britain (the *Sena*). He also lists the names of towns, although some of these are generic names such as *Dunon* 'fort' and *Rēgia* 'royal site'.[25] There is one town in the vicinity of Dublin that is called Eblana and which Patrizia De Bernardo Stempel explains as 'the Crowded Place', summoning up images of Iron Age tourists attempting to forge their way up Grafton Street. How many of the names can be provided with convincing etymologies is somewhat debatable, but many have been provided with Celtic etymologies and at least some have been equated with known places and names later encountered in early Irish history.[26] Unfortunately, a study of this earliest source of Irish names throws up an unexpected problem in our search for the origins of the Irish language.

P-Celts in Ireland

In 1946 Thomas O'Rahilly examined Ptolemy's list of names and argued that while many of the names could be supplied with Celtic etymologies, not one of the names was demonstrably Goidelic and seven of the names were best identified as Brittonic.[27] His most obvious example is the tribal name Manapioi which, as we have seen above should have been **Manaqii* if it were Irish but shows the characteristic $*k^w > p$ shift that helps define Brittonic. This is further supported by the fact that Ptolemy also lists a tribe called the Menapii in Gaul. Similarly, the Brigantes were a well-known British tribe (northeast England) that Ptolemy also located in Ireland. Another tribe ascribed to Ireland, the Gagganoi, is also known across the sea in northwest Wales where Ptolemy designates the Lleyn peninsula as the 'headland of the Gangani'. On the surface of it O'Rahilly's evidence pointed to a conclusion that could certainly warm the heart of any unionist: the earliest linguistic evidence for the names of the peoples and places of Ireland suggested that Ireland was *originally* British and that the Irish were latecomers!

While some of O'Rahilly's ultimate conclusions (see below) are usually rejected, most recent scholars do accept the presence of P-Celtic names in Ireland.[28] In the most recent examination of Ptolemy's Ireland, Patrizia De Bernardo Stempel identifies five tribes and one town as Gallo-British, i.e. Brigantes, Koriondoi, Ganganoi, Velaboroi and the Manapioi who also held the 'town' of Manapia.[29] De Bernardo Stempel also emphasizes that these form a coherent set of tribal groups settled adjacent to one another in the south of Ireland, and we have already reviewed in Chapter 5 the evidence for Romano-British settlement in the island. The possibility of British settlers in Ireland is widely accepted and was employed by both O'Rahilly and later scholars to explain why there are a good number of British loanwords in Irish. These are not likely to have been the only British in Ireland, as we could add the probable presence of some British warlords and monks and, of course, British slaves resident in Ireland around the time of St Patrick.[30] To these we might also add both personal names and genealogical traditions that trace some Irish families back to Gaul.[31]

As for O'Rahilly's lack of Goidelic names, De Bernardo Stempel does identify six Goidelic names, largely place names but including one possible tribal name, the Robogdioi of the northeast.[32] Most of the place names are located in Ulster. For the rest of the names, distinguishing between Goidelic and Brittonic is impossible.

In general, the evidence of Ptolemy is usually taken to indicate that by about the 1st century AD we can say with some certainty that a Celtic language was spoken in Ireland. We cannot say whether it was the only language spoken. In addition to Proto-Irish there is some evidence for a P-Celtic language, and there may have been remnants of an earlier non-Indo-European language as well (see below). We also do not know how much earlier whatever Celtic language or languages we are dealing with was brought to Ireland. To get a better handle on the problem we need to delve still earlier into the linguistic history of Irish.

Indo-Europeans

The linguistic relations of Irish are not limited to the Celtic group but extend to the entire Indo-European language family. Indo-European is the largest language family in the world in terms of speakers and comprises almost but not quite all the language groups of Europe, e.g. Germanic (English, Dutch, German, Scandinavian), Italic (Latin, the modern Romance languages of Italian, French, Spanish, Portuguese, Romanian, etc.), Baltic (Lithuanian, Latvian), Slavic (Russian, Polish, Czech, etc.), Albanian and Greek, and languages both ancient and modern found in western Asia

(Hittite, Phrygian, Armenian), further east (Iranian, Sanskrit) and in the western extremity of China (Tocharian). This means that the language of Niall of the Nine Hostages shares the same distant linguistic ancestor with his contemporaries, the Tocharians of the Tarim basin of China,[33] although they are so far apart (c. 6,500 km) that if one shouted a word loud enough in the land of the Tocharians it would take over five hours to be heard in Dublin. In Table 9.4 we compare some basic vocabulary in Old Irish, the not-so-distant Latin and the far-off Tocharian.

Table 9.4 Old Irish, Latin and Tocharian B

Old Irish	Latin	Tocharian B	English
athair	pāter	pācer	father
máthair	māter	mācer	mother
bráthair	frāter	procer	brother
ab	amnis	āp	river
cré	crēta	kwriye	clay
mí	mēnsis	meñe	moon
cú	canis	ku	dog
ech	equus	yakwe	horse
oss	–	okso	ox
oí	ovis	āu	sheep
étan	ante	ānte	forehead, before

Membership in the Indo-European family provides us with a crude but useful constraint on the time and place of the earliest Celts in Ireland. As Irish is a branch of Celtic and Celtic is a branch of Indo-European, it can hardly have arrived in Ireland before the spread of the Indo-European languages.

Language in space

Does the Irish language provide any evidence to suggest from which direction it arrived in Ireland? Consider for a moment the origins of English. We know that it is a Germanic language, part of a group comprising German, Frisian, Dutch, the Scandinavian languages and ancient Gothic. Of all these languages, the nearest relation to English is Frisian, a language spoken in the north of the Netherlands and the adjacent area of northern Germany.[34] The next 'closest' language to English is Low

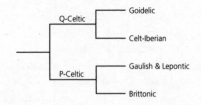

9.4. Traditional Celtic tree linking Goidelic and Celt-Iberian.

German. On the basis of this one could surmise that as English is intrusive to Britain, it probably came from near the area where we now find Frisian and Low German, which is precisely what both the historical records and all other evidence indicates. Can we take a similar line with Irish?

Unfortunately, there are two major and quite opposed schools of thought regarding the relationships between the Celtic languages. The first, the more traditional model,[35] regards the 'q/p' split as a significant factor in the subdivision of the Celtic languages which indicates two major branches of Celtic (9.4). Here we see that Irish is regarded as a conservative language along with the Celtic language(s) of Iberia. We can see immediately where this might lead: the ancestor of the Irish language must have come from Iberia, and the traditional legend of the Sons of Míl has therefore been verified by linguistics. But this could also be read another way. Recall that in order to follow a family line in genetics, we tracked the sequence of mutations – and the same goes for linguistic relationships. Conserving the $*k^w$ sound gives no indication of a shared innovation (= mutation) and only indicates that the ancestors of the Celts in Iberia and Ireland were not affected when the $*k^w > p$ shift spread through France, Italy and Britain. Moreover, we even find traces of Q-Celtic still in Gaul in the first centuries BC, and many would actually argue that the shift from $*k^w$ to $*p$ is fairly trivial as it also occurs in Indo-European languages in Italy and to some extent in Greece. In short, Irish and Hispano-Celtic are grouped together because they are peripheral to the spread of $*k^w > p$ and not because Irish derived from an earlier form of Celt-Iberian or Hispano-Celtic.

The second model, championed by Kim McCone and Peter Schrijver,[36] suggests that the Celtic languages should be split into two different groups according to the scheme in 9.5. Here we see that the split occurs geographically, with the Insular Celtic languages forming their own subgroup. In this model, we should expect that Britain and Ireland shared the same source for their Celtic languages, and it is plausible that whatever 'Celticized' Britain then had the same effect on Ireland. What this model does not do is provide a secure anchor for Insular Celtic in either Gaul or Iberia.

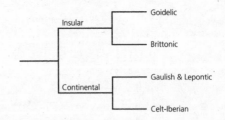

9.5. Revised Celtic tree linking Goidelic with Brittonic.

Patrick Sims-Williams's recent attempt to deal with all these issues concluded that 'attempts to prove the existence of either Gallo-Brittonic or Insular Celtic have failed so far'.[37] In the end, one can probably devise any number of scenarios. For example, the traditional model could still be seen to show that the conservative variety of Q-Celtic passed through Iberia and then went on to Ireland, or, alternatively, that a conservative version of Celtic initially spread to Iberia and across the Channel to both Britain and Ireland and that P-Celtic then spread from Gaul to Britain but not to Ireland.[38] In short, there is no widely accepted geographical homeland for Irish that can be established purely on the basis of the interrelationships among the Celtic languages.

Time depth

In order to trace the spread of the Celtic language to Ireland in space, we need to know roughly *when* it spread in time. While we can assign dates to the various stages of the written language because we can examine texts, unfortunately it is far more difficult – many would say impossible – to provide dates for prehistoric languages. Attempts have been made to do this, but the results rarely command much acceptance.

One technique, often cited but usually rejected (at least in the field of the Indo-European languages), is glottochronology. This assumes that vocabulary shared between two languages that came from the same source language (e.g. French and Italian both come from Latin) disintegrates at a constant rate over time. In more precise terms, two languages originally sharing the same basic vocabulary will see that vocabulary 'decay' at roughly the rate of 14% every thousand years for a select basic test vocabulary of 100 words. Conversely, two closely related languages that have replaced about 14% of their core vocabulary should have split from one another about a thousand years ago. Various linguists have sought to calculate, for example, when the Goidelic and Brittonic languages separated from one another. Back in 1964

David Greene put the split between Q- and P-Celtic at about 700 BC.[39] In a study of 2006, Novotna and Blažek calculated that Goidelic, Brittonic and Gaulish all separated from one another *c.* 1100 BC.[40] This is not too far off another study by Gray and Atkinson, who placed the separation of Goidelic and Brittonic as having occurred *c.* 2,900 years ago, i.e. *c.* 900 BC.[41] On the other hand, employing a different method, Forster and Toth computed that Celtic should have spread to Britain some time between *c.* 4700 and 1700 BC, i.e. somewhere between the Mesolithic and the Bronze Age![42] This would see Insular Celtic split from Gaulish first and then the two Insular Celtic branches diverging on their respective islands. However, many linguists do not accept that there is a core vocabulary which provides a valid basis for calculating a date of separation nor that all languages replace this so-called 'basic' vocabulary at the same rate. Moreover, even if the assumptions underlying glottochronology were correct, the practical problems of actually analysing the data are often so difficult that any results are far from precise.

A second approach to the dating of the Celtic languages involves comparing their reconstructed vocabulary against the evidence of archaeology to determine when (and possibly where) an ancestral language was spoken. It should be emphasized that one or two words are not likely to be definitive; after all, the Irish retained Proto-Celtic *natrik-* in Old Irish *nathir* 'serpent', the one item of fauna that Ireland is famously lacking. But if we take the reconstructed vocabulary as a whole, we can narrow down the date by which the ancestor of the Irish language was likely to be spoken in Ireland. First, all Indo-European languages share a series of common words for domesticated plants and animals as well as some of the material culture associated with agriculture. This includes the names for animals that were only introduced into Ireland at the beginning of the Neolithic. For example, there are several words associated with the cow in early Irish that are cognate (i.e. share the same ancestral word) with names for the same animals in other Indo-European languages, e.g. Old Irish (OIr) *bó* 'cow' and Sanskrit (Skt) *gau-* 'cow', OIr *dam* 'bull' and Skt *damya-* 'young bull', and even the Middle Irish (MIr) *búachaill* 'herdsman, boy' which compares with Greek *boukólos* 'cowherd'. We also have the names of other animals, e.g. OIr *erp* 'she-goat' and Skt *āreya-* 'ram', OIr *ói* 'sheep' and Skt *ávi-* 'sheep', and OIr *ech* 'horse' and Skt *áśva-* 'horse'. Other words that are associated with things or activities that should not have been present in Ireland until the Neolithic would be the plough (the MIr noun *arathar* 'plough' and MIr verb *airid* 'ploughs', which are cognate with Greek *árotron* and *aróō*). Within an Irish context none of these (except the cow bones from Ferriter's Cove) should date earlier than 4000 BC.

Now what does all this mean in terms of dating the Irish language? Here we can try a thought experiment. Let us propose that the earliest inhabitants of Ireland spoke Irish, i.e. that Irish was spoken from *c.* 8000 BC. How would we then explain that we have a word for the plough, inherited from Proto-Indo-European, when the Mesolithic colonists of Ireland lived over 4,000 years before the plough came to Ireland? This would require about 160 generations of Irelanders carefully passing down a word in their vocabulary for a tool they neither have nor need. Because of such words – and there are quite a number associated with farming and stock-raising – we can feel confident that the earliest Irelanders who occupied Ireland throughout the Mesolithic did not speak Irish or a language directly ancestral to it. This means that for 40% of the time that Ireland has been occupied, it has not been occupied by anyone who spoke anything remotely related to Irish. We can confidently narrow the development of the Irish language to the period between *c.* 4000 BC and AD 100. Can we constrain this date any further?

Among the items known to Celtic-speakers before they arrived in Ireland was the 'wagon' (OIr *carr*, cf. Gaulish *Karróduunon*), whose earliest form was borrowed by the Romans into Latin (*carrus*); they also shared a word for the 'chariot' (OIr *carpat*, cf. Gaulish *carpento-*) and possibly MIr *cul* (cognate with one of the Indo-European words for 'wheel') if it does mean 'chariot'. Wheeled vehicles do not appear in Atlantic Europe until after 3000 BC, i.e. after the introduction of farming in Ireland, and there is no certain evidence of wheeled vehicles in Ireland until about the 1st millennium BC.

The names of metals in Irish should be instructive, since we have no evidence for metallurgy in Ireland before the Beaker period (*c.* 2500 BC). All branches of the Celtic languages share a common word for 'silver', e.g. Hispano-Celtic *arkanta*, Gaulish *argento-*, Old Irish *arggat*, Middle Welsh *aryant*, and these derive from a Common Celtic word **arganto-* 'silver' which in turn simply continues a much earlier word that has survived in a number of other Indo-European branches, e.g. Latin *argentum*, Armenian *arcat'*, Sanskrit *rajatám*. So we can claim that the earliest Celts knew 'silver' as a metal (and not just as a colour). How early did anyone know of a metal such as silver in western Europe? The earliest evidence dates to the late 3rd millennium BC on the Continent and the earliest silver known in Ireland may date to the Late Bronze Age,[43] although it does not occur in any significant amount until the first centuries AD when Ireland sees Roman silver imports.

Some words for metals were probably created later than Proto-Indo-European but earlier than the dispersal of the Celtic languages. We have Proto-Celtic **loudyo* (Old Irish *luaide* 'lead') which is related to Latin *plumbum* 'lead', possibly loaned into both language groups from some other source. We do not find the use of lead in Irish metallurgy until about *c*. 1500 BC onward. One of the most recent words for a type of metal is Common Celtic **isarno* 'iron', which is found in Gaulish (*isarno*), Old Welsh *haern* and Old Irish *iärn*, and this should date to about the 1st millennium BC. Incidentally, the words for 'lead' and 'iron' were borrowed by the neighbouring Germanic-speaking peoples, which is why we find both of them in English. All of these metal names suggest a Late Bronze Age or Iron Age date.

In general, some of the late cultural vocabulary could date to the Late Bronze Age while other words fit more easily within the Iron Age. They suggest that any attempt to place the Irish language within Ireland much before about 1500–1000 BC runs into increasingly serious linguistic objections. These dates also concur with the range of dates most often suggested on either impressionistic[44] or glotto-chronological grounds (for anyone who believes) for determining the split of the Celtic branches. We are dealing with a line of evidence whose logic is a bit fluid, so we cannot be totally doctrinaire about the implications of such dates. But we can under-stand why linguists object to setting the arrival of the 'Proto-Irish' in the Neolithic or even the Early Bronze Age. And there is further linguistic evidence that suggests a Celtic language entered Ireland later rather than earlier.

Just as in genetics, where one may argue that the most recent divisions are marked by the least number of mutations between two samples, so also in linguistics it is reasoned that the more similar two languages are to one another, the less time they have been apart. When we first encounter the languages of Ireland, Britain and Gaul, they often appear remarkably similar and not that far removed from their recon-structed ancestral form (Proto-Celtic) (Table 9.5).

Table 9.5 Comparison of earliest Celtic languages

Proto-Celtic	Ogam	Gaulish	English
*baito-	*battigni*	*baitos*	stupid
*barro-	*-bar*	*-barrus*	point
*biwo-	*bivi-*	*biuonia*	alive
*brokko-	*broci*	*broco-*	badger
*dallo-	*dali*	*dallo*	blind
*drūto-	*druta*	*drutos*	foolish
*dubu-aidu-	*dovaidona*	*dovedōn*	dark fire
*ekʷo-	*eqo-*	*epos*	horse

Proto-Celtic	Ogam	Gaulish	English
*genos-	gena	genus	family
*glano-	glannani	glanis	clean
*gustu-	-gusso(s)	gussu-	force
*kasso-	cas-oni	casses	curly?
*katu-	cattu-	catu-	battle
*ki	ci	koui	this
*kunos	cuna-	cuno-	hound
*kʷenno-	cenni	penno	head
*kʷritu-	qritti	pritios	poetry
*Lugu-	Lugu	Lugus	Lug
*maglo-	magli	maglus	noble
*makʷo-	maqi	mapo-	son
*medu	meddo	medu	mead
*meli	meli	meli	honey
*olyo-	ol-	ollos	large, all
*rīg-	rigas	rix	king
*rowdo-	rod	roudius	red
*tigerno-	tigern	tigerno-	lord
*trexs(n)o-	trena	trennus	strong
*wekʷo-	veq	uepo	face
*windo-	vendo	vindo	white

These comparisons even go down to the level of proper names, such as the Irish *Cuna-cenni* = Gaulish *Cunopennus* 'dog-head'; Irish *Lugudeccas* = Gaulish *Lucudeca* 'Lug's servant'; Irish *Meddo-geni* = Gaulish *medu-genos* = Hispano-Celtic *mezukenos* 'honey-born'. This degree of similarity does not suggest that Irish and Gaulish, for example, had been apart for millennia before they entered the written record and, as Ancient British is midway between these two, it is even less likely that Irish and British had long been separated. Indeed, Peter Schrijver has argued that the first serious difference, other than the split between '*q*' and '*p*', between British and Irish does not appear until the 1st century AD.[45] Schrijver concludes from this that the linguistic identity of Irish and British Celtic up to so recent a period (i.e. the 1st century AD) is irreconcilable with the idea that the ancestor of Irish and the ancestor of British Celtic had been geographically separated by the Irish Sea for any length of time, for had that been the case, at least some linguistic differences, however trivial, should have arisen.

Another reason for opting for a more recent date is the fact that Old Irish was a monolithic language, lacking regional dialects. Today, of course, the Irish language can be divided broadly into Munster, Connacht or Ulster dialects, and we find the same phenomenon of regional dialects in English across Britain. But even when we delve into the earlier history of English or any of the other languages attested in the Middle Ages, we still find regional dialects. As these are not evident in Ireland, Schrijver argues that Old Irish is essentially the same as Proto-Irish, the ancestral language from which we would derive all the Goidelic languages. This is again an argument for a very shallow time depth for Irish: had it been in Ireland long before it emerged in the written record, we should have expected regional differences in the language. The one counter to this has been the suggestion that the Irish learned classes were so intimately interconnected and organized as a class that they somehow avoided the type of changes found in other countries.[46]

Schrijver's dates could pitch the spread of a Celtic language to Ireland as late as the 1st century AD, although it would allow for an earlier date provided it did not become implausibly early. We have also seen that the evidence of cultural vocabulary suggests a ballpark date of the Late Bronze Age or Iron Age for the split between Proto-Irish and the other Indo-European languages.

There is one objection to these approaches. The nature of our earliest Irish, British and Gaulish evidence tends to be formal inscriptions, and it is possible that these could fail to indicate the full range of differences that might have existed in the way the various Celtic languages were actually spoken at the time. One could argue that the Celtic language was much older in Ireland and Britain but, like Gaulish, the earliest written records were undertaken by druids or other members of the learned class who preserved an archaic form of the Celtic language,[47] just as Latin was employed for inscriptions long after most people could read them. Elsewhere in the Indo-European world we know religious texts such as the *Rig Veda* in India that are still recited in their original (Vedic) form although the language of the Vedas has been dead for thousands of years. In short, it could be suggested that the similarity between the earliest Celtic languages was at least partially because they were all dipping into their common ancient language. John Koch has argued that the difference between Ogam Irish and Old Irish seen in Table 9.1 was not the result of an abrupt change over the course of one or two centuries but rather a shift from what linguists regard as a higher register (elite), the archaic Ogam Irish, to a lower register, Old Irish, the language of the people that had been around for centuries but had not yet been recorded in written form.[48]

This objection could somewhat mitigate Schrijver's argument for the late split between Irish and British, but before we accept the higher register theory we might recall that the place names listed by Ptolemy from the 2nd century or earlier appear to be archaic and certainly show no sign of the later changes attributed to Old Irish. Why should the names of places and people, presumably articulated between Irish and British sailors, have been communicated in 'ye olde language'?

In general, almost any approach to dating the divisions between Proto-Irish and the other Celtic languages tends to fall somewhere within or close to the 1st millennium BC. The evidence of language does not put a straitjacket on other lines of evidence, but it would seem to suggest that bringing a Celtic language into Ireland becomes linguistically increasingly difficult to accept the earlier one recedes from c. 1000 BC. We have already seen that the evidence of the shared vocabulary of all the Indo-European languages, including Celtic, indicates that there could not have been any separation of the Celtic group before the emergence of farming. The dating evidence also makes it very difficult to uphold a Neolithic date for the entry of Irish, which would set the physical split between the earliest speakers of Irish, British and Gaulish, for example, to c. 4000 BC. This date is just bearable for the entire Indo-European language family, but not for the split between daughter languages many times removed from Proto-Indo-European. And even the higher versus lower register objection to Schrijver's conclusions looks a bit threadbare if we have to presume the 'auld tongue' was preserved for up to 4,000 years.

Now the irony, of course, in pitching the spread of a Celtic language into Ireland after the Neolithic – say, in the Late Bronze or Iron Age, the traditional 'windows' for the arrival of the Irish language – is that these are periods for which both the archaeologists and the geneticists are hard pressed to find serious evidence of significant movements of population or any other major cultural intrusions.

Enter archaeology

We have taken the evidence of language about as far as we can. Although we will soon be looking for the spread of a language, often it has been the archaeologist rather than the linguist who has taken up the challenge of tracing the expansion of the Celtic languages, despite the claim by the archaeologist Stuart Piggott that 'the solution is not in the hands of the archaeologists'.[49] Thomas O'Rahilly put it more bluntly when he wrote that the problem of the origin of the Irish language was:

beyond the range of archaeology. No archaeologist by examining an archaeological object – whether a bone or a brooch, a sword or a sickle – can possibly tell us that the object in question belonged to one who spoke a particular variety of Celtic.[50]

The solution may well not be in the hands of the archaeologist, but the temptation to try to resolve the issue is strong; to cite Piggott's contemporary, Terence Powell: 'The question of the former homelands of the Irish Celts presents no very great problem, although the archaeological evidence is still regrettably meagre.'[51] Obviously, the spread of a language suggests the spread of some people at least, along with their culture, so archaeologists do not feel totally isolated from the topic. We have seen earlier in the rhetoric of Macalister what type of evidence is most likely to impress an archaeologist. He once argued that the Beaker culture was 'the only catastrophe of ancient times subversive enough to have effected such a complete change of language'.[52] The archaeologist would reason that at some time the entire linguistic landscape of Ireland was changed and the existing population adopted an entirely new language. In order for this to happen, we should expect a major break in the archaeological record indicating a substantial foreign invasion that thoroughly transformed the culture of Ireland. In short, nothing less than a major break in the archaeological record will convince us that there was a total change in the language of Ireland.[53]

Unfortunately, no matter where in the world one is working, the archaeologist will find very little evidence of the large-scale cultural change that such reasoning generally demands. Whether we are talking about the arrival of the Indo-European languages in India, Iran, Turkey, Greece or Italy, there is a consistent lack of the type of overwhelming evidence for an invasion and language shift that would satisfy most archaeologists. Almost any novelty in the archaeological record can be dismissed as the result of trading connections, diffusion, emulation or some other process that hardly confirms the shock to the system that a total shift in language seems to imply. Moreover, there is almost always enough continuity with the previous period to suggest the possibility that whatever change was introduced, it did not completely alter the cultural (or linguistic?) landscape. In other words, if we set out to find what many archaeologists demand, we are almost certain to fail, especially if we look at the Bronze and Iron ages.

Let us return briefly to the issue of P-Celtic in Ireland. We have seen above that linguists accept the presence of a number of British tribes in southern Ireland on the basis of Ptolemy's map and other sources. Recall also that in Chapter 6, where I reviewed the evidence for population movements into Ireland during the Iron Age, I could at best squeeze out a fairly lukewarm acceptance that there was probably some movement of people from Britain to Ireland during the La Tène and in the first centuries BC, probably in the form of traders and artisans. This is as far as the archaeological evidence seemed to permit, but put a 'p' in a name (Manapia) or find an Irish tribe with the same name as a British one (Brigantes) and we find linguists surrendering more than a quarter of the island to British tribes. There is no way I could have postulated such a British migration in Chapter 6 purely on the basis of the archaeological evidence. To lose one British tribe might be a misfortune, but to lose five tribes does seem like carelessness. And here I am limiting the case for a Brittonic presence to purely phonological evidence, because we could add an even greater British presence if we also admitted historical tradition which would render almost the entire eastern coast from County Louth (Setantii) south, including the Lagini (Leinstermen) and the Dumnoni north of Dublin, the offspring of British colonists.[54] Are archaeologists really that bad at identifying population incursions? (Don't try to answer that yet.) So how can we resolve this non-alignment of the archaeological and historical evidence?

The first approach is a simple denial: there really were no P-Celtic tribes in Ireland. We simply dismiss the names of the tribes as inaccurately transcribed or transmitted in such a way as to mislead us. For example, it is probable that Ptolemy's names originated with the testimony of British seamen, who naturally would have pronounced Irish names as in their own language ('you say Manaqii, I say Manapii').[55] After all, the Irish reversed the process when they took names beginning with 'p' from Britain and changed them to 'c', e.g. Patricius (Patrick) became Irish Cothriche, and when an Irish speaker erected an ogam in Britain in memory of Voteporix (Latin Voteporigis), he translated the name into Irish Votecorigas.[56] The problem with this rebuttal is that we are not simply dealing with sounds ('p' for 'q'), but names that appear to be the same as those of other Celtic tribes in both Britain and western Gaul.

The second tactic is to agree that the names are indeed similar but are not historically related. Brigantes, for example, can be explained as either 'the high ones' or the 'hillfort-dwellers', and it is not beyond chance that more than one group of people might choose to identify themselves with such a name or have the name applied to them by someone else. While this is true, once again the proximity argument comes into play: what are the chances of two peoples on either side of the Irish Sea having the same name yet not be related?

If my objections hint of desperation, there is a serious reason. If one does conclude from this evidence that Menapi from Gaul (probably the most consistently obstinate opponents of Caesar's conquest),[57] the troublesome Brigantes of north Britain[58] and the Gangani of western Britain all crossed the water to settle in Ireland, why isn't there serious archaeological evidence for these migrations? Whether you imagine that a whole segment of a tribe moved or only an elite who established their tribe (New Brigantes?) and convinced the locals to join, there simply is no convincing archaeological evidence that this actually happened. Material culture from the Brigantes territory, for example, certainly included beehive querns[59] which, as we have already seen, are restricted to the northern two-thirds of Ireland, outside the territory of the Irish Brigantes. Nor do we find the abundant chariot gear anywhere in Ireland that is typical of northern Britain. And while Brigantian ceramics may be crude, at least they exist in Britain, while the Irish Iron Age remains stubbornly without pottery. The best we can cite is a metal container from Ballydavis, Co. Laois, which is paralleled by a similar object from Yorkshire dated to the 1st century BC and a number of northern British artifacts from a cemetery at Lambay suggesting 'just a warrior with a few of his followers, or even just with his family'.[60] Not even the most gullible archaeologist would regard these finds as sufficient to prove the movement of an entire tribe. It is little wonder, then, that archaeologists reviewing such evidence might refer to 'the intriguing but yet unproven possibility that parts of Ireland were settled by European and British tribes'.[61]

Attempting to deal with Ptolemy's map and even the most general archaeological evidence leads to a quagmire of possible interpretations. As an illustration, let us just for the hell of it accept the evidence for P-Celtic tribes in Ireland and see where this has got scholars in the past (9.6). If we follow De Bernardo Stempel's interpretation of Ptolemy's map, we are left with the image of Ireland *c.* AD 100 occupied by British tribes in the south and Goidelic tribes in the north: Belfast = true green Irishmen, Wexford = west Brits. Now recall that in terms of the archaeological evidence, the north is associated with the distribution of La Tène artifacts while Munster lacks evidence of the La Tène artistic horizon. So we have established a correlation:

north = Goidelic = La Tène
south = Brittonic = non-La Tène.

We can see acceptance of this correlation in Terence Powell's solution to Irish origins, in which he attempted to marry the Ulster Cycle of tales with archaeology. This series

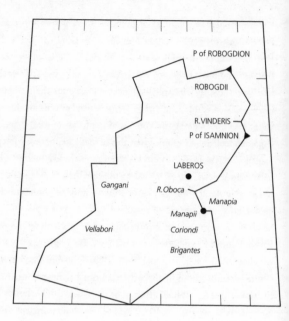

9.6. Brittonic (*italic*) and Goidelic (upper case) names from Ptolemy's map of Ireland.

of tales, ostensibly set to around the first centuries BC and AD but, at least in terms of material culture, depicting early medieval Irish society,[62] primarily concerns the hostile relations between the Black North (the Ulstermen) and their neighbours, especially the people of Connacht. The society depicted in the tales was dubbed that of the 'Overlords' by Powell, and as the principals were mainly located in Ulster and Connacht he treated this whole area as an Overlord culture which mirrored the distribution of La Tène artifacts. For Powell this was enough to establish that the homeland of the Irish language lay among the La Tène tribes of southwest Scotland and northern Britain.[63]

But this hardly squares with the assumption that at the time of Ptolemy Britain was clearly Brittonic and hence, to quote Gearóid Mac Eoin, 'it is clear that if there were a La Tène incursion into the north of Ireland from Britain the language of the newcomers would have been P-Celtic'.[64] So if you wanted to throw in a dash of McEvoy and Bradley's genetic evidence for a possible movement from Britain to northeast Ireland, you would be finding support for the movement of British-speaking populations into what the place names suggest was actually Goidelic territory. Conversely, let us recall that the area that produces our P-Celtic tribes in the south of Ireland is precisely the area where we find our most abundant evidence for the earliest native Irish writing, the ogam stones (Fig. 9.2). So we now have models that involve explaining the Irish language by having it introduced from Britain with the La Tène culture (which should have been British or Gallo-British and not Irish) as well as Brittonic tribes from Britain who abandoned their La Tène material culture to take up residency in southern Ireland where, several centuries later, they are erecting ogams in the Irish language and even trying to export the Irish language back (?) to Britain.

Are we are getting too wrapped up in the distinction between Goidelic and Brittonic? Recall that Peter Schrijver argued that the distinction was minimal before the 1st century AD. He also suggested that the language we reconstruct as Proto-Irish is a better fit for the ancient language of Britain than Ancient British itself, as the latter was heavily influenced by Latin by the time we acquire any extensive texts. He argues that the British population who shifted to Old English spoke a language whose sound system resembled Primitive Irish and that this provides a possible indication of the source of Proto-Irish in Ireland. If one surveys the initial area of Anglo-Saxon speech in Britain (from Hadrian's Wall south to the Isle of Wight), 'there is one particular section in the northeast where the match between Old Irish and Old English phonetics is so close that it stands a better chance than any other of being the area of origin of Irish': Northumbria (cue tabloid headlines: 'The Irish are really Geordies!').[65] And here we find ourselves back in the general territory of the Brigantes who, we would imagine, should have been speaking Brittonic in the 1st century AD.

Just about every proposition cited above appears to have led to a counter-intuitive conclusion. We are dealing with far too many unknowns here to make much sense of the data. For example, the tribes with British or Continental names are almost invariably assumed to be refugees from the Roman conquest of Gaul and Britain, because that provides them with a convenient excuse to come to Ireland, yet it is possible that some of these tribes settled in both Britain and Ireland within the same few generations, centuries earlier when some of them were still Q-Celtic. The archaeological evidence is certainly not giving us many hints as to when these 'British' tribes settled. In any event, when the number of unknowns seems to be expanding exponentially it is usually best to go back to first principles and remind ourselves that we are dealing with the spread of a language and not necessarily a tribal name, origin myth, architecture, artifacts or burials. So it is reasonable first to consider what might have actually happened on the ground when a language disperses. Only then can archaeologists decide whether there is anything in their toolkit that can deal with the issues.

How a language spreads

The Irish language was not 'native' to Ireland, but evolved from a Celtic predecessor that was carried into the island long after its initial settlement. The new language must have acquired a foothold in Ireland, more likely multiple staging areas, from which it spread across the island. There are two ways in which the language might be carried and these essentially replay many of the invasion scenarios that we have encountered in earlier chapters. The earliest speakers of Proto-Irish may themselves have spread across the island, replacing the earlier inhabitants either through warfare or successful competition (by having a more productive economy, or more children, etc.), or the language may have spread from these earliest immigrants to native populations who gradually adopted it themselves. The first option in its most extreme form is regarded as the least likely, both in theory and archaeological support, i.e. that some invading population slaughtered the earliest inhabitants. That there may have been a major economic shift that favoured the Proto-Irish overwhelmingly over the native Irelanders is, however, regarded as a suitable model and one that we will review below. The second process, involving the cultural assimilation of the native Irelanders, is also entirely plausible. Consider the spread of English in Ireland, where the main vehicle for its early spread involved Irishmen learning the new language either from their English-speaking neighbours or, probably more often, from their own countrymen who had become bilingual in Irish and English. The latter is logical, as there were not yet schools in Ireland in which one might learn English (that would come with a vengeance in 1831, when English became the language of instruction in the National Schools). As we will now see, this bilingualism is also one of the key factors in the spread of a language.

Unless a population is entirely exterminated, a new language will spread across a pre-existing population who first become bilingual in both their native language and the new (target) language. This is the initial stage of two languages in contact as we might imagine operating in Ireland. During this period native Irelanders adopted Proto-Irish, generally in order to satisfy specific social needs or aspirations. They may have spoken their native language at home and with their friends, but if there was an economic advantage in trade, for example, they might well have learned Proto-Irish. We all employ our language in a variety of social contexts (for example, at home, a livestock show, the office, a sporting event, a political rally, or in a religious ceremony or folk song). All of these are termed social 'domains', and often the target language will be especially associated with a specific social domain in which participation requires use of the new language. For this reason, a native speaker picks up the new target language for a given social domain. Although this situation may remain stable for a long time, it often results in the spread of the target language into other social domains until we find what linguists call 'societal bilingualism', when everyone can speak the target language as well as their own. The more social domains that employ the target language, the more likely it is for the native language to retract into fewer and fewer social domains, both in terms of place and age of the speaker, as parents prepare their children linguistically for a world increasingly dominated by the target language. In the end, the only native speaker may be an 80-year-old woman living in a country farmhouse who sings songs in the 'auld language' to her uncomprehending grandchildren. With her death we witness a complete language shift to the target language and the death of the native language.

Ireland offers a good example of language shift though, thankfully, not language death, in the spread of English. First introduced in the 12th century, the English language established itself precariously with the settlement of the clients of the Normans. We do not generally set the major expansion of the target language (English) to this period, as the 'Old English' settlers often adopted the Irish language of the surrounding countryside – so much so that the Statutes of Kilkenny (1366) were enacted to prevent the further erosion of the English language and identity in a sea of Irish culture, as the language of the initial English settlers, 'Yola', was only preserved in certain urban pockets. Rather, the decline of Irish and the rise of English are more properly seen to have begun in the 17th century, when there were much more massive plantations of English-speaking settlers, and a combination of restrictive laws against the Irish language, the confiscation of Irish lands and the later introduction of an English-based school system, coupled with the famine, all played their part in reducing the number of Irish-speakers. Whether because they were voluntarily seeking social advancement or were constrained by economic circumstances to find work in English-speaking towns, the numbers of native speakers of Irish rapidly declined. Irish went from being the predominant language c. 1700 to being the primary language of only a quarter of the population by 1850 and then of only about 5% by 1900.[66] Comparable processes occurred with Scots Gaelic and Welsh, although each also had other factors at work. For example, Welsh was far more integrated into the social domain of religion than Irish, and this has always encouraged the maintenance of Welsh.

The lessons that linguists have learned from studying language shift elsewhere in the world are not sufficient to give us a solid basis for estimating how it behaved in the past. The types of pressures experienced by modern Native Americans or

Australian Aborigines, for example, can hardly be projected into prehistoric Ireland. Moreover, linguistic studies do not reveal a series of clear-cut rules regarding how many newcomers are required to cause language shift, the precise nature of the social relationships between the two communities of speakers, etc. Everyone admits that economic factors, demography and status may be important factors in any explanation for why anyone abandons their own language and adopts another, but precisely how we can measure these factors is far from clear.[67] Nevertheless, we can at least try recalling the processes involved and the most likely factors that would have encouraged the spread of Proto-Irish.

Expressions of language shift

The success of Proto-Irish indicates that when it came into contact with the native language(s) of Irelanders, it had a competitive advantage. As languages are not intrinsically superior or inferior to one another, the advantage was a social one, i.e. the Irelanders regarded learning Proto-Irish a useful investment of their time. As we have seen, it probably entered Ireland either by filling an existing social domain or by creating a new social domain that attracted the native Irelanders. For example, they could have been enticed into adopting Proto-Irish by a desire to improve their means of subsistence or their security, to acquire goods, gain status through new social institutions or participate in new religious rituals.

Subsistence change

The first probable language shift in Ireland should have occurred with the beginning of the Neolithic, when we find not only the introduction of a far more efficient economy but also a radical transformation of architecture, material culture and religious behaviour, all brought to Ireland from some Continental source either directly or, more likely, through Britain. The impact of the new economy has been played out within the historical record, so we can imagine how this might have happened. For example, the Yaaku, a hunting-gathering people of East Africa, actively participated in the destruction of their own language when they decided to adopt both the pastoral economy and lifestyle of the Maasai.[68] It is highly probable that the introduction of the Neolithic to Ireland saw a major language shift, and some archaeologists have regarded this as sufficient evidence to presume that the Neolithic saw the introduction of a Celtic language and the formation of Irish. Indeed, one of the more popular models of the spread of the world's language families ties many of them

(Indo-European included) to the spread of agriculture.[69] Yet while this may appear to be the most striking change in the archaeological record, it is hardly the only window for language change.

Let us recall from the previous chapter that the Neolithic also appeared in the Carpathian basin, the present home of the Hungarians, yet from the time that we first encounter peoples from this area in written records (*c.* 400 BC, or 5,000 years after the Neolithic arrived in this region) we can name a succession of about nine different peoples and languages from two different language families that occupied the region *before* the Hungarians themselves (representative of yet another language family) arrived around AD 900. There is hardly a place in southern Europe (the only area our written records really cover) that has not experienced language shift over the past 2,000 years. It is obvious that the thorough cultural transformation associated with the spread of the European Neolithic may well have been a vehicle for new languages, but it is hardly the last one, and we have seen that there are serious problems setting the date of Proto-Irish back to *c.* 4000 BC. In short, while a major change in subsistence *c.* 6,000 years ago may have brought about a change in the language of the Irelanders, it might have had nothing to do with the spread of the (later) Irish language.

Exchange

Another possible mechanism for the introduction of Proto-Irish is exchange. As we have seen, ever since the Neolithic Ireland has clearly been in contact with both Britain and the Continent. As John Waddell has observed, during the Bronze Age the elites of Ireland were kitting themselves out in both weapons and ornaments in the same manner as their counterparts across the water, and there are any number of distribution maps that speak for the interconnectedness of Ireland and Britain and, to a lesser extent perhaps, of Ireland and the Continent (Figs 4.11, 5.16).[70] Waddell also emphasizes the importance of water transport and how it might have provided a means for the spread of the Celtic language(s) along Atlantic Europe. The nuts and bolts of this model have never really been presented in detail, but we might imagine something like the following.

Ireland was in constant (although perhaps regionally variable) contact with Britain from at least the beginning of the Neolithic, a fact that can be clearly seen in distribution maps of shared ceramic types, polished stone axes, megalithic tombs, etc. Often the distributions are regionally confined to one side or the other of the Irish Sea, e.g. portal tombs or Collared Urns (Fig. 4.14). In short, there had been a network of social contacts for thousands of years. At some time a Celtic language spread from the Continent to Britain along these networks as a *lingua franca* or trade language that facilitated communication between peoples along the Atlantic façade of Europe. This is regarded as a possible vehicle for the spread of a Celtic language to Ireland.

A model of this type has seen rising popularity, but I wonder how convincing it really is? First, Celtic elites transplanted to Ireland are likely to have faced the same cultural fate as the earliest English settlers in Ireland, i.e. they could just as easily have 'gone native'. It is also difficult to see precisely how the acquisition of the new language would have enhanced the status of the resident population. While there was certainly trade with Britain, the overwhelming majority of objects found in Ireland dating to the Bronze Age or the Iron Age were locally made: there was no need to chat up the sword-monger in a foreign language. Moreover, neither Irish nor any of the other Celtic languages looks much like the trade languages that spring up to facilitate communication among people who lack a common speech – such as a pidgin, created between multiple partners who want to trade with one another. In this case the vocabulary may come primarily from one language while the grammar, which is generally radically simplified, may come from either. Irish is not a simplified language (as anyone who has ever studied Old Irish can painfully attest) and its vocabulary essentially retains the full range of its Proto-Indo-European ancestor, like any other Indo-European language. In short, Irish is not some compromise that facilitated Beaker-users or Hallstatt traders to flog their wares. Also, we must consider how the entire island came to adopt the new language, and it is difficult to see how a language ascribed to an elite or a trading port would trickle down to the natives who would not obviously benefit from acquiring it. During the Iron Age the ancient Greeks maintained extensive trading colonies (emporia) in both southern France and Iberia, but this did not result in a major spread of the Greek language outside the walls of their towns.

Finally, there is the conundrum of time depth. Close contacts have existed between Ireland and Britain ever since the Neolithic, so when did Proto-Irish spread? The earlier the *lingua franca* appears, the earlier it becomes the native language of Ireland, and we have to set the clock of linguistic change ticking between Ireland, Britain and the Continent. An archaeologist could probably put the case for exchange more easily in the Neolithic (stone axes) or Early Bronze Age (metal) than later and, as we have already seen, this does involve some serious problems of time depth. Although exchange contacts with the outside world may well have played a role in introducing Proto-Irish to Ireland, it is far from obvious how this would actually lead to language shift across all Ireland.

Social prestige or identification

The most likely mechanism for the introduction of Proto-Irish is social prestige, i.e. the local population wanted to learn Proto-Irish (at least for use in certain social domains) because it gave them access to something that they did not have before. There are a variety of possible 'desirables' that may have attracted the natives to acquire Proto-Irish. For example, the Proto-Irish-speakers may have introduced a type of social organization that the local Irelanders regarded as an improvement on whatever system they had before. On an island where settlements were dispersed and leadership roles limited, a new system that encouraged much more intense or frequent social interactions (perhaps feasts or parties) could well seem attractive. From a male point of view, there might have been new sodalities, i.e. corporate groups such as war bands, that a young male might join and move up the social scale as a raider or warrior, acquiring booty and prestige at the same time. Another obvious social 'carrot' could be a new religion that offered a more compelling ideology, more emotionally charged ceremonies, greater prestige and a network of other social factors. The spread of most of the world's major religions frequently carried a linguistic dimension (e.g. Latin for Christianity, Spanish and Portuguese for Catholicism in South America, Arabic for Islam) as well as an entire cultural infrastructure. The cumulative result of these social factors would be that the native Irelanders would wish to identify with and behave like the bearers of Proto-Irish.

From an archaeological perspective, the new social system or ideology might be expressed in symbolic items. In today's world these form the modern regalia of institutions, such as maces, ceremonial swords or items of clothing. For the prehistoric period a good example might be the gold lunulae that we find in the Early Bronze Age, which do not appear to have been personal property as they are not found accompanying burials. The difficulty here is in understanding what meaning was invested in any particular object in prehistory. Bronze and Iron Age Ireland throws up numerous items of ornament that might have served primarily symbolic or ideological purposes. In addition to objects we might look for new architectural forms (megalithic tombs, stone circles, hillforts, Iron Age enclosures) that would provide both occasions for ritual expression and central places to attract an otherwise dispersed population.

Possible language shifts in prehistoric Ireland

The initial occupation of Ireland *c.* 8000 BC will have brought a population speaking an unknown language to Ireland. However, the possibility that this may actually have been the direct ancestor of Irish – an Indo-European language that could not have spread before the Neolithic – is so remote that we can dismiss it and conclude that at least for the first 40% of Ireland's settlement, it was not occupied by people who spoke anything remotely resembling Irish. Although we will postpone reviewing some of the suggested candidates until the end of this chapter, we can start by speculating about the number of languages spoken in Mesolithic Ireland and how they might have behaved.

The Mesolithic language

To begin with, from an archaeological standpoint there is only one cultural tradition in the Early Mesolithic associated with the earliest colonists. The same types of stone tools can be found all over the island and this suggests that we are dealing with a common origin for the entire population of Ireland at this time. A common origin would suggest a common linguistic background, so we find it easier to assume that a single language was introduced into Ireland.

The next question is whether this language is likely to have fragmented into markedly different dialects or languages. Generally, when a language spreads over a wide area, there will arise regional variations depending on the strength of the effects of geography (especially physical barriers), the economic system (whether it promotes frequent contacts with neighbours or encourages regionally sedentary and closed systems) or social factors (the emergence of elites who promote their own way of speaking). The Irish landscape lacked the type of really formidable physical barriers that might have forced the isolation of regional groups of speakers. The only exception to this is probably the forested landscape itself that could have impeded movement. But this was probably offset by a mobile economic system that required families and bands or groups of families to relocate seasonally. On the basis of ethnographic analogy we would expect out-marriage among these families so that there would be general mixing of the population, both genetically and socially, over time. Finally, we have no reason to expect that the economic system of Mesolithic Ireland produced anything other than egalitarian societies; the types of elites who promote the usage of their own regional dialects would not appear at least until the emergence of farming communities.

In a study of the size of language areas in North America, Raymond Newell and Trinettre Constandse-Westermann observed that the typical Native American tribal language averaged 8,191 sq km and ranged from 140 to 478,564 sq km.[71] In terms of area, Ireland at c. 84,000 sq km is well above the average but also still within the range of a single language group. From the standpoint of population size, their dialect tribes ranged anywhere from *c.* 150 to 7,200 people, which would be the right order of magnitude for the estimated population size of Ireland. A cruder index perhaps has been an estimate for speakers of Australian languages that generally range from 1,000 to 3,000 people. Ireland would possibly be at the upper range here. A single linguistic area would seem to be the best bet, although it is by no means certain.

A single linguistic area or language does not mean that the language did not change over time. As we have seen, all spoken languages are in a constant state of change, and over the period of some 160 generations from the beginning to the end of the Mesolithic we could certainly expect that the language spoken by *c.* 4000 BC was very different from that carried into Ireland 4,000 years earlier.

The Neolithic language

As we have seen, the first probable language *shift* should have occurred with the arrival of farming communities in Ireland. From the viewpoint of assessing migrations from the archaeological record, this is the closest thing to a 'smoking gun' that we will find. As we have seen in Chapter 3, the Neolithic involved a radical transformation of both the material and spiritual culture of Ireland's Mesolithic natives, and much of the new culture can be traced to earlier societies in Atlantic Europe. In terms of the different mechanisms of language shift listed above, it probably ticks every box (subsistence change, new exchange systems, new ceremonies, subscription to a new cultural identity). It should also be emphasized that within the Neolithic itself there were further potential enticements to language shift. This might be seen in the variety of megalithic tombs, most of which have British or Continental parallels. For example, Irish passage tombs are part of a more general Atlantic phenomenon and ultimately have their origins on the Continent, and there is some evidence that there were continued contacts between people who built passage tombs in different parts of western Europe. It is certainly possible that their spread involved the introduction of a language not necessarily identical to that which may have spread with Ireland's earliest farmers. That the distribution of passage tombs is largely confined to the northern half of Ireland is not reason enough to exclude it from introducing a language that spread over the entire island: it is always possible that whatever hypothetical language we attribute to the passage-tomb builders may have spread southward at a later date but was by then connected with an entirely different physical expression. Alternatively, of course, the spread of the various tomb types may not have been associated with any new languages.

The succession of potential religiously motivated language shifts continues into the late Neolithic when Ireland adopts both Grooved Ware pottery and the ceremonial structures associated with it, in this case suggesting the possibility of yet another language being introduced, possibly from northern Britain.

The Bronze and Iron Age language

The introduction of copper metallurgy and the new ceramics associated with the Beaker period suggests yet another arena for language shift around 2500 BC. This again moves Ireland potentially beyond a migration from Britain back into a larger European context and one that is spatially associated with many areas in which we later find Celtic languages.[72] In terms of providing a possible vehicle for another language shift, the Beaker horizon would seem to provide a serious case, as it has clear foreign connections and some changes in material culture (beakers, arrowheads, copper metallurgy), although it lacks other elements of behaviour associated with the Beakers such as single burials under mounds. The successive Early Bronze Age funerary wares such as the bowls (Food Vessels) and the various urn types all throw up distribution maps that also suggest some form of cultural interaction and possibly population movement between Britain and Ireland. However, although there is a succession of Bronze Age metal types with clear parallels between Ireland and either Britain or the Continent, these have traditionally been regarded as evidence for exchange contacts rather than horizons for the introduction of new peoples or new languages.

The rise of the hillforts at c. 1000 BC poses interesting problems and possibilities. On the one hand, we have seen that treating the hillforts as evidence for foreign contacts is *just* possible, but the evidence is hardly compelling. On the other hand, the hillforts do reflect new central places in the landscape of Ireland, just the type of venue that might have prompted a language shift *if* they were associated with a new language. They are the archaeological expression of potentially several social domains – religious ceremonies, exchange, social hierarchies – and so it is not difficult to imagine them as places where the local population might be enticed to adopt the new language of the people who introduced them (assuming they were introduced from abroad).

The introduction of iron metallurgy from around the 7th century BC onward would probably be regarded as a very weak explanation for language shift, although sneaking the Proto-Irish into Ireland in the midst of a dark age does have certain attractions. At one time the association between 'Celts' and the introduction of iron metallurgy was considered to be sufficient for explaining the arrival of Irish: Celtic smiths forged iron swords that permitted Celtic warriors to subdue Ireland and spread their language. Now we find that the evidence for iron metallurgy appears several centuries before the appearance of La Tène weapons (which would hardly be superior to a much larger Late Bronze Age bronze sword).

By the first centuries BC we find the Iron Age enclosures, the so-called 'royal sites', such as Navan, Tara, Knockaulin and Rathcroghan. These also could certainly have reflected yet another ceremonial domain and, if their distribution in the countryside had been denser, it would make a fairly compelling case for the type of social domain that might well have been associated with the spread of Proto-Irish. The problem here, even more so than for the hillforts of the Late Bronze Age, is that it has so far been impossible to find a source for these structures outside of Ireland.

The last possible horizon for the introduction of Proto-Irish would be the last century BC and 1st century AD, when we have evidence for contacts between both 'native' Iron Age and Roman populations in Britain. If the Proto-Irish relocated from Britain to Ireland at this time, their identity could have been concealed under one or more of the tribal names that we find in Ptolemy, although the archaeological evidence for such movements, as we have seen, is extremely weak.

The right window?

In providing a list of possible 'windows' for the introduction of Irish we can see that the archaeological record offers multiple opportunities for language shift in Ireland, although only one of these is likely to be associated with the direct ancestor of Irish. We have seen that there are reasonable linguistic arguments that suggest that introducing a Celtic language to Ireland during the first millennium BC is a better bet than at any time earlier, but linguists, left to their own devices, cannot really pinpoint the time and place of the spread of Celtic into Ireland. Moreover, from an archaeological perspective we have a series of possible horizons in which to introduce the Irish language, but we cannot be certain that we have identified the right one or even that any of our potential horizons actually resulted in the spread of a new language. While the course of least resistance – ascribing the Celtic language to the introduction of the Neolithic – might seem like the simplest solution, we have already seen that applied elsewhere (e.g. Hungary) it results in utter nonsense. So in the end we have two techniques or approaches to the problem, linguistics and archaeology, neither of which can yield a comfortable solution on its own. The immediate temptation is to find a solution by combining the evidence of both disciplines and I am on the point of doing this, but first a word of warning: I am also fully aware that combining two unknowns is hardly going to yield a conclusive answer.[73]

If we agree that the linguistic evidence for the late time depth of Proto-Irish is accepted, then the most likely set of windows for the introduction of Irish should fall roughly from about 1000 BC to the 1st century BC. Although earlier horizons (Neolithic, Beaker) may be 'juicier', they are just too early to be the ones that resulted in the spread of Proto-Irish. After all, we are not simply looking for evidence of language shift but specifically of the *last* instance of language shift in Ireland before the intro- duction of English. In addition, although we have discussed matters in terms of four potential 'events' during this period, i.e. hillforts (1000 BC), iron metallurgy (600 BC), La Tène metalwork and/or Iron Age ritual centres (*c.* 300–100 BC) and refugees from Roman Britain (*c.* AD 1–100), the period in question is short enough that the process could have covered more than one of these 'events'. Christopher Hawkes once coined the term 'cumulative Celticity' to describe the process by which Ireland eventually underwent this shift,[74] and within the period envisaged this concept could be helpful. Anyway, here is my best shot, warts and all.

Initial spread

At about 1000 BC the institution of the hillfort spread across all of Ireland. It lacked an obvious local predecessor and may have derived from the earliest manifestations of hillforts in southern Britain. In a land where settlement was typically (although not exclusively) dispersed, the hillforts offered a new central place, a venue in which the surrounding population could gather for religious ceremonies, exchange or feasts. In short, the hillfort offered a variety of new social domains that were attrac- tive to the native Irelanders. In addition, the appearance of the hillforts coincides with the rise of sword warfare in Ireland, and it is also possible that we now see the emergence of specific warrior groups who may have attracted or compelled the locals to join. Moreover, this is the period of emerging elites across Europe, and where new opportunities for wealth and prestige existed these, at least, provided the type of temptations required to attract native Irelanders to a new social system and the language that came with it. The elites who occupied the sites remained in charge even after the short duration of the hillforts had ceased around 800 BC, and they were the patrons of the newly introduced iron metallurgy that began about 600 BC and spread out beyond the earlier perimeter of the hillfort social system.

Warts: While the appearance and spread of the hillfort across all Ireland admi- rably satisfies the requirement for identifying a substantial new social domain, its foreign origin does depend on a less-than-secure acceptance of long-distance contacts with southern Britain and the Continent. Moreover, the collapse of the Irish hillfort (at least on the basis of the few sites excavated) complicates issues no end. However, there is perhaps opportunity here, and a partial cultural isolation of Ireland from Britain after 800 BC may also have ensured that it remained peripheral and 'untainted' by the tendency to pronounce one's 'q's' as 'p's', which enjoyed a certain European vogue during the Iron Age.

Consolidation

By the 3rd century BC elites in Ireland took up a new expression of their social identity by importing and then emulating the La Tène style, very much in the same way as their neighbours in Britain. Unlike Britain, however, the social and/or religious elites created a new ritual site, the Iron Age ceremonial enclosure that provided a few very highly visible central places and a new social domain. The creation of these new sites, involving the incorporation of earlier ritual monuments (at Tara) or their emulation (at Navan), signified a new ideology that embraced the traditional ancient provinces of Ireland.

Warts: obviously, had we good foreign parallels for the Irish ceremonial sites we could have suggested a much more recent introduction of Proto-Irish along the lines envisaged perhaps by Peter Schrijver, i.e. an origin in the first centuries BC. The current model proposed above establishes Proto-Irish in the island for at least a thousand years before it separates from Brittonic, and yet it is reputedly almost identical to Brittonic in the 1st century AD. On the other hand, there may again be opportunity in the archaeological evidence. A horizon of Iron Age ceremonial centres suggests at least the possibility of a prestige dialect gradually encompassing all of Ireland in the last few centuries BC. The spread of a single prestige dialect associated with these centres might then explain why Proto-Irish looks so recent and Old Irish so uniform. In short, the ceremonial centres in effect may have reset the clock for Proto-Irish and account at least for the lack of dialects in early Irish.

Pre-Celtic languages

As we have seen, the evidence surveyed so far makes it clear that the Irish language has not been spoken by all the Irelanders who occupied the island. Indeed, if one opts for a relatively late 'coming of the Celtic language' to Ireland at around 1500 BC or even more recently, then Ireland has been 'Irish' for only about the last third of its occupation, and therefore it must have been occupied by speakers of other languages for most of the period of its settlement. Linguists have long understood this, and there is an extensive history of research into uncovering relics of the earlier language(s). The results of such studies, however, are extremely problematic, and most cautious linguists would probably agree with Gearóid Mac Eoin, who wrote that 'Irish has not yet been reliably shown to contain any word, placename, personal name, or syntactic construction which has been convincingly credited to the language which preceded it in Ireland'.[75] Nevertheless, there is some unreliable evidence.

In various guises, there are two main language groups which have been attributed to pre-Celtic Ireland: Basque and Hamito-Semitic. The first marks an attempt to associate the earliest language in Ireland with the modern Basque language whose earliest recorded ancestor is Aquitainian, a language recorded in southwest France by the Romans.[76] The theory today is closely related to the evidence of genetics and suggestions that, after the Ice Age, most of western Europe was populated by peoples who had expanded from a climatic refuge in Iberia/southern France. As the Basque language has often been regarded as a survivor from the Palaeolithic, surrounded by a sea of Indo-European languages (Celtic, Italic), it is presumed to be the sole survivor from this process of colonization. If this is so, then the language of the late Palaeolithic inhabitants of Britain and the earliest Mesolithic occupants of Ireland should have been distantly related to Basque. Irish then is the result of the spread of a Celtic language to an island previously occupied by speakers of a Basque-like language.[77] The hard evidence for this is absolutely minimal. There are, for example, some words in Irish that appear to be very similar to Basque, e.g. Irish *aínder* 'married woman, virgin', Basque *andere* 'lady, wife', although the Irish word may be a loan from Welsh *anner* 'heifer'.[78] In fact, even if speakers of Basque itself settled in Ireland *c.* 8000 BC, the chances of us recovering any traces of it after more than 8,000 years (when we obtain our earliest written records) are really quite small.

An alternative identification of Ireland's 'indigenous language' is to assign it to the Hamito-Semitic family (more often now called the Afro-Asiatic family) which embraces many of the languages of southwest Asia (Akkadian, Hebrew, Arabic) and those of northern Africa (Egyptian, Berber, Chadic, etc.). This theory has a long history – Charles Vallancey was comparing Irish with Phoenician (actually Maltese) in 1772 – that has been sustained by a lot of research, debate and ridicule.[79] From time to time it also emerges in contemporary accounts of witnessing someone conversing 'intelligibly in Irish with some natives of Morocco'.[80] It can be presented in one of two ways: either the original occupants of Ireland were speakers of an Afro-Asiatic language, or Ireland (and Britain) was colonized at some time after its initial settlement (the Neolithic?, the earliest megalithic tombs?) by Afro-Asiatic-speakers

moving along the Atlantic façade of Europe. The evidence supporting this movement relies primarily, indeed almost exclusively, on traits found in the Insular Celtic
languages that appear to set them apart from the usual varieties of Indo-European
languages. Although these have been revisited a number of times by earlier scholars,
the current state of debate is largely anchored around an unpublished PhD dissertation by Orin Gensler.[81] We are in somewhat tricky territory here, because neither
the dissertation nor, as far as I am aware, any substantial article based on it has been
published by the author. On the other hand, the work has taken on a life of its own
that goes far beyond those of us who have a copy on our bookshelf,[82] and it has often
been treated as a work in the public domain.

Gensler tried to remove many of the objections to earlier unsystematic attempts
to demonstrate a relationship between Insular Celtic and the Afro-Asiatic family. His
approach was to isolate out 17 features that set Irish and Welsh 'radically out of place
in a European landscape'[83] and then survey how frequently these typological features
appeared, not simply among the Afro-Asiatic languages (the usual approach that
almost guaranteed a self-fulfilling prophecy), but also in a sample of languages from
all over the world. Just to give one of the less (linguistically) challenging examples,
we find in both Afro-Asiatic and Old Irish the metaphorical use of kinship terms:
for example, in Hebrew *ben mavet* 'son of death', i.e. 'one deserving of death', and *bat
'ayin* 'daughter of eye', i.e. the pupil; in Old Irish *mac báis* 'son of death', i.e. wicked
man, and *mac imblissen* 'son of iris', i.e. pupil.[84] Gensler concluded that while some
of the features might be found scattered elsewhere around the world, they were still
most strongly concentrated among the Afro-Asiatic languages, which suggests some
form of contact relationship between an Afro-Asiatic language and the Insular Celtic
languages. Gensler did not himself propose a prehistoric scenario to explain the
relationship, although he did emphasize that we were dealing with a substrate phenomenon, i.e. there was a period in which an Afro-Asiatic-like language was spoken in
Britain and Ireland and although its speakers shifted their language to Celtic, certain
structural features of their native language percolated through into Irish and Welsh.
So we might envisage something along the lines of Theo Vennemann's description of
Atlantic Europe as being initially Basque-like (in the Palaeolithic and Mesolithic) followed by the dispersal of farming communities from the Mediterranean who carried
an Afro-Asiatic (Semitic) language to Britain and Ireland (where he even explains the
name of Ireland *Ériu* as Semitic **'iy-weri'um* 'Isle of Copper').[85]

In 2007 Graham Isaac launched a fairly devastating critique of Gensler's 17 features
by illustrating how most of the evidence could be dismissed as trivial (because it

makes a comparison that occurs so widely it cannot be used to demonstrate a genetic relationship), dependent (i.e. a fair number of items on the list follow naturally from the presence of another item, which inflates the number of peculiar traits) and vacuous (because the trait only occurs sporadically in Insular Celtic or Afro-Asiatic, or it does so at a date that makes no sense in the context of prehistoric contacts).[86] In the end, Isaac only accepts three features from the list as having any bearing on the Afro-Asiatic contact theory, but when we attempt to model the theory on the ground it simply looks less and less plausible. If, for example, we assume that the Neolithic spread through the Mediterranean from southwest Asia and that the language of these farmers was Afro-Asiatic, we should expect that we would also have evidence for their language in Greece, Italy, Iberia and at least the southern half of France as well as their substrate impact on the languages of Britain and Ireland. We don't. So let us narrow things down and imagine (somehow) that a language crossed from North Africa to Iberia as the staging area for an expansion to Britain and Ireland. The problem here is that we have languages attested in Iberia (and southernmost France) from the Iron Age onward where we find Aquitainian (Basque) to the north and Iberian to the south and neither of these are Afro-Asiatic. So which came first? If we say that it was Basque and Iberian, we should expect clear evidence of the more recent and certainly more numerous North African languages. If we have the North Africans in first, then they were obliterated by Basques and Iberians who came from who knows where.[87] To make matters even worse, the Hispano-Celtic language of Iberia (by Gensler's own words) also lacks any evidence of the Afro-Asiatic substrate.[88] From an archaeological point of view, we are left clinging to the incongruous image of a Barbary ape (from Navan) traversing Ireland and teaching Hamito-Semitic to an eager population.

Another major issue is the brusque restructuring of both Goidelic and Brittonic, usually assumed to have occurred *c.* AD 500–600. This might be admitted as further evidence for the recent dating of Goidelic and Brittonic. The argument goes like this: the Celtic languages of both Britain and Ireland were radically altered (the 'mangling' that we saw in Table 9.1) because most of the population of Ireland had only recently learned a Celtic language, and they were speaking it with a very heavy local accent. We have already seen that some of these changes have been ascribed to Afro-Asiatic, but here the identity of the substrate is irrelevant. Try to imagine the entire population of Ireland adopting Chinese over the course of a few generations and what that might do to the Chinese system of tones. That the substrate Irelanders' language may have been radically different from Celtic is certainly possible, but Ranko Matasović has suggested a different possibility: speakers of British, Irish, Vulgar Latin and, by AD 400, Anglo-Saxon were all interacting with one another, and many of the changes that we find in the two Insular Celtic branches look precisely like the changes we might expect when a variety of languages form an interrelated speech area. A similar phenomenon occurred among the languages of the Balkans, and Matasović argues that the situation in Britain and Ireland would also have been ripe for language contacts.

Matasović has also considered the fundamental question of whether there was a single substrate language in Britain and Ireland before the spread of Insular Celtic. Finding an unknown substrate, as we have seen, is hard enough, but he believes the answer is no. Place names or general terms for topography are often one of the few surviving indicators of a previous language – and even if Irish should endure language death, there would still be ample vestiges of its prior existence in the place names of Ireland (Bally, Kill, Inch, etc.). Had the same language been spoken in both Britain and Ireland before Insular Celtic, we might have expected similar names for the topography of both islands, but Matasović finds no evidence for this.[89]

There seems no doubt that Ireland possessed pre-Irish languages. That Irish picked up some of the words from earlier languages is also quite probable, but determining specifically which words were borrowed from an earlier language is no easy task. One of the problems concerns the logic of the entire exercise. If an Irish word lacks a clear etymology, i.e. if it cannot be traced back through the other Celtic languages and then on into Indo-European (e.g. Old Irish *fer* 'man' < Proto-Celtic **wiros* < Proto-Indo-European **wiros*), we must then begin a series of evaluations. For example, the word may go back to Proto-Celtic or even some earlier stage and still not be regarded as inherited from Proto-Indo-European. The Celts, along with the Germanic-speakers and possibly Italic, all possess common vocabulary which some suspect to have been picked up from non-Indo-European languages of western Europe. As a number of items of this vocabulary relate to the names of birds (e.g. heron, blackbird, lark), Peter Schrijver has suggested that this substrate might be termed the 'language of the birds'.[90] So here we see an argument for the earliest Celtic-speakers in Ireland importing non-Indo-European names for birds, but these words may still have had nothing whatsoever to do with the language of earlier non-Irish Irelanders.

At the other end of the scale, we confront words that only occur in Irish (or the other Goidelic languages that originated in Ireland) that lack a good etymology. Peter Schrijver has identified a number of such words, all within the same semantic field (fishing). The words in question (*partán* 'crab', *gliomach* 'lobster', *faochán* 'periwinkle', and *bratán* 'salmon')[91] are at least the types of local words that might be absorbed into a newly introduced target language. To these we might add Gearóid Mac Eoin's suggestion that both place names (Aife, Bréife, Grafrenn, Life, etc.) and a number of obscure words (*bréife* 'ring', *cuifre* 'ale', etc.), all with an 'f' in the middle of the word, may also reflect loanwords, borrowed from a substrate that employed a sound not originally found in the Irish language.[92] These studies, however, are still in their infancy, and only when we can produce both systematic semantic and structural evidence for words that appear in Irish, lack an etymology and are not found in Brittonic will we be able to draw any serious conclusions about the pre-Irish languages of Ireland.

Conclusions

→ The Irish language is a member of the Celtic branch of the Indo-European language family.

→ The earliest certain evidence for a Celtic language in Ireland dates to *c.* AD 100 (Ptolemy's map).

→ Over the course of its occupation the peoples of Ireland probably experienced language shift a number of times.

→ It is highly improbable that a language directly related to Irish was spoken in Ireland during the Mesolithic (8000–4000 BC).

→ The shift from hunting-gathering to farming *c.* 4000 BC probably resulted in a language shift in Ireland. There are good reasons to regard the Neolithic language as not Irish.

→ There were a series of possible windows for language shift or at least the introduction of new languages during the later Neolithic (e.g. Grooved Ware) and Early Bronze Age (Beaker), but the dates of these events appear too early to be associated with the spread of the language directly ancestral to Irish.

→ The most probable period of the introduction of Irish lies between *c.* 1000 BC and the 1st century BC. During this time there is evidence that both Goidelic and Brittonic tribes were settled in Ireland.

→ One of the most plausible mechanisms for language shift during the target period was the appearance and spread of hillforts and a class of elite warriors *c.* 1000 BC.

→ The rise of Iron Age ritual centres in the first centuries BC may also have been a vehicle for language shift and stimulated the consolidation of the Goidelic language.

CHAPTER TEN

The Origins of the Irish

What are the origins of the Irish? By now the complexity of the question should be appallingly apparent. If we attempt to trace the genealogy of our target Irishman, Niall of the Nine Hostages, his ancestral trail would split within a single generation as his father was born in Ireland (presumably) while his mother was British. Potentially, his 'Irish' bloodline could have extended back some 330 generations to the time when Ireland was first settled, and his genetic ancestors could have ranged from descendants of the first colonists who moved north after the Ice Age to Near Eastern farmers who had moved into central Europe, or indeed anyone else in Europe who intermixed with his ancestors before they came to Ireland or who themselves came to Ireland to settle. Almost any aspect of Niall involves a new ancestral trail. While his chemical composition was essentially drawn from Irish geology, the foods that powered his body had different genetic origins. While tucking into a meal of wild boar may have found him consuming an animal whose own local ancestors went back to the Irish Mesolithic, his beef, bread and beer were all introduced from outside Ireland after 4000 BC, while the horse he rode was not introduced until after 2500 BC. By the 5th century AD his dress had been heavily influenced by the fashions of Roman Britain, as had the weapons he held in his hand. Politically, he was a king (*rí*) of a tribe (*túath*), a member of an institution that clearly came from the earlier Indo-European world (the Irish word for 'king' is cognate with Latin *rex* and Sanskrit *rāj-*, while the Irish word for 'tribe' is cognate with Lithuanian *tautà* 'people'), no doubt modified from whatever its original significance by its use within a distinctly Irish political landscape. He would still cling to a religion that had been partly introduced ultimately from Celtic Europe but that had since engaged with native religions and a landscape covered with ceremonial monuments of past faiths. His language was derived from the earlier Indo-European language family yet had picked up numerous 'foreign' words as its speakers had crossed Europe and then, presumably, absorbed many more words from the residue of all the various languages that had preceded Proto-Irish in Ireland. And this is only scratching the surface of all that went into the making of our target Irishman.

Nevertheless, some form of conclusion is needed, and while there is no use pretending that I have been able to give a full – much less a fully credible – set of answers to the questions of Irish origins, I hope at least we can see something of the shape of the answers.

The unfolding of the Irish

The early Irish of the 5th century AD were physically composed of elements initially brought together when two landmasses collided with one another about 450 million years ago to form the foundations of Ireland. The subsequent millions of years of geological change that ultimately evolved into the island of Ireland not only provided more of the primal 'stuff' of the earliest Irish, but also created a landscape that has helped shape the natural and cultural environment of all its occupants. The dearth of native flora and (especially) fauna made Ireland a fairly unattractive prospect at the time of its earliest human colonization. Its postglacial landscape made it far easier to promote a pastoral rather than a strictly agrarian economy with the increase in population that might have supported. On the other hand, the emergence of sources of copper and gold heavily influenced the cultural trajectory of the entire island from c. 2500 BC onward and encouraged the emergence of stratified societies.

The earliest human occupants of Ireland only settled there c. 10,000 years ago in a landscape that was markedly poorer in terms of natural resources than their homeland, which may have been located in the now submerged portions of the Isle of Man basin. The island of Ireland forced these first colonists to modify their behaviour and economy, and by 9,000 years ago a distinctly Irish Mesolithic culture had developed. Many geneticists have reasonably suggested that the bloodlines of these earliest Irelanders can be traced primarily to human populations that occupied Atlantic Europe or, at least, western Europe during the last Ice Age and expanded from refuges in southern Europe. But how much 'blood' of these earliest settlers was in Niall or runs through modern Irish populations is still impossible to determine for certain and may remain so until we discover more human remains from this earliest period and are able to analyse their ancient DNA. The language of these hunter-gatherers was most likely unrelated to the Irish language or any of its prehistoric ancestors.

About 6,000 years ago the entire economy and culture of Ireland were radically changed as farming was introduced during the Neolithic (c. 4000–2500 BC). This transformation was instigated by at least some farming populations who entered Ireland from Britain, bringing to an end what appears to have been a period of relative isolation that had lasted from *c.* 7000 to 4000 BC. After this period, contact between Ireland and Britain (and to some extent also between Ireland and Continental Europe) becomes a major theme, underwritten by an archaeological record that tracks almost constant exchanges of material culture and cultural behaviour between the two islands. Analysis of the genetics of modern Irish populations has suggested that a significant minority of the earliest farmers in Ireland possessed a genetic background that may not have entered Europe until the Neolithic and derived more immediately from southwest Asia. The distinction between these farmers and other populations is probably limited entirely to the genetic signature of their mtDNA and Y chromosome. By the time the first farmers entered Ireland it is very probable that any farmers of ultimate southwest Asian descent were culturally thoroughly mixed with 'native European' populations who had adopted agriculture from their neighbours. With the increase in population brought on by the shift to agriculture, it is certainly possible that Niall's generation and modern generations of Irish continue at least in part the genetic signature of some of these first farmers. Again, future developments in ancient DNA should provide a much more concrete picture. The sweeping cultural change initiated by the spread of farming is likely to have resulted in the first case of language shift in Ireland, although again it is fairly unlikely that the language of Ireland's first farmers was related to any of the linguistic predecessors of Irish.

About 2500 BC Ireland entered the Bronze Age, adopting both copper metallurgy and the use of an international style of ceramics that had spread over most of western Europe. Despite acceptance of the new Beaker ceramic style, it does not seem that Ireland accepted the whole associated ideology, such as the specific Beaker burial that was widespread in Britain and neighbouring areas on the Continent. For this reason the case for yet another language shift in Ireland, while still quite possible, is perhaps weaker than it was for the Neolithic, especially when we have to consider that the spread of Beaker-users may have mapped on to the earlier distribution of people associated with Grooved Ware and its new ceremonial horizon. The latter not only indicates a change in pottery but also the introduction of new communal ritual practices that might be better associated with language shift than the Beaker horizon but is so localized in Britain and Ireland that it could hardly be ancestral to the Irish language.

During the Late Bronze Age Ireland, like most of western Europe, was transformed into a society characterized by warrior elites, the conspicuous consumption of metallic wealth and the erection of hillforts. While direct evidence for foreign contacts is sporadic, the spread of hillforts across Ireland would at least be congruent with the creation of a new social domain associated with the new elites and, possibly, the spread of a new language. Linguistically, this could correlate with the initial expansion of a Celtic language to Ireland. During this period the material culture of Ireland is expressed in tools, weapons and ornaments that have clear connections with Britain and Continental Europe, but items of local inspiration are also indicated.

The Iron Age is still one of the poorest-known periods of Irish prehistory, although now we can at least see some evidence that the use of iron was spreading across Ireland in the centuries from *c.* 600 BC onward. By about the 3rd century BC elites in Ireland began kitting themselves out in the La Tène style, which was particularly associated with horse gear. This art style, of Continental and British inspiration but delivered almost exclusively in a local Irish form, was largely confined to the northern two-thirds of Ireland. Current archaeological evidence admits at most the entrance of small bands of elites and their craftsmen, but there is nothing to support a major settlement of a foreign population (the 'Celts'). On the other hand, the evidence of tribal names would appear to suggest that broad areas – a third or more of the island – were occupied by tribes presumably speaking the Celtic languages or dialects of Britain or the Continent. It is possible that during the last centuries BC the horizon of large ritual enclosures, the so-called provincial royal sites such as Tara and Navan, indicates a new expression of religious ceremonialism and/or political ideology across Ireland which may have prompted yet another possible language shift or, perhaps, the consolidation of the Goidelic 'dialect' over the dialects of competing Brittonic tribal groups. To this we might also add the erection of massive linear earthworks that would also have drawn populations together. Archaeology provides some evidence for traders and perhaps small groups of settlers from Roman Britain in the first centuries AD. In the centuries leading up to the death of Niall, Ireland became progressively more Romanized and soon afterwards incorporated into its traditions a new religion brought from southwest Asia and much of the material culture from the adjacent Roman province.

It should be emphasized that neither in the Neolithic nor throughout any subsequent period was Ireland ever the mere passive recipient of the cultures of the Continent and Britain, but was always an active player also exporting goods across the water to both Britain and the Continent. More importantly, the creation of the Irish was never solely the product of outside influences or peoples, but invariably involved an internal dynamic of adjustment to continuously changing conditions, both environmental and social. This book may well be criticized for focusing so much attention on assessing the various hypotheses for immigration into Ireland (where do the Irish come *from*?) and not devoting much space to exploring the 'genius' of the Irish (or Irelanders) in developing their own cultural identity. But this narrower focus has already required a book, and unless we can deal with what was brought to Ireland from the outer world, we will be poorly equipped to understand the larger picture.

The Irish discover themselves

In the introduction I indicated that it would be nearly impossible to direct the goals of this book around a classical ethnic definition of the Irish, i.e. one in which the people of Ireland had discerned that they were a single people. But having chewed off so much already, there is little reason not to tackle this final problem, albeit very briefly: did Niall think he was Irish?

While books abound with titles referencing the 'Irish Nation' or (wince) 'Irish Race', the concept of nationalism is generally regarded as modern, the product of the emergence of nation states or aspirations to become such a state that began about the 17th century. In Ireland, for example, explicit references to an Irish nation (*náision*) only emerge at the beginning of the 17th century in the context of the Counter-Reformation, to quote one pamphlet: 'I call the Irish Catholics the nation of Ireland, because Protestants therein are deemed generally but intruders and newcomers'.[1] The religious tag was critical here: even Geoffrey Keating, that great receptacle of 17th-century Irish learning, had a vision of an Irish people that included both native Gaels and those of Norman lineage (such as himself) who were Catholic and embraced the Irish language, but excluded newcomers such as the 'unassimilated English and Protestant'.[2] This type of definition illustrates how a sense of nationality often focuses not on who one believes oneself to be, but who one wants to exclude; the 'Us-versus-Them' approach has often been a driving force in the creation of national identities. We find a good example of this when Daniel Binchy suggested in the 1970s that an Irish sense of national identity may have been forged as early as the 9th century in the face of the Viking incursions into Ireland.[3]

Donnachadh Ó Corráin would put the evidence for an Irish national identity back to at least the 7th century.[4] Ó Corráin emphasized the impact of Christianity on Irish thought as it plugged them into a system of belief that already provided an origin for all humans and peoples. As the Franks and Saxons were recognized 'nations', so also should the Irish find their own place in this greater system, and hence all the diverse peoples and tribes of Ireland could be assimilated into the Irish origin myth provided in the *Lebor Gabála*. Moreover, the rise of Niall's descendants saw at least greater ideological attempts to aspire to an all-island kingship. This would place the Irish of pre-Norman times in a much larger world than that summarized in 1911 by G. H. Orpen: 'The Irishman's country was the *túath* or territory belonging to his tribe'.[5]

What word the Irish used to refer to themselves is problematic. As we have already seen, the Irish borrowed the Welsh pejorative *gwyddel* ('raiders') to provide their own self-designation *goídel*, and this term only seems to have entered Irish about the 7th century. In texts cited by Ó Corráin to indicate the concept of an all-embracing 'nation', we find reference to Niall's son occupying Tara as the *caput Scottorum*, 'capital of the Irish', and Diarmait mac Cerbaill, Niall's great-grandson, is described as the *totius Scotiae regnatorem*, 'king of all Ireland'. Throughout the Middle Ages the common designations for the people of Ireland were *mic Milidh*, 'sons of Míl', which again emerges earliest in the 7th century, and *fir Éireann*, 'men of Ireland'. It should be said that while this latter term can refer to all the people of Ireland, in the Ulster tales it is also at times restricted to designate only the southern opponents of the Ulstermen.

But could the people of Niall's world have also possessed an Irish national consciousness, or what Ó Corráin describes as a 'feeling of identity', that we might understand as 'nationality'? Here we are not talking of a political concept but rather a cultural one, i.e. the people of Ireland might still regard themselves as members of their different tribes but also recognize a cultural kinship that united all the occupants of the island irrespective of their regional political differences.

In his final (posthumous) book, Proinsias Mac Cana argued that a 'consciousness of Irish nationality' could be found based on language and the pagan system of religion that preceded Christianity.[6] We have already seen that at least the initiation of a Celtic language in Ireland precedes Niall and must have been in Ireland by the 1st century AD and presumably earlier. Unlike Peter Schrijver, who argued that the lack of dialects in early Irish hinted at its comparative recentness, Mac Cana envisaged a learned class (druids, poets) so closely interconnected and so dominant across the island that they were able to prevent the type of linguistic divisions found elsewhere and so they integrated the entire island into a single system of values, despite the fact that Ireland was strongly divided politically into frequently warring tribal groups.[7] Perhaps we might consider the city states of ancient Greece in a similar way, frequently at each other's throats and boasting a wide variety of different political institutions but sharing many elements of a common religion and language (though here with very marked dialectal differences) and coming together at the Olympic games.

So what is the earliest evidence for an ideology that seems to extend beyond tribal affiliations and embrace the entire island? The Irish word for 'province' is *cúigeadh* (Old Irish *coiced*) which derives from the word for 'five' (*coic*) and hence actually means a 'fifth', i.e. Ireland was envisaged as comprising five-fifths. The concept of the totality of Ireland being divided into five provinces has been described as 'the oldest certain fact in the political history of Ireland'.[8] This 'fact' saw Ireland divided into the five provinces: Connacht, Ulster, Leinster and Munster, with Meath as a separate province at the centre. These were far more than regional political divisions such as counties – they were part of a cultural cosmology, a way of partitioning the world in which each province was embued not only with a directional significance but also a conceptual characteristic (Table 10.1).[9]

Table 10.1 **The five provinces**

Province	Direction	Characteristic	Capital	Site
Connacht	West	*Fis* 'Learning'	Crúachain	Rathcroghan
Ulster	North	*Cath* 'Battle'	Emain Macha	Navan Fort
Leinster	East	*Bláth* 'Prosperity'	Dún Ailinne	Knockaulin
Munster	South	*Séis* 'Music'	Caseal	Cashel
Meath	Middle	Kingship	Temair	Tara

The five-province division was certainly a governing principle for discourse on the make-up of Ireland throughout the Middle Ages. Its existence as a system, ideological or political, presupposes a vision of Ireland as a subdivided unity. It does not provide evidence for an Irish 'nation', but it does underwrite the concept of what Mac Cana regarded as a 'national consciousness', an awareness that the occupants of Ireland constituted an individual people and were not merely an assortment of tribes who accidentally shared the same island. How early then is this provincial concept?

Its ascription to the earliest period of historical sources has generally meant that the concept has been presumed to be 'prehistoric' or, worse, dating back to 'time immemorial' (not much use to an archaeologist). Almost all discourse regarding its antiquity has been in the hands of historians, so there have not been many attempts to ground any proof of the provincial concept in the archaeological record. In the most thorough analysis of the issues within an archaeological context, Nick Aitchison has argued that the concept of Ireland being divided into five provinces is a product of Niall and his descendants, who attempted to anchor their own claims to political superiority in a supposedly ancient system that they themselves had fabricated.[10]

There seem to be two main elements to Aitchison's dismissal of any prehistoric existence for the provincial concept. The first concerns the archaeological sites that are the emblematic capitals of each of the provinces. The historical evidence depicts these as provincial political capitals, the residences of kings, and the scene of assemblies and battles during the medieval period. The archaeological evidence, on the other hand, suggests that the so-called 'royal capitals' were no later than the Iron Age (therefore they could not have provided the scene for activities set in the Middle Ages) and that they were ceremonial rather than defensive or residential. The second element is that the concept of the five provinces with a centre at Tara served so well the political ambitions of the Uí Néill to dominate Ireland, placing them in control of the centre of the entire system. The five-province system could not lie in the Iron Age 'because its ideological function and political context lie in the early medieval period and this cosmological scheme could scarcely have developed without relating to an ideology that reflected genuine political aspirations'.[11] In short, the cosmological scheme of the five provinces was part of an 'Uí Néill ideology'. If we follow this interpretation, it was the descendants of Niall who created for Ireland its earliest 'national consciousness'.

Before questioning this interesting interpretation, we need to dispense with some of the other issues on which most authors probably agree. First, the concept of a five-part world view focused on a centre surrounded by four directional and symbolic regions is widely found, both in the Indo-European world (especially ancient India) and outside it (e.g. China). There is nothing exclusively 'Irish' about it: it is an almost natural way of shaping a politico-cosmology. Second, we are dealing with an ideology and not a political system and so, whenever it came into existence, it need not have reflected a concrete political reality with a central high king surrounded by four provincial kings. Third, Munster as one of the provinces is problematic in almost every imaginable way. The sources are ambivalent as to where its emblematic capital was located (though Cashel is the main contender) or whether Munster constituted more than one province. Testing the date of the provincial system is probably best confined to the four more northerly provinces and their capitals. And fourth, the medieval Irish frequently engaged in reconstructing a fictional past for their monuments. The site of Navan Fort, for example, bears little evidence for the imagined buildings that were portrayed in the Ulster tales.

On the other hand, I think that a case can still be made that the provincial system as an ideology extended all the way back into the Iron Age. If the identification of the provincial capitals, what Aitchison has described as the 'monumental linchpins – the *quintessence* – of the five-fold division of Ireland',[12] was merely an Uí Néill ploy to superimpose a familiar cosmological system on their landscape, a critical element would obviously be the selection of these 'linchpins'. The Uí Néill could potentially have selected any ancient monuments that were impressive enough to meet their needs. They could have chosen their 'legendary' provincial centres from more than 70 hillforts and earlier ceremonial enclosures such as the Giant's Ring near Belfast. Yet the Uí Néill spin-doctors just happened to select at least three monuments (and probably the fourth – Rathcroghan) that all date to the Iron Age, the sparsest period in Irish prehistory for leaving remains of settlement. Moreover, the similarities between what should have been random sites, especially Navan and Knockaulin, are so striking that they must surely be related; the most recent remote sensing of Rathcroghan (published long after Aitchison's book appeared) renders the Connacht capital far more comparable to the others as well.[13] Even without the lens of later historical sources, an archaeologist surveying the archaeology of the Irish Iron Age would be tempted to interpret these sites as major centres in the same way that archaeologists have analysed Neolithic megaliths or Bronze Age hillforts as some form of political or ceremonial centre. As the Uí Néill managed to identify these monuments in the early Middle Ages, perhaps we should be impressed less with their achievements as political propagandists and more with their extraordinary abilities as archaeologists! In short, the four more northerly centres do not appear to be the product of later random selection; the Uí Néill were tapping into an earlier system.

Aitchison rightly recognizes one of the really critical issues with erecting such a system: irrespective of whether it was established in the Iron Age or the Middle Ages, just how does one generate five sites on the landscape that represent this five-part politico-cosmology? In Aitchison's theory, the driving force was the need of the Uí Néill to anchor their political aspirations in a mythic past (if they control the centre at Tara, the rest of Ireland should naturally be subservient to them).[14] So how can we imagine that the people of Ireland could have set up a five-province system in prehistory when we will assume that they actually believed in the politico-cosmology?

Mac Cana reminds us that, in order to scale the universe down to their ideology, the Irish would have had to set apart special sacred places and also recreate the cosmological relationships in their own territory. And when people migrate, they may be expected to 're-cosmicize the national territory…by creating new ritual centres'.[15] What we might imagine, then, is that during the Iron Age the five-province cosmological principle spread across Ireland (or at least the northern two-thirds, if Munster is excluded) as an ideology. Indeed, it may have been part of the 'big idea' that attracted the Irelanders to embrace a new language. All the sites that have seen excavation show signs of occupation, including presumably some form of ritual use, prior to the Iron Age horizon of their henges, large circular structures and mounds. Only one of them, Tara, already had a mound, while both Navan and Rathcroghan created mounds over earlier timber structures. This could suggest that there was an attempt to emulate on the periphery what already existed at Tara: i.e. in terms of the architectural components of the horizon, Tara probably had primacy. So during the last centuries BC populations in Leinster, Ulster and Connacht accepted this new vision of a five-part Ireland and erected similar ceremonial centres in areas that seemed most appropriate. In the case of Ulster and Connacht, the sites selected were already established ceremonial centres that were modified to serve as expressions of the new ideology. A common cultural idea – accepted across an island whose leaders spoke a Celtic language and which shared cultural institutions found among their Celtic-speaking neighbours in both Britain and on the Continent – would probably meet Mac Cana's quest for establishing a prehistoric Irish 'national consciousness'. If you accept this, then there is at least a case to be made that some form of Irish national consciousness had already taken shape by the first centuries BC.[16] And for that reason, I suspect that when Niall ended his days and went to the House of Donn, he entered it as an Irishman.

A Brief Update to the 2017 Edition

Earliest Human Occupation

In 2015 Peter Woodman published a major review of the evidence for the earliest human occupation of Ireland, including an assessment of the likelihood of discovering traces of Pre-Mesolithic settlement.[17] Although nothing really solid had yet been uncovered, there was still some optimism that such evidence might be found in the future. The 'future' occurred almost as soon as the book was off the press, when an article was submitted to *Quaternary Science Reviews* that pushed back the date of humans in Ireland by about 2,500 years.[18] The patella (kneecap) of a brown bear from an excavation of the Alice and Gwendoline Cave in Co. Clare had been recovered in 1903 and even then was known to exhibit five scratch marks of a stone tool. The bone was rediscovered in the National Museum of Ireland in 2011 and subsequent radiocarbon analysis indicated that it dated to c. 10,500 BC. It would seem that at least some hunters had crossed the sea to become Irelanders during the Upper Palaeolithic and future dating of cave specimens may well reveal more evidence of their presence.

Ancient DNA

When Chapter 8, on the evidence of DNA, was written our knowledge of Ireland's genetic history was based entirely on attempts to read history from the modern spatial distribution and frequency of genes in Ireland and the rest of Europe. This left us with a picture where the major genetic components of the modern population of Ireland were thought to derive either from the earliest Mesolithic settlers or from the Neolithic and I concluded (reluctantly) that most studies had 'failed to find any significant evidence of migrations after the Neolithic'.[19] The principal haplogroup among Irish males, for example, was R1b, usually attributed to the earliest (Mesolithic) occupants of Ireland although some argued that it derived from Neolithic settlers.

More recent scientific advances in the recovery and sequencing of ancient DNA from early sites have permitted the phenomenal growth of palaeogenetics, the study of the genetics of past societies, a discipline whose discoveries erase earlier models on a monthly basis. Since the 1980s, ancient DNA from populations ranging from Neanderthals to the present had been gradually recovered and identified across parts of Eurasia, but the first results from Ireland only appeared in 2016.[20] These comprised four samples: one woman from Ballynahatty, Co. Down, dating to the Neolithic c. 3300–3000 BC, and three males from an Early Bronze Age cemetery (c. 2000–1500 BC) from Rathlin Island, Co. Antrim. The Neolithic woman revealed a predominantly Near Eastern origin and she was, as so many other Neolithic samples are, most similar to a modern Sardinian, who has become the genetic archétype for the first farmers in the Mediterranean and Atlantic Europe.[21] She had dark brown hair and brown eyes.

The three males excavated from Rathlin Island, with genes for light-coloured hair and brown eyes, all belonged to the male haplogroup R1b which comprises about 80% of all modern Irish males. As we have seen, in my original account this haplogroup was believed to derive from the original Mesolithic inhabitants of Ireland as a result of the expansion of human populations from Iberia and southern France after the last Ice Age. Now the story has become much more interesting.

In 2015 there appeared two groundbreaking articles based on ancient DNA analysis undertaken at Harvard (and Jena)[22] and Copenhagen.[23] In samples collected across Eurasia, they both found evidence for a major migration from the steppelands north of the Black Sea to Western Europe (Germany) around 3000 BC. About 80% of the burials from one culture in Germany showed evidence of a steppe ancestry and this persisted into the Early Bronze Age Beaker culture of the region and subsequent metal-using societies. The haplogroup borne by these steppe intruders and passed on to Central and West Europeans was R1b, the same haplogroup recovered from Rathlin Island. Although there may be problematic traces of this haplogroup in Europe before this steppe expansion,[24] its presence is no longer seen as a residue of either the Mesolithic or Neolithic expansions but rather the result of these late expansions from the European steppelands. The Rathlin Island burials were accompanied by Food Vessels whose ancestor, the Beaker horizon, was the likely bearer of the new gene. The current working hypothesis, then, is that c. 3000–2500 BC a large area of Europe, including Ireland, was genetically transformed by immigrants from the east. The implications for Irish origins are both profound and perplexing.

The European vector of R1b was most likely the Beaker horizon and, while my earlier account of the Beakers in Chapter 4 argued that there must have been some immigration to explain the presence of Irish Beakers, I doubt that anyone imagined such a massive influx as to thoroughly reshape Ireland's genetic history. Most intriguing is the evidence that the modern genetic profile of Irish males seems to begin only with the Early Bronze Age. The question, however, is whether the genetic shift was very rapid or merely a gradual process over several thousand years.

If there was a massive migration to Ireland, archaeologists have failed to recognize it in the archaeological record (which, mind you, does not mean that it did not happen). But it is also entirely possible that we are witnessing a persistent east to west movement of R1b males from Atlantic Europe (where, like Ireland, R1b may be found at levels over 80%) through Britain (present levels of over 60%) and on into Ireland. This would constitute a series of migration streams beginning with the Beakers but persisting through the Bronze and Iron ages. Obviously, when we have a far larger DNA sample of Bronze Age males we will have a much better idea whether the genetic shift in Ireland was rapid or slow and which populations of Western Europe are the most likely ancestors to these Irish immigrants.

The current model indicated by the genetic evidence suggests then that Ireland has experienced three major palaeogenetic phases. The earliest saw the initial settlement of Ireland by populations originally stemming from southwest Europe after the last Ice Age. Four thousand years later there was probably an influx of farmers who would trace their origins back to the Near East and who may well have entered

Ireland along the Mediterranean and then northwards up the Atlantic coast. This is what we find in the single Neolithic burial analyzed. The genetic types that we presume date back to the Mesolithic and Neolithic now comprise about 20% of the Irish population (though we cannot be certain that all the Mesolithic DNA groups were local and not picked up along the way by later groups). The third phase was initiated *c.* 2500–2000 BC with the arrival of immigrants whose ancestors lay in the distant steppelands of the Ukraine and southern Russia; they crossed Europe, also accumulating the genetic signatures of its earlier inhabitants, before arriving in Ireland. Eventually they came to constitute about 80% of the Irish population.

And what about language?

The genetic evidence has some bearing on the origins of the Irish language because two of the migration phases coincide with the two main competing theories concerning the origins and expansions of the Indo-European languages, which includes the Celtic languages. One theory holds that the ancestor of what would eventually emerge as Irish spread during the Neolithic from Turkey, both across the Balkans and Central Europe and south along the Mediterranean and then the Atlantic, arriving in Ireland *c.* 4000 BC. The alternative associates the Indo-European languages with the movement of peoples from the European steppe westwards into Europe (our R1b event of *c.* 3000 BC), arriving in Ireland sometime after 2500 BC. As literacy did not appear in Central Europe until it was already entirely occupied by Indo-European languages, little can be said about the merits of this hypothesis on the basis of direct linguistic evidence. On the other hand, the route of farmers from the Near East across the Central and West Mediterranean does reveal written evidence from the Iron Age in precisely the same regions as the earliest Neolithic settlements. Here, for example, we find the ancestor of Basque in southern France and an extinct Iberian language along the east coast of Spain, both of which are clearly non-Indo-European. And in islands such as Sardinia where occupation appears to be minimal before the settlement of farmers, we recover in place names and indigenous words in Sardinian traces of what is known as Palaeo-Sardo, again a non-Indo-European language.[25] This evidence appears to associate one or more *non*-Indo-European languages (to what extent these languages may be related to one another is controversial) with the areas of earliest Mediterranean farmers. If this be accepted, it makes it unlikely that the Celtic languages, including Irish, originated among the earliest farming communities in southwest Europe.[26]

Notes

Preface (pp. 6–7)
1 Mallory 1985.
2 Mallory 1991.
3 Mallory 2006.

Introduction (pp. 8–10)
1 A worthy exception is Shane Hegarty (2009), who asks many of the right questions.
2 The standard accounts are Waddell (2010), Cooney and Grogan (1999), O'Kelly (1989), Harbison (1988) and Herity and Eogan (1977). More popular accounts include Flanagan (1998), Ryan (1994) and McCaffrey and Eaton (2002).
3 See, for example, De Paor 1986, Loughrey 1988, Hegarty 2009.
4 Gallagher 2007.
5 See Mac Cana 2011.
6 O'Rahilly 1946, 216; Byrne 1973, 71.

Chapter 1 (pp. 11–36)
1 For a general account of the formation and evolution of the Earth, see Marshak 2001. The basic accounts of Irish geology have been taken from Woodcock and Strachan 2000, Holland 2001, Mitchell and Ryan 1997, Mitchell 2004, and more popular accounts in Feehan 1997, McKeever 1999 and Williams and Harper 2003.
2 Winn 2006, 68.
3 Comerford 2003, 1.
4 O'Sullivan and Breen 2007, 15. Measuring coastlines is a notorious problem involving fractals, as can be seen by the very different estimate in Wikipedia of 1,448 km. There France and Spain are given much longer coasts than Ireland, while O'Sullivan and Breen claim that Ireland's coast is longer than that of either.
5 Ward and Brownlee 2003, 30; a larger amount is estimated in Marshak 2001.
6 Winn 2006, 55–56 (Leighlinbridge, Co. Carlow).
7 Ward and Brownlee 2003, 31.
8 This is the shortest estimate I have found (Smith 2010, 147, correcting an erroneous estimate

of 25 mm); but there are sources indicating as much as 2 cm per year.
9 There are footprints 7 cm long of an early reptile (but not yet a dinosaur) from near Scrabo, Co. Down, and the discovery of dinosaur remains at Portmuck. We will obviously discount the (unintentionally) amusing discovery of a dinosaur and its mother off the west coast of Ireland in the British monster film *Gorgo* (originally banned in Finland!).
10 See C. R. Scotese's 'Pangea Ultima' image at http://www.scotese.com/future2.htm.
11 Woodman *et al.* 1997.
12 Dates kindly supplied by Valerie Hall, Queen's University Belfast.
13 Viney 2003 provides a good summary of some of these issues.
14 Mitchell and Ryan 1997, 107.
15 Wingfield 1995.
16 Lambeck and Purcell 2001.
17 Devoy 1995.
18 Edwards and Brooks 2008.
19 Cooper *et al.* 2002.
20 Edwards and Bradley 2009.
21 Ward and Brownlee 2003, 81–85.

Chapter 2 (pp. 37–70)
1 The earliest radiocarbon date for human settlement in Ireland is from Mount Sandel, Co. Londonderry, where the start date for the settlement falls in the range 7790–7635 BC (Bayliss and Woodman 2009).
2 Wales was first settled *c.* 250,000 years ago by early Neanderthals; modern humans are recorded from *c.* 26,000 years ago at Paviland Cave (Lynch *et al.* 2000, 5).
3 I exclude here the genuine artifacts such as hand-axes from Dún Aonghusa and Argalin whose contexts are so problematic that they cannot be regarded as valid evidence for occupation of Ireland.
4 Mitchell and Ryan 1997, 79–80. A more recent discovery comes from near Scrabo, Co. Down, where it was probably redeposited during the Midlandian glaciation.
5 Early Modern humans were

already in Britain by *c.* 44,000–42,000 years ago (Higham *et al.* 2011).
6 Woodman 2003.
7 Costa *et al.* 2005, 22; Woodman (pers. comm.) now suggests 7800(?)–6800(?) BC for the Early Mesolithic, but the arguments for these dates have not yet been published.
8 Woodman 1985; the only full synthesis of the Irish Mesolithic is Woodman 1978a.
9 Woodman at http://www.excavations.ie/Pages/Details.php?Year=&County=Limerick&id=2067.
10 Collins and Coyne 2003.
11 German *Irländer*, Swedish *Irländare*.
12 Translation from Viney 2003; for a short account of this remarkable thinker, see Duddy 2002, 1–17.
13 Woodman and McCarthy 2003, 36–37.
14 See Woodman *et al.* 1997; McCormick 1999; Davenport *et al.* 2008; Searle 2008; Sleeman 2008.
15 Estimates of modern animal populations from Sleeman and Yalden 2009.
16 Figures taken from Sleeman 2008, 78.
17 Ellis *et al.* 2003, 117–18; there is also mention of another site (Marsh Benham) with an 'animal bone assemblage of unknown size dominated by wild boar' (119).
18 Bay-Petersen 1978.
19 Yalden 1999, 72.
20 McCormick 1999. See also McCormick 2004.
21 Van Wijngaarden-Bakker 1989; Kelly 2008.
22 http://caloriecount.about.com/calories-eel-mixed-species-i15026.
23 Woodman *et al.* 1999.
24 O'Sullivan and Breen 2007, 39.
25 McClean 1993.
26 Warren 2005, 13.
27 Tolan-Smith 2008, 144.
28 O'Sullivan and Breen 2007, 53–57.
29 Macalister 1921, 58–59.
30 Herity and Eogan 1977, 17.
31 Woodman 1978a, 208.
32 Harbison 1988, 24.
33 Tolan-Smith 2008, 151: "To

et to Ireland in the mid-eighth
millennium cal BC involved a sea
crossing, and it is reasonable to
assume that the passage was made
from Southwest Scotland, from
which the coast of Ireland is visible
on most days.'

4 Ballantyne 2004.
5 Ashmore 2004, 90.
6 Mellars 2004, 169.
7 Mellars 2004, 169–70.
8 Edwards 2004.
9 Warren 2005, 37.
10 E.g. Bayliss and Woodman
2009, 117.
11 Mellars 2004, 173.
12 Wickham-Jones 2004.
13 Woodman 2004, 291; Bayliss
and Woodman 2009, 117.
14 Saville 2004b, 189.
15 See Saville 2004b for the Scottish
Mesolithic industry.
16 Saville (2009, 55), who
emphasizes that he has 'been at
pains to contradict earlier attempts
to link the Irish and Scottish
Mesolithic…by stressing the paucity
of hard evidence for any cultural
similarities on either side of the
North Channel before the Neolithic
period'.
17 Scotland and northern Britain
do possess ground stone tools,
but only Ireland produces an
abundance of ground stone axes
(Clarke 2009, 19).
18 Woodman 2004, 294–95.
19 At Mount Sandel there were
523 scalene triangles, 315 rods and
100 needle points (Woodman 1985,
54), while the ratios at Scottish
sites such as Bolsay Farm on Islay
and Staosnaig on Colonsay were
590/294/9 and 47/142/6 respectively
(Finlay 2009, 23).
50 McCartan 2003; 2004.
51 Accounts of Manx toolkits in
McCartan 2004; Woodman 1978b;
1987.
52 David and Walker 2004, 303.
53 David and Walker 2004, 317.
54 Woodman 1986, 10.
55 Gouletquer and Monnier 1976;
Kayser 1991, 203–4; Valdeyron
2008, 194.
56 Kayser 1991, 199.
57 Tolan-Smith 2008, 146.
58 Peter Woodman, pers. comm.
59 Woodman (1986, 10) regarded
the Isle of Man origin 'the most

attractive proposition'.
60 Coles 1998; Pollard 2008, 6–7.
61 Anthony 1990, 903–4.
62 Woodman 1986, 11–15.
63 O'Sullivan and Breen 2007, 39.
64 Mitchell and Ryan 1997, 118–20;
see also Harbison 1988, 24, who
contemplates the possibility of the
extinction of the first colonists and
resettlement by a second wave 'who
plucked up the courage to cross
the sea'.
65 Costa et al. 2005, 23.
66 Woodman 1978b, 133.
67 'It is an old maxim of mine
that when you have excluded the
impossible whatever remains,
however improbable, must be the
truth' (A. Conan Doyle, 'Adventure
of the Beryl Coronet', 1892).
68 Reviewed most recently in
Costa et al. 2005.
69 Riede 2011, 316–18.
70 Woodman 1981.
71 Woodman 1981, 103.
72 Gamble 1999.
73 Lynch et al. 2000, 28.
74 Assuming a woman might
produce somewhere between two
and three children who survived
to adulthood; see Hasan 1973, 540.

Chapter 3 (pp. 71–104)
1 Bhreathnach 1995, 22.
2 Barker 2006, 414.
3 R. A. S. Macalister conflated
the origins of the Mesolithic with
the Neolithic, although he did
attribute the changes generally
associated with the Neolithic to
'later colonies [who] found their
way into Ireland and introduced the
more developed arts'; their source
was 'the larger island', Britain, that
had also provided the source for
Ireland's first occupants (Macalister
1921, 69). Michael Herity's account
implicitly opts for the same answer,
as Ireland's earliest Neolithic pottery
'assemblage is clearly related to those
of the British Primary Neolithic'
(Herity and Eogan 1977, 24), while
Peter Harbison offered slightly
more discussion of Neolithic origins
and opted for 'somewhere in the
northern half of Britain' (Harbison
1988, 30). Michael O'Kelly (1989,
29) had the native Irish Mesolithic
populations obtaining their
Neolithic from abroad, but he was

silent as to the actual source. In the
first edition of the standard textbook
of Irish prehistory, John Waddell
(1998, 25) reprised the traditional
view that the Neolithic was
introduced to Ireland by 'the arrival
of pioneering farming communities',
but when it comes to the specifics
'what precisely happened is still
quite unclear'. In the new edition of
2010 he still suggests colonization
as a possibility but emphasizes that
different facets of the Neolithic may
have been introduced at different
times (2010, 26).
4 Warren 2008, 8.
5 See Robb and Miracle 2007.
6 Fischer 1970.
7 The six or seven houses excavated
at Corbally, Co. Kildare, are not
likely to have been occupied all
at the same time (Whitehouse
2011, 58).
8 Other than the pig, all other
domesticates must have been
brought to Ireland and derive
genetically from the earliest
domesticates in southwest Asia.
There may well have been local
domestication of wild pigs in
Europe (Tresset and Vigne 2007,
193–94), but there is insufficient
evidence to pronounce on the
source of the domestic pig in
Ireland.
9 Schulting 1998.
10 Kooijmans 2007, 306.
11 Zvelebil and Rowley-Conwy
1984.
12 O'Kelly 1981, 118; see also
O'Kelly 1989, 29–30.
13 Woodman et al. 1999.
14 Scarre 2007, 252.
15 Hartz et al. 2007, 579.
16 Woodman and McCarthy 2003.
17 Thomas 2008, 64 indicates
that some Later Mesolithic tools
from Ireland have been found in
southwest Scotland.
18 There are a few more very early
sites but all of these have been
challenged; see Woodman et al.
1999, 144–51.
19 Woodman 1976, 303.
20 For example, in Iberia (Arias
2007, 56–57), where we have
imported pottery on otherwise
Mesolithic sites.
21 Piggott 1954.
22 Piggott 1954, 369–70.

23 E.g. Case 1969.

24 O'Sullivan 2000.

25 Woodman 1976, 301.

26 Tresset 2000, 17, lists four models:

1) population replacement;

2) rapid acculturation of native groups after arrival of farmer colonists;

3) 'direct interaction between farming pioneers and native hunter-gatherers'; 4) indirect interaction via long-distance exchange.

27 Cooney 2007, 560.

28 Gronenborn 2007, 87; Crombé and Vanmontfort 2007, 273.

29 DeBoer 1990.

30 Warren 2008, 8.

31 See the reviews by Whittle 2007, Hey and Barclay 2007, 400 and Whittle et al. 2011.

32 See Waddell 1998, 25–26 for some examples.

33 There are various models for the dates of the start and end of the enclosures; see the exhaustive discussion of all this in Whittle et al. 2011.

34 See Cooney et al. 2011, 665–68 for a variety of attempts to deal with the Magheraboy dates.

35 Rowley-Conwy (2011, S443) goes so far as to write that 'we must face the surprising possibility that Ireland "went agricultural" before Britain; if true, it would be the biggest leapfrog migration in Europe and the ultimate testimony to the importance of the hide boat'.

36 Robb and Miracle 2007, 111. A more recent estimate for the Neolithic cultures of the carinated bowl tradition, which would include Britain and Ireland, is an average rate of 2.3 km per year (Bocquet-Appel et al. 2012, 536).

37 Bayliss et al. 2011, 800–1.

38 Thomas 2008.

39 Rowley-Conwy 2004; 2011, S442–43.

40 Thomas 2008, 65.

41 Rowley-Conwy 2004, S97.

42 Cooney and Mandal 1998.

43 Sheridan 2004a, 16.

44 Simpson and Meighan 1999.

45 See, for example, the island of Jersey, which received 28% of its axes from Brittany, 16% from Normandy and a sizeable proportion from other sources,

despite the fact that it was a major exporter of dolerite axes; Cunliffe 2001, 207.

46 See, for example, Sheridan 2004a; Cooney 2000, 102–3.

47 Anthony 1990.

48 Whittle 2007, 393.

49 Whittle 2007, 393.

50 Marchand 2007; Scarre et al. 2003, 76–80.

51 Cunliffe 2001, 68.

52 Case 1969, 5.

53 O'Sullivan and Breen 2007, 74–77.

54 Cunliffe 2002, 94, citing Avienus.

55 Or somewhat earlier, see Scarre et al. 2003.

56 Scarre 2007, 256.

57 Sheridan 2000, 12.

58 Sheridan 2000. But the same cannot be said for such major classes of stone tools as arrowheads, where those of western France are quite different from those of Britain and Ireland (Marchand 2007, 236–39).

59 Cunliffe 2001, 173, 180–1.

60 Bradley 2007, 20.

61 Whittle et al. 2011, 872.

62 Sheridan 2004a, 10.

63 Dupont et al. 2009, 107–8.

64 Whittle et al. 2011, 849–52.

65 Sheridan 2007, 461.

66 Sheridan 2007, 464.

67 Sheridan 2004a, 14.

68 Sheridan 2007, 468–70.

69 Marchand 1999, 313–19.

70 Hasan 1973, 540.

71 Perles 2001, 45.

72 Doyle and Ó Néill 2003.

73 Baum and Bar-Gal 2003, 73; but this is contradicted by Rothschild 2003, 115, who argues that it has existed since the Ice Age. Of course, it may still have been associated with wild cattle or another animal carrier of the disease that was absent from Ireland (Rothschild suggests that American Indians acquired tuberculosis from hunting bison), hence new colonists could still have introduced the disease.

74 Mercer 1999; Schulting 2006.

75 Schulting and Wysocki 2005.

76 Moore 2004, 151: 'There is no evidence that it was the indigenous hunter-gatherers of the Later Mesolithic who attacked these sites.'

77 McCormick 2009.

78 Bonsall et al. 2001.

79 Guilaine 2003, 83–101.

80 Cauvin 2000.

81 Asouti 2006.

82 Thomas 1981, 295.

83 See McGrail 1983 for detailed discussion of the requirements of ancient navigators.

84 For example, Cunliffe 2001, 196; Bradley 2007, 134.

85 Sheridan 2004b, 35.

Chapter 4 (pp. 105–28)

1 Joynt 1910, 111.

2 Harrison 1980, 9.

3 Abercromby 1912.

4 The first actual Beaker find may have been from Moytirra, Co. Sligo, and Macalister himself recovered a Beaker in 1913 from Longstone Furness, Co. Kildare, although he did not recognize it for what it was (Carlin 2011a, 29–30).

5 Macalister 1928, 52.

6 Macalister 1949, 87–88; compare the language of Christopher and Jaquetta Hawkes only two years earlier, commenting on British Beakers: 'once arrived, these several waves of energetic conquerors soon occupied the greater part of Britain, ruthlessly dispossessing the Neolithic communities of their best pastures, and also no doubt their herds, and sometimes their women' (Hawkes and Hawkes 1947, 54).

7 Harbison 1975, 113.

8 Herity and Eogan 1977, 117.

9 Herity and Eogan 1977, 132.

10 The so-called wristguards may have served a different (possibly ornamental) purpose, as there are a variety of reasons to suspect that they could not have actually functioned as wristguards.

11 See Gallay 2001, 54–55 for the association between Beaker people and the European languages.

12 See Brodie 1994 for a discussion of the British evidence.

13 Childe 1949, 119.

14 Neither of which are 'Beakers', as the gypsies derived from northern India and entered Europe in the Middle Ages and the tinkers are a modern travelling folk.

15 Waddell 1998, 123; 2010, 130.

16 Harbison (1988, 92) thought that it might be 'premature to be sure whether the advent of Beaker pottery brought with it incursions

of new "Beaker people" (if such existed)'. Similarly, O'Kelly (1989, 71–72) refers to earlier theories involving a 'Beaker Folk' expanding into Ireland but in general opts for the spread of a prestige ware that may have had some impact on technology but did not really affect the lives of the native population. See also Cooney and Grogan with regard to the appearance of metallurgy and beakers, who argue that their presence is less likely to 'represent the presence of new individuals or groups on the island' but rather that they reflect a 'package of material culture centring on Beaker pottery which spread along networks of contact established between social elites in different areas' (1999, 83–84). But the concept of Beaker migrations was still obviously present in Lawrence Flanagan's account of Irish prehistory in 1998 (81–82). Flanagan admitted that there were apparent difficulties in establishing the nature of the Beaker People's 'colonisation of Ireland' and that perhaps the concept of colonisation directly, and solely, from Britain should be discarded, or at least modified – even though the distribution not only of Beaker pottery but of the rest of the Beaker-compatible equipment does seem so strongly to suggest it.'

7 Such conclusions are based on the analysis of strontium signatures in teeth and bones that are laid down according to the geological impact of water sources. And the impact of migrating populations might be minimized: the chemical evidence from tooth enamel can only deal with first-generation migrants, so any later generations would pass for 'local' (Price et al. 2004, 30).

8 Fitzpatrick 2011.
9 Tusa 2001.
10 Clarke 1976.
11 There is some evidence for the circulation of Beakers in Brittany, although these seem to be isolated cases (Salanova 2001, 95–96). However, when similar tests have been applied in, for example, the Netherlands, Switzerland and Hungary, the pottery appears to

have been of local manufacture, although there has been some evidence that pots may have been imported from c. 200 km away along the Rhine drainage (Drenth and Hogestijn 2001, 325; Kalicz-Schreiber and Kalicz 2001, 448; Convertini 2001; Othenin-Girard 1998, 58; Rehman et al. 1992).
22 Case 1995, 26; Brodie 1994, 17; Carlin 2011b, 228.
23 Nicolis 2001, 217; Vander Linden 2004, 38.
24 Gibson 2002, 88–89. They may have taken something on the order of four to six hours to produce (Brodie 1994, 15–16). A study of British Beakers by Humphrey Case suggests that they generally held between 500 and 1,250 ml of whatever they contained (Brodie 1998, 47), and analysis of the size of the Beakers indicates that adult males received the largest, followed by females and the smallest accompanied children (Brodie 1998, 48).
25 Salanova 2001, 99.
26 Burgess 1976.
27 Dickson 1978; Brodie 1994, 19–20; see Brodie 1998, 48 for alternative hypotheses.
28 Harrison and Heyd 2007, 206.
29 Vander Linden 2006, 89. There is also suggestion of some form of porridge from a British Beaker, but other clearly non-consumables have been found in Beakers such as the skeleton of an infant, cremations and objects of flint (Brodie 1998, 48).
30 Gibson 2002, 91.
31 Declan Hurl, pers. comm.
32 Case 2004b, 202.
33 Vander Linden 2006, 56.
34 ander Linden 2006, 40–41; see also Besse (2004, 127) where the common wares associated with Beakers can be regarded as products of gradual transition in northwest Europe but, because of the lack of local antecedents, are regarded as the products of migration in southern Europe.
35 See, for example, Case 2004c, 11–15.
36 Müller and van Willigen 2001.
37 Carlin 2011a, 13.
38 Carlin 2006.
39 Carlin 2006, 59–60. Carleton

Jones (2004, 60–61) excavated a house on Roughan Hill in the Burren where he found a roughly circular structure, 6 or 7 m in diameter, that rested on stone foundation walls. With the exception of a single (later) potsherd, all other ceramic remains were Beakers and he argued that the structure belonged to the Beaker period, but even this site is not securely 'Beaker' as Carlin (2011a, 73) argued that 'there is no definite evidence to indicate that a Beaker structure was present'.
40 Waddell 1998, 117; more recently Allen 2005.
41 Eogan and Roche 1997, 223–60.
42 Possibly 293 (Neill Carlin, pers. comm.)
43 Chapple et al. 2009, 5–36.
44 Eogan 1984, 308–12.
45 Van Wijngaarden-Bakker 1986. This comes from an admittedly mixed layer and may, therefore, belong to a later period. Horse remains have also been recovered from an Early Bronze Age Irish Bowl burial in an earlier Neolithic tomb at Audleystown, Co. Down (Jope 1954), but the remains are lost and this cannot be verified.
46 McCormick and Murray 2007, 143.
47 Harrison 1980, 84–91; Vander Linden 2006, 148–54.
48 Carlin 2011a, 155.
49 Vander Linden (2001, 274) describes Ireland as 'culturally autonomous during the Beaker phase'.
50 For example, the use of megalithic tombs in southern France for Beaker burials is the norm (87% of Beaker burials are in collective tombs; Guilaine et al. 2001, 248), and they are widely found in earlier megalithic tombs in Brittany as well (Helgouac'h 2001, 294–95). Beakers are also routinely found in earlier megalithic tombs in Denmark and northern Germany (Vander Linden 2006, 46).
51 Carlin and Brück (in press).
52 Brindley and Lanting 1991/92, 25.
53 The association of wedge tombs with Beakers, however, is not without some problems. For example, of the 30 wedge tombs

excavated, only about half (13) contained evidence of Beakers, and it would seem that the other half did not require Beakers to accompany the dead. This might be a regional practice, as none of the 8 tombs excavated in the far southwest of Ireland have yielded remains of Beakers (O'Brien 1999, 274). The insertion of Beakers in a megalithic tomb is unusual for Britain, although a minority do occur in such tombs in western and northern Britain (Case 2004a, 196). But we should note that the British tombs are not wedge tombs and we have already seen that Beaker-using populations were very much attracted to the ritual monuments that preceded them.

54 Harrison 1980, 9.

55 Mount 2000, 57.

56 O'Brien 2001.

57 Warner et al. 2009.

58 Burmeister 2000, 548.

59 Härke in a critique of Burmeister (Burmeister 2000, 558).

60 O'Brien 1992, 132.

61 Vander Linden 2004, 41–42.

62 Gibson 2004.

63 That we might expect such foreign burials (if they existed) is supported by evidence from Scotland, where a Beaker grave from Argyll would appear to be a dead ringer for a Dutch Beaker burial (timber chamber, ring ditch with posts) and where there are some other such foreign Beaker burials that suggest immigrants (Sheridan 2008).

64 Vander Linden 2006, 85.

65 Salanova 2004, 63–66.

66 Harbison 1979, 98–99. On the other hand, Irish bracers tend to be two-holed, the customary type of western France but not of neighbouring Britain.

67 Salanova 2004, 69–71.

68 Case 1995, 20–21. As for architectural remains, also often treated within the context of folk vernaculars, we have so little evidence that we cannot even discuss it, and even if we did it might not be all that informative as immigrants may adopt any system that works for their new environment (Burmeister 2000, 541).

69 Needham 2002, 105.

70 Timberlake 2002, 328–29.

71 In Hungary, for example, we find traditional Beaker burials alongside native cremation burials (Vander Linden 2006). Moreover, the Bell Beakers of Hungary are entirely confined to the region of Budapest. This suggests that here we may be dealing with an intrusive culture, perhaps in confrontation with a native population. In other areas the local Late Neolithic population had a deep impact on the Beakers, for example in Sicily, where we find Beaker pottery that has been painted and also mass burials, characteristics of earlier native Sicilian populations (Vander Linden 2006, 98–102). Here again Beaker occupation is restricted to the west of the island. In France, elements of early Beaker material may be found on native sites, or sites may show a mixed culture, or we have exclusively Beaker sites (Vander Linden 2006, 76).

72 Earlier works such as Harbison 1979 emphasized that the Beakers were largely a northern phenomenon.

73 There are settlements of the Beaker period which have yielded no pottery, e.g. Knock Dhu, Co. Antrim.

74 Neill Carlin, pers. comm.

75 With the exception of the odd possible Grooved Ware influence on a Beaker pot (Brindley 1999, 31).

76 Case 1995, 25–26.

77 Gibson 2002, 88–89.

78 DeBoer 1990.

79 Vander Linden 2001, 272–73.

80 Vander Linden 2001, 271–74.

81 Brodie 1994, 29.

82 Harrison and Heyd 2007, 206–7.

83 Brodie 1994, 30.

84 Waddell 1998, 133–37.

85 Taylor 1970.

86 Anthony 1990.

87 Brindley 2007, 331.

Chapter 5 (pp. 129–56)

1 *The American Heritage Dictionary of the English Language* (1969), 691. Boston, Houghton Mifflin Harcourt.

2 Macalister 1921, 26 and 37. Macalister dismissed a Bronze Age invasion because he believed that there was little evidence to suggest

that the 'round-headed' Bronze Age stock who had replaced the 'long-headed' Neolithic people of Britain had had a similar effect on Ireland.

3 Herity and Eogan's textbook on Irish prehistory envisaged waves of Beaker Folk, Food Vessel People and Urn People, but there is really no further mention of invaders: 'In Ireland the evidence available need not cause one to postulate the arrival of immigrant bands, perhaps some craftsmen' (Herity and Eogan 1977, 181). While Michael O'Kelly mentions 'outside contacts and influences' during the Bronze Age, he does not entertain the idea of invaders (O'Kelly 1989, 150).

4 See O'Sullivan and Breen 2007, 93–99 for the types of boat in the Bronze Age and their possible social context; see also Henderson 2007, 48–56 for a summary account of Atlantic seafaring in the Late Bronze and Iron ages.

5 Although tin has been found in Ireland, there is no archaeological evidence to indicate that it was exploited in antiquity; see Cahill 2009, 6–7.

6 See, for example, Kristiansen 1998, 52–56.

7 Harding 2000, 279, beating even the Danes and north Germans and 2.6 times more than in Britain.

8 O'Kelly 1989, 151.

9 Or possibly 1600–1100 BC (Waddell 2010, 187).

10 For the association between the environmental situation and Bronze Age archaeological periods, see Plunkett 2008.

11 The use of these items is not entirely clear and, although they occur primarily with adult males, there are some instances of a woman and in one instance even a child with a razor (Cooney and Grogan 1994).

12 Or 1150–1000 BC (Waddell 2010, 187).

13 Eogan 2009.

14 For general accounts of hoards and votive offerings, see Bradley 1990; Harding 2000, 352–68; and for Ireland see Eogan 1983 and Bourke 2001.

15 Henderson 2007, 47.

16 Kristiansen 1998, fig. 74; Henderson 2007, 77.

7 Ó Néill 2009.
8 Whether in fact there was only one house on such sites depends on the area around the house being adequately searched for other houses; generally, this is an assumption that should be rejected.
9 Doody 2000.
10 O'Neill 2009.
11 Ginn and Rathbone 2012.
12 Brunicardi 1914, 191–95.
13 Henderson 2007, 100.
14 Ginn (in press) argues that houses in some of these clusters date to different periods.
15 To the fulachta fiadh we might also add another site: the stone circle, which occurs in concentrations in south Munster and has repeatedly indicated dates of c. 1000 BC.
16 Eogan 1983; Bourke 2001.
17 Grogan 2005.
18 For Late Bronze Age France, which we would expect to have considerably greater carrying capacity than Ireland, Brun 1993, 172) works with a notional community of 200–400 people per 7-km radius (c. 154 sq km). Extrapolating this estimate to the Mooghaun area would then give a population of c. 580 to 1,160, and for Ireland as a whole we might project somewhere between 10,000 and 215,000 people. For some regions of Europe estimates have ranged around 1.5 to 3 people per sq km (Harding 2000, 383), which would provide Ireland with a rough figure of 125,000 to 250,000. Harding (2000, 426) also summarizes a study of hillfort distribution in south Württemburg where hillforts were distributed between 5 and 10 km apart, controlling territories of c. 20 to 80 sq km with populations of several thousand each.
19 Eoin MacNeill estimated 80 tribes, but most Irish traditional historians, following a 12th-century poem, opted for 184 or 185; Francis John Byrne suggested 'no less than 150 kings in the country at any given date between the fifth and twelfth centuries'. See Ó Corráin (1978, 10–11) for a critical discussion of these estimates.
20 Brück 2007, 31.

31 For various functions see Osgood 1998, 71–75; Osgood and Monks 2000, 14–15; Henderson 2007, 115–16.
32 See Grogan 2005, vol. 2, 111–29 for a survey of Irish hillforts.
33 Condit and O'Sullivan 1999; for Britain see Brück 2007, 31.
34 The circumference of a 5-hectare hillfort would require its occupants to defend a line about 792 m long.
35 Grogan 2005, vol. 2, 123; also Condit and O'Sullivan 1999, 35. But note that Ó Néill (2009, 47) suggests that this is truer of the earliest hillforts and that through time the number of structures may have increased.
36 Harding (2000, 306), for example, considers it preferable to regard Dún Aonghusa as 'essentially ceremonial in origin'.
37 Henderson 2007, 120.
38 In Ireland we learned this the hard way: years ago almost every archaeologist who set out to excavate an Iron Age hillfort in Ireland found that it dated to the Bronze Age. This was the case with Barry Raftery at Rathgall, Co. Wicklow, and Richard Warner at Clogher, Co. Tyrone (Warner 2009, 507); by the time I began excavations at Haughey's Fort, Co. Armagh, the pattern was fairly clear.
39 Raftery 1994, 60. Raftery is well aware of the difficulties that this would make for relating the language of Ireland with that of Britain and beyond (1994, 62).
40 Hamilton and Manley 2001, 7.
41 Cunliffe 1991, 344.
42 For example, an oval enclosure at Ram's Hill, whose first phase dates to c. 1370–920 cal BC (Needham and Ambers 1994, 234); see also Osgood 1998, 55–64, for the earliest British hillforts.
43 Grogan 2005, vol. 2, 129–32.
44 Cunliffe 1991, 39–41; Bradley 2007, 206–9.
45 Waddell 1998, 270–73.
46 Mallory 1995, 76.
47 Bradley 2007, 208; Osgood (1998, 66) cites the Norton Fitzwarren hoard as the sole example from Britain.
48 Waddell 1998, 252–53.
49 Lynn 2003, 51–54.

50 Warner 2006; MacDonald and Ó Néill 2009.
51 Lynn 2003, 53–54.
52 At French hillforts such as Fort Harroud, sword moulds suggest that swords were manufactured on site for export (Brun 1993, 178).
53 Hamilton and Manley 2001, 11.
54 Waddell 1998, 354–57; to this list could also be added Lyles Hill, Co. Antrim.
55 Hamilton and Manley 2001, 11–13.
56 Lynch et al. 2000, 150–51.
57 Megaw and Simpson 1979, 288.
58 Primas 2002, 43–50; see also Osgood and Monks 2000, 10–15, 65–70; Harding 2000, 291–306.
59 Primas 2002, 57.
60 Osgood 1998, 71; see also 64.
61 Grogan and Roche 2009, 131.
62 Lynch et al. 2000, 199.
63 Raftery 1995b.
64 Waddell 1991, 8–13; 1991/92.
65 Waddell 1991/92, 36.
66 Harding 2000, 408.
67 Waddell 1991/92, 36–38.
68 Ehrenberg 1989, 82.
69 Bradley 2007, 217, 219.
70 Bourke 2001.
71 Primas 2002, 54.
72 Koch 1991, 17–18.
73 Kristiansen and Larsson 2005.
74 Waddell 1998, 226.
75 Martin 2009, 136.
76 Martin 2009, 141.
77 Prüssing 1991, 22–26.
78 Thale in Sachsen-Anhalt, Basedow in Mecklenburg, and Pössneck-Schettwein in Thuringia; see Martin 2009, 52, 54, 56.
79 Kristiansen 1998, 89.
80 Kristiansen and Larsson 2005, 43.
81 Bourke 2001, 139, 151–53.
82 Brück 1995, 249; Brück 2008, 649.
83 Cooney and Grogan 1994, 146–48.
84 Brück 1995, 262.
85 Waddell 1991/92, 31–35.

Chapter 6 (pp. 157–200)
1 Macalister 1949, 213; Harbison 1988, 168–69; O'Kelly 1989, 258.
2 Quinn 2005, 242.
3 For example, Macalister 1935, 91; Harbison 1988, 168–72; O'Kelly 1989, 248–50; Waddell 2010, 302–5.
4 Jackson 1964.

5 Ó hÓgáin 1990, 356.
6 Henderson 2007, 116.
7 Henderson 2007, 116–19.
8 Needham 2007, 50–52.
9 Needham 2007, 54.
10 Kristiansen 1998, 241–48.
11 Macalister 1949, 215.
12 The Gündlingen sword is regarded as a 'pseudo-type' of sword, as it actually comprises a number of different sword shapes; Milcent 2008, 235.
13 Burgess 1974, 213. Interestingly enough, Macalister (1928, 134) thought the Hallstatt C artifacts 'were just the kind of objects that are most likely to be transferred from one country to another by way of trade'.
14 Burgess 1980, 177.
15 Raftery 1994, 30; Cooney and Grogan 1994, 174–79; similar criticism can be found for the same evidence and arguments in Scotland, cf. Ralston and Ashmore 2007, 230. On the other hand, see Scott 1990, 47, who accepts an 'intrusion of adventurers'.
16 Haselgrove and Pope (2007, 4) suggest that the Gündlingen swords in Britain were among the objects that were 'symbolically charged' and hence remained in bronze rather than in iron.
17 A possible iron Hallstatt C sword was recovered from the River Shannon (Scott 1990, 48).
18 Milcent 2008.
19 Cunliffe 2001, 320.
20 Burgess 1974, 211.
21 Bourke 2001, 46.
22 Kristiansen 1998, 240. It has also been suggested that the presence of the swords in rivers may have been connected with a burial rite in which the cremated remains of warriors were placed in rivers with their weapons (Cunliffe 1991, 499).
23 Eogan 1983, 15 lists two hoards with Class 4 swords and other items; there are also seven hoards exclusively composed of Class 4 swords and one with four Gündlingen-type swords.
24 O'Connor 2007, 68.
25 There is one example of a hoard containing a Hallstatt item along with native bronzework (Eogan 1983, 94). There is also a Hallstatt C chape found with largely Late

Bronze Age objects at Navan Fort (Raftery 1997a, 92–93).
26 Raftery 1994, 26–32.
27 Henderson 2007, 118–19.
28 Warner 1998.
29 Mallory and McNeill 1991, 140–42.
30 Becker et al. 2008.
31 Becker et al. 2008, 37–38 indicate that all these sites show later occupation, which may suggest that the radiocarbon dates are the result of the 'old wood effect'.
32 Becker et al. 2008, 16.
33 The main accounts of Navan are to be found in Waterman 1997 and Lynn 2003; the Knockaulin excavations are in Johnston and Wailes 2007; for Tara see Newman 1997 and Roche 2002; and the impressive Rathcroghan survey is in Waddell et al. 2009.
34 Newman 1998, 133.
35 Rathcroghan lacks (so far) evidence of a figure-of-eight structure, but there are traces of a single large structure with a funnel-shaped entrance. See Waddell et al. 2009, 192–93.
36 Grogan 2008, 30–33.
37 O'Sullivan 2005.
38 Wailes 1990, 10.
39 Newman 1998, 139.
40 Newman 1998, 133.
41 Hicks (2011) has argued for a close association between henges and later (historically known) assembly sites.
42 Harding 2009, 186–98 discusses some evidence for figure-of-eight structures in Britain and Ireland, indicating how they continued into the early medieval period.
43 Waterman 1997, 221–23.
44 Cunliffe 1997, 207–8.
45 Harding 2009 discusses the major Irish Iron Age structures but does not offer any serious British parallels.
46 Harding 2009, 219–32.
47 Cunliffe 1991, 512; Armit 2007, 137.
48 Roche 2002.
49 Harding 2009, 119–23.
50 Raftery 1994, 112.
51 Weir 1995, 106–12.
52 http://www.ucd.ie/archaeology/research/researcha-z/ironageireland/.
53 The earliest evidence for

wheeled vehicles in Britain was recovered from Blair Drummond Moss and dates to c. 1255–815 BC (Cowie and Shepherd 2003, 156.)
54 A popular account can be found in Raftery 1990; the full account of the major programme of trackway excavations is Raftery 1996.
55 Raftery 1996, 223–26, 421–22.
56 Macalister (1935, 83–85) also envisaged Germanic warriors introducing iron metallurgy (not art), but this was largely on spurious racial grounds.
57 De Bernardo Stempel 2000, 100.
58 O'Sullivan and Breen 2007, 100–102.
59 Wise 2006.
60 See, for example, Sharples 2007 on English linear earthworks and other major building projects of the Iron Age.
61 Cunliffe 1991, 532.
62 Giles 2007, 106–9; Armit 2007, 134–35.
63 Kytmannow 2008, 112.
64 Becker 2009, fig. 3b; W. O'Brien 2009; see also Raftery 1998.
65 Raftery 1995a, 5.
66 At least it is not evident on the ground. One way to include Munster is to presume that it also had La Tène artifacts but that local ritual practice did not encourage their deposition as votive offerings, so we have not been able to find them. I prefer to argue that the objects were never there in the first place, as many objects that we do recover were probably simply 'lost', and I can't imagine the Irelanders of Munster being any less likely to lose objects than anyone else in Ireland. During the Bronze Age they were perfectly capable of leaving bronze objects behind.
67 Raftery 1984.
68 Raftery 1984, 313.
69 Dunmore, Co. Galway, did produce a linchpin, believed to be imported from southeast England (Raftery 1984, 332–33).
70 Figures for British objects compiled from http://www.britishmuseum.org/research/research_projects/project_archive/technologies_of_enchantment/the_celtic_art_database.aspx.
71 Phil McDonald, pers. comm.
72 Actually from Ardnaglug, Co.

Roscommon (Halpin and Newman 2006, 17).

73 See Raftery 1984 for detailed discussion of La Tène imports.

74 E. O'Brien 2009.

75 Caulfield 1977.

76 Warner 1991; 2002.

77 Warner 2002, 130.

78 Rynne 1961.

79 Raftery 1984, 327.

80 Raftery 1984, 328–33.

81 Raftery 1994, 200–202.

82 Warner 1983; Rynne 1983.

83 Raftery 1997b.

84 Cooney and Grogan 1994, 199.

85 Cunliffe 1991, 498–510.

86 Macalister 1928, 19–20.

87 See Mytum 1992 for a detailed analysis of the Romano-British impact on Ireland.

88 Mytum 1992, 21.

89 Warner (2009, 512) has recently suggested that the 'Romanization' of Irish culture should be set a century earlier and that we should conclude the native Iron Age at c. 300 rather than setting it to the notional date of the spread of Christianity.

90 Di Martino 2003, 115.

91 Becker et al. 2008, 17.

92 Becker et al. (2008, 25) cite c. 35 Developed (= La Tène c. 400–1 BC) settlements but only c. 27 Late Iron Age settlements.

93 Raftery (1995a, 6) provides examples of the same Irish La Tène objects being dated anywhere from the 1st to the 6th centuries AD.

94 According to Julius Caesar.

95 Strabo and most Greek texts, which reflect a Greek attempt to render *Iweriu, one of the native names for Ireland. Ptolemy came closest with Iwernia (Freeman 2001a, 67).

96 In Sacram (sic insulam dixere prisci) according to Rufus Festus Avienus, who probably translated an earlier Greek hiera nēsos 'holy island' where hiera represents a Greek version of the early Irish name Iérnē (Freeman 2001a, 29).

97 Mikrà Brettanía according to Ptolemy, as the smaller of the Brettanic/Pretannic islands (Freeman 2001a, 65).

98 Pseudo-Hegesippus, who extended the common early designation of the Irish as Scotti to the island from whence they came

(Freeman 2001a, 98).

99 Freeman 2001a, 97.

100 Strabo, who thought that Ireland lay about 800 km north of the centre of Britain (Freeman 2001a, 40). Here the people lived a wretched existence because of the cold.

101 Freeman 2001a, 46.

102 Freeman 2001a, 101.

103 Freeman 2001a, 49.

104 Freeman 2001a, 87.

105 Or not so anonymous if one accepts Richard Warner's thesis that the king in question was known in later Irish literature as Tuathal Techtmar (Warner 1995). Dermot MacMurrough was the exiled Irish king who solicited the Anglo-Normans to help him regain his throne.

106 Translation in Freeman 2001a, 62.

107 Freeman 2001a, 62–63; Di Martino 2003, 6–7.

108 Translation in Freeman 2001a, 57.

109 General accounts can be found in Raftery 1994, 206–19; Freeman 2001a, 1–13; Di Martino 2003.

110 Raftery 1994, 215–16.

111 Raftery 1994, 210.

112 Thomas 1981, 297.

113 O'Sullivan and Breen 2007, 102–4.

114 Di Martino 2003, 129.

115 Edwards 1990, 1–2.

116 Di Martino 2003, 50.

117 Thomas 1981, 297.

118 Thomas 1981, 300–306.

119 Warner 2009, 512.

120 Warner 2009, 513.

121 Di Martino 2003, 28–32, provides an account of the press speculation.

122 O'Brien 1992.

123 Armit 2007, 137.

124 Mytum 1992, 25–26.

125 Mytum 1995, 15.

126 Laing (1985, 274) sees no evidence before the 5th century.

Chapter 7 (pp. 201–14)

1 McCone 1990, 30.

2 McCone 1990, 77.

3 The critical (and much criticized) edition of the LG is Macalister 1938–56; a more readable translation is by John Carey (1995a).

4 A 17th-century attempt to compile a record of the entire course of Irish history from Noah's Flood to 1616. Online at http:// www.ucc.ie/celt/online/T100005A/.

5 LG III.27.

6 O'Brien 1976.

7 Carey 1995a, 55.

8 Carey 2005, 37–38.

9 There is also evidence for a third son, Ír, who was the ancestor figure of the Ulstermen; Carey 2005, 37.

10 Warner 1990 argues for accepting some dates; Mallory 1993 argues against.

11 Comerford 2003, 51–84.

12 Caulfield 1981, 212–13.

13 Dillon and Chadwick 1972, 37.

14 Oppenheimer 2010, 144.

15 O'Rahilly 1946, 193–208.

16 McCone 1990.

17 McCone 1990, 67–68. In the Cogadh Gáedhel re Gallaibh, an early 12th-century account of Brian Boru's wars against the Vikings, Brian's lineage (the Uí Briain) describe themselves as 'the sons of Israel of Ireland' (Ó Corráin 1978, 35). Of course, from the perspective of the much later British Israelites, begun by an Irishman (John Wilson) in 1840, the Irish were included among the Ten Lost Tribes, and there is a long tradition in Ireland of ascribing monuments to the prophet Jeremiah who supposedly fled to Ireland with the daughters of the last king of Judah (see Fritze 2009, 113–15).

18 E.g. Carey 1994; 1995b; 2010.

19 Carey 2001.

20 Wiseman and Wiseman 1980, 93.

21 Agricola 24. Oxford Translation at http://www.gutenberg.org/dirs/etext05/7aggr10.txt.

22 Orosius Book 1 (Orosius 1964, 16).

23 Hillgarth 1984.

24 Etymologies xiv.vi.5, translated by Barney et al. 2002, 294.

25 Carney (1971, 73) suggested that the Sons of Míl legend was created by Senchán Torpéist c. AD 630.

26 Translated portions marked in quotes and derived from Hopkins and Koch 1995, 272.

27 Here I follow the essentially identical discussions of Donn in Carey 1995b and Mac Cana 2011,

222–25.

28 Joynt 1910, 101.

29 Carey 1995b, 58.

Chapter 8 (pp. 215–42)

1 Grattan 1853, 199.

2 The index was based on measuring the width, multiplying it by 100, and then dividing the number by the length. A mesocephalic or mesaticephalic ranges from 76 to 81 for males and 75 to 83 for females; a value below this is dolichocephalic and a value above is brachycephalic.

3 De Lapouge 1899. R. A. S. Macalister used skull measurements to determine how the Bronze Age was introduced into Ireland and concluded that 'we infer that the Bronze Age culture was introduced into Ireland by trade rather than by conquest or invasion, and that, until the process of contamination began after the Anglo-Norman conquest, no brachycephalic race found a footing in the country' (Macalister 1921, 37).

4 Taylor 1921, 107, table vii.

5 Beddoe 1885, 270.

6 Beddoe 1885, 10.

7 To some extent, this is still so. For example, the tendency of blue-eyed adolescent Nordic to be shy has been explained genetically (Ridley 1999, 166–67).

8 Beddoe 1885, 10.

9 Beddoe 1885, 261.

10 Cunningham and Haddon 1892.

11 Hooton and Dupertuis 1955, 7. Data from the Harvard Mission was later analysed to suggest that the midlands of Ireland differed from the periphery and that this might have been the result of Viking settlement (Relethford and Crawford 1995).

12 cf. Beddoe 1898.

13 *Echtra Mac Echdach Mugmedóin* 6, 14 (Joynt 1910).

14 Martin 1935, 157–60.

15 Brothwell 1985.

16 Brodie 1994.

17 Wheets 2004.

18 Haldane 1940; Sokal 1989.

19 Mourant et al. 1976, 67–68.

20 Ridley 1999, 141, 144. Type O is also more susceptible to cholera than types A or B, but this too would not have been a problem for the ancient Irish.

21 For example, Hackett et al. 1956.

22 Bodmer 1993, 48–49.

23 Cavalli-Sforza et al. 1994, 268–69.

24 Cavalli- Sforza et al. 1994, 291–92.

25 Tong et al. 2010.

26 Zschocke et al. 1997; Tyfield 1997.

27 Although now it seems to have turned up among Uyghurs in Xinjiang, China (Yu et al. 2009).

28 An X chromosome has 1,218 genes while a Y chromosome only has about 128 genes.

29 Jobling et al. 2004, 414–21.

30 Sykes 2001.

31 The dates for Table 8.1 follow those published more recently in Soares et al. 2009, table S5, rather than those in Sykes 2006.

32 Except for haplogroup X, which is found in the ancient DNA of Hungarians.

33 As I could not find a published source, the haplogroup percentages are taken from http://www.eupedia.com/europe/european_mtdna_haplogroups_frequency.shtml.

34 Sykes 2006, 190–92.

35 McEvoy et al. 2004, 695.

36 Oppenheimer 2006, 166.

37 Oppenheimer 2006, 134–37.

38 Oppenheimer 2006, 538, n. 57.

39 Busby et al. 2011.

40 This is easier done in theory than practice, as many surnames in Ireland may have a variety of derivations and it is exceedingly difficult to know when the right one has been identified. For example, the surname Barr might be Irish (Ó Báire), Scottish (Barr), English (Barr) or Norman (De Barra). A survey by the author of 1,824 Northern Irish surnames revealed that 24% could have derived from both Irish and at least one other nationality.

41 Hill et al. 2000.

42 http://www.insideireland.com/sample19.htm.

43 McEvoy and Bradley 2006.

44 Moore et al. 2006.

45 McEvoy et al. 2008.

46 Or northwest Irish/lowland Scots variety, see http://www.familytreedna.com/public/R1b1c7.

47 Indeed, the blog 'Niall not the daddy of R-M222' (2 October 2011) suggests that the distribution of M222 both in Ireland and in Britain (with substantial percentages in southern Scotland and Yorkshire) may be more in keeping with a La Tène migration from Britain.

48 This is the official designation (of 29 September 2011) on http://www.isogg.org/tree/ISOGG_HapgrpR.html. The instability of haplogroup designations is a phenomenon in itself. In Myres et al. 2011, 97, it is listed as R1b1b1a1b2a; the Wikipedia entry (of 26 September 2011) has R1b1a2a1a1b4b, but the entry for 23 January 2009 was R1b1b2a1b6b.

49 Myres et al. 2011; percentage figures from en.wikipedia.org/wiki/Haplogroup–R1b_(Y-DNA) (23 February 2012).

50 Myres et al. 2011, 100.

51 Balaresque et al. 2010; Myres et al. 2011, 95.

52 See Eupedia: 'Origins, age, spread and ethnic association of European haplogroups and subclades' (http://www.eupedia.com/europe/origins_haplogroups_europe.shtml#R1b) for one (speculative?) account of the very late spread of variants of the R1b haplogroup in western Europe.

53 Busby et al. 2011.

54 Haak et al. 2010, 8, who also note that some of these types (U4 and U5) are absent from the major Neolithic culture of central Europe; this was ancestral to the earliest farmers of Britain and Ireland.

55 Haak et al. 2010, 9. Among the mtDNA haplogroups found in Ireland, U4, U5a and U5a1 have all been found among hunter-gatherer populations in northern and eastern Europe (Bramati et al. 2009; Malmstrom et al. 2009).

56 McEvoy and Bradley 2010, 117, where they label the haplogroup I1c.

57 Rosser et al. 2000.

58 Tömöry et al. 2007.

59 Tömöry et al. 2007, 354.

60 Only 13% of modern Hungarian haplotypes could be found among the ancient sample and only 23% of the ancient types survive among modern Hungarians; Tömöry et al. 2007, 362. A somewhat similar

exercise comparing medieval and modern Icelanders has revealed that the original settlers are genetically more like their source populations (modern Scots, Irish and Scandinavians) than are modern Icelanders (Helgason et al. 2009).
51 Csányi et al. 2008.
52 See Nash 2006.
53 See also Jobling et al. 2004, 9, where they demonstrate that 'What was the ancestral biological homeland of population X?' is a meaningless question.
54 A good European-wide summary of this model can be found in Soares et al. 2010.
55 Analysis of pottery from Donegore Hill, Co. Antrim (Jessica Smyth, pers. comm).
56 A good European-wide survey from this perspective can be found in Haak et al. 2010; see also Myres et al. 2011 and Balaresque et al. 2010.

Chapter 9 (pp. 243–86)
1 Comerford 2003, 121–52; for the Irish quote see Thompson 2006, 83.
2 Or Fénius Farsaid, the father of Gáedel Glas, who instructed his son in distilling the Irish language from the 72 spoken at the Tower of Babel.
3 For example, McDonnell 2011, 22; K. O'Brien 2009, 14; Ó hÓgáin 2002, 104.
4 Collis 2003, 16–25 provides a useful summary of the Greek and Roman sources.
5 Collis 2003, 100–103.
6 There is one long shot: Parthenius of Nicaea, a 1st-century BC poet writing in Greek, who left us with a very brief sketch of the origin of the Celts. While wandering through the land of the Celts he met Celtine, the daughter of King Bretannus, by whom he had a son named Celtus from whom the Celts derive their name (Lightfoot 1999, 357). The problem is that we have no idea where Bretannus lived, although it is presumed that he is the ancestor of the Britains. One would have expected that Bretannus is the lesser character here and that he might have descended from Celtus, not the other way round, a situation for which the modern editor of Parthenius can 'find no satisfactory explanation' (Lightfoot 1999, 533).

But what we do seem to have here is some early association between the ancestor of the Britons and the Celts.
7 It should be emphasized that the concept of a periphery uniting against a central Saxon foe is much older. The 10th-century Armes Prydein 'Prophecy of Britain', for example, has the Welsh along with allies from Ireland, Strathclyde, Cornwall and Brittany joining battle against the Anglo-Saxons to regain possession of Britain.
8 MacNeill 1919, 9.
9 Mac Eoin 2007, 114.
10 MacNeill 1919, 11. The explanation for this is that the names for Ireland and the Irish, Hibernia and Scotti, appeared to have been related to Iberia and Scythia, but Celtae lacked a comparable term in Irish.
11 Sims-Williams 1998, 13.
12 Chapman 1992; Sims-Williams 1998; James 1999; and Collis 2003 cover much of this; for a specifically Irish context see Ó Donnabháin 2000.
13 McDonnell 2011, 23.
14 Brinton 1890, 155. Of course, 'The German, the Englishman and the Anglo-American now control the politics of the world, and their contributions to every department of literature, science and the arts have been the main stimuli of the marvelous progress of the 19th century' (p. 164).
15 Karl 2010, 47; see also Evans 1992, 6.
16 Even by the end of the 18th century Celtic was regarded as a possible member of the same language family as Greek, Latin and Sanskrit. The major early scientific work, however, began with the Danish linguist Rasmus Rask in 1817, followed by the Swiss linguist Adolphe Pictet (1836) and the German Franz Bopp (1837). On the other hand, there were also the Celtomaniacs such as the Scottish scholar James Grant (1814, 27–28) who imagined that the Celtic languages reflected some arcane primeval language that could 'explain' the other languages of Europe. See Pedersen 1962, 53–63.
17 The technical terms are apocope and syncope.

18 Campbell (2001) has argued that Argyll was Goidelic since the Iron Age and was not the product of a migration/invasion from Ireland.
19 Linguistic revenge was visited on the Welsh when the outside world accepted the Anglo-Saxon pejorative term for them, Wælisc, i.e. foreigner.
20 In Old English the earlier *k^w developed into hw, e.g. hwa, hwēol, hwīl, the letters of which we now reverse as 'who', 'wheel' and 'while'.
21 Freeman 2001b.
22 Koch 2009; 2010.
23 Freeman 2001b.
24 Toner 2000; De Bernardo Stempel 2000.
25 Or Rēgia may be a Celtic word, 'the ruling one' (De Bernardo Stempel 2007, 149).
26 The classic studies are O'Rahilly 1946, 1–42; Mac an Bhaird 1991–93; Toner 2000; De Bernardo Stempel 2000; 2007.
27 O'Rahilly 1946, 1–42.
28 For example, Sims-Williams 2007, 329–30.
29 De Bernardo Stempel 2007.
30 Matasović 2007, 96.
31 Meyer 1910, 208.
32 The Robogdioi, unfortunately, have been provided with so many conflicting etymologies that one sometimes gets the feeling we have not really moved on much from Cormac's 9th-century glossary. Pokorny 1954 (and Schrijver 2009, 205) took the name to mean 'very poor'; O'Rahilly (1946, 295) interpreted it to mean 'traveller (by horse or chariot)'; De Bernardo Stempel (2007, 154) explained it as those 'who fight in front' or 'mighty fighters', while Graham Isaac (in a 2008 seminar at Queen's University Belfast) reconstructed it as 'ones characterized by great slaying'.
33 As a proper designation of a branch of Indo-European, Tocharian is just as problematic as Celtic (see Mallory and Mair 2000, 333–34).
34 A frequently cited example of their similarity is 'Brea, bûter en griene tsiis is goed Ingelsk en goed Frysk', i.e. 'Bread, butter and green cheese is good English and good Frisian'.
35 Schmidt 1977.

36 McCone 1996, 98–104; Schrijver 1995, 463–65.
37 Sims-Williams 2007, 345.
38 Adams (1970) discusses a variety of possible permutations, as does O'Rahilly (1946, 419–43) in his review of earlier theories of Goidelic origins.
39 Greene 1964, 12.
40 Novotna and Blažek 2006.
41 Gray and Atkinson 2003, 437.
42 Forster and Toth 2003.
43 If there is silver inlay in Irish Late Bronze Age hair-rings; Waddell 1998, 248.
44 For example, David Greene (1983, 132), who regards 600 BC 'the least unacceptable solution'.
45 Schrijver 2009, 205.
46 Mac Cana 2011, 275–78.
47 Koch 1994.
48 Koch 1994.
49 Piggott 1983, 148.
50 O'Rahilly 1946, 434.
51 Powell 1950, 193.
52 Macalister 1949, 87–88.
53 Cf. Raftery 1951, 180: 'A military invasion or a folk migration sufficiently powerful to cause a complete linguistic, cultural, and racial change in the population of a country would require to be great, both in numbers and prestige, to have sufficient organization to make a permanent conquest, to control the social life of a community....'
54 Ó hÓgáin 2002, 105, 193–95.
55 Ó Corráin 1992, 3.
56 Matasović 2007, 96.
57 For a detailed though clearly partisan account of the importance of the Manapi see Mongan 1995.
58 And possibly the neighbouring Coritani: see De Bernardo Stempel 2007, 156.
59 Hartley and Fitts 1988, 10; Cunliffe 1991, 180.
60 Rynne 1976, 242.
61 Halpin and Newmann 2006, 17.
62 Mallory 1992; 1998.
63 Powell 1950, 185.
64 Mac Eoin 1986, 171.
65 Schrijver 2009, 209.
66 Todd 1989, 14–15.
67 Mesthrie 2001, 494–95.
68 Brenzinger et al. 1991.
69 Renfrew 1987.
70 Waddell 1995; 1999.
71 Constandse-Westermann and Newell 1989.

72 Gallay 2001.
73 O'Rahilly (1946, 435) cites Iorwerth C. Peate's injunction that 'modern archaeologists should abandon all attempts to equate invasions for which there is archaeological evidence with philological events for the dating of which there is no evidence'.
74 Hawkes 1973.
75 Mac Eoin 2007, 119.
76 Trask 1997.
77 Wiik 1999; 2002; Vennemann 2003 offer broad perspectives in support of this theory.
78 Schrijver 2002. Quinn (2005, 140–41) lists some comparisons between Irish and Maltese, a Semitic language, but these are generally based on mere sound similarities and result in Irish words with known Indo-European etymologies (scian 'knife', cos 'leg') or borrowed from more proximate sources.
79 Vallancey 1772, with extensive comparison between Irish and Maltese plus some other, even more bizarre examples of very strange linguistic comparisons, e.g. the name of Saturn, who Vallancey describes as the god of bread-corn, is explained as a compound (Satharan) of Irish sat 'abundance' + aran 'bread', while Uranus, the god of land and sea, is from Irish uir 'land' + an 'sea' and Neptune is 'plainly derived from the Irish nimh a Deity, and ton the waves of the Sea'. (Vallancey 1772, 22–23).
80 MacAdam 1859, 195. As MacAdam concludes, these instances may merely involve people ignorant of both languages finding similarities because of the 'similarity of pronunciation'. But he also relates Eugene O'Curry's opinion that it would not be strange to find Irish spoken in North Africa because of 'the great number of Irish who had been carried off by the Corsairs, in the middle ages, to Africa' (p. 197). Far-fetched perhaps, but compare the luscious linguistic variety of Surinam that includes several African-based creoles such as Saramaka that were carried to the New World by slaves who had escaped. On the other hand, Irish pales compared with Welsh when it comes to reports of its use in

unexpected locations, as no fewer than 13 Native American tribes have been reported to speak Welsh (Fritze 2009, 77–79).
81 Gensler 1993 provides a history of research and a detailed (favourable) analysis of the Afro-Asiatic theory.
82 For which I must thank Orin.
83 Gensler 1993, 426.
84 Gensler 1993, 248–49.
85 Vennemann 1998; not a plausible explanation from a phonetic standpoint (see Isaac 2007, 51), nor from an archaeological standpoint if we imagine that an Afro-Asiatic language was associated with the spread of megaliths c. 3800 BC when copperworking does not emerge in Ireland until well over a thousand years later.
86 To be fair, Gensler anticipates many of these objections in the final chapter of his dissertation.
87 Isaac 2007, 47–48.
88 Gensler 1993, 452.
89 Matasović 2007, 109; 2009, 443.
90 Schrijver 1997.
91 Schrijver 2000 and 2005; against including partán see Isaac 2003, who suggests that it is a Latin loanword.
92 Mac Eoin 2007.

Chapter 10 (pp. 287–99)
1 Ó Buachalla 1995, 110.
2 Mac Cana 2011, 54.
3 Binchy 1976.
4 Ó Corráin 1978, 35.
5 Orpen 1911, vol. 1, 20.
6 Mac Cana 2011, 43.
7 See also Ó Corráin 1978 for similar ideas.
8 Binchy 1975, 124.
9 For discussions of the five provinces from the perspective of cosmologies see Rees and Rees 1961, 118–39; Aitchison 1994, 50–130; Mac Cana 2011, 91–108.
10 Aitchison 1994. See also Dillon and Chadwick (1972), who suggest that the creation of a fifth central province at Tara was instigated by the Uí Néill for their own political advantage.
11 Aitchison 1994, 122.
12 Aitchison 1994, 105.
13 Waddell et al. 2009.
14 Or as Ó Corráin (1978, 19)

out it: 'It was this mandarin class that elaborated the idea of the overkingship of all Ireland and projected it backwards into even the remote past'. But we should recall here that historical records only start about the time of the Uí Néill, so the political aspirations of Ireland's prehistoric populations are completely unknown to us.
15 Mac Cana 2011, 73.

16 It might be noted that the four northerly provincial centres all fall within the territory where La Tène metalwork was found, i.e. the La Tène horizon may not only reflect a prestige metalworking tradition but also was in some way attached to the new religious ideology. This may explain why it is difficult to produce a suitable or reliable capital for Munster.

17 Woodman 2015
18 Dowd and Carden 2016
19 Mallory 2013, 242
20 Cassidy et al. 2016
21 Pala et al. 2016, 367
22 Haak et al. 2015
23 Allentoft et al. 2015
24 Pala et al. 2016, 369
25 Blasco Ferrer 2015
26 Mallory 2013

Bibliography

Abercromby, J. (1912) A Study of the Bronze Age Pottery of Britain and Ireland and its Associated Grave-goods. Oxford, Clarendon Press.

Adams, B. (1970) Language and man in Ireland. Ulster Folklife 15(15), 140–71.

Aitchison, N. B. (1994) Armagh and the Royal Centres in Early Medieval Ireland: Monuments, Cosmology and the Past. Woodbridge, Suffolk and Rochester, NY, Cruithne Press/ Boydell and Brewer.

Allen, M. J. (2005) Beaker settlement and environment in the chalk downs of southern England. Proceedings of the Prehistoric Society 71, 219–45.

Allentoft, M. E., M. Sikora, K.G. Sjögren, S. Rasmussen, M. Rasmussen, J. Stenderup, et al. (2015) Population genomics of Bronze Age Eurasia. Nature 522, 167–172.

Anthony, D. (1990) Migration in archaeology: the baby and the bathwater. American Anthropologist 92, 895–914.

Arias, P. (2007) Neighbours but diverse: social change in north-west Iberia during the transition from the Mesolithic to the Neolithic (5500–4000 cal BC). In Whittle and Cummings (eds), 53–71.

Armit, I. (2007) Social landscapes and identities in the Irish Iron Age. In Haselgrove, C. and T. Moore (eds) The Later Iron Age in Britain and Beyond, 130–39. Oxford, Oxbow.

Ashmore, P. (2004) Dating forager communities in Scotland. In Saville (ed.), 83–94.

Asouti, E. (2006) Beyond the Pre-Pottery Neolithic B interaction sphere. Journal of World Prehistory 20, 87–126.

Balaresque, P., G. R. Bowden, S. M. Adams, H-Y. Leung, T. E. King, Z. H. Rosser, J. Goodwin, J-P. Moisan, C. Richard, A. Millward, A. G. Demaine, G. Barbujani, C. Previderè, I. J. Wilson, C. Tyler-Smith and M. A. Jobling (2010) A predominantly Neolithic origin for European paternal lineages. PLoS Biology 8(1), e1000285.

Ballantyne, C. (2004) After the ice: paraglacial and postglacial evolution of the physical environment of Scotland, 20,000 to 5000 BP. In Saville (ed.), 27–43.

Barker, G. (2006) The Agricultural Revolution in Prehistory. Oxford, Oxford University Press.

Barney, S. A., J. A. Beach and O. Berghof (2002) Etymologies of Isidore of Seville. Cambridge, Cambridge University Press.

Baum, J. and G. K. Bar-Gal (2003) The emergence and co-evolution of human pathogens. In Greenblatt, C. and M. Spigelman (eds) Emerging Pathologies: Archaeology, Ecology and Evolution of Infectious Disease, 67–78. Oxford, Oxford University Press.

Baumgarten, R. (1984) The geographical orientation of Ireland in Isidore and Orosius. Peritia 3, 189–203.

Bay-Petersen, J. L. (1978) Animal exploitation in Mesolithic Denmark. In Mellars, P. (ed.) The Early Postglacial Settlement of Northern Europe, 115–45. London, Duckworth.

Bayliss, A., F. Healy, A. Whittle and G. Cooney (2011) Neolithic narratives: British and Irish enclosures in their timescapes. In Whittle et al. (eds), vol. 2, 682–847.

Bayliss, A. and P. Woodman (2009) A new Bayesian chronology for Mesolithic occupation at Mount Sandel, Northern Ireland. Proceedings of the Prehistoric Society 75, 101–23.

Becker, K. (2009) Iron Age Ireland: finding an invisible people. In Cooney et al. (eds), 353–61.

Becker, K., N. Ó Néill and L. O'Flynn (2008) Iron Age Ireland: Finding an Invisible People. Dublin, Heritage Council, Ireland.

Beddoe, J. (1885) The Races of Britain. Bristol, Arrowsmith.

Beddoe, J. (1898) On complexional differences between the Irish with indigenous and exotic surnames respectively. Journal of the Anthropological Institute of Great Britain and Ireland 27, 164–70.

Besse, M. (2004) Bell Beaker common ware during the third millennium BC in Europe. In Czebreszuk (ed.), 127–48.

Bhreathnach, E. (1995) Tara: A Select Bibliography. Dublin, Royal Irish Academy.

Binchy, D. (1975) The passing of the old order. In Ó Cuív, B. (ed.) The Impact of the Scandinavian

Invasions on the Celtic-speaking Peoples, c. 800–1100 AD, 119–32. Dublin, Institute for Advanced Studies.

Binchy, D. (1976) Irish history and Irish law: II. *Studia Hibernica* 16, 7–45.

Blasco Ferrer, Eduardo (2015) Paläosardisch und Paläobaskisch, in Mailhammer, Robert, Theo Vennemann Nierfeld, and Birgit Anette Olsen (eds) *The Linguistic Roots of Europe: Origin and Development of European Languages*, 155–200. Copenhagen, Museum Tusculanum Press.

Bocquet-Appel, J.-P., S. Naji, M. Vander Linden and J. Kozlowski (2012) Understanding the rates of expansion of the farming system in Europe. *Journal of Archaeological Science* 39, 531–46.

Bodmer, W. (1993) The genetics of Celtic populations. *Proceedings of the British Academy* 82, 37–57.

Bonsall, C., M. Macklin, D. Anderson and R. Payton (2001) Climate change and the adoption of agriculture in north-west Europe. *European Journal of Archaeology* 5(1), 7–21.

Boswell, J. (1785) *The Journal of a Tour to the Hebrides*. London, Charles Dilly.

Bourke, L. (2001) *Crossing the Rubicon: Bronze Age Metalwork from Irish Rivers*. Galway, Department of Archaeology, National University of Ireland, Galway.

Bradley, R. (1990) *The Passage of Arms: An Archaeological Analysis of Prehistoric Hoards and Votive Deposits*. Cambridge, Cambridge University Press.

Bradley, R. (2007) *The Prehistory of Britain and Ireland*. Cambridge, Cambridge University Press.

Bramati, B., M. G. Thomas, W. Haak, M. Unterlaender, P. Jores, K. Tambets, I. Antanaitis-Jacobs, M. N. Haidle, R. Jankauskas, C.-J. Kind, F. Lueth, T. Terberger, J. Hiller, S. Matsumura, P. Forster and J. Burger (2009) Genetic discontinuity between local hunter-gatherers and Central Europe's first farmers. *Science* 326, 137–40.

Brenzinger, M., B. Heine and G. Sommer (1991) Language death in Africa. In Robins, R. H. and E. M. Uhlenbeck (eds) *Endangered Languages*, 19–44. Oxford, Berg.

Brindley, A. (1999) Irish Grooved Ware. In Cleal, R. and A. MacSween (eds) *Grooved Ware in Britain and Ireland*, 23–35. Oxford, Oxbow, Neolithic Studies Group Seminar Paper 3.

Brindley, A. L. (2007) *The Dating of Food Vessels and Urns in Ireland*. Galway, Department of Archaeology, National University of Ireland, Bronze Age Studies 7.

Brindley, A. and J. Lanting (1991/92) Radiocarbon dates from wedge tombs. *Journal of Irish Archaeology* 6, 19–26.

Brinton, D. G. (1890) *Races and Peoples: Lectures on the Science of Ethnography*. New York, Hodges.

Brodie, N. (1994) *The Neolithic-Bronze Age Transition in Britain*. Oxford, BAR British Series 238.

Brodie, N. (1998) British Bell Beakers: Twenty-five years of theory and practice. In Benz, M. and S. van Willigen (eds) *Some New Approaches to the Bell Beaker 'Phenomenon': Lost Paradise…?*, 43–56, Oxford, BAR International Series 690.

Brothwell, D. (1985) Variation in early Irish populations: a brief survey. *Ulster Journal of Archaeology* 48, 5–9.

Brück, J. (1995) A place for the dead: the role of human remains in Late Bronze Age Britain. *Proceedings of the Prehistoric Society* 61, 245–77.

Brück, J. (2007) The character of Late Bronze Age settlement in southern Britain. In Haselgrove and Pope (eds), 24–38.

Brück, J. (2008) A comparison of Chancellorsland Site A with contemporary settlements in southern England. In Doody, M. (ed.) *The Ballyhoura Hills Project*, 642–52. Bray, Wordwell.

Brun, P. (1993) East-West relations in the Paris Basin during the Late Bronze Age. In Scarre, C. and F. Healy (eds) *Trade and Exchange in Prehistoric Europe*, 171–82. Oxford, Oxbow.

Brunicardi, J. (1914) The shore-dwellers of ancient Ireland. *Journal of the Royal Society of Antiquaries of Ireland* 4.3, 185–213.

Burgess, C. (1974) The Bronze Age. In Renfrew, C. (ed.) *British Prehistory: A New Outline*, 165–232. London, Duckworth.

Burgess, C. (1976) The Beaker phenomenon: some suggestions. In Burgess, C. and R. Miket (eds) *Settlement and Economy in the Third and Second Millennia BC*, 306–23. Oxford, BAR 33.

Burgess, C. (1980) *The Age of Stonehenge*. London, Dent.

Burmeister, S. (2000) Archaeology and migration: approaches to an archaeological proof of migration. *Current Anthropology* 41, 539–67.

Busby, G. B. J., F. Brisighelli, P. Sanchez-Diz, E. Ramos-Luis, C. Martinez-Cadenas, M. G. Thomas, D. G. Bradley, L. Husmao, B. Winney, W. Bodmer, M. Vennemann, V. Coia, F. Scarnicci, S. Tofanelli, G. Vona, R. Ploski, C. Vecchiotti, T. Zemunik, I. Rudan, S. Karaxhanak, D. S. Toncheva, P. Anagnostou, G. Ferri, C. Rapone, T. Hervig, T. Moen, J. F. Wilson and C. Capelli (2011) The peopling of Europe and the cautionary tale of Y chromosome lineage R-M269. *Proceedings of the Royal Society* (in press)

Byrne, F. J. (1973) *Irish Kings and High-Kings*. London, Batsford.

Cahill, M. (2009) Tinkering with torcs: an unusual Bronze Age hoard from Kilsallagh, Co. Longford. In Finlay et al. (eds), 3–11.

Campbell, E. (2001) Were the Scots Irish? *Antiquity* 75, 285–92.

Carey, J. (1994) *The Irish National Origin-Legend: Synthetic Pseudohistory*. Cambridge, Department of Anglo-Saxon, Norse and Celtic, University of Cambridge, Quiggin Pamphlets on the Sources of Mediaeval Gaelic History 1.

Carey, J. (1995a) *Lebor Gabála Érenn. The Book of Invasions*. In Koch, J. T. and J. Carey (eds) *The Celtic Heroic Age: Literary Sources for Ancient Celtic Europe and*

Early Ireland and Wales, 213–66. Malden, Mass., Celtic Studies Publications.

Carey, J. (1995b) Native elements in Irish pseudohistory. In Edel, D. (ed.) *Cultural Identity and Cultural Integration: Ireland and Europe in the Early Middle Ages*, 45–60. Dublin, Four Courts Press.

Carey, J. (2001) Did the Irish come from Spain? *History Ireland* 9(3), 8–11.

Carey, J. (2005) *Lebor Gabála* and the legendary history of Ireland. In Fulton, H. (ed.) *Medieval Celtic Literature and Society*, 32–48. Dublin, Four Courts Press.

Carey. J. (2010) Donn, Amairgen, Íth and the prehistory of Irish pseudohistory. *Journal of Indo-European Studies* 38, 319–41.

Carlin, N. (2006) The Beaker complex in Ireland. http://www.m3motorway.ie/Archaeology/Section2/Skreen3/file,16726,en.pdf (Appendix 15, 51–96).

Carlin, N. (2011a) A Proper Place for Everything: The Character and Context of Beaker Depositional Practice in Ireland. Unpublished PhD dissertation, University College Dublin.

Carlin, N. (2011b) Into the West: placing Beakers within their Irish contexts. In Jones, A. and G. Kirkham (eds) *Beyond the Core: Reflections on Regionality in Prehistory*, 87–100. Oxford, Oxbow.

Carlin, N. and J. Brück (2012) Searching for the Chalcolithic: continuity and change in the Irish Final Neolithic/Early Bronze Age. In Allen, M. J., J. Gardiner, A. Sheridan and D. McOmish (eds) *Is There a British Chalcolithic: People, Place and Polity in the Later 3rd Millennium*. London, Prehistoric Society Research Paper No. 4.

Carney, J. (1971) Three Old Irish accentual poems. *Ériu* 22, 65–73.

Case, H. (1969) Settlement patterns in the north Irish Neolithic. *Ulster Journal of Archaeology* 32, 3–27.

Case, H. (1995) Irish Beakers in their European context. In Waddell and Shee Twohig (eds), 14–29.

Case, H. (2004a) Beaker burial in Britain and Ireland. In Besse, M. and J. Desideri (eds) *Graves and Funerary Rituals during the Late Neolithic and the Early Bronze Age in Europe (2700–2000 BC)*, 195–201. Oxford, BAR International Series 1284.

Case, H. (2004b) Bell Beaker and Corded Ware burial associations: a bottom-up rather than top-down approach. In Gibson, A. and A. Sheridan (eds) *From Sickles to Circles: Britain and Ireland at the Time of Stonehenge*, 201–14. Stroud, Tempus.

Case, H. (2004c) Beakers and the Beaker culture. In Czebreszuk (ed.), 11–34.

Case, H. (2004d) The Beaker culture in Britain and Ireland: groups, European contacts and chronology. In Nicolis, F. (ed.) *Bell Beakers Today*, 361–77. Trento, Provincia.

Cassidy, Lara M., Rui Martiniano, Eileen M. Murphy, Matthew D. Teasdale, James P. Mallory, Barrie Hartwell, and Daniel G. Bradley (2016) Neolithic and Bronze Age migration to Ireland and the establishment of the insular Atlantic genome. *Proceedings of the National Academy of Sciences* 113 (2) 368–373.

Caulfield, S. (1977) The beehive quern in Ireland. *Journal of the Royal Society of Antiquaries of Ireland* 107, 104–38.

Caulfield, S. (1981) Celtic problems in the Iron Age. In Ó Corráin, D. (ed.) *Irish Antiquity: Essays and Studies Presented to Professor M. J. O'Kelly*, 205–15. Cork, Tower Books.

Cauvin, J. (2000) *The Birth of the Gods and the Origins of Agriculture*. Cambridge, Cambridge University Press.

Cavalli-Sforza, L. L., P. Menozzi and A. Piazza (1994) *The History and Geography of Human Genes*. Princeton, Princeton University Press.

Chapman, M. (1992) *The Celts: The Construction of a Myth*. Basingstoke, Macmillan.

Chapple, R. M., C. Dunlop, S. Gilmore and L. Heaney (2009) *Archaeological Investigations along the A1 Dualling Scheme, Loughbrickland to Beech Hill, Co. Down, N. Ireland, 2005*.

Oxford, BAR British Series 479.

Childe, V. G. (1949) *Prehistoric Communities of the British Isles*. London and Edinburgh, Chambers.

Clarke, A. (2009) Craft specialisation in the Mesolithic of Northern Britain: the evidence from the coarse stone tools. In Finlay *et al.* (eds), 12–21.

Clarke, D. L. (1976) The Beaker network – social and economic models. In Lanting, J. and J. van der Waals (eds) *Glockenbecher Symposion, Oberried 1974*, 459–77. Bussum, Fibula-Van Dishoeck.

Coles, B. (1998) Doggerland: a speculative survey. *Proceedings of the Prehistoric Society* 64, 45–81.

Collins, T. and F. Coyne (2003) Fire and water...Early Mesolithic cremations at Castleconnell, Co. Limerick. *Archaeology Ireland* 17(2), 24–27.

Collis, J. (2003) *The Celts: Origins, Myths and Inventions*. Stroud, Tempus.

Comerford, R. (2003) *Ireland*. London, Hodder Arnold.

Condit, T. and A. O'Sullivan (1999) Landscapes of movement and control: interpreting prehistoric hillforts and fording-places on the River Shannon. In *Discovery Programme Reports* 5, 25–39. Dublin, Royal Irish Academy.

Constandse-Westermann, T, and R. Newell (1989) Social and biological aspects of the Western European Mesolithic population structure: a comparison with the demography of North American Indians. In Bonsall, C. (ed.) *The Mesolithic in Europe*, 106–15. Edinburgh, John Donald.

Convertini, F. (2001) Production de la céramique campaniforme dans l'axe Rhin-Rhône. In Nicolis (ed.), vol. 2, 547–60.

Cooney, G. (2000) *Landscapes of Neolithic Ireland*. London and New York, Routledge.

Cooney, G. (2007) Parallel worlds or multi-stranded identities? Considering the process of 'going over' in Ireland and the Irish Sea zone. In Whittle and Cummings (eds), 543–66.

Cooney, G., A. Bayliss, F. Healy, A. Whittle, E. Dahanher, L. Cagney,

J. Mallory, J. Smyth, T. Kador and M. O'Sullivan (2011) Ireland. In Whittle *et al.* (eds), vol. 2, 562–669.

Cooney, G., K. Becker, J. Coles, M. Ryan and S. Sievers (eds) (2009) *Relics of Old Decency: Archaeological Studies in Later Prehistory*. Dublin, Wordwell.

Cooney, G. and E. Grogan (1994) *Irish Prehistory: A Social Perspective*. Dublin, Wordwell.

Cooney, G. and E. Grogan (1999) *Irish Prehistory: A Social Perspective*, rev. edn. Dublin, Wordwell.

Cooney, G. and S. Mandal (1998) *The Irish Stone Axe Project*. Bray, Wordwell.

Cooper, J. A. G. *et al.* (2002) Inner shelf seismic stratigraphy off the north coast of Northern Ireland: new data on the depth of the Holocene lowstand. *Marine Geology* 186, 369–87.

Costa, L., F. Sternke and P. Woodman (2005) Microlith to macrolith: the reasons behind the transformation of production in the Irish Mesolithic. *Antiquity* 79, 19–33.

Cowie, T. and I. Shepherd (2003) The Bronze Age. In Edwards, K. and I. Ralston (eds) *Scotland after the Ice Age: An Environmental and Archaeological History, 8000 BC–AD 1000*, updated edn, 151–68. Edinburgh, Edinburgh University Press.

Crombé, P. (2009) Early pottery in hunter-gatherer societies of western Europe. In Jordan, P. and M. Zvelebil (eds) *Ceramics before Farming*, 477–98. Walnut Creek, Ca., Left Coast Press.

Crombé, P. and B. Vanmontfort (2007) The neolithisation of the Scheldt basin in western Belgium. In Whittle and Cummings (eds), 263–85.

Crystal, D. (2000) *Language Death*. Cambridge, Cambridge University Press.

Csányi, B., E. Bogácsi-Szabó, G. Tömöry, Á. Czibula, K. Priskin, A. Csösz, B. Mende, P. Langó, K. Csete, A. Zsolnai, E. K. Conant, C. S. Downes and I. Raskó (2008) Y-chromosome analysis of ancient Hungarian and two modern Hungarian-speaking populations from the Carpathian Basin. *Annals of Human Genetics* 72, 519–34.

Cunliffe, B. (1991) *Iron Age Communities in Britain*, 3rd edn. London and New York, Routledge.

Cunliffe, B. (1997) *The Ancient Celts*. Oxford, Oxford University Press.

Cunliffe, B. (2001) *Facing the Ocean: The Atlantic and its Peoples, 8000 BC–AD 1500*. Oxford, Oxford University Press.

Cunliffe, B. (2002) *The Extraordinary Voyage of Pytheas the Greek*. London and New York, Penguin and Walker.

Cunliffe, B. and J. T. Koch (eds) (2010) *Celtic from the West: Alternative Perspectives from Archaeology, Genetics, Language and Literature*. Oxford, Oxbow, Celtic Studies Publications No. 15.

Cunningham, D. J. and A. C. Haddon (1892) The Anthropometric Laboratory of Ireland. *Journal of the Anthropological Institute of Great Britain and Ireland* 21, 35–39.

Czebreszuk, J. (ed.) (2004) *Similar but Different: Bell Beakers in Europe*. Poznan, Adam Mickiewicz University.

Davenport, J. L., D. P. Sleeman and P. C. Woodman (eds) (2008) *Mind the Gap: Postglacial Colonization of Ireland*. Irish Naturalists' Journal, Special Supplement.

David, A. and E. Walker (2004) Wales during the Mesolithic period. In Saville (ed.), 299–337.

De Bernardo Stempel, P. (2000) Ptolemy's Celtic Italy and Ireland: a linguistic analysis. In Parsons, D. and P. Sims-Williams (eds) *Ptolemy: Towards a Linguistic Atlas of the Earliest Celtic Place-names of Europe*, 83–112. Aberystwyth, CMCS Publications.

De Bernardo Stempel, P. (2007) Pre-Celtic, Old Celtic layers, Brittonic and Goidelic in ancient Ireland. In Cavill, P. and G. Broderick (eds) *Language Contact in the Place-Names of Britain and Ireland*, 137–63. Nottingham, English Place-Name Society.

De Lapouge, G. V. (1899) *L'Aryen: son role social*. Paris, Fontemoing.

De Paor, L. (1986) *The Peoples of Ireland*. London, Harper Collins.

DeBoer, W. (1990) Interaction, imitation, and communication as expressed in style: the Ucayali experience. In Conkey, M. and C. Hastorf (eds) *The Uses of Style in Archaeology*, 82–104. Cambridge, Cambridge University Press.

Devoy, R. J. N. (1995) Deglaciation, Earth crustal behaviour and sea-level changes in the determination of insularity: a perspective from Ireland. In Preece, R. C. (ed.) *Island Britain: A Quaternary Perspective*, 181–208. London, Geological Society.

Di Martino, V. (2003) *Roman Ireland*. Cork, Collins Press.

Dickson, J. (1978) Bronze Age mead. *Antiquity* 52, 108–13.

Dillon, M. and N. Chadwick (1972) *The Celtic Realms*, 2nd edn. London, Weidenfeld and Nicolson.

Doody, M. (2000) Bronze Age houses in Ireland. In Desmond, A., G. Johnson, M. McCarthy, J. Sheehan and E. Shee Twohig (eds) *New Agendas in Irish Prehistory*, 135–59. Bray, Wordwell.

Dowd, Marion and Ruth F. Carden (2016) First evidence of a Late Upper Palaeolithic presence in Ireland. *Quaternary Science Reviews* 139, 158–163.

Doyle, L. and J. Ó Néill (2003) Foragers, farmers and pathogens. *Archaeology Ireland* 17(4), 31–33.

Drenth, E. and W. J. H. Hogestijn (2001) The Bell Beaker culture in the Netherlands: the state of research in 1998. In Nicolis (ed.), vol. 1, 309–32.

Duddy, T. (2002) *A History of Irish Thought*. London and New York, Routledge.

Dupont, C., A. Tresset, N. Desse-Berset, Y. Gruet, G. Marchand and R. Schulting (2009) Harvesting the seashore in the Late Mesolithic of northwestern France: a view from Brittany. *Journal of World Prehistory* 22, 93–111.

Edwards, C. J. and D. Bradley (2009) Human colonisation routes and the origins of Irish mammals. In McCartan, S., R. Schulting, G. Warren and P. Woodman (eds) *Mesolithic Horizons*, 217–24. Oxford, Oxbow.

Edwards, K. (2004) Palaeoenvironments of the Late Upper Palaeolithic and Mesolithic periods in Scotland and the North Sea area: new work, new thoughts. In Saville (ed.), 55–72.

Edwards, N. (1990) *The Archaeology of Early Medieval Ireland*. London, Batsford.

Edwards, R. and A. Brooks (2008) The island of Ireland: drowning the myth of an Irish land-bridge? In Davenport *et al.* (eds), 19–34.

Ehrenberg, M. (1989) The interpretation of regional variability in British and Irish Bronze Age metalwork. *Bronze Age Studies* 6, 77–88.

Ellis, C. J., M. J. Allen, J. Gardiner, P. Harding, C. Ingram, A. Powell and R. Scaife (2003) An Early Mesolithic seasonal hunting site in the Kennet Valley, southern England. *Proceedings of the Prehistoric Society* 69, 107–35.

Eogan, G. (1983) *The Hoards of the Irish Later Bronze Age*. Dublin, University College.

Eogan, G. (1984) *Excavations at Knowth: 1*. Dublin, Royal Irish Academy.

Eogan, G. (2009) The small metal tools of the Irish Bronze Age: an outline review. In Cooney *et al.* (eds), 107–26.

Eogan, G. and H. Roche (1997) *Excavations at Knowth: 2*. Dublin, Royal Irish Academy.

Evans, D. E. (1992) Celticity, identity and the study of language – facts, speculation and legend. *Archaeologia Cambrensis* 140, 1–16.

Feehan, J. (1997) The heritage of the rocks. In Foster, J. W. (ed.) *Nature in Ireland*, 3–22. Dublin, Lilliput Press.

Finlay, N. (2009) Futile fragments? Some thoughts on microlith breakage patterns. In Finlay *et al.* (eds), 22–30.

Finlay, N., S. McCartan, N. Milner and C. Wickham-Jones (2009) (eds) *From Bann Flakes to Bushmills*. Oxford, Oxbow,

Prehistoric Society Research Paper No. 1.

Fischer, D. H. (1970) *Historians' Fallacies*. New York, Harper and Row.

Fitzpatrick, A. P. (2011) *The Amesbury Archer and the Boscombe Bowmen: Bell Beaker Burials on Boscombe Down, Amesbury, Wiltshire*. Salisbury, Wessex Archaeology, Wessex Archaeology Report 27.

Flanagan, L. (1998) *Ancient Ireland*. Dublin, Gill and Macmillan.

Forster, P. and A. Toth (2003) Toward a phylogenetic chronology of ancient Gaulish, Celtic, and Indo-European. *Proceedings of the National Academy of Science of the USA* 100(15), 9079–84.

Freeman, P. (2001a) *Ireland and the Classical World*. Austin, University of Texas Press.

Freeman, P. (2001b) *The Galatian Language*. Lewiston, NY and Lampeter, Mellen Press.

Fritze, R. H. (2009) *Invented Knowledge: False History, Fake Science and Pseudo-religions*. London, Reaktion.

Gallagher, F. (2007) Introduction. In Hall, 3.

Gallay, A. (2001) L'énigme campaniforme. In Nicolis (ed.), vol. 1, 41–57.

Gamble, C. (1999) *The Palaeolithic Societies of Europe*, 2nd edn. Cambridge, Cambridge University Press.

Gensler, O. (1993) A Typological Evaluation of Celtic/Hamito-Semitic Syntactic Parallels. Unpublished PhD dissertation, University of California, Berkeley.

Gibson, A. (2002) *Prehistoric Pottery in Britain and Ireland*. Stroud, Tempus.

Gibson, A. (2004) Burials and Beakers: seeing beneath the veneer in late Neolithic Britain. In Czebreszuk (ed.), 173–92.

Giles, M. (2007) Refiguring rights in the Early Iron Age landscapes of East Yorkshire. In Haselgrove and Pope (eds), 103–18.

Ginn, V. (in press) The fusion of settlement and identity in dispersed and nucleated

settlements in Bronze Age Ireland. *Journal of Irish Archaeology*.

Ginn, V. and S. Rathbone (2012) *Corrstown: A Coastal Community*. Oxford, Oxbow.

Gouletquer, P. and J. Monnier (1976) Les civilisations de l'Epipaléolithique et du Mésolithique en Armorique. In de Lumley, H. (ed.) *La préhistoire française*, vol. 1, 1456–60. Paris, CNRS.

Grant, J. (1814) *Thoughts on the Origin and Descent of the Gael*. London, Underwood.

Grattan, J. (1853) On the importance to the archaeologist and ethnologist of measuring human crania and of recording the results; with a description of a new craniometer. *Ulster Journal of Archaeology* 1, 198–208.

Gray, R. and Q. Atkinson (2003) Language-tree divergence times support the Anatolian theory of Indo-European origin. *Nature* 426, 435–39.

Greene, D. (1964) The Celtic languages. In Raftery, J. (ed.) *The Celts*, 9–21. Cork, Mercier.

Greene, D. (1983) The coming of the Celts: the linguistic viewpoint. In Mac Eoin, G. (ed.) *Proceedings of the Sixth International Congress of Celtic Studies*, 131–37. Dublin, Institute for Advanced Studies.

Grogan, E. (1996) Neolithic houses in Ireland. In Darvill, T. and J. Thomas (eds) *Neolithic Houses in Northwest Europe and Beyond*, 41–60. Oxford, Oxbow.

Grogan, E. (2004) Irish Middle Bronze Age burial traditions. In Roche *et al.* (eds), 61–71.

Grogan, E. (2005) *The North Munster Project*, 2 vols. Bray, Wordwell, Discovery Programme Monograph 6.

Grogan, E. (2008) *The Rath of the Synods, Tara, Co. Meath: Excavations by Seán P. Ó Ríordáin*. Dublin, Wordwell.

Grogan, E. and H. Roche (2009) An assessment of Middle Bronze Age domestic pottery in Ireland. In Cooney *et al.* (eds), 127–36.

Gronenborn, D. (2007) Beyond the models: 'Neolithisation' in Central Europe. In Whittle and Cummings (eds), 73–98.

Guilaine, J. (2003) *De la vague à la tombe: La conquête néolithique de la méditerranée*. Paris, Seul.

Guilaine, J., F. Claustre, O. Lemercier and P. Sabatier (2001) Campaniformes et environment culturel en France méditerranéenne. In Nicolis (ed.), vol. 1, 229–75.

Haak, W., O. Balanovsky, J. J. Sanchez, S. Koshel, V. Zaporozhchenko, C. J. Adler, C. S. I. Der Sarkissian, G. Brandt, C. Schwarz, N. Nicklisch, V. Dresely, B. Fritsch, E. Balanovska, R. Villems, H. Meller, K. W. Alt, A. Cooper and the Genographic Consortium (2010) Ancient DNA from European Early Neolithic farmers reveals their Near Eastern affinities. *PLoS Biology* 8(11), e1000536.

Haak, W., I. Lazaridis, N. Patterson, N. Rohland, S. Mallick, B. Llamas, *et al.* (2015) Massive migration from the steppe was a source for Indo-European languages in Europe. *Nature* 522, 207–211.

Hackett, W. E. R., G. W. P. Dawson and C. J. Dawson (1956) The pattern of the ABO blood group frequencies in Ireland. *Heredity* 10, 69–84.

Haldane, J. B. S. (1940) The blood-group frequencies of European peoples and racial origins. *Human Biology* 12, 457–80.

Hall, M. (2007) *Is There a Shared Ulster Heritage?* Belfast, Island Publications/Farset Community Think Tanks Project.

Halpin, A. and C. Newman (2006) *Ireland: An Oxford Archaeological Guide to Sites from Earliest Times to AD 1600*. Oxford, Oxford University Press.

Hamilton, S. and J. Manley (2001) Hillforts, monumentality and place: a chronological and topographic review of first millennium BC hillforts of south-east England. *European Journal of Archaeology* 4(1), 7–42.

Harbison, P. (1975) The coming of the Indo-Europeans to Ireland: an archaeological assessment. *Journal of Indo-European Studies* 3, 101–19.

Harbison, P. (1979) Who were Ireland's first metallurgists?

In Ryan, M. (ed.) *The Origins of Metallurgy in Atlantic Europe*, 97–105. Dublin, Stationery Office.

Harbison, P. (1988) *Pre-Christian Ireland*. London, Thames & Hudson.

Harding, A. (2000) *European Societies in the Bronze Age*. Cambridge, Cambridge University Press.

Harding, D. (2009) *The Iron Age Round-house*. Oxford, Oxford University Press.

Harrison, R. J. (1980) *The Beaker Folk*. London, Thames & Hudson.

Harrison, R. and V. Heyd (2007) The transformation of Europe in the Third Millennium BC: the example of 'Le Petit-Chasseur I + II' (Sion, Valais, Switzerland). *Praehistorische Zeitschrift* 82, 129–214.

Hartley, B. R. and R. L. Fitts (1988) *The Brigantes*. Stroud, Sutton.

Hartz, S., H. Lübke and T. Terberger (2007) From fish and seal to sheep and cattle: new research into the process of neolithisation in northern Germany. In Whittle and Cummings (eds), 567–94.

Hasan, F. (1973) On mechanisms of population growth during the Neolithic. *Current Anthropology* 14, 535–40.

Haselgrove, C. and R. Pope (2007) Characterising the Earlier Iron Age. In Haselgrove and Pope (eds), 1–23.

Haselgrove, C. and R. Pope (eds) (2007) *The Earlier Iron Age in Britain and the Near Continent*. Oxford, Oxbow.

Hawkes, C. (1973) Cumulative Celticity in pre-Roman Britain. *Études Celtiques* 13, 607–27.

Hawkes, J. and C. Hawkes (1947) *Prehistoric Britain*. London, Chatto and Windus.

Hegarty, S. (2009) *The Irish (& other Foreigners) from the First People to the Poles*. Dublin, Gill and Macmillan.

Helgason, A., C. Lalueza-Fox, S. Ghosh, S. Sigurðardóttir, M. L. Sampietro, E. Gigli, A. Baker, J. Bertranpetit, L. Árnadóttir, U. Þorsteinsdóttir and K. Stefánsson (2009) Sequences

from first settlers reveal rapid evolution in Icelandic mtDNA pool. *PLoS Genetics* 5(1), e1000343.

Helgouac'h, J. (2001) Le cadre culturel du campaniforme armoricain. In Nicolis (ed.), vol. 1, 289–99.

Henderson, J. (ed.) (2000) *The Prehistory and Early History of Atlantic Europe*. Oxford, BAR International Series 861.

Henderson, J. C. (2007) *The Atlantic Iron Age*. London and New York, Routledge.

Herity, M. and G. Eogan (1977) *Ireland in Prehistory*. London, Routledge and Kegan Paul.

Hey, G. and A. Barclay (2007) The Thames Valley in the late fifth and early fourth millennium BC: the appearance of domestication and the evidence for change. In Whittle and Cummings (eds), 399–422.

Hicks, R. (2011) The sacred landscape of ancient Ireland. *Antiquity* 64(3), 40–45.

Higham, T., T. Compton, C. Stringer, R. Jacobi, B. Shapiro, E. Trinkhaus, B. Chandler, F. Gröning, C. Collins, S. Hillson, P. O'Higgins, C. Fitzgerald and M. Fagan (2011) The earliest evidence for anatomically modern humans in northwest Europe. *Nature* 479, 521–24.

Hill, E., M. Jobling and D. Bradley (2000) Y-chromosome variation and Irish origins. *Nature* 404, 351–52.

Hillgarth, J. N. (1984) Ireland and Spain in the seventh century. *Peritia* 2, 1–16.

Holland, C. H. (ed.) (2001) *The Geology of Ireland*. Edinburgh, Dunedin.

Hooton, E. A. and C. W. Dupertuis (1955) *The Physical Anthropology of Ireland*. Cambridge, Mass., Peabody Museum of Archaeology and Ethnology, Harvard University.

Hopkins, P. S. and J. T. Koch (1995) Historia Brittonum. In Koch, J. T. and J. Carey (eds) *The Celtic Heroic Age: Literary Sources for Ancient Celtic Europe and Early Ireland and Wales*, 270–85. Malden, Mass., Celtic Studies Publications.

Isaac, G. R. (2003) Varia I: some Old Irish etymologies and some conclusions drawn from them. *Ériu* 53, 151–55.

Isaac, G. R. (2007) Celtic and Afro-Asiatic. In Tristram (ed.), 25–80.

Jackson, K. H. (1964) *The Oldest Irish Tradition: A Window on the Iron Age.* Cambridge, Cambridge University Press.

James, S. (1999) *The Atlantic Celts: Ancient People or Modern Invention?* London, British Museum Press.

Jobling, M. A., M. E. Hurles and C. Tyler-Smith (2004) *Human Evolutionary Genetics: Origins, Peoples and Disease.* New York, Garland.

Johnston, S. and B. Wailes (2007) *Dún Ailinne: Excavations at an Irish Royal Site, 1968–1975.* Philadelphia, University of Pennsylvania Museum of Archaeology and Anthropology, University Museum Monograph No. 129.

Jones, C. (2004) *The Burren and the Aran Islands: Exploring the Archaeology.* Cork, Collins Press.

Jope, E. M. (1954) Animal bones from the chambers in Audleystown cairn. *Ulster Journal of Archaeology* 17, 53–56.

Joynt, M. (1910) Echtra Mac Echdach Mugmedóin. *Ériu* 4, 91–111.

Kalicz-Schreiber, R. and N. Kalicz (2001) Were the Bell Beakers social indicators of the Early Bronze Age in Budapest? In Nicolis (ed.), vol. 2, 439–58.

Karl, R. (2010) The Celts from everywhere and nowhere: a re-evaluation of the origins of the Celts and the emergence of Celtic cultures. In Cunliffe and Koch (eds), 39–64.

Kayser, O. (1991) Le Mésolithique Breton: un état des connaissances en 1958. In *Mésolithique et néolithisation en France et dans les régions limitrophes*, 197–211. Paris, CTHS.

Kelekna, P. (2009) *The Horse in Human History.* Cambridge, Cambridge University Press.

Kelly, T. (2008) The origin of the avifauna of Ireland. In Davenport et al. (eds), 97–107.

Koch, J. T. (1991) Eriu, Alba, and Letha: when was a language ancestral to Gaelic first spoken in Ireland? *Emania* 9, 17–27.

Koch, J. T. (1994) Windows on the Iron Age: 1964–1994. In Mallory, J. P. and G. Stockman (eds) *Ulidia: Proceedings of the First International Conference on the Ulster Cycle of Tales*, 229–37. Belfast, December Publications.

Koch, J. T. (2009) *Tartessian: Celtic in the South-west at the Dawn of History.* Aberystwyth, Celtic Studies Publications No. 13.

Koch, J. T. (2010) Paradigm shift? Interpreting Tartessian as Celtic. In Cunliffe and Koch (eds), 185–301.

Kooijmans, L. (2007) The gradual transition to farming in the Lower Rhine Basin. In Whittle and Cummings (eds), 287–309.

Kristiansen, K. (1998) *Europe before History.* Cambridge, Cambridge University Press.

Kristiansen, K. and T. Larsson (2005) *The Rise of Bronze Age Society.* Cambridge, Cambridge University Press.

Kytmannow, T. (2008) *Portal Tombs in the Landscape.* Oxford, BAR British Series 455.

Laing, L. (1985) The Romanization of Ireland in the fifth century. *Peritia* 4, 261–78.

Lambeck, K. and A. P. Purcell (2001) Sea-level change in the Irish Sea since the Last Glacial Maximum: constraints from isostatic modelling. *Journal of Quaternary Science* 16, 497–506.

Lightfoot, J. L. (1999) *Parthenius of Nicaea.* Oxford, Clarendon Press.

Loughrey, P. (1988) (ed.) *The People of Ireland.* Belfast, Appletree Press.

Lyle, P. (2003) *The North of Ireland.* Harpenden, Terra Publishing.

Lynch, F., S. Aldhouse-Green and J. Davies (2000) *Prehistoric Wales.* Stroud, Sutton.

Lynn, C. J. (1991) Knockaulin (Dún Ailinne) and Navan: some architectural comparisons. *Emania* 8, 51–59.

Lynn, C. J. (1994) Hostels, heroes and tales: further thoughts on the Navan mound. *Emania* 12, 5–20.

Lynn, C. J. (2003) *Navan Fort: Archaeology and Myth.* Bray, Wordwell.

MacAdam, R. (1859) Is the Irish language spoken in Africa? *Ulster Journal of Archaeology* 7, 195–200.

Macalister, R. A. S. (1921) *Ireland in Pre-Celtic Times.* Dublin and London, Maunsel and Roberts.

Macalister, R. A. S. (1928) *The Archaeology of Ireland.* London, Methuen.

Macalister, R. A. S. (1935) *Ancient Ireland: A Study in the Lessons of Archaeology and History.* London, Methuen.

Macalister, R. A. S. (1938–56) *Lebor Gabála Érenn*, 5 vols. Dublin, Irish Texts Society.

Macalister, R. A. S. (1949) *The Archaeology of Ireland*, 2nd rev. edn. London, Methuen.

Mac an Bhaird, A. (1991–93) Ptolemy revisited. *Ainm* 5, 1–20.

Mac Cana, P. (2011) *The Cult of the Sacred Centre: Essays on Celtic Ideology.* Dublin, Institute for Advanced Studies.

MacDonald, P. and J. Ó Néill (2009) Investigation of the find-spot of the Tamlaght hoard, Co. Armagh. In Cooney et al. (eds), 167–79.

Mac Eoin, G. (1986) The Celticity of Celtic Ireland. In Schmidt, K. H. (ed.) *Geschichte und Kultur der Kelten*, 161–74. Heidelberg, Winter Universitätsverlag.

Mac Eoin, G. (2007) What language was spoken in Ireland before Irish? In Tristram (ed.), 113–25.

MacNeill, E. (1919). *Phases of Irish History.* Dublin, Gill and Son.

Mallory, J. P. (1985) The origin of the Irish. *Journal of Irish Archaeology* 2, 65–69.

Mallory, J. P. (1991) Two perspectives on the problem of Irish origins. *Emania* 9, 53–58.

Mallory, J. P. (1992) The world of Cú Chulainn: the archaeology of *Táin Bó Cúailnge.* In Mallory, J. P. (ed.) *Aspects of the Táin*, 103–59. Belfast, December Publications.

Mallory, J. P. (1993) The archaeology of the Irish Dreamtime. *Proceedings of the Harvard Celtic Colloquium* 13, 1–24.

Mallory, J. P. (1995) Haughey's Fort and the Navan Complex in the Late Bronze Age. In Waddell and Shee Twohig (eds), 73–86.

Mallory, J. P. (1998) The Old Irish chariot. In Jasasnoff, J., H. Melchert and L. Oliver (eds) *Mír Curad: Studies in Honor of Calvert Watkins*, 451–64. Innsbruck, Innsbrucker Beiträge zur Sprachwissenschaft.

Mallory, J. P. (1999) Language in prehistoric Ireland. *Ulster Folklife* 45, 3–16.

Mallory, J. P. (2006) Irish origins: the archaeological, linguistic and genetic evidence. In Turner, B. (ed.) *Migration and Myth: Ulster's Revolving Door*, 97–111. Downpatrick, Ulster History Trust.

Mallory, J. P. and V. H. Mair (2000) *The Tarim Mummies: Ancient China and the Mystery of the Earliest Peoples from the West*. London, Thames & Hudson.

Mallory, J. P. (2013) The Indo-Europeanization of Atlantic Europe, in Koch, John T. and Barrie Cunliffe (eds) *Celtic from the West 2*, 17–39. Oxford, Oxbow.

Mallory, J. P. and T. McNeill (1991) *The Archaeology of Ulster*. Belfast, Institute of Irish Studies.

Malmstrom, H., M. T. P. Gilbert, M. G. Thomas, M. Brandström, J. Storå, P. Molnar, P. K. Andersen, C. Bendixen, G. Holmlund, A. Götherström *et al.* (2009) Ancient DNA reveals lack of continuity between Neolithic hunter-gatherers and contemporary Scandinavians. *Current Biology* 19, 1–5.

Marchand, G. (1999) *La Néolithisation de l'ouest de la France*. Oxford, BAR International Series 748.

Marchand, G. (2007) Neolithic fragrances: Mesolithic-Neolithic interactions in western France. In Whittle and Cummings (eds), 225–42.

Marshak, S. (2001) *Earth: Portrait of a Planet*. New York and London, Norton.

Martin, C. A. (1935) *Prehistoric Man in Ireland*. London, Macmillan.

Martin, J. (2009) *Die Bronzegefasse in Mecklenburg-Vorpommern, Brandenburg, Berlin, Sachsen-Anhalt, Thüringen und Sachsen*. Stuttgart, Steiner, *Prähistorische Bronzefunde* II, 16.

Matasovic, R. (2007) Insular Celtic as a language area. In Tristram (ed.), 93–112.

Matasovic, R. (2009) *Etymological Dictionary of Proto-Celtic*. Leiden, Brill.

McCaffrey, C. and L. Eaton (2002) *In Search of Ancient Ireland: The Origins of the Irish, from Neolithic Times to the Coming of the English*. Chicago, New Amsterdam Books.

McCartan, S. (2003) Mesolithic hunter-gatherers in the Isle of Man: adaptions to an island environment? In Larsson, L., H. Kindgren, K. Knutsson, D. Loeffler and A. Akerlund (eds) *Mesolithic on the Move*, 331–39. Oxford, Oxbow.

McCartan, S. (2004) The Mesolithic in the Isle of Man. In Saville (ed.), 271–83.

McClean, R. (1993) Eat your greens: an examination of the potential diet available in Ireland during the Mesolithic. *Ulster Journal of Archaeology* 56, 1–8.

McCone, K. (1990) *Pagan Past and Christian Present in Early Irish Literature*. Maynooth, An Sagart.

McCone, K. (1996) *Towards a Relative Chronology of Ancient and Medieval Celtic Sound Change*. Maynooth, Department of Old Irish, St Patrick's College.

McCormick, F. (1999) Early evidence for wild animals in Ireland. In Benecke, N. (ed.) *The Holocene History of the European Fauna*, 355–71. Rahden, Verlag Marie Leidorf.

McCormick, F. (2004) Hunting wild pig in the Late Mesolithic. In Roche *et al.* (eds), 1–5.

McCormick, F. (2009) The Faunal Remains from Kilshane. Unpublished report.

McCormick, F. and E. Murray (2007) *Excavations at Knowth: 3. Knowth and the Zooarchaeology of Early Christian Ireland*. Dublin, Royal Irish Academy.

McDonnell, V. (2011) *Ireland: Our Island Story*. Cork, Collins Press.

McEvoy, B. and D. Bradley (2006) Y-chromosomes and the extent of patrilineal ancestry in Irish surnames. *Human Genetics* 119, 212–19.

McEvoy, B. and D. Bradley (2010) Irish genetics and Celts. In Cunliffe and Koch (eds), 107–20.

McEvoy, B., M. Richards, P. Foster and D. Bradley (2004) The *longue durée* of genetic ancestry: multiple genetic marker systems and Celtic origins on the Atlantic façade of Europe. *American Journal of Human Genetics* 75(4), 693–702.

McEvoy, B., K. Simms and D. Bradley (2008) Genetic investigation of the patrilineal kinship structure of Early Medieval Ireland. *American Journal of Physical Anthropology* 136, 415–22.

McGrail, S. (1983) Cross-Channel seamanship and navigation in the late first millennium BC. *Oxford Journal of Archaeology* 2, 299–337.

McKeever, P. (1999) *A Story through Time*. Dublin and Belfast, Geological Survey of Ireland and Geological Survey of Northern Ireland.

Megaw, R. and V. Megaw (1989) *Celtic Art*. London, Thames & Hudson.

Megaw, V. and D. Simpson (eds) (1979) *Introduction to British Prehistory: From the Arrival of Homo Sapiens to the Claudian Invasion*. Leicester, Leicester University Press.

Mellars, P. (2004) Coastal occupation and the role of the Oronsay middens. In Saville (ed.), 167–83.

Mercer, R. (1999) The origins of warfare in the British Isles. In Carman, J. and A. Harding (eds) *Ancient Warfare*, 143–56. Oxford, Oxbow.

Mesthrie, R. (2001) Language maintenance, shift, and death. In Mesthrie, R. (ed.) *Concise Encyclopedia of Sociolinguistics*, 493–98. Amsterdam and New York, Elsevier.

Meyer, K. (1910) Gauls in Ireland. *Ériu* 4, 208.

Milcent, P.-Y. (2008) À l'Est rien de nouveau: Chronologie des armes de poing du premier âge du Fer médio-atlantique et genese des standards materiels élitaires hallstattiens et lateniens. In *Construire le temps: Histoire et méthodes des chronologies et calendriers des derniers millénaires avant notre ère en Europe occidentale*, 231–50. Glux-en-Glenne, Centre archéologique européen, Collection Bibracte 16.

Mitchell, F. and M. Ryan (1997) *Reading the Irish Landscape*. Dublin, Town House.

Mitchell, W. I. (ed.) (2004) *The Geology of Northern Ireland*. Belfast, Geological Survey of Northern Ireland.

Mongan, N. (1995) *Menapia Quest*. Dublin, Herodotus.

Moore, D. (2004) Hostilities in Early Neolithic Ireland: trouble with the neighbours – the evidence from Ballyharry, County Antrim. In Gibson, A. and A. Sheridan (eds) *From Sickles to Circles: Britain and Ireland at the Time of Stonehenge*, 142–54. Stroud, Tempus.

Moore, L., B. McEvoy, E. Cape, K. Simms and D. Bradley (2006) A Y-chromosome signature of hegemony in Gaelic Ireland. *American Journal of Human Genetics* 78, 334–38.

Mount, C. (2000) Exchange and communication: the relationship between Early and Middle Bronze Age Ireland and Atlantic Europe. In Henderson (ed.), 57–72.

Mourant, A. E., A. Kopec and K. Domaniewska-Sobczak (1976) *The Distribution of the Human Blood Groups and other Polymorphisms*, 2nd edn. Oxford, Oxford University Press.

Müller, J. and S. van Willigen (2001) New radiocarbon evidence for European Bell Beakers and the consequences for the diffusion of the Bell Beaker phenomenon. In Nicolis (ed.), vol. 1, 59–80.

Myres, N. M., S. Rootsi, A. A. Lin, M. Järe, R. J. King, I. Kutuev, V. M. Cabrera, E. K. Khusnutdinova, A. Pshenichnov, B. Yunusbayev, O. Balanovsky, E. Balanovska,

P. Rudan, M. Baldovic, R. J. Herrera, J. Chiaroni, J. Di Cristofaro, R. Villems, T. Kivisild and P. A. Underhill (2011) A major Y-chromosome haplogroup R1b Holocene era founder effect in Central and Western Europe. *European Journal of Human Genetics* 19, 95–101.

Mytum, H. (1992) *The Origins of Early Christian Ireland*. London, Routledge.

Mytum, H. (1995) Across the Irish Sea: Romano-British and Irish settlements in Wales. *Emania* 13, 15–22.

Nash, C. (2006) Irish origins, Celtic origins: population genetics, cultural politics. *Irish Studies Review* 14, 11–37.

Needham, S. (2002) Analytical implications for Beaker metallurgy in North-West Europe. In Bartelheim, M., E. Pernicka and R. Krause (eds) *Die Anfänge der Metallurgie in der Alten Welt*, 99–134. Rahden, Verlag Marie Leidorf.

Needham, S. (2005) Transforming Beaker culture in North-West Europe: processes of fusion and fission. *Proceedings of the Prehistoric Society* 71, 171–217.

Needham, S. (2007) 800 BC, The Great Divide. In Haselgrove and Pope (eds), 39–63.

Needham, S. and J. Ambers (1994) Redating Rams Hill and reconsidering Bronze Age enclosure. *Proceedings of the Prehistoric Society* 60, 225–43.

Newman, C. (1997) *Tara: An Archaeological Survey*. Dublin, Royal Irish Academy, Discovery Programme Monograph 2.

Newman, C. (1998) Reflections on the making of a 'royal site' in early Ireland. *World Archaeology* 30, 127–41.

Nicolis, F. (2001) Some observations on the cultural setting of the Bell Beakers of Northern Italy. In Nicolis (ed.), vol. 1, 207–27.

Nicolis, F. (ed.) (2001) *Bell Beakers Today: Pottery, People, Culture, Symbols in Prehistoric Europe*, 2 vols. Trento, Servizio Beni Culturali.

Novotna, P. and V. Blažek (2006) On application of glottochronology for Celtic languages. In *Celto-Slavica: Second International Colloquium of Societas Celto-Slavica*, 11–36. Moscow, Institut Jazykoznanija.

O'Brien, E. (1992) Pagan and Christian burial during the first millennium AD. In Edwards, N. and A. Lane (eds) *The Early Church in Wales and the West*, 130–37. Oxford, Oxbow.

O'Brien, E. (2009) Re-evaluation of find-spot and context for the anthropoid hilted sword, Ballyshannon, Co. Donegal. In Cooney et al. (eds), 193–98.

O'Brien, K. (2009) *The Story of Ireland*. Dublin, O'Brien Press.

O'Brien, S. (1976) Indo-European eschatology: a model. *Journal of Indo-European Studies* 4, 295–320.

O'Brien, W. (1999) *Sacred Ground: Megalithic Tombs in Coastal South-west Ireland*. Galway, Department of Archaeology, National University of Ireland, Bronze Age Studies 4.

O'Brien, W. (2001) New light on Beaker metallurgy in Ireland. In Nicolis (ed.), vol. 2, 561–76.

O'Brien, W. (2009) Hidden 'Celtic' Ireland: indigenous Iron Age settlement in the south-western peninsulas. In Cooney et al. (eds), 437–48.

Ó Buachalla, B. (1995) Irish Jacobitism and Irish nationalism: the literary evidence. In O'Dea, M. and K. Whelan (eds) *Nations and Nationalisms: France, Britain, Ireland and the Eighteenth-century Context*, 103–15. Oxford, Voltaire Foundation.

O'Connor, B. (2007) Llyn Fawr metalwork in Britain: a review. In Haselgrove and Pope (eds), 64–79.

Ó Corráin, D. (1978) Nationality and kingship in pre-Norman Ireland. In Moody, T. W. (ed.) *Nationality and the Pursuit of National Independence*, 1–35. Belfast, Appletree Press.

Ó Corráin, D. (1992) Celtic Ireland: the earliest accounts. In Foster, R. (ed.) *The Oxford History of Ireland*, 1–43. Oxford, Oxford University Press.

O'Dea, M. and K. Whelan (eds) (1995) *Nations and Nationalisms: France, Britain, Ireland and the Eighteenth-century Context.* Oxford, Voltaire Foundation.

Ó Donnabháin, B. (2000) An appalling vista? The Celts and the archaeology of later prehistoric Ireland. In Desmond, A., G. Johnson, M. McCarthy, J. Sheehan and E. Shee Twohig (eds) *New Agendas in Irish Prehistory,* 189–96. Bray, Wordwell.

Ó hÓgáin, D. (1990) *Myth, Legend and Romance: An Encyclopaedia of the Irish Folk Tradition.* London, Ryan.

Ó hÓgáin, D. (2002) *The Celts: A History.* Cork, Collins Press.

O'Kelly, M. (1981) The megalithic tombs of Ireland. In Renfrew, C. (ed.) *The Megalithic Monuments of Western Europe,* 113–26. London, Thames & Hudson.

O'Kelly, M. J. (1989) *Early Ireland.* Cambridge, Cambridge University Press.

O'Loughlin, T. (1999) An early thirteenth-century map in Dublin: a window into the world of Giraldus Cambrensis. *Imago Mundi* 51, 22–40.

Ó Néill, J. (2009) Inventory of Bronze Age Structures. Unpublished report, Dublin, Heritage Council, Ireland.

O'Rahilly, T. (1946) *Early Irish History and Mythology.* Dublin, Institute for Advanced Studies.

Ó Ríordáin, B. and J. Waddell (1993), *The Funerary Bowls and Vases of the Irish Bronze Age,* Galway, Galway University Press, Bronze Age Studies.

O'Sullivan, A. (2000) Last foragers or first farmers? In Young, R. (ed.) *Mesolithic Lifeways: Current Research from Britain and Ireland,* 153–64. Leicester, University of Leicester, School of Archaeological Studies, Leicester Archaeology Monographs 7.

O'Sullivan, A. and C. Breen (2007) *Maritime Ireland: An Archaeology of Coastal Communities.* Stroud, Tempus.

O'Sullivan, M. (2005) *Duma na nGiall. The Mound of the Hostages, Tara.* Bray, Wordwell.

Oppenheimer, S. (2006) *The Origins of the British.* London, Robinson.

Oppenheimer, S. (2010) A reanalysis of multiple prehistoric immigrations to Britain and Ireland aimed at identifying the Celtic contributions. In Cunliffe and Koch (eds), 121–50.

Orosius, P. (1964) *The Seven Books of History against the Pagans,* trans. R. J. Deferrari. Washington, DC, Catholic University of America Press.

Orpen, G. H. (1911–20) *Ireland under the Normans,* 4 vols. Oxford, Clarendon Press.

Osgood, R. (1998) *Warfare in the Late Bronze Age of North Europe.* Oxford, BAR International Series 694.

Osgood, R. and J. Monks (2000) *Bronze Age Warfare.* Stroud, Sutton.

Othenin-Girard, B. (1998) A Bell Beaker settlement at Alle, Noir Bois (Jura Switzerland). In Benz, M. and S. van Willigen (eds) *Some New Approaches to the Bell Beaker 'Phenomenon': Lost Paradise…?,* 57–71, Oxford, BAR International Series 690.

Pala, Maria, Pedro Soares and Martin B. Richards (2016) Archaeogentic and palaeogenetic evidence for metal age mobility in Europe, in Koch, John T. and Barrie Cunliffe (eds) *Celtic from the West 3,* 351–384. Oxford, Oxbow.

Pedersen, H. (1962) *The Discovery of Language: Linguistic Science in the Nineteenth Century,* trans. J. W. Spargo. Bloomington, Indiana University Press.

Perles, C. (2001) *Early Neolithic Greece.* Cambridge, Cambridge University Press.

Piggott, S. (1954) *Neolithic Cultures of the British Isles.* Cambridge, Cambridge University Press.

Piggott, S. (1965) *Ancient Europe.* Edinburgh, Edinburgh University Press.

Piggott, S. (1983) The coming of the Celts: the archaeological argument. In Mac Eoin, G. (ed.) *Proceedings of the Sixth International Congress of Celtic Studies,* 138–48. Dublin, Institute for Advanced Studies.

Plunkett, G. (2008) Land-use patterns and cultural change in the Middle to Late Bronze Age in Ireland: inferences from pollen records. *Vegetational History Archaeobotany* 18, 273–95.

Pokorny, J. (1954) Die Geographie Irlands bei Ptolemaios. *Zeitschrift für celtische Philologie* 12, 94–120.

Pollard, J. (ed.) (2008) *Prehistoric Britain.* Oxford, Blackwell.

Powell, T. G. E. (1950) The Celtic settlement of Ireland. In Fox, C. and B. Dickens (eds) *The Early Cultures of North-west Europe,* 173–95. Cambridge, Cambridge University Press.

Price, T. D., C. Knipper, G. Grupe and V. Smrcka (2004) Strontium isotopes and prehistoric human migration: the Bell Beaker period in central Europe. *European Journal of Archaeology* 7(1), 9–40.

Primas, M. (2002) Taking the high ground: Continental hill-forts in Bronze Age contexts. *Proceedings of the Prehistoric Society* 68, 41–59.

Prüssing, G. (1991) *Die Bronzegefasse in Österreich.* Stuttgart, Steiner, *Prähistorische Bronzefunde* II, 5.

Quinn, B. (2005) *The Atlantean Irish: Ireland's Oriental and Maritime Heritage.* Dublin, Lilliput Press.

Raftery, B. (1972) *Iron Age Ireland.* Dublin, Folens.

Raftery, B. (1984) *La Tène in Ireland: Problems of Origin and Chronology.* Marburg, Veröffentlichung des Vorgeschichtlichen Seminars Marburg 2.

Raftery, B. (1990) *Trackways through Time.* Dublin, Headline.

Raftery, B. (1994) *Pagan Celtic Ireland: The Enigma of the Irish Iron Age.* London, Thames & Hudson.

Raftery, B. (1995a) Pre- and Protohistoric Ireland: problems of continuity and change. *Emania* 13, 5–9.

Raftery, B. (1995b) The conundrum of Irish Iron Age pottery. In Raftery, B., V. Megaw and V. Rigby (eds), *Sites and Sights of the Iron Age: Essays on Fieldwork and Museum Research Presented to Ian Mathieson Stead,*

149–56. Oxford, Oxbow, Monograph 56.

Raftery, B. (1996) *Trackway Excavations in the Mountdillon Bogs, Co. Longford, 1985–1991.* Dublin, Department of Archaeology, University College Dublin.

Raftery, B. (1997a) Discussion of diagnostic finds. In Waterman, 90–95.

Raftery, B. (1997b) Implications of the monkey bones from Site B. In Waterman, 121–24.

Raftery, B. (1998) Observations on the Iron Age in Munster. *Emania* 17, 21–24.

Raftery, J. (1951) *Prehistoric Ireland.* Dublin, Batsford.

Ralston, I. and P. Ashmore (2007) The character of Earlier Iron Age societies in Scotland. In Haselgrove and Pope (eds), 229–47.

Rees, A. and B. Rees (1961) *Celtic Heritage: Ancient Tradition in Ireland and Wales.* London, Thames & Hudson.

Rehman, F., V. J. Robinson and S. J. Shennan (1992) A neutron activation analysis of Bell Beakers and associated pottery from Czechoslovakia and Hungary. *Pamatky Archeologicke* 83, 197–211.

Relethford, J. and M. Crawford (1995) Anthropometric variation and the population history of Ireland. *American Journal of Physical Anthropology* 96, 25–38.

Renfrew, C. (1987) *Archaeology and Language: The Puzzle of Indo-European Origins.* London, Jonathan Cape.

Ridley, M. (1999) *Genome: The Autobiography of a Species in 23 Chapters.* London, Fourth Estate.

Riede, F. (2011) Climate and demography in early prehistory: using calibrated 14C dates as population proxies. *Human Biology* 81, 309–37.

Robb, J. and P. Miracle (2007) Beyond 'migration' versus 'acculturation': new models for the spread of agriculture. In Whittle and Cummings (eds), 99–115.

Roche, H. (2002) Excavations at Ráith na Ríg, Tara, Co. Meath, 1997. In *Discovery Programme Reports* 6, 19–165. Dublin, Royal Irish Academy.

Roche, H., E. Grogan, J. Bradley, J. Coles and B. Raftery (eds) (2004) *From Megaliths to Metal: Essays in Honour of George Eogan.* Oxford, Oxbow.

Rosser, Z., T. Zerjal, M. Hurles, M. Adojaan, D. Alavantic, A. Amorim, W. Amos, M. Armenteros, E. Arroyo, G. Barbujani *et al.* (2000) Y-chromosomal diversity in Europe is clinal and influenced primarily by geography, rather than language. *American Journal of Human Genetics* 67, 1526–43.

Rothschild, B. (2003) Infectious processes around the dawn of civilization. In Greenblatt, C. and M. Spigelman (eds) *Emerging Pathologies: Archaeology, Ecology and Evolution of Infectious Disease,* 103–16. Oxford, Oxford University Press.

Rowley-Conwy, T. (2004) How the West was lost: a reconsideration of agricultural origins in Britain, Ireland, and southern Scandinavia. *Current Anthropology* 45 (Supplement), S83–113.

Rowley-Conwy, T. (2011) Westward ho! The spread of agriculture from Central Europe to the Atlantic. *Current Anthropology* 52 (Supplement), S431–51.

Ryan, M. (1994) *Irish Archaeology Illustrated,* new edn. Dublin, Town House/Country House.

Rynne, E. (1961) The introduction of the La Tène into Ireland. In *Bericht über den V. Internationalen Kongress für Vor- und Frühgeschichte: Hamburg, 1958,* 705–9. Berlin, Gebr. Mann.

Rynne, E. (1976) The La Tène and Roman finds from Lambay, County Dublin: a re-assessment. *Proceedings of the Royal Irish Academy* 76C, 231–44.

Rynne, E. (1983) Some early Iron Age sword-hilts from Ireland and Scotland. In O'Connor, A.

and D. V. Clarke (eds) *From the Stone Age to the 'Forty-five,* 188–96. Edinburgh, John Donald.

Sacchi, D. (1976) Les civilisations de l'Epipaléolithique et du Mésolithique en Languedoc occidental (Bassin de l'Aude) et en Roussillon. In de Lumley, H. (ed.) *La préhistoire française,* vol. 1, 1390–97. Paris, CNRS.

Salanova, L. (2001) Technological, ideological or economic European union? The variability of Bell Beaker decoration. In Nicolis (ed.), vol. 1, 91–102.

Salanova, L. (2004) The frontiers inside the western Bell Beaker block. In Czebreszuk (ed.), 63–75.

Saville, A. (ed.) (2004a) *Mesolithic Scotland and its Neighbours.* Edinburgh, Society of Antiquaries of Scotland.

Saville, A. (2004b) The material culture of Mesolithic Scotland. In Saville (ed.), 185–220.

Saville, A. (2009) Speculating on the significance of an axehead and a bead from Luce Sands, Dumfries and Galloway, south-west Scotland. In Finlay *et al.* (eds), 50–58.

Scarre, C. (2007) Changing places: monuments and the Neolithic transition in western France. In Whittle and Cummings (eds), 243–61.

Scarre, C., P. Arias, G. Burenhult, M. Fano, L. Oosterbeek, R. Schulting, A. Sheridan and A. Whittle (2003) Megalithic chronologies. In Burenhult, G. (ed.) *Stones and Bones,* 65–111. Oxford, Archaeopress, BAR International Series 1201.

Schmidt, K. H. (1977) *Die Festlandkeltischen Sprachen.* Innsbruck, Innsbrucker Beiträge zur Sprachwissenschaft.

Schrijver, P. (1995) *Studies in British Celtic Historical Phonology.* Amsterdam, Rodopi.

Schrijver, P. (1997) Animal, vegetable and mineral: some Western European substratum words. In Lubotsky, A. (ed.) *Sound Law and Analogy,* 293–314. Amsterdam, Rodopi, Leiden Studies in Indo-European 9.

Schrijver, P. (2000) Non-Indo-European surviving in Ireland

in the first millennium AD. *Ériu* 51, 195–99.

Schrijver, P. (2002) Irish *ainder*, Welsh *anner*, Breton *annoar*, Basque *andere*. In Restle, D. and D. Zaefferer (eds) *Sounds and Systems: Studies in Structure and Change*, 205–19. Berlin and New York, Mouton de Gruyter.

Schrijver, P. (2005) More on Non-Indo-European surviving in Ireland in the first millennium AD. *Ériu* 55, 137–44.

Schrijver, P. (2009) Celtic influence on Old English: phonological and phonetic evidence. *English Language and Linguistics* 13, 193–211.

Schulting, R. (1998) Slighting the sea: stable isotope evidence for the transition to farming in northwestern Europe. *Documenta Praehistorica* 25, 203–18.

Schulting, R. (2006) Skeletal evidence and contexts of violence in the European Mesolithic and Neolithic. In Gowland, R. and C. Knüsel (eds) *Social Archaeology of Funerary Remains*, 224–37. Oxford, Oxbow.

Schulting, R. and M. Wysocki (2005) 'In this chambered tumulus were found cleft skulls…': an assessment of the evidence for cranial trauma in the British Neolithic. *Proceedings of the Prehistoric Society* 71, 107–38.

Scott, B. (1990) *Early Irish Ironworking*. Belfast, Ulster Museum.

Searle, J. B. (2008) The colonization of Ireland by mammals. In Davenport *et al.* (eds), 109–15.

Sharples, N. (2007) Building communities and creating identities in the first millennium BC. In Haselgrove and Pope (eds), 174–84.

Sheridan, A. (1985/86) Megaliths and megalomania: an account, and interpretation, of the development of passage tombs in Ireland. *Journal of Irish Archaeology* 3, 17–30.

Sheridan, A. (2000) Achnacreebeag and its French connections: vive the 'Auld Alliance'. In Henderson (ed.), 1–16.

Sheridan, A. (2004a) Neolithic connection along and across the Irish Sea. In Cummings, V. and C. Fowler (eds) *The Neolithic of the Irish Sea*, 9–21. Oxford, Oxbow.

Sheridan, A. (2004b) Going round in circles? Understanding the Irish Grooved Ware 'complex' in its wider context. In Roche *et al.* (eds), 26–37.

Sheridan, A. (2007) From Picardie to Pickering and Pencraig Hill? New information on the 'Carinated Bowl Neolithic' in northern Britain. In Whittle and Cummings (eds), 441–92.

Sheridan, A. (2008) Upper Largie and Dutch-Scottish connections during the Beaker period. In Fokkens, H., B. J. Coles, A. L. van Gijn, J. P. Kleijne, H. H. Ponjee and C. G. Slappendel (eds) *Between Foraging and Farming: An Extended Broad Spectrum of Papers Presented to Leendert Louwe Kooijmans*, 247–60. Leiden, University of Leiden, Analecta Praehistorica Leidensia 40.

Simpson, D. D. A. and I. Meighan (1999) Pitchstone – a new trading material in Neolithic Ireland. *Archaeology Ireland* 13, 26–30.

Sims-Williams, P. (1998) Celto-mania and Celto-scepticism. *Cambrian Medieval Celtic Studies* 36, 1–35.

Sims-Williams, P. (2007) Common Celtic, Gallo-Brittonic and Insular Celtic. In Lambert, P-Y. and G-J. Pinault (eds) *Gaulois et Celtique Continental*, 309–54. Geneva, Droz, École Pratique des Hautes Études.

Sleeman, D. P. (2008) Quantifying the prey gap for Ireland. In Davenport *et al.* (eds), 77–82.

Sleeman, D. P. and D. Yalden (2009) Ireland's mammals: an annotated list. In Finlay *et al.* (eds), 211–19.

Smith, C. (2010) *The Naked Scientist*. London, Little, Brown.

Soares, P., A. Achilli, O. Semino, W. Davies, V. Macaulay, H-J. Bandelt, A. Torroni and M. B. Richards (2010) The archaeogenetics of Europe. *Current Biology* 20, R174–83.

Soares, P., L. Ermini, N. Thomson, M. Mormina, T. Rito, A. Rohl, A. Salas, S. Oppenheimer,

V. Macaulay and M. Richards (2009) Connecting for purifying selection: an improved human mitochondrial molecular clock. *American Journal of Human Genetics* 84, 740–59.

Sokal, R. (1989) Update to Haldane's 'Blood-Group Frequencies of European Peoples and Racial Origins'. *Human Biology* 61, 691–702.

Sykes, B. (2001) *The Seven Daughters of Eve*. London and New York, Bantam Press and Norton.

Sykes, B. (2006) *Blood of the Isles*. London, Corgi.

Taylor, G. (1921) The evolution and distribution of race, culture, and language. *Geographical Review* 11, 54–119.

Taylor, J. (1970) Lunulae reconsidered. *Proceedings of the Prehistoric Society* 36, 38–81.

Thomas, C. (1981) *Christianity in Roman Britain to AD 500*. London, Batsford.

Thomas, J. (2008) The Mesolithic-Neolithic transition in Britain. In Pollard (ed.), 58–89.

Thompson, T. F. (2006) *Ireland's Pre-Celtic Archaeological and Anthropological Heritage*. Lewiston, NY and Lampeter, Mellen Press.

Timberlake, S. (2002) Ancient prospection for metals and modern prospection for ancient mines: the evidence for Bronze Age mining within the British Isles. In Bartelheim, M., E. Pernicka and R. Krause (eds) *Die Anfänge der Metallurgie in der Alten Welt*, 327–57. Rahden, Verlag Marie Leidorf.

Todd, L. (1989) *The Language of Irish Literature*. Basingstoke, Macmillan.

Tolan-Smith, C. (2008) Mesolithic Britain. In Bailey, G. and P. Spikins (eds) *Mesolithic Europe*, 132–57. Cambridge, Cambridge University Press.

Tömöry, G., B. Csányi, E. Bogácsi-Szabó, T. Kalmár, Á. Czibula, A. Csösz, K. Priskin, B. Mende, P. Langó, C. S. Downes and I. Raskó (2007) Comparison of maternal lineage and biogeographic analyses of ancient and modern Hungarian populations. *American Journal of Physical Anthropology* 134, 354–68.

Toner, G. (2000) Identifying Ptolemy's Irish places and tribes. In Parsons, D. and P. Sims-Williams (eds) *Ptolemy: Towards a Linguistic Atlas of the Earliest Celtic Place-names of Europe*, 73–81. Aberystwyth, CMCS Publications.

Tong, P., J. Prendergast, A. Lohan, S. Farrington, S. Cronin, N. Friel, D. Bradley, O. Hardiman, A. Evans, J. Wilson and B. Loftus (2010) Sequencing and analysis of an Irish human genome. *Genome Biology* 11, R91.

Trask, R. L. (1997) *The History of Basque*. London, Routledge.

Tresset, A. (2000) Early husbandry in Atlantic areas: animal introductions, diffusions of techniques and native acculturation at the north-west fringe of Europe. In Henderson (ed.), 17–32.

Tresset, A. and J.-D. Vigne (2007) Substitution of species, techniques and symbols at the Mesolithic-Neolithic transition in western Europe. In Whittle and Cummings (eds), 189–210.

Tristram, H. L. C. (ed.) (2007) *The Celtic Languages in Contact*. Potsdam, Potsdam University Press.

Tusa, S. (2001) Mediterranean perspective and cultural integrity of Sicilian Bell Beakers. In Nicolis (ed.), vol. 1, 173–86.

Tyfield, L. A. (1997) Phenylketonuria in Britain: genetic analysis gives a historical perspective of the disorder but will it predict the future for affected individuals? *Journal of Clinical Pathology* 50, 169–74.

Valdeyron, N. (2008) The Mesolithic in France. In Bailey, G. and P. Spikins (eds) *Mesolithic Europe*, 182–202. Cambridge, Cambridge University Press.

Vallancey, C. (1772) *An Essay on the Antiquity of the Irish Language*. Dublin, Powell.

Van Wijngaarden-Bakker, L. (1986) The animal remains from the Beaker settlement at Newgrange, Co. Meath: final report. *Proceedings of the Royal Irish Academy* 86C, 17–111.

Van Wijngaarden-Bakker, L. (1989) Faunal remains and the Irish Mesolithic. In Bonsall, C. (ed.) *The Mesolithic in Europe*, 125–33. Edinburgh, John Donald.

Vander Linden, M. (2001) Perpetuating traditions, changing ideologies: the Bell Beaker culture in the British Isles and its implications for the Indo-European problem. In Huld, M. E., K. Jones-Bley, A. Della Volpe and M. Robbins Dexter (eds), *Proceedings of the Twelfth Annual UCLA Indo-European Conference*, 269–86. Washington, DC, Institute for the Study of Man.

Vander Linden, M. (2004) Polythetic networks, coherent people: a new historical hypothesis for the Bell Beaker phenomenon. In Czebreszuk (ed.), 35–62.

Vander Linden, M. (2006) *Le phénomène campaniforme dans l'Europe du 3ème millénaire avant notre ère*. Oxford, Archaeopress, BAR International Series 1470.

Vennemann, T. (1998) Zur Etymologie von Eire, dem Namen Irlands. *Sprachwissenschaft* 23(4), 461–69.

Vennemann, T. (2003) *Europa Vasconica – Europa Semitica*. Berlin and New York, Mouton de Gruyter.

Viney, M. (2003) *I.reland*. Belfast, Blackstaff.

Waddell, J. (1991) The question of the Celticization of Ireland. *Emania* 9, 5–16.

Waddell, J. (1991/92) The Irish Sea in prehistory. *Journal of Irish Archaeology* 6, 29–40.

Waddell, J. (1995) Celts, Celticisation and the Irish Bronze Age. In Waddell and Shee Twohig (eds), 158–69.

Waddell, J. (1998) *The Prehistoric Archaeology of Ireland*. Galway, Galway University Press.

Waddell, J. (1999) Celts: maritime contacts and linguistic change. In Blench, R. and M. Spriggs (eds) *Archaeology and Language IV: Language Change and Cultural Transformation*, 125–37. London and New York, Routledge.

Waddell, J. (2010) *The Prehistoric Archaeology of Ireland*. Dublin, Wordwell.

Waddell, J., J. Fenwick and K. Barton (2009) *Rathcroghan: Archaeological and Geophysical Survey in a Ritual Landscape*. Dublin, Wordwell.

Waddell, J. and E. Shee Twohig (eds) (1995) *Ireland in the Bronze Age*. Dublin, Stationery Office.

Wailes, B. (1990) Dún Ailinne: a summary excavation report. *Emania* 7, 10–21.

Wainwright, G. J. (1979) *Mount Pleasant, Dorset: Excavations 1970–1971*. London, Society of Antiquaries.

Ward, P. and D. Brownlee (2003) *The Life and Death of Planet Earth*. London, Piatkus.

Warner, R. (1983) Ireland, Ulster and Scotland in the Earlier Iron Age. In O'Connor, A. and D. V. Clarke (eds) *From the Stone Age to the 'Forty-five*, 160–87. Edinburgh, John Donald.

Warner, R. (1990) The 'prehistoric' Irish annals? *Archaeology Ireland* 4(1), 30–33.

Warner, R. (1991) Cultural intrusion in the Early Iron Age: some notes. *Emania* 9, 44–52.

Warner, R. (1995) Tuathal Techtmar: a myth or ancient literary evidence for a Roman invasion? *Emania* 13, 23–32.

Warner, R. (1998) Is there an Iron Age in Munster? *Emania* 17, 25–29.

Warner, R. (2002) Beehive querns and Irish 'La Tène' artefacts: statistical test of their cultural relatedness. *Journal of Irish Archaeology* 11, 125–30.

Warner, R. (2006) The Tamlaght hoard and the Creeveroe axe: two new finds of Late Bronze Age date from near Navan, Co. Armagh. *Emania* 20, 20–28.

Warner, R. (2009) Clogher in late prehistory. In Cooney *et al.* (eds), 507–18.

Warner, R., R. Chapman and M. Cahill (2009) The gold source found at last? *Archaeology Ireland* 23(2), 22–25.

Warren, G. (2005) *Mesolithic Lives in Scotland*. Stroud, Tempus.

Warren, G. (2008) The Adoption of Agriculture in Ireland: What are the Key Research Challenges? Draft report, University College

Dublin, Department of Archaeology.

Waterman, D. (1997) *Excavations at Navan Fort 1961–71* (ed. C. J. Lynn). Belfast, Stationery Office, Northern Ireland Archaeological Monograph No. 3.

Weir, D. (1995) A palynological study of landscape and agricultural development in County Louth from the second millennium BC to the first millennium AD. In *Discovery Programme Reports* 2: *Project Results 1993*, 77–126. Dublin, Royal Irish Academy.

Wheets, J. (2004) A Dental Anthropological Approach to Issues of Migration and Population Continuity in Ancient Ireland. Unpublished PhD thesis, Pennsylvania State University.

Whitehouse, N. (2011) Cultivating Societies: Assessing the Evidence for Agriculture in Neolithic Ireland. Unpublished report, Dublin, Heritage Council and Society of Antiquaries, Ireland.

Whittle, A. (2007) The temporality of transformation: dating the early development of the southern British Neolithic. In Whittle and Cummings (eds), 377–98.

Whittle, A., A. Bayliss and F. Healy (2011) Gathering time: the social dynamics of change. In Whittle *et al.* (eds), vol. 2, 848–914.

Whittle, A. and V. Cummings (eds) (2007) *Going Over: The Mesolithic-Neolithic Transition in North-west Europe.* Oxford, Oxford University Press, Proceedings of the British Academy 144.

Whittle, A., F. Healy and A. Bayliss (eds) (2011) *Gathering Time: Dating the Early Neolithic Enclosures of Southern Britain and Ireland*, 2 vols. Oxford, Oxbow.

Wickham-Jones, C. (2004) Structural evidence in the Scottish Mesolithic. In Saville (ed.), 229–42.

Wiik, K. (1999) Europe's oldest language? At http://www.finlit.fi/booksfromfinland/bff/399/wiik.htm.

Wiik, K. (2002) *Eurooppalaisten Juuret.* Jyväskylä, Atena.

Williams, M. and D. Harper (2003) *The Making of Ireland: Landscapes in Geology.* London, Immel.

Wingfield, R. T. R. (1995) A model of sea-levels in the Irish and Celtic seas during the end-Pleistocene to Holocene transition. In Preece, R. C. (ed.) *Island Britain: A Quaternary Perspective*, 209–42. London, Geological Society.

Winn, C. (2006) *I Never Knew that about Ireland.* London, Ebury.

Wise, P. (2006) Northern Linear Earthworks: Reassessing their Function in the Irish Iron Age Landscape using GIS Techniques. Unpublished MLit dissertation, National University of Ireland, Galway.

Wiseman, A. and P. Wiseman (trans.) (1980) *The Battle for Gaul.* London, Chatto and Windus.

Woodcock, N. and R. Strachan (eds) (2000) *Geological History of Britain and Ireland.* Oxford, Blackwell.

Woodman, P. C. (1976) The Irish Mesolithic/Neolithic transition. In de Laet, S. (ed.) *Acculturation and Continuity in Atlantic Europe*, 296–307, Brugge, De Tempel.

Woodman, P. C. (1978a) *The Mesolithic in Ireland.* Oxford, BAR British Series 58.

Woodman, P. C. (1978b) A re-appraisal of the Manx Mesolithic. In Davey, P. (ed.) *Man and Environment in the Isle of Man*, 119–39. BAR British Series 54.

Woodman, P. (1981) The post-glacial colonisation of Ireland: the human factors. In Ó Corráin, D. (ed.) *Irish Antiquity: Essays and Studies Presented to Professor M. J. O'Kelly*, 93–110. Cork, Tower Books.

Woodman, P. C. (1985) *Excavations at Mount Sandel, 1973–77.* Belfast, HMSO.

Woodman, P. (1986) Problems in the colonisation of Ireland. *Ulster Journal of Archaeology* 49, 7–17.

Woodman, P. (1987) Excavations at Cann ny Hawin, a Manx Mesolithic site, and the position of the Manx microlithic industries. *Proceedings of the Prehistoric Society* 53, 1–22.

Woodman, P. (2003) Colonising the edge of Europe: Ireland as a case study. In Larsson, L., H. Kindgren, K. Knutsson, D. Loeffler and A. Akerlund (eds) *Mesolithic on the Move*, 57–61. Oxford, Oxbow.

Woodman, P. (2004) Aspects of the Mesolithic in Ireland. In Saville (ed.), 285–97.

Woodman, Peter (2015) *Ireland's First Settlers. Time and the Mesolithic.* Oxford, Oxbow.

Woodman, P. C., E. Anderson and N. Finlay (1999) *Excavations at Ferriter's Cove, 1983–95.* Bray, Wordwell.

Woodman, P. C. and M. McCarthy (2003) Contemplating some awful(ly interesting) vistas: importing cattle and red deer into Prehistoric Ireland. In Armit, I., E. Murphy, E. Nelis and D. Simpson (eds) *Neolithic Settlement in Ireland and Western Britain*, 31–39. Oxford, Oxbow.

Woodman, P., M. McCarthy and N. Monaghan (1997) The Irish Quaternary faunal project. *Quaternary Science Reviews* 16, 129–59.

Yalden, D. (1999) *The History of British Mammals.* London, Poyser.

Yu W. Z., Qiu D. H., Song F., Liu L., Liu S. M., He X. J., Jin Y. W., Zhang Y. L., Zou H. Y., He J., Lei Q. and Liu X. W. (2009) Characteristics of the PAH gene mutation in Chinese patients with phenylketonuria in Xinjiang [in Chinese], *Zhonghua Yi Xue Yi Chuan Xue Za Zhi* 26(1), 26–30.

Zschocke, J., J. P. Mallory, H. G. Eiken and N. C. Nevin (1997) Phenylketonuria and the peoples of Northern Ireland. *Human Genetics* 100, 189–94.

Zvelebil, M. and P. Rowley-Conwy (1984) The transition to farming in northern Europe: a hunter-gatherer perspective. *Norwegian Archaeological Review* 17, 104–28.

Sources of Illustrations

Unless otherwise credited, line illustrations are courtesy the author.

1.1 after Lyle 2003, 36; *1.2* after Woodcock and Strachan 2000, 26, fig. 2.5b; *1.3* after Woodcock and Strachan 2000, 17, fig. 1.9; *1.4* after Mitchell 2004, 69, fig. 6.1; *1.5* after Woodcock and Strachan 2000, 29, fig. 2.6a; *1.6* after Woodcock and Strachan 2000, 306, fig. 16.6; *1.7* after Mitchell 2004, 145, fig. 11.1; *1.8* after Mitchell 2004, 149, fig. 12.1; *1.9* after Lyle 2003, 52, fig. 5.12; *1.10* after Lyle 2003, fig. 5.2; *1.11* after http://www.scotese.com/future2.htm; *1.12* after Mitchell and Ryan 1997, 67, fig. 50; *1.13* after Devoy 1995, 182, fig. 1; *1.14* after Mitchell and Ryan 1997, 107, fig. 73; *1.15* after Devoy 1995, 185, fig. 3b; *2.2* after Mitchell and Ryan 1997, 80, fig. 57; *2.3* after Woodman 1985, 133, fig. 66; *2.4* courtesy P. C. Woodman; *2.5* sea levels: after Ashmore 2004, 91, fig. 6.8; *2.6* after Woodman 1985, 37, fig. 24.4; 39, fig. 25.0; 52, fig. 33.2; 40, fig. 26.2; *2.7* rod: after Woodman 1985, 44, fig. 28.5; needle point: fig. 28.25; scalene: after Woodman 1978a, 223, fig. 3; scraper: after Woodman 1985, 42, fig 27.2; *2.8* after Woodman 1985, 49, fig. 31; *2.10* after McCartan 2004, 275, fig. 15.4.8; *2.11* after David and Walker 2004, 316, fig. 17.11; *2.12* axe: after David and Walker 2004, 326, fig. 17.17.1; scalene triangle, denticulate: after Lynch *et al.* 2000, 35, fig 1.10.c; *2.13* after Sacchi 1976, 1395, fig. 4; *3.2* after Grogan 1996, 56; *3.3* javelin: after O'Kelly 1989, 39, fig. 16.6; *3.5* after Waddell 2010, 44, fig. 2.9; *3.6* after Crombé 2009, 487, fig. 17.5; *3.7* Irish bowl from Browndod, Co. Antrim: after Herity and Eogan 1977, 33, fig.

9.1; British bowl from Dyffryn Ardudwym, Mer, Wales: after Lynch *et al.* 2000, 60, fig. 2.5.1; *3.8* after Whittle, Bayliss and Healy 2011, 869, fig. 15.8; *3.11* after Sheridan 1985/86, 18, fig. 1; *3.12* after Sheridan 2000, 8, fig. 2.4; *3.13* after Sheridan 1985/86, 18, fig. 1; *3.14* courtesy B. Hartwell; *3.15* courtesy B. Hartwell; *4.1* after Harrison 1980, 13, fig. 2; *4.3 Dublin Penny Journal*, 1832; *4.4* after Case 2004d, 373, fig. 1.5; *4.5* after Waddell 2010, 127; arrowhead: fig. 4.2; 'wristguard': fig. 4.1; early gold ornament: fig. 4.12.4; *4.6* after Herity and Eogan 1977, 118, fig. 43; *4.7* after Waddell 2010, 127; button: fig. 4.6.3; dagger: fig. 4.6.6; *4.8* after Harbison 1988, 117, fig. 67; *4.9* after Waddell 2010, 146, fig. 4.13.1; *4.10* after Waddell 2010, 144, fig. 4.12.7; *4.11* after Waddell 2010, 146, fig. 4.13.4; *4.12* after Waddell 2010, 153, fig. 4.16.2; *4.13* bowl: after Ó Ríordáin and Waddell 1993, 206, fig. 232; vase: after Ó Ríordáin and Waddell 1993, 247, fig. 432; Food Vessel urn and Collared Urn: after Herity and Eogan 1977, 151, fig. 56; *4.14* after Waddell 2010, 159, fig. 4.19.2; *5.1* after Waddell 2010, 196, fig. 6.6; Mallory and McNeill 1991, 113, fig. 3.40, and 112, fig. 3.39; *5.2* after Waddell 1998, 212, fig 6.17; *5.4* Mallory and McNeill 1991, 137, fig. 4.40; *5.5* after Herity and Eogan 1977, 211, fig. 87; *5.6* after Megaw and Simpson 1979, 314, fig. 6.31.1; *5.8* figure courtesy of V. Ginn; *5.9* after Waddell 1998, 182, fig. 5.3; *5.11* after Waddell 2005, vol. 2, 119, fig. 7.2; *5.12* after Waddell 1998, 284, fig. 7.38; *5.13* a: after Bradley 2007, 209, fig. 4.11; b: after Waddell 1998, 284, fig. 7.38; *5.14* a: after Bradley 2007, 209, fig. 4.11; b: courtesy author; *5.16*

after Waddell 1998, 200, fig. 6.9; *5.17* after Bradley 2007, 219, fig. 4.15; *5.18* after Warner 2006, 22, fig. 5; *6.1* after Piggott 1965, 239, fig. 134; *6.2* after Waddell 1998, 292, fig. 8.1; *6.3* after O'Connor 2007, 69, fig. 5; *6.5* after Lynn 2003, 47, fig. 27; *6.6* after Lynn 1991; Navan: 54, fig. 2; Dún Ailinne: 55, fig. 3; *6.7* after Waddell 2010, 373, fig. 9.26; *6.8* after Waterman 1997, 222, fig. 87; *6.9* after Harding 2009, 225, fig. 44a; *6.10* Navan Fort: after Waterman 1997, 5, fig. 3; Mount Pleasant: after Wainwright 1979, 36, fig. 20; fig. 51; *6.12* after Megaw, R. and V. 1989, xxiv, fig. 0.1; *6.13* after Raftery 1994, 227, fig. 143; *6.14* after Raftery 1994, 109, fig. 59; *6.15* after Raftery 1994, 110, fig. 61; *6.16* after Raftery 1984, 58, fig. 38; *6.17* after Raftery 1984, 176, fig. 93; *6.18* after Raftery 1984, 160, fig. 85; *6.19* after Raftery 1994, 139, fig. 79; *6.20* after Raftery 1994, 143, fig. 83; *6.21* after Raftery 1994, 145, fig. 87; *6.22* after Raftery 1994, 123, fig. 73; *6.23* after Warner 2002, 126, fig. 1; *6.24* after Raftery 1994, 162, fig. 102; *6.25* after Raftery 1994, 193, fig. 117; *6.27* after Raftery 1994, 206, fig. 131; *7.2* after O'Loughlin 1999, 40, pl. 2; *8.1* after Cavalli-Sforza *et al.* 1994, 268, fig. 5.5.1; *8.2* after Cavalli-Sforza *et al.* 1994, 269, fig. 5.5.2; *8.3* after Cavalli-Sforza *et al.* 1994, 292, fig. 5.11.1; *8.4* after Zschocke *et al.* 1997, 191, fig. 1; *8.5* after Oppenheimer 2006, 135, fig. 3.6d; *8.6* after Myres *et al.* 2011, 1, fig. 1; *8.7* after Myres *et al.* 2011, fig. 1m; *9.2* after Mytum 1992, 32, fig. 2.3; *9.3* after Raftery 1994, 205, fig. 130; *9.4* after Novotna and Blažek 2006, 11; *9.5* after Novotna and Blažek 2006, 11.

Index